Deng Xiaoping

DENG XIAOPING

Chronicle of an Empire

Ruan Ming

translated and edited by
Nancy Liu, Peter Rand, and
Lawrence R. Sullivan

with a Foreword by Andrew J. Nathan

Westview Press
Boulder • San Francisco • Oxford

Copyright © 1992, 1994 by Editions Philippe Picquier

This English edition published in 1994 in the United States of America by Westview Press, Inc., 5500 Central Avenue, Boulder, Colorado 80301-2877, and in the United Kingdom by Westview Press, 36 Lonsdale Road, Summertown, Oxford OX2 7EW

Chinese edition published in 1992 by Shih-pao Publishing Company, Taipei, Taiwan
French edition published in 1992 by Editions Philippe Picquier under the title *Deng Xiaoping: Chronique d'un empire 1978–1990*

Library of Congress Cataloging-in-Publication Data
Ruan, Ming, 1931–
  [Teng Hsiao-p'ing ti kuo. English]
  Deng Xiaoping : chronicle of an empire / Ruan Ming ; translated
and edited by Nancy Liu, Peter Rand, and Lawrence R. Sullivan ; with a
foreword by Andrew J. Nathan.
      p.   cm.
  Includes index.
  ISBN 0-8133-1920-X. — ISBN 0-8133-1921-8 (paper)
    1. Teng, Hsiao-p'ing, 1904–   . 2. China—Politics and
government—1976–   I. Liu, Nancy.   II. Rand, Peter.   III. Sullivan,
Lawrence R.   IV. Title.
DS778.T39R813   1994
951.05'8'092—dc20   94-1944
                                                                          CIP

Printed and bound in the United States of America

 The paper used in this publication meets the requirements of the American National Standard for Permanence of Paper for Printed Library Materials Z39.48-1984.

10   9   8   7   6   5   4   3   2   1

Contents

Foreword

Ruan Ming provides a shrewd, insightful, readable, and convincing analysis of politics in the era of Deng Xiaoping. He takes as his central theme how Deng pragmatically accommodated with conservative forces in the Chinese Communist Party and lost the chance to put China on the road to democracy and thus links events in the economy, foreign affairs, and ideology. By weaving in the story of the power struggles among major figures, Ruan provides a persuasive synthesis of what the Deng years meant to China's development and how China worked in these years.

Ruan's account is full of new information from internal publications, documentary sources, and personal observation. Ruan was not at the inner core of power: He was an associate of Hu Yaobang who helped draft key documents and who knew many of the key players, especially in Hu's circle. But he was close enough to the center to have advantages in both documentation and astuteness over Western observers. For example, his account challenges the dominant Western view of Chen Yun as a reformer trying to move China away from Stalinism, albeit cautiously, and of Zhao Ziyang as committed to political democracy, and reveals much that is new about Chen's and Zhao's aims and strategies. Foreign analysts understood only murkily events that Ruan analyzes with clarity, such as the Zhao Yiya incident of 1982.

Ruan portrays a fiercer struggle over reform than the West perceived. The conventional view is that after 1978 all the Chinese leaders agreed on reform, but disagreed on pace and methods. Ruan sees a battle for China's soul between real Stalinists on one side and true democrats, led by his mentor, Hu Yaobang, on the other, with Deng in the middle. He argues that China's 1979 Vietnam incursion was the crucial point at which Deng shifted from trying to democratize China to trying to consolidate his dictatorship. This convincing interpretation carries implications for our understanding of Deng's place in history, China's historic course, and theories of reform in communist systems.

Ruan shows how power worked in Deng's China. First, meetings, propaganda discussions, and the drafting of documents were occasions for testing the balance of sentiment and power in the broad, ill-defined party core where decisions were made. Second, interventions by senior leaders could block initiatives by other senior leaders—for example, when the senior general Nie

Rongzhen did not want to allow the purge of a liberal intellectual, Sun Changjiang, the purge was aborted. Third, contending factions carried out an endless chess game over positions. The Chen Yun group, the malevolent antagonist of democracy in Ruan's narrative, worked its way by a series of strategic alliances through which it knocked off one after another of Deng's paladins of reform.

Fourth, Deng was always the trump card. Ruan never fully explains the mystery of Deng Xiaoping's power—perhaps no one can—but he shows how all the factions went running to Deng with their problems and tried to manipulate his perceptions of the others. One group would take an article by a member of another group to Deng and claim that the article was an attack on him. As Ruan presents him, Deng was easily swayed and easily angered. A nod from him on any subject closed discussion. Ruan's metaphor of an empire is appropriate, for the machinations he describes are those of court politics.

Because Deng tried to balance factions and keep power, he failed to see that China needed to move away from dictatorship and toward democracy. On many occasions, such as the epic battle over the special economic zones, in which Ruan participated and on which he provides much fresh information, the ultimate issue was ideological. The irony of Deng's political pragmatism was that it blinded him to the importance of the issues the conservatives presented when they paraded them in the guise of personal power politics. Deng's pragmatism was not about the liberation of thought, as often described in China, or about economic efficiency, as commonly argued in the West, but about staying in power: not about guiding China across the river of reform to a specified place on the other bank, but about crossing the river without slipping on the rocks. In Ruan's view, it was the lack of any other principle than power that led to Deng's finding himself presiding over the tragedy of 1989.

Written in a lively narrative style, the book contains vivid memoiristic scenes, such as the description of a meeting Ruan attended at which Hu Qiaomu wept crocodile tears, and an account of the process by which Ruan himself was expelled from the Chinese Communist Party. As in a Chinese novel, each chapter centers on a phase of political struggle, describing its key characters and its setting, stratagems, and outcomes and leading compellingly to the next chapter. Ruan pauses in appropriate places to give the histories and sketch the personalities of key players.

Ruan has a point of view on matters large (China is inevitably headed for democracy), medium (Zhao Ziyang's fast-growth strategy was bad for the environment and workers' health), and small (Hu Qiaomu was insincere when he wept). He thinks highly of Hu Yaobang and deplores his enemies, led by Chen Yun, Deng Liqun, and Hu Qiaomu. In the last section of the book, when Hu Yaobang is dead, Ruan turns his disdain on Hu's last betrayer, Zhao

Ziyang, and his brain trusters, some of whom are today Ruan's colleagues in exile.

Ruan Ming left China in 1988 to take up a one-year Luce Fellowship at Columbia, during which I had the privilege of numerous conversations with him about the extraordinary crisis then unfolding in his country. He subsequently did research at the University of Michigan and Harvard University and is now at the Princeton China Initiative. At each institution, colleagues have found Ruan Ming to be a man of extraordinary intelligence, with outstanding insight into the personalities, issues, power and cultural considerations, and ideological discourse that make up Chinese politics today.

Since arriving in the United States, Ruan Ming has written three important books. The first was *Hu Yaobang at the Turning Point of History*, a study of the policies and politics of Party General Secretary Hu. The present book was published in Chinese and in French and is now before readers in this English version. He has also published *Essays on Chinese Communist Personalities* and is now working on *The Mao Zedong Empire*.

Ruan Ming's work has won respect from academics. His arguments are sophisticated, penetrating, and eloquently argued. His facts are reliable, often sourced to eyewitness experiences that he recorded in notebooks. In the vast literature on Deng's reforms, we have little on high politics, and nothing with such a keenness of discernment, covering such a long time span, and achieving such broad thematic synthesis. This book offers at once an absorbing narrative of China's recent political history, a vivid picture of the game of politics in China, and a powerful analysis of Deng Xiaoping's influence on China's historical trajectory.

Andrew J. Nathan
Columbia University

Note from the Translators and Editors

The power of *Deng Xiaoping: Chronicle of an Empire* resides as much in the lively flavor of its language as in its penetrating analysis of China's politics and its leaders during the first ten years of the reform era. In translating Ruan Ming's fascinating and insightful book, therefore, we have striven to realize the dry humor and scathing commentary that punctuate his narrative. This has called for an effort beyond the literal job frequently expected of standard Chinese political translation. In the course of rendering Ruan Ming's original Chinese idiom into something comparable for the pleasure and instruction of his English-language readers we have, in consultation with the author, employed a variety of literary allusions and a bit of poetic license.

The notes at the end of each chapter are from the original text by Ruan Ming. We have added a series of asterisked footnotes that explain difficult terms, obscure historical events, and esoteric Chinese Communist ideological concepts. Quotations in the text without citations are drawn from Ruan Ming's personal notes and accounts of conversations between the author and individuals such as Hu Yaobang. A historical chronology of the major events for the period 1976–1993 is also provided along with a glossary of dramatis personae.

We are grateful for the assistance of Susan McEachern of Westview Press; to Mark Selden of the State University of New York at Binghamton; to Adelphi University, Garden City, New York, for its generous financial assistance; to the Fairbank Center for East Asian Research, Harvard University; and to Nancy Hearst, the very capable Fairbank Center China librarian. Most of all, we are indebted to Ruan Ming for his intimate portrayal of the personalities and political forces at work in contemporary China.

Nancy Liu
Peter Rand
Lawrence R. Sullivan

Historical Chronology: 1976–1993

1976

January 8: Death of Zhou Enlai.

April 5: "Tiananmen incident": On the day of the Qing Ming festival honoring the dead, mass demonstrations break out in memory of Zhou Enlai on Tiananmen Square and are suppressed by state militia.

April 7: Deng Xiaoping suspended from all work.

September 9: Death of Mao Zedong.

October 6: Arrest of the "Gang of Four" (Jiang Qing, Zhang Chunqiao, Yao Wenyuan, and Wang Hongwen).

1977

February 7: *People's Daily* editorial lauds the "two whatevers."

March 10–22: Central Work Conference at which the "two whatevers" supported by Hua Guofeng and Wang Dongxing are reaffirmed and Wang Zhen and Chen Yun demand Deng Xiaoping's rehabilitation.

July 16–21: Third Plenum of the Tenth Party Congress restores Deng Xiaoping to the Politburo Standing Committee vice chairman of the CCP and vice chairman of the Military Commission and appoints him to positions of vice premier and army chief of staff. Hua Guofeng is confirmed as Party chairman and chairman of the Central Military Commission.

August 4–8: Science and Education Work Forum at which Deng Xiaoping pushes for major reforms and praises intellectuals.

August 12–18: Eleventh Party Congress. Hua Guofeng praises Mao Zedong's contributions to Marxism-Leninism.

Sources used in preparing this chronology include: Kenneth G. Lieberthal and Bruce J. Dickson, *A Research Guide to Central Party and Government Meetings in China, 1949–1986* (Armonk, N.Y.: M. E. Sharpe, 1989); the annual editions of *China Briefing*, ed. Steven M. Goldstein, Anthony J. Kane, John S. Major, and William A. Joseph (Boulder: Westview Press, 1984–1992); and "Quarterly Chronicle and Documentation," *The China Quarterly*, School of Oriental and African Studies, London.

1978

April 27–June 6: All-Military Conference on Political Work at which Deng Xiaoping criticizes leftists in Party leadership.

May 10: The editorial "Practice Is the Sole Criterion of Truth" is published.

August 3: Luo Ruiqing dies in a West German hospital.

November 10–December 15: Central Party Work Conference focuses on debate over the "criterion of truth." Deng gives speech supporting shift of Party work from promoting class struggle to socialist modernization.

December 18–22: Third Plenum of the Eleventh Party Congress inaugurates major reforms in agricultural and economic policies focusing on the "four modernizations."

December 25: Politburo meeting appoints Hu Yaobang as secretary in chief of the Party and Hu Qiaomu and Yao Yilin to the positions of deputy secretaries in chief. Wang Dongxing is dropped from his post as head of the General Office of the CCP.

1979

January 27: Deng Xiaoping voices praise for Democracy Wall in Beijing.

January 29: Deng travels to the United States.

January 18–April 3: Conference on Guidelines in Theory Work. First session from January to February concentrates on democracy and freedom of thought. Second session takes more conservative turn highlighted by Deng's speech "Uphold the Four Cardinal Principles," delivered on March 30.

February 17: China invades northern territory of Vietnam.

March 16: Chinese forces retreat from Vietnamese territory.

April 5–28: Central Work Conference at which Party conservatives criticize the reforms inaugurated by the 1978 Third Plenum. Three-year period of readjustment proposed.

September 25–28: Fourth Plenum of the Eleventh Party Congress promotes Zhao Ziyang and Peng Zhen to the Politburo. Other old cadres, such as Yang Shangkun and Jiang Nanxiang, are added to the Central Committee. Agricultural policies are revised.

1980

February 23–29: Fifth Plenum of the Eleventh Party Congress adopts "Guiding Principles for Political Life in the Party." Zhao Ziyang and Hu Yaobang are added to the Standing Committee of the Politburo and the Party Secretariat is reestablished. Wang Dongxing, Ji Dengkui, Wu De, and Chen Xilian are removed from Party and state posts. Yang Dezhi replaces Deng Xiaoping as army chief of staff.

April 1: Hu Qiaomu attacks Party Propaganda Department.

April 8–30: All-Military Conference on Political Work. Wei Guoqing pushes slogan to "promote proletarian ideology and eliminate bourgeois ideas." Deng does not attend.

May: Deng at the behest of old comrade Li Weihan disassociates himself from leftist slogan on "promoting proletarian ideology" pushed by Wei Guoqing.

May 31: Deng attacks "feudalism" in the Party but critical elements of the speech are later excised from his *Selected Works.*

June 10: Politburo Standing Committee holds special meeting to discuss the issue of eliminating "feudalism" from the Party.

July: Political crisis in Poland erupts.

August 18–23: Enlarged Meeting of the Politburo. Deng's speech "On the Reform of the System of Party and State Leadership" is delivered. Zhao Ziyang is slated to replace Hua Guofeng as premier. Proposals are made for a bicameral National People's Congress (NPC) and tricameral CCP, complete with checks and balances.

August 30–September 10: Third Session of the Fifth NPC. Intense debate is allowed among delegates over the issue of reforming the political system.

September 23–24: Central Secretariat meeting decides to apply flexible and open policies in Guangdong and Fujian provinces. Agricultural responsibility system is strengthened.

November 10–December 5: Series of Politburo meetings where Hu Yaobang is charged with routine work of the Politburo and Deng Xiaoping is put in control of the Central Military Commission.

November 20–December 29: Trial of the "Gang of Four."

December 16–25: Central Work Conference. Hu Qiaomu launches his "struggle against bourgeois liberalism." Deng Xiaoping, Zhao Ziyang, and Chen Yun all endorse economic retrenchment.

1981

January 14–February 1: All-Military Political Work Conference. Wei Guoqing insists that the military must adhere to the "Four Cardinal Principles" enunciated by Deng Xiaoping while he also criticizes bourgeois ideology.

March 27: The "struggle against bourgeois liberalism" is mentioned by Deng Xiaoping for the first time.

March 30: CCP and State Council call for diversified agricultural economy.

June 27–29: Sixth Plenum of the Eleventh Party Congress revises and then passes the "Resolution on Certain Questions in the History of Our Party Since the Founding of the PRC." Hu Yaobang is promoted to Party chairman.

July: Party conservatives attack special economic zones (SEZs) while Deng Xiaoping remains silent on the issue.

July 17: Deng Xiaoping castigates liberal intellectuals such as Guo Luoji and Wang Ruoshui in a speech titled "Concerning Problems on the Ideological Battlefront" to Central Propaganda Department leaders.

August 3–8: Forum on Problems on the Ideological Battlefront is held to launch attacks on "bourgeois liberalism."

December 15–23: Central Committee discussion meeting at which Chen Yun criticizes Hu Yaobang's alleged mistakes in economic policy. Chen also asserts a primary role for the state in the economy and opposes any further expansion of the SEZs.

1982

January 11–13: Enlarged Meeting of the CCP Politburo issues "Directive on Strengthening Political and Legal Work."

January 14: Meeting of the Central Secretariat at which Hu Yaobang calls for utilizing foreign investment in China's economic modernization.

January 25: Ad hoc meeting of the State Planning Commission. Chen Yun asserts that economic planning must remain supreme in the countryside despite the creation of the agricultural responsibility system.

February 11–13: Open Forum on Guangdong and Fujian provinces. Hu Yaobang focuses on the problem of corruption.

April 10: Politburo meeting discusses "economic crime" and calls for harsh punishments to be meted out by the Central Discipline Inspection Commission of the CCP.

July 30: Enlarged Politburo meeting discusses ways to end life tenure for leaders.

August 6: Seventh Plenum of the Eleventh Party Congress. Hua Guofeng attacks the slogan "practice is the sole criterion of truth."

September 1–11: Twelfth Party Congress. Party chairmanship is abolished and replaced by weaker post of general secretary. Chen Yun clique launches several campaigns against "bourgeois liberalism."

December 31: Enlarged Politburo meeting emphasizes the importance of raising divergent views at inner-Party meetings.

1983

January 7–22: National Conference on Ideological and Political Work. Hu Yaobang and Deng Liqun clash on the role of ideological and political work in China's modernization.

March: Academic Forum at the Central Party School to commemorate the one hundredth anniversary of Marx's death. Zhou Yang raises issue of humanism and alienation.

October 11–12: Second Plenum of the Twelfth Party Congress. On the issue of Party rectification, Chen Yun calls for getting rid of the "three categories of people." Deng Xiaoping's speech at the plenum on "cleaning up spiritual pollution" is not published until after the fall of Hu Yaobang in early 1987.

November: Enlarged meeting of the Politburo decides to limit cleaning up spiritual pollution to the fields of art and literature.

1984

January: Hu Qiaomu's article "On Humanism and Alienation" is published.

January 24–February 23: Deng Xiaoping tours several southern SEZs.

February 24: Central forum on the role of SEZs produces "heated" discussion on the policy of opening up China to the outside world.

March 26–April 6: Forum convened by the Central Secretariat and State Council on the SEZs opens up fourteen more coastal cities to foreign investment.

April 30: Enlarged Politburo meeting validates decision of March-April forum on the SEZs. *People's Daily* calls for a fundamental negation of the Cultural Revolution.

June 1: Central Committee Document Number One on agriculture is published calling for strengthening and improving the rural responsibility system.

October 1: At the National Day review in Beijing, Deng's popularity reaches its zenith.

October 20: Third Plenum of the Twelfth Party Congress adopts "Resolution on the Structural Reform of the Economy."

December 29–January 5: Fourth Conference of the All-China Writers' Association is held in Beijing and calls for greater autonomy for writers.

1985

January: Deng Xiaoping's book *Build Socialism with Chinese Characteristics* is published.

January 1: CCP and State Council jointly issue "Ten Policies on Further Enlivening the Rural Economy," calling for expansion of the free rural economy.

January 25–31: State Council meets on developing the Yangtze and Pearl River deltas.

March 2–7: National Forum on Science and Technology in Beijing calls for radical changes in these two areas.

March 27–April 10: Third Session of the Sixth NPC calls for initial steps toward price reform.

May 23–June 6: Central Military Commission decides to demobilize up to one million People's Liberation Army (PLA) troops and to retire older officers.

June: Restructuring of the administrative organs of the People's Communes is completed.

June 29: State Council decides to enlarge the Xiamen (Amoy) SEZ.

September 18–23: National Conference of the CCP. Chen Yun attacks "Resolution on the Structural Reform of the Economy" and criticizes Party members for loss of communist ideals.

1986

January 6–9: Central Cadres Conference focuses on "instability" in the national economy and criticizes "lax" work among Party organs.

June 28: Politburo Standing Committee meeting at which Deng Xiaoping gives speech on reform of the political structure and on strengthening legal consciousness. He also criticizes interference of the Central Discipline Inspection Commission in Party rectification.

September 28: Sixth Plenum of the Twelfth Party Congress adopts "Resolution on the Guiding Principles for Construction of Socialist Spiritual Civilization."

December: Student demonstrations break out in Hefei, Anhui province, and quickly spread to other cities, including Beijing.

December 30: Deng criticizes Hu Yaobang's handling of liberal intellectuals in the CCP, such as Wang Ruowang.

1987

January 4: Politburo Standing Committee meeting with several members absent relieves Hu Yaobang of his duties as general secretary of the CCP. Fang Lizhi, Wang Ruowang, and Liu Binyan are expelled from the CCP for advocating "bourgeois liberalism."

January 10–15: "Party life meeting" led by Bo Yibo openly criticizes Hu Yaobang.

January 16: Hu Yaobang's formal resignation announced.

January 28–29: Zhao Ziyang announces the reasons for Hu Yaobang's dismissal to high-level cadres in Central Committee Document Number Four.

April: Series of conferences on ideological and political work convened by leftists to continue criticism of "bourgeois liberalism" as direct CCP control is established over newspapers and periodicals, including literary publications.

July 1: Deng Xiaoping's August 1980 speech "On Reform of the System of Party and State Leadership" is reissued.

August: Su Shaozhi, the director of the Institute of Marxism–Leninism–Mao Zedong Thought, is expelled from his post; Wang Ruoshui and other intellectuals are expelled from the party.

October 20: Seventh Plenum of the Twelfth Party Congress confirms Hu Yaobang's resignation as general secretary and appoints Zhao Ziyang as acting general secretary.

October 25–November 1: Thirteenth Party Congress. Zhao announces current state of development as the "primary stage of socialism." Deng Liqun fails to be elected to the Central Committee under a more open election procedure.

November 2: First Plenum of the Thirteenth Party Congress elects Zhao Ziyang as general secretary of the CCP. Sixth NPC Standing Committee approves Li Peng as acting premier.

1988

March 25–April 13: First Session of the Seventh NPC formally approves Li Peng as premier, Yang Shangkun as president, and Wang Zhen as vice president. Proposals are made by Zhao Ziyang's think tanks to establish a professional civil service in China.

April: Hainan Island is granted status as a separate province. State Statistical Bureau warns of inflationary pressure.

July 1: *Red Flag* terminates publication and is replaced by *Qiushi* (*Seeking Truth*).

August 15–17: After fierce debates among top leadership at Beidaihe summer retreat, commitment is made to pursue price reform, but decision is quickly withdrawn.

September 26–30: Third Plenum of the Thirteenth Party Congress calls for emphasis on stabilizing the economy with some leaders calling for greater "centralism and centralized leadership."

1989

January 6: Fang Lizhi submits petition to Deng Xiaoping seeking release of Wei Jingsheng and a general amnesty for political prisoners.

February 16: Chinese dissidents begin petition drive seeking amnesty for China's political prisoners.

April 15: Death of Hu Yaobang.

April 22: On official day of mourning for Hu Yaobang, massive crowds of students fill Tiananmen Square.

April 26: *People's Daily* editorial, based on a speech by Deng Xiaoping, condemns student demonstrations as "anti-Party, anti-socialist turmoil."

May 4: Zhao Ziyang at Asian Development Bank meeting in Beijing speaks positively about the student movement. More than three hundred journalists demand freedom of the press.

May 5: Zhao Ziyang calls for dialogue and most students return to classes, although a minority remain in Tiananmen Square.

May 12–19: Students initiate hunger strike as intellectual and cultural elites urge government to inaugurate a dialogue with student protesters.

May 18: Dialogue is held between Premier Li Peng and students led by Wu'er Kaixi.

May 19: Zhao in a pre-dawn appearance in Tiananmen Square appeals for students to leave. Students vote to end the hunger strike as later in the day martial law is declared in parts of Beijing.

May 26: Zhao Ziyang is reportedly placed under house arrest. Chen Yun delivers speech indicating his support for Li Peng and Yang Shangkun.

June 3–4: PLA troops force their way into Tiananmen Square and outlying parts of the city, killing several hundred or perhaps thousands of students and city residents.

June 23–24: Fourth Plenum of the Thirteenth Party Congress votes to strip Zhao Ziyang of all his posts and appoints Jiang Zemin as general secretary of the Party.

November 7: More than two million rural enterprises are shut down.

November 6–9: Fifth Plenum of the Thirteenth Central Committee. Deng Xiaoping resigns as chairman of the Central Military Commission.

December 22: Ceauşescu government in Romania is overthrown.

1990

January 2: Two-year austerity program announced.

January 6: Chinese police put on alert following the collapse of communist government in Romania.

March 20: At Third Session of the Seventh NPC Li Peng calls for tighter control of "hostile elements."

April 3: Jiang Zemin named as chairman of the state Central Military Commission.

April 14: Mourning for Hu Yaobang is banned.

June 23: Wang Zhen in the *People's Daily* attacks moderates in the government as hostile anti-Party forces.

October 22: *People's Daily* announces a new campaign against crime and "liberal" influences such as pornography.

December 25–30: Seventh Plenary Session of the Thirteenth Central Committee adopts economic blueprint for the Eighth Five-Year Plan, which stresses stability and self-reliance.

1991

January–February: Trials are held of various 1989 democratic movement participants.

March 3: At a national meeting on economic reform, Li Peng supports further reforms to decentralize the economy.

April 8: Shanghai mayor Zhu Rongji and head of the State Planning Commission Zou Jiahua are appointed as vice premiers.

May 6: New press code encourages journalists to spread Marxism-Leninism.

May 29: Secret emergency directive issued to all Party and government offices to guard against hostile forces that seek to overthrow the government.

July 1: Jiang Zemin views the country's "central political task" to be opposition to alleged Western plots against China.

August: Attempted coup d'état against Soviet leader Mikhail Gorbachev collapses.

September: Chen Yun's son, Chen Yuan, draws up document "Realistic Responses and Strategic Options for China Following the Soviet Union Upheaval."

October 6: State announces increases in payments to farmers for grain as of January 1992.

October 25: Internal CCP document accuses the Bush administration of attempting to bring about the collapse of communism through "peaceful evolution."

1992

January 13: Bao Tong, adviser to Zhao Ziyang, is charged with subversion.

January 19–21: Deng Xiaoping tours Shenzhen SEZ in southern China and calls for further economic reforms.

February 23: *People's Daily* attacks hard-line views and calls for bolder economic reforms.

March 14–15: Supporters of economic reforms attack conservative attempts to reverse economic reform policies.

March 16: Death of Wang Renzhong.

June 14: Liberal scholars hold unofficial forum to condemn continuing power of the hard-liners in the CCP.

September 28: Death of Hu Qiaomu.

October 12–18: Fourteenth Party Congress is held and enshrines the principle of a "socialist market economic system" for China's future development. Central Advisory Commission chaired by Chen Yun is abolished and Yang Shangkun is dropped from the Party Central Military Commission.

November: Deng Xiaoping gives speech admonishing people to follow the "three don'ts," that is, do not revise the political interpretation of the 1989 Beijing massacre, do not tolerate "bourgeois liberalism," and do not replace any more leading leftists.

1993

March 12: Death of Wang Zhen.

December 26: China marks the one-hundredth anniversary of the birth of Mao Zedong.

Deng Xiaoping

Introduction

Late in spring 1989 an eighty-four-year-old man announced his impending resignation as chairman of China's Central Military Commission, his last official position. Then to the surprise of the entire world, he mobilized several tens of thousands of troops to surround his own capital city of Beijing. After a more than two-week standoff between troops and demonstrators, he ordered infantry and tank units to recapture Tiananmen Square by force, resulting in the massacre of thousands of innocent civilians. At the same time, he forced from power his own designated successor of the past two years: General Secretary Zhao Ziyang. Although unwilling to accept the appellation of supreme leader, between 1980 and 1989 he had successively driven from office three of China's top leaders: Hua Guofeng, Hu Yaobang, and now Zhao Ziyang. This elderly man, whose absolute power doesn't come with a crown, is none other than Deng Xiaoping.

On two separate occasions between May 31 and June 16, 1989, during and after ordering the slaughter in Beijing, Deng issued the extraordinary declaration that he was "transferring political power."[1] Though from the very start of the reform movement in December 1978, Deng had always refused the formal position of supreme leader, it was he who "in practice held the key position." Whereas Mao Zedong had been the "core of the first generation" of the Chinese Communist Party [CCP] leaders, according to Deng, he himself had embodied the "second generation." Now the "third generation" of leaders would be centered around the newly designated General Secretary Jiang Zemin.[2] What had occurred in *reality*, however, was that the Deng Xiaoping empire had now replaced the empire of Mao Zedong.

The last act of Mao's empire had been the events on the day of the April 5 Qing Ming festival in 1976. Yet back then Mao had been content to order in the militia with their truncheons to disperse the masses on Tiananmen Square. Blood was shed, but no one died. Arrests were made, but not a soul was executed. This time around, however, Deng deployed tanks, machine guns, automatic weapons, and flame throwers to slaughter people. Waves of house-to-house searches swiftly followed, together with arrests, summary executions, and extensive investigations. The old Chinese adage describes it as "stamping out trouble at its source." It was a bloody tragedy, and there is not yet an end in sight.

This same Deng Xiaoping was once famous for avidly promoting both the policy of reform and opening up China to the outside world. Twice he was chosen as *Time* magazine's Man of the Year, an honor that made him immensely proud. Deng had also won the love and respect of China's farmers, workers, students, and intellectuals. Five years earlier when in great majesty, Deng reviewed military marchers from the top of the Gate of Heavenly Peace in Beijing, pennants fluttering in the parading crowd called out in written characters, "How are you Xiaoping!" No average Chinese person in recent memory had publicly greeted a leader in such an informal way, and it showed just how close Deng was at one time to the hearts of the people.

This complicated character has played a role as both reformer and despot. At several crucial junctures in China's recent history, I had the chance to observe him close up. The first was in 1956 soon after Deng was appointed general secretary [*zong shuji*] of the Communist Party Central Committee by Mao Zedong at the Eighth Party Congress. This was during the period of Mao's great love affair with Deng. From that time date Mao's famous speeches, the "Double Hundred Policy" and "On the Ten Major Relationships." These gave every sign that Mao was ready to begin de-Stalinization on the political, economic, and cultural fronts. Preparing the way for opening up relations with the West, Mao asserted: "Our policy is to learn from the strong points of all nationalities and all countries, learn all that is genuinely good in the political, economic, scientific, and technological fields and in literature and art."[3]

Mao was the first leader in the history of the world communist movement who had successfully resisted Stalin in the 1930s and 1940s. At the time, the young Deng Xiaoping had supported Mao in opposing Stalin—thereby defeating the Wang Ming line in the Chinese Communist Party. It was for that reason, in fact, that Deng was purged from his position along with Mao Zedong's younger brother Mao Zetan.[4] But after the Korean War, as relations with the West were completely severed, Mao gave up on his New Democracy policy and embraced Stalin. By 1956, however, Stalin was dead and the Korean War was history, so contacts with the West could be restored. Now Mao planned to follow his own way, and his "Double Hundred Policy" and "On the Ten Major Relationships" were aimed at the Soviet Union and China's Stalinists. From the Korean War onward, Mao had been determined to eliminate dogmatism just as he had altered Wang Ming's Stalinist policies in the 1930s and 1940s.

The political events in Poznan and Budapest in 1956, however, quickly put Mao in a severe dilemma: On the one hand, to carry out domestic reform, Stalinist dogmatism had to be criticized; on the other, such criticism would assist those forces committed to democracy and liberalism in Poland and Hungary. Mao's reaction to the political developments in Poland and Hungary was peculiar: During the outbreak of the Poznan riots, Khrushchev had threatened intervention by sending Soviet army units to the Polish border. Mao stopped him, explaining that Gomulka was a comrade and the Polish issue was a conflict among the people. During the Hungarian fighting, however, although Khrushchev had originally planned to stay out of the fray, Mao sent Zhou Enlai as his envoy to persuade Khrushchev to order in troops, claiming that the situation in Hungary amounted to a counterrevolutionary riot and that Nagy was an enemy of communism.

In China, the only effect of these challenges to communist rule in Eastern Europe was modest ideological unrest on university campuses. With some students boycotting classes and signing petitions, Mao Zedong charged Deng to go and make a speech at Beijing's Qinghua University, where at that time, I was the secretary of Qinghua's New Democratic Youth League. Prior to Deng's coming, the university president, Jiang Nanxiang, sent me to the leadership compound at Zhongnanhai in central Beijing to provide Deng with an initial report on the students' thinking.

When I arrived the first question posed to me by this VIP was: "How old are you?" "Twenty-five," I replied. "You're certainly qualified; my age is just the reverse, fifty-two." Pointing at his ear, Deng then remarked: "Speak louder I'm a bit hard of hearing." I gave him a very short report on the nature of questions raised by the students after the outbreak of the disorders in Poland and Hungary. Deng then noted that the Party Central Committee was preparing a major statement to answer the many questions raised about recent international and domestic events. The central issue, Deng continued, was the question of Stalin. Khrushchev and Tito's method of "knocking Stalin down with one stroke," he complained, had resulted in the Polish and Hungarian situations, something Premier Zhou had criticized Khrushchev about while in Moscow. China's proposal on handling the issue of Stalin, Deng asserted, was to: "first protect, and second criticize." Right now, Deng noted: "There is turmoil in Eastern Europe, but in China we have relative stability, except for some unrest in the universities. Chairman Mao has ordered all Central Committee members and provincial Party secretaries to give reports at universities, and he has asked that I be the first one to do it. That's why I'll be coming to your place next week once the official statement is published."

From what Deng said, I had the impression that his focus had shifted from internal to international affairs: from the dead Stalin to the live Khrushchev. Ever since Stalin's death, new and more deeply troubling divisions had emerged between China and the Soviet Union, replacing the old conflicts of the Stalin era. Mao's new ideas on reform as depicted in his speeches "On the Ten Major Relationships" and the "Double Hundred Policy," obviously aimed at Stalinism, were in danger of disappearing under the huge shadow of Khrushchev's knocking off Stalin in one stroke.

In December 1956, the day after the Central Committee published its major editorial criticizing Khrushchev and defending Stalin titled "More on the Historical Experience of the Dictatorship of the Proletariat," Deng arrived at Qinghua. After he briefly toured the university labs, I accompanied him to the auditorium, where his speech on the editorial lasted for a good five hours, the longest lecture I ever heard from Deng. Mao would later pay great attention to this speech, as is evident in volume 5 of his *Selected Works,* where it's mentioned three times, something quite extraordinary for Mao.[5] In affirming the positive role of Stalin and the Soviet road to socialism, while also condemning Khrushchev and Tito, Deng's speech marked a historical turning point as criticism in China now shifted from Stalinist dogmatism to Khrushchev's revisionism. This clearly preordained the political storm that would break out in the summer of 1957, the anti-rightist campaign.

The second time I met Deng was in July 1962, when I listened to his speech at the Seventh Plenum of the Third Communist Youth League. Though now employed at the CCP Propaganda Department, I still attended Youth League conferences as my term as secretary in the league had not yet ended. It was at this conference that Deng first uttered the famous line: "It doesn't matter if the cat is yellow or black as long as it catches the mouse" (when the phrase was publicized, the cat's color was changed from yellow to white).

This all occurred during a period of general political relaxation following the Three Difficult Years 1959–1962, when the Party leadership abstained from criticizing "Khrushchev's revisionism." At the Seven Thousand Cadres Conference held earlier in January–February 1962, Mao had acknowledged the errors in his work over the past few years. Later in May when Mao was away from Beijing, Liu Shaoqi, Zhou Enlai, Chen Yun, and Deng Xiaoping convened a small work conference where "leftist" errors in the Party were subject to severe criticism by among others, Mao's secretary, Tian Jiaying (who later committed suicide at the beginning of the Cultural Revolution). He proposed that opposition be mobilized against the "leftist" disease, which was a view totally contrary to Mao's persistent anti-rightist position. During the discussion on the revival of agricultural production, the participants in this conference also advocated a policy of legalizing the household contract system [*baochan daohu*] so as to increase incentives among the peasants for greater production. Building on the comments he had made to the Youth League conference, Deng said:

> New conditions have appeared in the villages. I believe that altogether the various types of household contracts now make up more than twenty percent of the villages in agriculture. In deciding on the best production system, we might have to embrace the attitude of adopting whichever method develops agricultural production most easily and rapidly and whichever method the masses desire most.

We must make the illegal legal. To quote an old saying from Sichuan province once uttered by Comrade Liu Bocheng: "It doesn't matter if the cat is yellow or black as long as it catches the mouse."

Deng's speech hit the nail on the head and was warmly received by all the participants. The suffocating atmosphere that had followed the 1957 anti-rightist campaign and the 1959 campaign opposing rightist trends was suddenly swept away. But although Youth League cadres sensitive to such changes felt that a new era of ideological emancipation was about to unfold out of Deng's speeches, it all proved to be a flash in the pan.

Deng made his comments on the morning of July 7, 1962. That evening after returning from his inspection tour of Hunan, Mao immediately informed Liu Shaoqi, Zhou Enlai, and Deng Xiaoping that his investigations of rural conditions in the province had convinced him that the poor and lower-middle peasants opposed the single-family household system, and thus Mao demanded that the collective economy be consolidated. This was obviously a view diametrically opposed to the proposals held by the rest of the Standing Committee of the Politburo.

So what resulted from this conflict? Not a soul stood up to challenge Mao. On the same night and again the next morning, Deng told Hu Yaobang over the phone to delete the "yellow cat, black cat" phrase from his speech and to add a paragraph focusing on the consolidation of the collective economy. In my own notebook, however, I still have a copy of the original speech containing the yellow cat, black cat phrase.[6]

This sudden alteration by Deng demonstrated that Mao was preparing for a new ideological storm in tune with his general anti-rightist position. Soon afterward, Mao ordered the publication of his famous speech delivered at the leadership's summer resort in Beidaihe, "Never Forget Class Struggle"; in it he vehemently criticized tendencies toward the single-household system and the temptation to reverse verdicts, that is, to rehabilitate his earlier critics, especially Marshal Peng Dehuai. With the attacks on Khrushchev quickly resumed, Mao had launched his ship toward the unprecedented "Great Proletarian Cultural Revolution."* As for Deng's "yellow cat, black cat" speech, although altered and revised to fit Mao's prescriptions, it did not escape Mao's vigilance. A major target of Mao's call to "Bombard the Headquarters" in his famous big-character poster issued on August 5, 1966, Deng Xiaoping was thus purged for a second time.

---

*Ruan Ming frequently employs quotation marks around this and other political terms concocted in China (e.g., Gang of Four) as a way to express his general distaste for such ideologically charged jargon in China's contemporary politics. In other words, the "Cultural Revolution" was neither about culture nor was it a revolution.

Sixteen years passed before I saw Deng again; this time he was an elderly man of seventy-four. It was now December 1978, a time when, following the smashing of the leftist "Gang of Four," China was at a critical political crossroads. Hua Guofeng and Wang Dongxing's proposals for the "two whatevers" and the call for "continuing the revolution under proletarian dictatorship"—policies that had been followed in Mao's later years—were now meeting with enormous resistance from the common people. Both the Xidan Democracy Wall movement in Beijing and the Central Work Conference held just prior to the 1978 Third Plenum of the Eleventh Party Congress couched their opposition to the "two whatevers" policy in practically the same language of calling for democracy and reform.* Yet the Work Conference could not proceed until Deng gave his speech. Hu Qiaomu had prepared a draft for Deng that sought a middle way between endorsing and opposing outright the "two whatevers."[7] Dissatisfied with this approach, Deng showed a copy of the speech to Hu Yaobang and commented: "This is not very useful. Qiaomu's line of argument just won't work. Look for someone to rewrite it."

On the morning of December 1, Hu Yaobang called me to his room at the Jingxi Hotel [a military hostel], where after showing me Hu Qiaomu's version, he proposed I produce an alternative draft. I was a little confused since I didn't really understand Deng's train of thought. And although Hu Yaobang provided some of his own proposals, I was still unsure whether I could write the kind of powerful speech that was needed at the time. Thus I decided to consult with Lin Jianqing, who was then working for the Policy Research Office of the State Council [*Guowuyuan Yanjiushi*] under Deng's direction. Together we worked out an outline around the theme of negating the policies of the "two whatevers" and the theory of "continuing the revolution under proletarian dictatorship," while emphasizing democracy and modernization. The next day, Lin Jianqing sent me an urgent message indicating that Deng had some new ideas and I should go to Zhongnanhai right away. There Deng received all those who had drafted various versions of the speech. Obviously excited, he mentioned eight important issues, with the focus on ideological emancipation and democracy.

Deng was obviously preparing for a decisive battle at the Third Plenum. His demeanor gave me the impression that this time he was finally acting on his own. During the Cultural Revolution when Mao had condemned the Secre-

---

*The December 1978 Third Plenum of the 1977 Eleventh Party Congress brought Deng Xiaoping to the fore as China's paramount leader and launched China's economic reforms. It also effectively destroyed the political force of the leftist faction in the CCP that had affirmed Mao's infallibility with the notion of the "two whatevers"—"Whatever policies Mao had decided, we shall resolutely defend; whatever instructions he issued, we shall steadfastly obey." *People's Daily* (*Renmin ribao*), February 7, 1977.

tariat headed by Deng as an "independent kingdom," Deng had not really been all that independent. Indeed, the Deng I had met on the first occasion had been a proud follower of Mao. During the transition from criticizing Stalinist dogmatism to criticizing Khrushchev's revisionism, Deng had in fact served as the frontline commander in Mao's two big battles against rightists and revisionism.[8] On the second occasion, in 1962, Deng seemingly possessed something of an independent mind and understood that to "go forward, one has to retreat."[9] Yet after being attacked by Mao, who was unwilling to retreat an inch, Deng immediately ordered revisions of his speech to suit Mao.

At the time of Deng's next reappearance, in 1973, I was exiled in Ningxia province and under the supervision of a military surveillance group sent by Jiang Qing and Yao Wenyuan to oversee members of the Party Propaganda Department, and I didn't meet Deng in person. But I heard that the price of his rehabilitation had been the admission of being a "capitalist roader," along with a promise "never to reverse the verdicts." Yet when Deng once again began to take an independent line in 1975, Mao commented: "Never reverse the verdicts? I don't buy it." Mao quickly followed by launching a campaign to criticize Deng and the rightist trend of reversing verdicts that led to Deng's purge for a third time.

After Mao's death, however, acting on a belief that Mao's successor Hua Guofeng "doesn't possess a scant of independence except on the issue of the two whatevers,"[10] Deng considered himself the only person qualified to determine China's fate. But I personally think that at that time Deng had not yet decided on the role he would play in China's history. Perhaps his desire to become the democratic leader who would terminate Mao Zedong's empire was greater than any contrary temptation to build his own empire. Indeed, his emphasis on democracy (exhibited in the following quote) left a deep impression on me:

> Democracy must be emphasized in all situations especially in this era. The reason why centralization was practiced for so long was due to the lack of democracy. Since everybody is still afraid to speak out because of their lingering fears, we are unable to come up with decent ideas. What we should fear most is the masses refusing to speak up. "The loudest thunder comes from dead silence."[11] We're not afraid of the masses speaking up, what we do fear is "ten thousand horses standing mute." Thus in order to develop the economy, we must have democratic elections, democratic management, and democratic oversight. Factories should be supervised by the workers and the rural areas by the entire society. We should also emphasize the legal system. The reality of democracy must be stabilized in legal form. It must be institutionalized so that it is protected by the system. We should emphasize civil law, criminal law, and all kinds of special regulations.

One must understand that the period after Mao's death in 1976 was a time in Chinese history when just about anything could be said. On the streets and even in Central Committee meetings, just about anyone could criticize the great heroic leader Hua Guofeng, who held the three key positions of Party chairman, chairman of the Central Military Commission, and state premier. Forced into a self-criticism and abandonment of the "two whatevers,"[12] Hua agreed to hold a public debate among the entire population to reevaluate the Cultural Revolution and the major political and historical issues that had preceded it. Indeed, the scale and influence of changes inaugurated in that period far surpassed the criticism of Stalin and Wang Ming's dogmatism during the 1942–1944 Rectification campaign.

After listening to Deng's talk in early December 1978, we speech writers were able to complete a draft in one day. It was obvious that Deng was very concerned with this speech, as he had us revise it three times. Just as we were completing the last revision (on December 9), Deng proposed that we add something to the end of the speech along the lines of "under the leadership of Comrade Hua Guofeng's guidance of the Party Central Committee and State Council, we must alter China's backward state, move forward, and build our country into a strong and modernized socialist state!" This made me realize that Deng had not yet decided to remove Hua from his leadership position.[13]

Deng was very pleased with our draft, but I was a bit dissatisfied. It was still possible for Hu Qiaomu to alter it any which way by eliminating some of the better ideas and replacing them with his own thoughts. But Deng didn't really pay much attention to these kinds of details. On December 13, 1978, after Deng had given the speech, he immediately asked that we draft the formal report of the Third Plenum such that the most important documents produced by the meeting consisted of Deng's speech and this formal report.[14] Deng's historical contribution at the Third Plenum was to express the common goals of Chinese society, the Democracy Wall movement, and the democratic forces within the Communist Party and to create a new political line separate from Mao Zedong that afterward turned into the line for reform and opening up to the outside world. Meanwhile, Hua Guofeng failed to establish an independent position as his idea of "grasp the key link of class struggle and bring about great order across the land" involved grasping a link that was in actuality Mao Zedong's. Deng Xiaoping's idea of emancipating thought and democracy totally destroyed Hua's "link."

Yet there remained the question of just what Deng Xiaoping was preparing to build on the ruins of Mao Zedong's empire. Was it to be a new democratic republic or his own new empire? During the period from December 1978 to January 1979, I couldn't conceive of the possibility that Deng wanted to do the latter. Even as he remained personal assistant to Hua Guofeng, Deng focused on changing the Maoist power structure and appeared willing to experiment with China traversing the road toward a democratic system. On January 27, 1979, when Hu Yaobang suggested to Deng that the Central Committee convene a theoretical work conference to discuss the current situation, Deng continued to concentrate on discussing the problem of democracy. As a member of the drafting group for this conference I had the opportunity to listen in as Deng said:

> Sixty years after the October Revolution, democracy has not been secured. In the first half of this year we should draw up a major document of twenty to thirty thousand words and publish it on May Fourth* noting that the dominant social and world historical trend has clearly been the development of democracy. The capitalist class thrives off the people and uses them to oppose feudal autocracy. They employ democracy to overcome all the exploiting classes that have existed in the past. Proletarian democracy must achieve an even higher stage of democratic development and in order to surpass the democracy of the capitalist class the good aspects of bourgeois democracy must be carried forward. In the past the proletariat has not succeeded because of Stalin's mistakes and our own.
>
> We must discuss the principles of the Paris Commune, one aspect being elections and another the wage system. But I oppose discussing only these two points, since the most important goal is to turn government officials from the rulers of society into its public servants. These first two aspects are merely derivative. How can we convert rulers into public servants? Perhaps we need to utilize these two aspects, a third one, or even some others.
>
> We want the people to be the rulers. But how can we make the people take on this role? The capitalists have ways of making themselves into rulers, namely elections and the legal system that they use to control the government. We must also think of methods for making the people see themselves as the rulers of the nation. Today I'm not quite clear about how to do this, so I would like you to organize twenty or thirty people to concentrate on writing this document.

Two days later (January 29) Deng Xiaoping traveled to the United States and had a heart-to-heart talk with U.S. military leaders concerning the Soviet Union. Deng then decided to launch his so-called war to "punish Vietnam." This conflict had a profound impact on the progress toward democracy in China after the Third Plenum, as it led Deng Xiaoping to shift emphasis from terminating the Mao Zedong empire to building his own Deng Xiaoping empire. Frequent warnings at the Xidan Democracy Wall to stop the "new autocracy" were like fuel added to the fire, as they provoked Deng to place restrictions on the very democracy movement that he had previously praised. The January 1979 Conference on Guidelines in Theory Work was also interrupted by the war. When the conference reconvened, what Deng presented was not a discussion of democracy but the "Four Cardinal Principles" of upholding socialism, the democratic dictatorship, Communist Party leadership, and Marx-

---

*The anniversary of China's 1919 student movement in Beijing, which proclaimed science and democracy as the goals of a modern China and ultimately led to the formation of the Chinese Communist Party in 1921 by such May Fourth luminaries as Chen Duxiu.

ist-Leninist-Maoist doctrine drafted by Hu Qiaomu that soon constituted the basic political principles of Deng's empire.

On March 30, 1979, I sat listening to Deng's speech at the Great Hall of the People. Watching his facial expressions, I felt as if I was reliving his five-hour speech given at Qinghua University more than twenty years before, when he had used very harsh tones to criticize Ma Yunfeng, a woman Party member from Beijing's Aeronautical Institute who had opposed Soviet intervention in Hungary. In the same speech, Deng first mentioned his criticism of modern revisionism in making critical comments about Tito. Now Deng was once again perpetuating Mao Zedong Thought, and so the fundamental question arose as to which era and what aspect of Mao Zedong Thought Deng would perpetuate. It must be recalled that in 1945 even Mao had once mentioned the establishment of a "free and democratic China," designing in great detail a new democratic road that was to differ substantially from Leninism and Stalinism. But the Korean War and Khrushchev had pushed Mao first to a position of anti-Americanism, anti-rightism, and anti-revisionism and ultimately to the bottomless pit of the "Cultural Revolution." Throughout that era, Deng had been Mao's magnificent general in the fight against rightism and revisionism.

Now the same majestic look came over Deng that I had seen more than twenty years earlier. Even the Four Cardinal Principles were quite similar to Mao's Six Criteria for doing a good job in the rural Socialist Education movement of the early 1960s that preceded the Cultural Revolution; both came from Hu Qiaomu's pen. I sat there wondering if China would face a new storm of anti-rightism and anti-revisionism and the reestablishment of the Mao Zedong empire. I sensed an indescribable surprise and sadness in Deng as the shadow of Khrushchev cast a pall over him, just as it had over the two previous generations of the Chinese leadership in the past two or three decades. One group feared the appearance of a Khrushchev in China; the other so dreaded becoming China's Khrushchev[15] that they lost all rational thought for China's fate. Isn't this what led all of them to try to establish an empire modeled on Stalin?

Developments after 1979 made apparent how complex a character Deng was. Sometimes he acted with a clear mind; at other times he appeared befuddled, driving both forward and backward in the huge cart of China's reform and opening up to the outside world. This changeableness has made people both hopeful and desperate. Perhaps Deng started to degenerate when at the end of 1986 he joined Chen Yun and Zhao Ziyang in forcing the former Party Chairman Hu Yaobang to resign. And not long after his honeymoon with Zhao Ziyang, he discovered that the theory of the "new authoritarianism" promoted by Zhao's "elites" was aimed not only at the students, intellectuals, workers, and peasants who were pursuing democracy and freedom, but also at him.

Originally, the democracy movement in the spring of 1989 was not targeted at Deng, nor was it planned by Zhao Ziyang. There was certainly room for Deng to retreat, for if he had acted on the democratic political reform principles that he himself had promoted earlier on, he could have joined with the common people in defeating the "new authoritarianism" and thus pushed China onto the road of true democracy, legality, and modernity. At this time, however, Deng was not the Deng of ten years before, when he had been a reformer rich in imagination and creative spirit. Now he was truly old and slow, surrounded by a bunch of egotistic, stupid, and corrupt bureaucrats, and thus he made the irreversible and erroneous decision of viewing the hot-blooded youth who were genuinely concerned with China's fate as enemies similar to his opponents on the Huaihai battlefront during the 1945–1949 Civil War. In mobilizing thousands of "People's Liberation Army" (PLA) troops to encircle and defeat the students, he wrote the most shameful page in the history of the People's Republic.

Deng's empire is sustained by the terror of iron and blood, but its foundation is cracking and will soon collapse. Deng's bloody game succeeded superficially, yet in reality it failed. Right now he's not only encircled by the entire population, but is also turning China into an isolated island in the great ocean of the world democratic movement.

Last winter [1988], I left my motherland and made my way to New York. Originally, I had planned to write a book based on my personal experiences titled *The Mao Zedong Empire*. But the blood spilled on June 4, 1989, prevented my writing such a work in tranquility, and thus I have decided to write this more significant work on Deng Xiaoping's empire, with plans to return to *The Mao Zedong Empire* later. Is it possible for a "third empire" to appear in the future? The main concern of my current research, this will be the theme of my last book and the culmination of my life's work.

Ann Arbor, Michigan, 1989

Notes

1. See "Deng Xiaoping's Conversation with Li Peng and Yao Yilin," May 31, 1989, and "Deng Xiaoping's Conversation with Jiang Zemin, Yang Shangkun, Li Peng, Wan Li, Qiao Shi, Yao Yilin, Song Ping, and Li Ruihuan," June 16, 1989, quoted in *The Mirror* (*Jingbao*), August 1989.

2. Ibid.

3. Mao Zedong, "On the Ten Major Relationships," in *Selected Works of Mao Zedong* (*Mao Zedong Xuanji*) (Beijing: People's Publishing House, 1977), vol. 5, p. 285.

4. At that time, this group was labeled the "Deng, Mao, Xie, and Gu anti-Party clique" and was composed of Deng Xiaoping, Mao Zetan, Xie Weijun, and Gu Bo.

5. See Mao Zedong, *Selected Works*, vol. 5, pp. 332–333, 354–355, 357.

6. Deng Xiaoping's famous "yellow cat, black cat" talk is now included in the *Selected Works of Deng Xiaoping: 1938–1965 (Deng Xiaoping Wenxuan: 1938–1965)* (Beijing: People's Publishing House, 1989), p. 305.

7. This draft by Hu Qiaomu aimed at incorporating Deng Xiaoping's speech into the realm of Hua Guofeng's leftist theory of "grasp the key link of class struggle and bring about great order across the land" and "the theory of continuing the revolution under proletarian dictatorship." Hu Qiaomu's version contained such notions as "realizing the continuation of the revolution under proletarian dictatorship; no matter what, we must not forget that class struggle persists in socialist society and power holders taking the capitalist road still reside in the Party; we must guard against the possibility of generating a new bourgeoisie; and don't forget the necessity of eliminating all activities by class enemies in the early stages," etc. Deng Xiaoping was very dissatisfied with this draft and thus gave it to Hu Yaobang for alteration, and he in turn passed it on to me for actual revision. Thus, Hu Qiaomu's draft is still in my possession.

8. In 1957, Deng Xiaoping was the primary person in charge of prosecuting the anti-rightist campaign that was launched by Mao Zedong against outspoken intellectuals. Then from 1960 to 1965 Deng Xiaoping was in charge of the debate between China and the Soviet Union launched by Mao Zedong. Deng was also director of the negotiating team sent to the Soviet Union and oversaw the drafting of articles on anti-revisionism.

9. Deng Xiaoping, *Selected Works*, p. 305.

10. "Deng Xiaoping's Conversation with Li Peng and Yao Yilin," p. 52.

11. "The loudest thunder comes from dead silence" [*Yu wusheng chu*] was borrowed by Deng Xiaoping from the title of a play that employed slogans from the April 1976 Tiananmen incident. The phrase originally came from Lu Xun's poem "The Loudest Thunder Comes From Dead Silence."

12. At the closing session of the Central Work Conference preceding the Third Plenum, Hua Guofeng held himself accountable for the errors of the "two whatevers" and engaged in a self-criticism.

13. Deng Xiaoping finally decided to remove Hua Guofeng from his leadership positions in early 1980. At this time, late 1978, preparations were made to restore the office of the Central Secretariat and to appoint Hu Yaobang general secretary as had already been decided at the Third Plenum. With Hua Guofeng's resignation as premier, Zhao Ziyang would assume this position. Thus the actual power of Hua Guofeng as Party chairman was weakened considerably. In consternation over this turn of events in early 1980, Hua Guofeng refused to attend the Spring Festival [Chinese New Year's] Tea Party, and therefore Deng had to convince Hu Yaobang to appear and make a speech and even egged him on to "go first!"

14. Originally a document drafting group had been formed for the Third Plenum, led by Wang Dongxing, who also was to serve as secretary in chief of the plenum, with Li Xin charged with drafting the documents. After their documents were rejected, this task shifted to Hu Yaobang, who was appointed as the new secretary in chief by the Central Committee.

15. During the discussion in 1980 of the "Resolution on Certain Questions in the History of Our Party Since the Founding of the People's Republic of China," many

cadres did not agree with including Mao Zedong Thought in the document. Hu Qiaomu's concept of "including the correct and excluding the incorrect in Mao Zedong Thought" was very vague. Moreover, Mao Zedong Thought had also been excised from the Party Constitution passed at the 1956 Eighth Party Congress. However, Deng insisted on including it. Deng's daughter, Deng Nan, once inquired of her father: "Isn't it true that you're afraid of being pegged like Khrushchev?" Deng could only smile without uttering a word.

PART I

The Basis of
Deng Xiaoping's Power
(1976–1979)

The course of history does not always proceed from the sun-ripened thoughts of great historical figures. Unforeseen incidents can suddenly alter the minds and moods of people, even their goals, and cause them to veer from their original principles. These sudden turnabouts by important figures can change the course of history. This is what happened in the past half a century under Franklin Roosevelt, Mao Zedong, and Deng Xiaoping.

The Atlantic Charter, signed aboard the cruiser *Augusta* in 1941, can be called the product of President Roosevelt's considered reflection.[1] It proposed the creation of a world order guaranteeing basic human rights and laid the foundation for an antifascist alliance. On the verge of victory, however, Roosevelt suddenly forsook Churchill at the wartime Yalta conference and signed a pact with Stalin that divided the postwar world into two parts and so enabled Stalin to build an empire that stretched from Eastern Europe across Mongolia to North Korea.

In 1945, the Seventh Congress of the Chinese Communist Party (CCP) proposed a China "free and democratic," such as that Mao Zedong imagined in the course of his own long reflections. This was a riposte flung from the depths of the caves of northern Shaanxi province at the giants of Yalta. When a Reuters correspondent in Chongqing, Sichuan, wanted to know what he meant by a "free and democratic" China, Mao replied: "It means that central and local governments must be chosen by universal vote and secret ballot. It means Sun Yat-sen's Three Principles of the People and Lincoln's principle of government by and for the people and the principles enumerated in Roosevelt's Atlantic Charter."[2] Mao called attention in these circumstances to the Atlantic Charter, an essential part of which Roosevelt had jettisoned at the Yalta conference, and by doing so he demonstrated that he possessed the wisdom and vision of a great historical figure.

When Kim Il Sung launched the Korean War, Stalin was fearful of getting sucked into it and goaded China to get involved. Thus, when MacArthur announced the invasion of Manchuria by United Nations' troops, Mao, after long hesitation, eventually sent "volunteers" to fight against the United States in support of Kim Il Sung's Korea.[3] From that time onward, China had to live with a long-term economic blockade by the West and was forced to accept support from the Soviet Union. Thus began the construction, on an imported Stalinist foundation, of Mao's empire.

China's evolution in the Deng era shared some similarities with that of the Mao era. Just as Mao twice blocked democracy only to sink into despotism during the Korean War in 1950 and again in 1956 during the Hungarian affair, Deng also halted the democratic progression embarked upon after the 1978 Third Plenum. In 1979, at the time of the Sino-Vietnamese War, and in 1980, at the time of the Polish crisis, Deng stopped the engine of progress toward democracy that he had thrown into gear. He thus set a course toward a new despotic empire. In the beginning, however, Deng had consolidated his power by relying on the forces of reform at the heart of the Party and on the democracy movement at the heart of Chinese society.

Notes

1. Prior to meeting with Churchill, Roosevelt had already proposed the four great freedoms in his State of the Union address to the U.S. Congress on January 6, 1941. These included freedom of speech, publication, and individual religious worship, as well as freedom from material want and fear for the entire world. These four great freedoms were reiterated in the Atlantic Charter.

2. Mao Zedong's article titled "Response to Twelve Questions Posed by Reuters" was not included in the 1950s version of his *Selected Works*, but it is included in a version I possess of the *Selected Works* published in 1948. The last line reads: "Roosevelt's four great freedoms." In September 1989 when I was in France I discovered a Japanese edition of the *Complete Works of Mao Zedong* (*Mao Zedong Quanji*) that includes this same article. The last line reads "Roosevelt's 'Atlantic Charter.'" Obviously, the 1948 edition of the *Selected Works* made this alteration to make it easier for readers to understand.

3. Mao was taken by surprise when Kim Il Sung launched the Korean War. After his initial defeat, Kim turned to Stalin, but Stalin, fearful of the United States, did not want to intervene militarily and instead pressured Mao to send troops. Mao mulled over the situation for three days and decided that if the Soviet Union provided air sup-

port China would send a volunteer force. But after initially agreeing, Stalin had second thoughts and withdrew his promise of Soviet air support. Mao then ordered a halt to the troop deployments and quickly dispatched Zhou Enlai to Moscow. After several exchanges between the two, Stalin was still hesitant. Later MacArthur's threat to cross China's defense line convinced Mao to take action. In the end, Mao decided to go it alone and thus sent Chinese volunteers to resist the United States and aid Korea.

1

Mao Dies and
Hua Guofeng Blocks
Deng Xiaoping's Return

A conflict between different factions over issues of ideology characterized political life in China during the two and a half years that elapsed between the death of Mao Zedong on September 9, 1976, and the Chinese offensive into Vietnam on February 17, 1979. In this decisive struggle, the alliance between Party intellectuals and the democratic reform movement at the heart of society played a determining role.

On October 6, 1976, a month after Mao's death, Hua Guofeng, Ye Jianying, and Wang Dongxing joined forces to arrest the "Gang of Four" (the four Central Politburo members, including Mao's widow, Jiang Qing).[1] Yet Hua Guofeng, who remained as the head of the new Central Committee, had no intention of modifying either the "revolutionary line" or its underlying theory of "continuing the revolution under proletarian dictatorship" that had been implemented in Mao's later years. Two days after the arrest of the "Gang of Four," on October 8, the Central Committee, the Standing Committee of the National People's Congress, the State Council, and the Central Military Commission issued two joint decisions: first, to build in Beijing a memorial hall for Mao's coffin—a coffin of rock crystal through which the masses could contemplate the face of the corpse—and second, to make preparations for the publication of the *Complete Works of Mao Zedong* and to publish volume 5 of the *Selected Works*. For this second enterprise, Hua Guofeng himself wrote an article entitled "Continue the Revolution Under the Dictatorship of the Proletariat to the End—A Study of Volume Five of the *Selected Works of Mao Tsetung*."* It must be said that at that time the Central

_____

*Peking Review, no. 19 (May 6, 1977): 15–27.

Committee considered the targets of "continuing the revolution under proletarian dictatorship" to be not only the "Gang of Four" but Deng Xiaoping as
well! They all fell under the same heading of "power holders responsible for
taking the capitalist road." When Wang Dongxing, the person in charge of
ideological matters, distributed the central document—"Expose the 'Gang of
Four,' Continue the Criticism of Deng, and Oppose the 'Rightist Trend of
Reversing the Verdicts'"—he insisted on three similarities between Deng and
the "Gang": "Deng Xiaoping, just like the Gang of Four, opposes Mao, his
thought, and his revolutionary line. We must not be lax about criticizing
Deng while denouncing the Gang of Four."[2]

Wang Dongxing had emerged as a fan of "palace intrigue" during the
"Cultural Revolution." He got his hands on the General Office of the Central
Committee and controlled Army Unit 8341, the Praetorian Guard of the
Central Committee. During Mao's later years, Wang presided over the chairman's immediate entourage. He manipulated Mao's every word and action.
Anybody, Jiang Qing included, who wanted to see Mao, first had to get
Wang's approval. At the time of Mao's death, Wang calculated the balance of
power and lined up next to Hua Guofeng. He commanded Army Unit 8341
at the time of the flashlight arrest of the Gang of Four, a bloodless coup. This
great exploit allowed him to advance to Party vice chairman and become a
sort of all-powerful right-hand man to Hua Guofeng. Wang had no thoughts
himself of becoming emperor. He wanted to play the role of the "pope" who
crowns the new emperor in the name of "god." He threw himself into the
business of carrying out Mao's last will and testament—"With you [Hua
Guofeng] in command, I am at ease"—and was entirely devoted to the erection of a new dynasty headed by Hua Guofeng. Wang was by no means a man
of letters, but he put himself body and soul into the seizing of ideological
power that was essential to the legitimacy of a new dynasty. From the struggles during the "Cultural Revolution," he had learned that whoever holds the
key to ideology possesses the "truth" and thus has the power of life and death
in political struggles. He often boasted in a lordly way to his entourage: "Who
truly knows the history of the 'Cultural Revolution?' Premier Zhou and Kang
Sheng are both dead. Chen Boda and Jiang Qing are in prison. Chairman
Hua came to work on the late side. As of now, nobody but me knows. I will
tell you when I have the time."[3]

The only one he was cautious about was Deng Xiaoping. After the
Tiananmen incident of 1976 he wanted to run Deng out of Beijing. But Deng
refused to leave and wrote directly to Mao Zedong demanding that he be allowed to stay in the capital. Mao gave his consent. Thus Wang Dongxing
feared two things: a political reinterpretation of the Tiananmen incident and
the reappearance of Deng on the political scene. He seized on every occasion
to oppose Deng. On November 18, 1976, at the first National Propaganda

Conference following the fall of the "Gang of Four," Wang declared:

> The Tiananmen incident was a counterrevolutionary riot. Chairman Mao said so.
> ... As for Deng Xiaoping, the chairman has already dealt with the matter in Docu-
> ment Number Four.[4] The content of this document is correct and must be de-
> fended because it was Mao's directive. ... Deng Xiaoping has made mistakes, and
> serious mistakes at that. He did not obey Chairman Mao. He's still up to the same
> old tricks. The chairman once said that we must keep Deng under observation,
> without, to be sure, taking away his Party membership. ... Comrade Hua
> Guofeng is farsighted, a worthy successor to the head of our Party, he is our bril-
> liant leader. Deng Xiaoping can't hold a candle to Hua. ... We've already tried
> Deng out. He's no good. He still doesn't understand the Cultural Revolution.[5]

Collaborating at that time with Wang Dongxing was Wu De, head of the
Beijing Revolutionary Committee. In a speech to the National People's Congress (NPC) in November 1976, Wu declared that the anti–"Gang of Four"
tendency in the Tiananmen incident was a mistake. The four were at the time
still leaders of the Central Committee. Opposing them was the same as "split-
ting the Central Committee!"[6] These two speeches aroused public wrath. On
the anniversary of Premier Zhou Enlai's death in January 1977, big-character
posters appeared publicly attacking Wang and Wu. They also called for a reversal of the verdicts on the Tiananmen incident and the rehabilitation of
Deng Xiaoping.

New weapons had to be found to smother the "will of the people." There
were two kinds. The spiritual weapon was the "two whatevers," and on the
material level, a brutal repression was undertaken, with arrests and executions.

On February 7, 1977, the editorials of the *People's Daily,* of the *Liberation
Army Daily,* and of the journal the *Red Flag* proclaimed: "Whatever policies
Mao had decided, we shall resolutely defend; whatever instructions he issued,
we shall steadfastly obey." Hence the famous "two whatevers."

The next day, February 8, the Central Committee published Central Document Number Five, entitled "Notification of the Central Committee on
Firmly Puncturing Political Rumors." The document stated:

> For some time slogans and big-character posters have appeared all over the place
> attacking and slandering leaders of the Central Committee. Certain rumors, po-
> litically very reactionary, have seriously distorted and damaged the glorious image
> of our great leader Chairman Mao and viciously attacked other leaders, dead and
> alive, of the Central Committee in a vain attempt to delude people's minds, insti-
> gate the masses, and divide the Central Committee headed by Chairman Hua
> Guofeng. ... This is a new way in which our class enemies both at home and
> abroad attack us. Party members on every level must pay attention and show vigi-
> lance; they must retaliate against these acts of sabotage by our class enemies. Pub-
> lic security organs must conduct inquiries into these political rumors and this type
> of big-character poster.

In this way, those who wrote big-character posters criticizing Wang Dongxing and Wu De and denouncing the fallen Kang Sheng as an éminence grise of the "Gang of Four" were all assailed in the same document as "venomous slanderers of Central Committee leaders, dead and alive, enemies both at home and abroad assaulting the Party" who thus became targets of ruthless retaliation.

Later, at the beginning of the Central Work Conference held in March 1977, certain members, such as Wang Zhen, brought up the problem of Deng Xiaoping's eventual return. Hua Guofeng responded severely with a speech prepared by Wang Dongxing's scribblers. The report dealt with the problem of the so-called dangerous political trend. Hua declared:

> Now we have found proof that shows that there's a small handful of counterrevolutionaries whose tactic consists of forcing the Central Committee to take a position on this problem. Under cover of calling for the return of Deng Xiaoping, they want to bring Wang Hongwen [a radical leftist leader during the Cultural Revolution] back to power and rehabilitate the "Gang of Four." That's why, if acting hastily, we let Deng come back to work, we'll fall into the trap of the class enemies and mess up the campaign exposing the "Gang of Four" and we'll lose the initiative.

At the same conference, Hua reiterated: "The criticism of Deng and the counterattack against efforts by the right to reverse the verdicts was made by the great leader Chairman Mao. This criticism is a must. ... Indeed it was a small handful of counterrevolutionaries who provoked the Tiananmen Square incident." Hua Guofeng also quoted Mao: "Lenin and Stalin are two knives we must never throw away." This showed that Hua not only upheld the "two whatevers" of Mao Zedong, but also wanted to add the "two whatevers" of Lenin and Stalin.[7]

Wang Dongxing was immensely pleased by the results of this conference. He gave a report on the meeting a few days later at the Great Hall of the People to Party members of units and organizations directly under the Central Committee. He demanded:

> Did any among you here go to Tiananmen Square to call for the return of Deng Xiaoping? As far as I know, there wasn't one. But don't think for a minute there aren't any problems just because no one went to the square to make high-minded speeches on this topic. Can you honestly say that no such thought crossed your mind? I doubt it. At the Central Work Conference quite a few of the old cadres expressed themselves on this subject with extreme vigor. I am happy to say that after Chairman Hua's speech, Wang Zhen made a self-criticism. This was classy! To let Deng Xiaoping resume work now would be to forget Mao. Aren't we supposed to carry out Chairman Mao's instructions?[8]

The most painful thing after that Central Work Conference was the crackdown on those young people who were accused of committing "vicious attacks." Some promising young opponents, who detested the Cultural Revolution and managed during the reign of Mao Zedong to avoid execution, were now ruthlessly put to death! This amounted to a continuation on an even larger scale of executions of truth seekers like Zhang Zhixin, who was liquidated during the Mao era.* To my knowledge, more than ten outstanding young people were killed after the 1976 Tiananmen demonstrations. The 1978 Third Plenum denounced these tragedies. At one point these people were going to be publicly exonerated, but there were all sorts of objections. Finally, only two names appeared in the newspapers, Wang Shenyou and Shi Yunfeng.⁹

While these executions were being carried out, Wang Dongxing also consolidated his power on the theory and propaganda front. He created a small theory squad [*lilun banzi*] headed by Li Xin (former secretary to Kang Sheng) and including Wu Lengxi, Hu Sheng, Xiong Fu, and others. All had been "anti-revisionism" scribblers under Kang Sheng at Diaoyutai, a state guest house and the headquarters of Jiang Qing in western Beijing.¹⁰ The new group led by Wang controlled all propaganda work dealing with theory.

When the editors of the *People's Daily* asked for instructions in order to criticize the leftist articles "On Exercising All-Round Dictatorship over the Bourgeoisie" by Zhang Chunqiao and "On the Social Basis of the Lin Biao Anti-Party Clique" by Yao Wenyuan, Wang Dongxing commented in a memorandum: "The Central Committee and our late lamented great leader and teacher Chairman Mao approved the publication of both these two texts. We should just criticize the wrong ideas without mentioning names." Later, the editors of the *People's Daily* wanted to criticize errors in the theory of "continuing the revolution under proletarian dictatorship." Members of the editorial board after research discovered the original copy of the editorial of November 6, 1967, in which this expression was used for the first time, an editorial simultaneously published in the *People's Daily,* and the *Red Flag.* It turned out that the editorial in question was never discussed by the Central Committee before publication and the text contained additions from the hands of Chen Boda and that of Yao Wenyuan. The expression "all-round dictatorship" [*quanmian zhuanzheng*] was not a quote from Mao, but an invention of Chen Boda and Yao Wenyuan, who ordered that these words be used in the newspaper as citations from Mao. When this investigative report by the *People's Daily* was printed in the bulletin of the Central Propaganda De-

---

*A woman staff member in the propaganda department of Liaoning provincial government whose expression of her inner thoughts regarding doubts and dissatisfaction with the party to a friend led to her arrest and an eventual death sentence. Before her execution, her vocal cords were severed so as to prevent Zhang from making any "counterrevolutionary" outbursts before the axe fell.

partment, Wu Lengxi rang up Zhu Muzhi and Hu Jiwei to reprimand them for their excessive curiosity, all the time pretending that he had proof that Chen Boda and Yao Wenyuan had acted with the consent of Mao, which of and by itself gave these "corrections" a certification of "excellent," as though carved in marble. Subject closed.

Notes

1. These four people included Politburo members Yao Wenyuan and Jiang Qing, Politburo Standing Committee member Zhang Chunqiao, and Party Vice Chairman Wang Hongwen.

2. "Speech by Wang Dongxing at the Great Hall of the People to Party Cadres of Units and Organizations Directly Under the Central Committee," October 1976.

3. "Speech by Wang Dongxing to the National Propaganda Conference," November 18, 1976.

4. Document Number Four issued by the Party Central Committee in 1976 contains Mao Zedong's criticisms of Deng Xiaoping, including Mao's comment, "Never reverse the verdicts? I don't buy it."

5. "Speech by Wang Dongxing to the National Propaganda Conference," November 18, 1976.

6. "Speech by Wu De at the Third Session of the Fourth National People's Congress," November 13, 1976.

7. "Speech by Hua Guofeng at the CCP Central Work Conference," March 1977.

8. "Speech by Wang Dongxing at the Great Hall of the People to Units and Organizations Directly Under the Central Committee Transmitting the Results of the Party Central Work Conference," March 1977.

9. Since the execution of those who were wrongly convicted was approved by leaders at the central and provincial levels who were still in positions of power in 1978, after these two cases were publicized the whole matter was dropped.

10. This group, responsible for drafting anti-revisionism articles, resided at Diaoyutai and took orders from Kang Sheng.

2

Hu Yaobang Paves the Way
for Deng's Return

At the very moment when partisans of the "two whatevers" were getting ready to strangle a China newly awakened from the nightmare of the "Gang of Four," Hu Yaobang took over at the Central Party School.* During the two years 1977–1978, in the middle of these troubles, Hu did a tremendous amount of ideological and organizational preparation for the 1978 Third Plenum, which changed the course of Chinese history. Hu Yaobang was the principal member of the reform force within the Party. It was his destiny to be one of the last intellectual idealists in the Party: He made it to the top, then shot through and vanished like a shooting star. To clarify my theses I shall present here briefly the two main historical components of the forces that originally shaped the Chinese Communist Party and laid the foundation of the democratic revolution in China.

The first component was formed by intellectuals holding to the ideals of freedom and democracy. They participated in the revolution not to escape their own poverty-stricken circumstances, but to devote themselves to these two ideals. Among them were quite a few people from privileged and famous families of the old society. Their goal was to eliminate the oppression of dictatorship and foreign imperialism in China. They wanted to banish the filthiness, the darkness of the old vile social forms and establish a new society, free, democratic, and equal. Their communism was that of Marx and Engels as laid out in the *Manifesto of the Communist Party:* They dreamed of a society in which "the free development of each [individual] is the condition for the free

---

*Located in the western suburbs of Beijing, the Central Party School is a training and political education center for Party cadres from the central and provincial levels of the CCP.

development of all."* They wanted to build a "community of free men" in which each member of society would enjoy more freedom than seemed possible under capitalism to express his or her intelligence and creativity. That's why they could not find satisfaction in the way the Chinese Communist Party exercised power. In pursuit of these more exalted objectives, they pushed for social reforms. The leaders of the first epoch of the Chinese Communist Party immediately following the 1919 May Fourth movement, such as Chen Duxiu, Li Dazhao, and others, raised the banner of freedom, democracy, and human rights. The Mao Zedong of 1945 and Deng Xiaoping of 1978 themselves, at a time when they were in a position to control the trend of history, brandished the standard of freedom and democracy to unite those forces that alone could further China's progress. Moreover, without this core constituency of loyal intellectuals devoted to freedom and democracy the Party could never have achieved victory or budged the Chinese people.

The second component consisted of the workers and peasants who suffered severe oppression. In general, they joined the Party in order to improve their own lives. The majority among them were peasants, who reflecting the CCP's long experience in revolutionary bases in rural areas and the policy of surrounding the cities from the countryside, ultimately became the dominant force in the Chinese communist army. Due to poverty and oppression, they were poorly educated and their immediate motive in joining the army was merely to "overthrow the landlords and bullies and divide the land." In fact, most of the peasant Party members returned to the rural areas after the CCP gained power and did not play an important role in China's political evolution.

The ratio of workers to others within the Party was minute, and the ratio of true industrial workers was even smaller. Nevertheless, during the Stalinist era (1930s–1940s), the Comintern emphasized the importance of recruiting proletarians as leaders into the communist parties of each country. In actual fact, the proletarian leaders in the Chinese Communist Party, such as Gu Shunzhang and Xiang Zhongfa, were nothing but thug proletarians [*liumang wuchanzhe*] who later became traitors. Further, these working-class Party members occupied important posts in the bosom of the Party because they had the confidence of the Chinese Twenty-Eight Bolsheviks leaders in Moscow. The latter counted on them to lead the struggle against the "opportunists," who were considered by definition to be intellectuals (whereas the great majority of communist peasants had almost no say in the various struggles initiated from top to bottom within the CCP).

----

*Karl Marx and Frederick Engels, "Manifesto of the Communist Party," in *Selected Works* (Moscow: Foreign Languages Publishing House, 1955), vol. 1, p. 54.

Under the cover of these internecine struggles, the mercenaries who knew how to flatter the leaders easily obtained promotion. Wang Zhen was a typical example of this kind of person. He was once a railway station janitor, but he called himself a true railway worker. This allowed him to secure the privileged position of prosecutor in Party struggles. Never finding himself on the wrong side, for example, he persecuted Wang Shiwei in Yan'an.*

In Yan'an in 1942, the Rectification campaign was originally aimed at putting an end to the Stalinist dogma of Wang Ming and to emancipate thought. But it also aroused the intellectuals to criticize the bureaucracy and the system of privilege in the Party. Wang Shiwei was a writer freshly arrived in Yan'an. He had written an essay, "Wild Lilies," in which he contrasted the nostalgia aroused by the memory of martyrs fallen for their ideals and the reality of life in the communist redoubt. He especially attacked the system of privileged rank by contrasting the reality of life among high-level cadres with the original ideals of the martyrs. Rationing, for instance, was supposedly egalitarian, but in reality, there were differentiations in food and in clothing, all according to rank. Special treatment was reserved for family members and relatives of high-level cadres.

Wang's criticisms were mild, and in fact were in the tradition of the third century B.C. poet Qu Yuan. Their author in any case had no intention of condemning Yan'an or the Communist Party. But it was enough to provoke the outrage of Wang Zhen. The latter was no more than thirty years old, like Wang Shiwei, but there the comparison stops. One was the "gun" of the proletariat and the other was merely a defenseless petty bourgeois intellectual. Wang Zhen rushed into Chairman Mao's cave and vented his spleen: "While we're fighting at the front those blankety-blanks dare to criticize us at the rear!" Mao desperately needed the support of people like Wang Zhen to defeat Wang Ming. He appointed Wang Zhen to the position of commander in chief of the Yan'an garrison and at the same time made him the director of the Yan'an Artistic Rectification Committee. Wang Zhen now directed the persecution of Wang Shiwei and other intellectuals. Rectification changed direction and instead of "dogmatism" it criticized "liberalism."

Wang Zhen called a meeting to denounce Wang Shiwei. Except for using expletives, Wang Zhen didn't really know how to conduct debates, so he

---

*A prodigious translator in Yan'an, Wang Shiwei was persecuted during the 1942–1944 Rectification campaign and ultimately executed—apparently without Mao's consent—for writing the short but biting "critical essays" (*zawen*) appropriately titled "Wild Lilies" that touched the raw nerve of the leadership. For a recent full investigation of the Wang Shiwei case by a contemporary Chinese journalist, see Dai Qing, *Wang Shiwei and "Wild Lilies": Rectification and Purges in the Chinese Communist Party, 1942–1944*, ed. David E. Apter and Timothy Cheek (Armonk, N.Y.: M. E. Sharpe, 1994).

called on Chen Boda to come to his rescue. Chen was one of Mao's secretaries in Yan'an, a spineless sort of theoretician whom Mao made his general amanuensis, but his presence at Wang Zhen's side nevertheless gave the meeting a certain cachet. Chen Boda also made the closing statement. Among the writers who were denounced along with Wang Shiwei were Ding Ling, Ai Qing, Xiao Jun, and others. However, apparently Wang Shiwei was the toughest nut to crack: He refused to admit his faults, to make a self-criticism. This quickly elevated the level of his crime, so much so that Wang was denounced as a "Trotskyite" and arrested. Some years later, when communist troops evacuated Yan'an during the 1945–1949 Civil War, Wang Shiwei was executed by his guards, He Long's men, in Shanxi province.[1]

When one ponders the history of the Party, Wang Zhen appears as one of the first "guns" specializing in attacks on intellectuals, with a career spanning almost fifty years. Persistent, indeed. At the 1978 Third Plenum, Deng Xiaoping proposed to appoint Wang Zhen to the Politburo, a recommendation that encountered violent opposition. Deng then declared: "Wang Zhen is our bazooka. Even though it often shoots off target, it's a lovely bazooka!" Wang Zhen was elected. This kind of bazooka was as indispensable to Mao as it was to Deng. Wang Zhen referred to himself as the knife-wielding, mythical guard Zhou Cang from the temple of the god of war Guandi. And in the attack on Hu Yaobang and Zhao Ziyang, he was always the first to hurl himself into the fray.

Before the Chinese Communist Party took control of China, these two forces—worker and intellectual—had always basically been united against the Japanese and the Nationalist government of Chiang K'ai-shek. The union of these two forces was necessary to achieve victory over Stalin and Chiang, although the heavy composition of thug proletarians helped to stimulate an atmosphere of violence and cruelty in the Party. Then, after the CCP took over, the conflict between ideal and power began to intensify, because the intellectuals wanted China to evolve into a free and democratic society, and the thug proletarians wanted to seize power in order to "sit on top of the mountains and rivers" like the heroes of traditional popular novels. Looking more and more like spoilsports, the intellectuals became the victims of successive political campaigns. Some intellectuals, however, such as Zhang Chunqiao, Yao Wenyuan, Chen Boda, Kang Sheng, Hu Qiaomu, Deng Liqun, and others, chose the side of power and became a species of cudgel that the despots could wield. These flunkies of the new court played a key role in the history of the Party, supporting despotic power and plotting persecutions against the "dissidents." All despotic empires need the plotting schemes of such intellectual flunkies.

Hu Yaobang was the type of intellectual leader who had not forgotten the ideals of freedom and democracy. Although from a "little red devil" [*hongxiaogui*] or young Red Army soldier background, he had attended middle

school and during the revolutionary period he was considered a minor intellectual. Not long after joining the Red Army, this was enough to make him a
target in the campaign to eliminate counterrevolutionaries. He was accused of
being a member of the Anti-Bolshevik League—and it was a near thing that
he wasn't shot.[2] Feng Wenbin, who had been a child laborer, saved Hu
Yaobang and brought him from the Fujian-Jiangxi border region to the Central Soviet Region, where he served in the Communist Youth League. The
Central organization of the Youth League wanted to send Hu to the Security
Department [*Baoweibu*]. Hu told the secretary of the league: "Make me do
anything you want, put me to work at the steel stencil or sweeping up, but
don't send me to the Security Department!" So he wrote on stencil steel
boards for half a year and was cleared of any political problems.

Hu Yaobang's experience gave him a profound understanding of the impact and meaning that imaginary crimes had on men and women. He was
thirsty for knowledge: He loved to reflect and he read voraciously and quickly.
Mao Zedong once said of him: "Likes to read but only focuses on the surface,
likes to talk and makes grandiose statements."

That was certainly not a positive evaluation, though it is full of humor and
warning. Mao found Hu to be young and superficial. Nevertheless, few Communist Party leaders worked and studied as hard as Hu. He read like crazy despite his hectic schedule. He read all kinds of books, including the works by
Marx and Lenin and famous classical and contemporary writings both Chinese and foreign. He confided to me that he regretted that he did not know a
foreign tongue well, but that they were too hard. He added that he was going
to read a translation by Zhu Shenghao of the complete works of Shakespeare.
And the fact that he enjoyed talking with intellectuals had a lot to do with his
respect for knowledge.

There are two traditions of reading in the Chinese Communist Party: One
is the kind promoted by Lin Biao and Chen Yun, who only focus on reading a
few lines and label this "intensive reading." Lin Biao read the "Three Constantly Read Articles,"[3] and Chen Yun focused on the "Five Philosophical Articles."[4] Both advocated reading a text again and again until one is able to re-
cite the whole thing from beginning to end. Chen Yun claimed that he really
"benefited a great deal" by reading the Five Philosophical Articles during the
1942–1944 Rectification movement in Yan'an.[5]

Such a dialectic is vicious in that it creates ideological ossification and cultural despotism. Mao Zedong himself read almost all the Chinese classics. In
his later years he did not read many foreign contemporary works, which had a
lot to do with the stiffening of his thinking in those years. But he read two issues of *Reference Materials* [*Cankao ziliao*][6] every day, articles of the kind that
helped him to understand international affairs better than domestic problems.
Hu Yaobang once considered inviting a man of letters to live with him and to

serve as his secretary to organize his reading. He even prepared a room for this purpose. But Deng Liqun thwarted the project.[7]

Moreover, Hu Yaobang attached great importance to field trips. His ambition was to traverse all the two thousand counties of China, and by the time of his political demise at the end of 1986, he had already visited more than sixteen hundred.

Hu Yaobang greatly valued the principles of freedom, democracy, and humanism. He profoundly hoped that the Chinese people could free themselves of the dictatorial yoke so that everyone could live like a human being. He enjoyed quoting a line from Marx's "Introduction to *A Contribution to the Critique of Hegel's 'Philosophy of Right'*": "Once the 'lighting of thought' has struck deeply into this native soil of the people the emancipation of Germans into men will be accomplished."[8] Hu Yaobang added: "Marx wrote this article in his youth in the 1840s when Germany was under the feudal system. Peasants were serfs and lived like slaves. We shouldn't degrade ourselves by being slaves."[9]

The arrival of Hu in 1977 at the Central Party School indeed offered a historic opportunity to change the fate of China. The problems were certainly innumerable, but among them two stood out: The first was the spiritual bondage. Without breaking the iron collar of the "two whatevers," the spirit of the entire Party and nation could not be emancipated. China's destiny was blocked. The other problem was that of the phony verdicts. More than one hundred million people continued to suffer directly or indirectly from the consequences of political prosecution and phony verdicts from the past.

Hu Yaobang had a sound view of things. Two crucial points concerned him: first to resolve the theory problem by breaking through Mao Zedong's "two whatevers" to emancipate the thought of the entire Party and nation, and then to rehabilitate the victims of the purges. In this way, forces long oppressed would be mobilized to create a new future for China.

The first person to challenge the "two whatevers" was none other than Deng Xiaoping. On April 10, 1977, Deng wrote a letter to the Central Committee in which he proposed that "we should use genuine Mao Zedong Thought taken as an integral whole [*zhunquede wanzhengde Mao Zedong sixiang*] to guide our Party, our military, our nation, and our people." According to Deng's later explanation, he wrote the letter after careful consideration with the intent of criticizing Hua Guofeng's "two whatevers."[10] Hua then dispatched Wang Dongxing and Li Xin[11] to have a talk with Deng, demanding that Deng take a clear-cut stand acknowledging the "two whatevers" and accepting the judgment on the Tiananmen incident as a "counterrevolutionary incident" that had aimed at "creating conditions" to support Deng's resumption of work. In reality, Deng was thus being forced to make the same confession that he had issued before returning to work the previous time. Deng refused point-blank. He replied on the spot that the "two whatevers" had damaged Mao Zedong Thought and that Mao himself would never have agreed with the idea. Deng also said that "the 'two whatevers' are unacceptable."[12] He added that if he followed the "two whatevers" to their logical conclusion he was condemned never to reappear on the political scene since Mao had dismissed him, and so he didn't understand the point of Wang and Li's visit to him.

Later Deng further explained his basic idea:

> In saying that we should use as our guide genuine Mao Zedong Thought taken as an integral whole, I mean that we should have a correct and comprehensive understanding of Mao Zedong Thought as a system and that we should be proficient at studying it, mastering it, and applying it as a guide to our work. Only in this way can we be sure that we are not fragmenting Mao Zedong Thought, distorting or debasing it.[13]

This notion of Deng's was certainly a step forward in comparison to the "two whatevers," but it was by no means a complete improvement. For instance, Mao's judgments of the 1976 Tiananmen incident and of Deng himself were isolated and incorrect judgments that had nothing to do with the comprehensive system of Mao Zedong Thought, and consequently, one cannot respect them. And this kind of reasoning can lead to other absurdities. Hu Qiaomu did not hesitate to coin a definition of "Mao Zedong Thought":

> Anything and everything, including Mao Zedong's antagonistic views toward some of Liu Shaoqi's thoughts, should, as long as they are correct, be contained in the holistic system of Mao Zedong Thought. As for erroneous things, even the theory of "continuing the revolution under proletarian dictatorship" that was formed within the system of Mao Zedong Thought, should now be expelled from the holistic system.

So the question immediately presented itself: How to differentiate accurate things from erroneous ones? Who decides? Of course, in the end it was Hu Qiaomu who decided. And if there was any disagreement, Hu Qiaomu took it to the ultimate authority: Deng Xiaoping.

Whereas Hua Guofeng and Wang Dongxing wanted to use Mao Zedong's authority to prevent alteration of past errors, Deng, aided by his view of Mao Zedong Thought as "an integral whole," attempted to establish a new authority. He wanted to be connected with the new leaders of the moment and to decide which of their solemn theories would be correct. In the end it was replacing an old yoke with a new one.

What really opened the gate to ideological emancipation was Hu Yaobang's promotion of the principle of "practice is the sole criterion of truth." It was no longer to be a matter of propping up the authority of an old or a new leader, but of submitting truth to the test of social and scientific practice. This thoroughly negated dogmatism and theoretical despotism and laid the ideological foundation for China to move forward to reform and opening up to the outside world.

It is for this precise reason that Hua Guofeng, Wang Dongxing, and their lackeys could accept Deng's remark about "an integral whole" but not Hu Yaobang's "practice criterion." The article written under the tutelage of Hu Yaobang by Hu Fuming titled "Practice Is the Sole Criterion of Truth" was published on May 10, 1978, in the Central Party School publication *Theory Trends* [*Lilun dongtai*], Number 60. On the next day, May 11, the *Enlightenment Daily* reprinted the article under the byline "special commentator," thus averting censure. On May 12, the article was simultaneously reprinted in the *People's Daily* and the *Liberation Army Daily*.

Around eleven that night, Wu Lengxi rang up Hu Jiwei, editor in chief of the *People's Daily* and severely condemned the article. Wu's entire telephone talk went as follows:

The article has committed an error of direction. Its theoretical plan is wrong. It constitutes a grave political problem. It's vicious, vicious. The article denies the relativity of truth and the universal truth of Marxism. The article pretends that Marxism must be proven true by long-term practice. According to this argument, Lenin's theory on the possibility for individual countries gaining revolutionary victory in the era of imperialism was only proven true after World War I and the October Revolution, which is to say that it was not the truth when Lenin first proposed it. In reasoning of this kind, the line of the Eleventh Congress now proposed by the Party is not the absolute truth, and can only be proven as such in twenty-three years time. How can you expect the masses to warmly support and follow this line?

The article advocates suspicion toward everything, says that truth is beyond belief and understanding and that relative truth is nonexistent, that truth is not true when it is first proposed and can only be proven after employing the criterion of practice. This is an error in principle.

The article is politically vicious. In the author's view, the "Gang of Four" were not revisionists but dogmatists, and they did not at all misrepresent Mao Zedong Thought, but were hooked on it. Thus what we should aim at is opposing dogmatism, not the "Gang of Four" or revisionism. The article also advocated that to break the spiritual choke hold of the "Gang of Four," we ought to oppose the notion that "only what's in the bible is correct." Their so-called notion of breaking through the forbidden zones is in actuality breaking through Mao Zedong Thought. The article concludes by affirming that at present "reliance on the ready-made regulations of Marxism, Leninism, and Mao Zedong Thought or even employing those regulations to limit, kill, and cut the infinitely rich and speedy revolutionary practice" is actually aimed at attacking Marxism-Leninism and Mao Zedong Thought.

Under the pretext of attacking dogmatism, the article is a merciless call to arms against Marxism-Leninism and Mao Zedong Thought. The article expands at great length on how Marx and Engels amended the *Manifesto* and how Mao Zedong amended his own articles. The article advocates that we nourish doubts about Chairman Mao's instructions and amend Mao Zedong Thought. Considering Mao's instructions incorrect, he thinks that we shouldn't follow them blindly and worship them like the bible. Obviously the author's attempt was to cut down the banner of Mao. The article also criticizes Lin Biao, who said "one line of Mao's is worth ten thousand lines" and "each line is a truth." Agreed, but does that mean that one line of Mao's is not worth any other, that each line is a countertruth?

Mao Zedong Thought is the foundation of our unity. How can our Party maintain unity if everyone is suspicious and attempts to amend Mao Zedong Thought and argues over which lines are correct and which are incorrect? If that's the case, how can we maintain stability and unity? That's why this political article aimed at cutting down the banner of Chairman Mao's Thought is vicious, vicious.

That was the signal for attack. From mid-May 1978 to the beginning of the Central Work Conference on November 11 of the same year, the debate in both the philosophical and political realms over "the criterion of truth" raged on. Generally speaking, the side that supported the idea of "practice is the sole criterion of truth" carried out a theoretical debate employing the weapon of philosophy. Partisans of the "two whatevers" used the weapon of authority to suppress this new exploration in theory. The end result was that for the very first time since the creation of the Mao Zedong empire, truth defeated authority.

Hua Guofeng did not publicly take part in the debate. He was represented by Wang Dongxing, Party vice chairman in charge of ideology, and by Zhang Pinghua, head of the Propaganda Department.

On May 17, Wang Dongxing made a speech to a meeting of propaganda personnel:

> We did not read the article "Practice Is the Sole Criterion of Truth" before its publication. As much in the Party as in the country, comment abounds. Basically it's directed against Mao Zedong Thought. From what Central Committee is it coming? Our task is to protect and support Mao Zedong Thought. We must now lead an investigation, learn the lessons, and adopt a common point of view. The *People's Daily* must show proof of Party spirit and the Propaganda Department must be on guard.

On the next day, May 18, Zhang Pinghua spoke directly about this article at a symposium of provincial- and municipal-level secretaries and directors of culture, education, and propaganda. He said:

> I have heard two opposing views on this matter. Some say the article is good, others agree that it's not. I myself am not all that clear about it. I propose to you that debates and the expression of different views are allowed within a narrow scope. Don't think that once it is published in the *People's Daily* and reprinted by the Xinhua News Agency that it then becomes a fixed theory. Debates can be held within a narrow scope over this and other articles such as the one in the *Peo-*

ple's Daily criticizing the "summit theory" (that's to say, the absolute superiority of Mao Zedong Thought). We welcome your reports as helpful to the Propaganda Department and if in your internal debates at the provincial level you arrive at other positions, let us know. When he was alive, Chairman Mao once said in a talk to provincial-level leaders that irrespective of the origin of a theory, even if from the Central Committee, we must take a close look at it and smell it instead of just following it blindly.

Hands clasped, Zhang Pinghua kowtowed to everyone and implored: "Take care of us, Take care of us!" In reality, he was preparing a great battle of encirclement and annihilation at the bosom of the Party, a battle against a crime called "cutting down the banner of Mao." In demanding to know which Central Committee this article came from, Wang Dongxing wanted to say that two factions now opposed each other at the top; he visibly sought to establish a line between Hu Yaobang's article and Deng Xiaoping. Although in reality Deng Xiaoping did not know that Hu Yaobang was going to publish the article, that didn't stop him from supporting it. In a talk at the All-Military Conference on Political Work on June 2, he declared: "They maintain that those who persist in seeking truth from facts, proceeding from reality, and integrating theory with practice are guilty of a heinous crime."* Deng's talk was obviously aimed at Wang Dongxing and Zhang Pinghua.

Wang Dongxing launched another attack on June 15 at a meeting with directors of the propaganda system and media personnel directly under the Central Committee. He specifically attacked articles written and inspired by Hu Yaobang:

> Something is very wrong with articles that carry the byline of "special commentator" [articles edited by Hu Yaobang were usually published in the *Theory Trends* and then reprinted by the *People's Daily* and the *Enlightenment Daily* in the name of a "special commentator" so as to avoid sending them to Wang's theory squad for approval]. They are emotional and lack Party principles. It seems that there is an element of agitation expressed through these articles that is wrong. We must study this. I have problems with it.

Wang also criticized a letter to youth by an old cadre (written by Hu Yaobang) published in the *People's Daily* on April 10, 1978, for "instigating young people to commit mistakes."

When Wang Dongxing and Zhang Pinghua launched this ideological attack, the comedy played by Hu Qiaomu and Deng Liqun was especially amusing. They pretended to be striving for peace and justice, but this was just hy-

---

*Deng Xiaoping, "Speech at the All-Military Conference on Political Work" (June 2, 1978), in *Selected Works of Deng Xiaoping: 1975–1982 (Deng Xiaoping Wenxuan: 1975–1982)* (Beijing: People's Publishing House, 1983), p. 109.

pocrisy, since they in fact represented the faction unconditionally partisan to the "two whatevers," the faction that wanted to suppress the right of speech by the defenders of "practice."

On June 20, five days after he got the signal for attack, Hu Yaobang summoned Wu Jiang and me to his house.[14] He told us that Hu Qiaomu had just left, that Hu Qiaomu had blamed us, Wu Jiang and myself, for provoking this debate. Hu Qiaomu did not want it to continue; also, he demanded that *Theory Trends* immediately put a stop to publishing controversial articles. Both Wu Jiang and I expressed disagreement with Hu Qiaomu's point of view. Hu Yaobang insisted: "Let's lie low for now. In the next two issues, *Theory Trends* can reprint some articles from local journals."

Fortunately, just as Hu Yaobang engaged in "a slight withdrawal," it happened that a great general—Luo Ruiqing—decided to come forward.[15] At that time, *Theory Trends* was preparing to publish an article challenging point by point the views of Wu Lengxi as contained in his telephone conversation on May 12, 1978. But in his talk with us on June 20, Hu Yaobang indicated his decision not to publish it. Nevertheless, Wu Jiang had the article sent to Luo Ruiqing indirectly through the offices of the *Liberation Army Daily*. Luo Ruiqing expressed full support of the article and asked the paper to publish it on June 24, 1978, signed as usual by a "special commentator." He declared, "It seems there are some who don't like 'special commentators.' Well, the *Liberation Army Daily* will publish this article under that kind of byline." Luo's clear-cut stand at that key juncture canceled Hu Qiaomu's efforts at mediation and calls for capitulation.

Luo Ruiqing was very cultivated and independent of spirit. He had a passion for theoretical knowledge, and his talk had an intellectual flavor. He also had a cordial friendship with Hu Yaobang. Before the Cultural Revolution, Hu often invited Luo to lecture on military affairs to the Youth League committee. The sight of the diminutive Hu talking to the huge Luo left a deep impression on the young people present. Later when Hu was appointed vice president of the Central Party School, he often consulted with Luo. Luo Ruiqing's strong support for Hu at this time had immense consequences for the political situation. When the *Liberation Army Daily* published the article by the "special commentator" challenging the proposals of Wu Lengxi, local newspapers and journals sounded the echo across China, and in the months to come—July, August, September, and October—provincial journals openly expressed their opinion on the issue in the local press.

This campaign to "express attitudes" [*biaotai*] was originally arranged by the propaganda chief Zhang Pinghua. However, its results were just the opposite of what his organization had hoped to achieve. Everyone supported the idea of practice as the sole criterion for truth. Those who opposed it didn't express their attitude at all. Such was the case at the *Red Flag*, which did not take a position. Its reporters wrote nothing, but passed the time spreading noise about "resisting this trend." The editor of the *Red Flag*, Xiong Fu, declared at a meeting on July 3, 1978: "We must get ready to use the big democratic method of the Great Proletarian Cultural Revolution to fight against unrepentant capitalist roaders such as Liu Shaoqi, Lin Biao, and the 'Gang of Four.'" He added: "The *Red Flag* must bloom on its own. We must not publicly approve this article. We must not be afraid of being isolated. After all, what's there to be afraid of?"

On the eve of the opening of the Central Work Conference in November, the editors of the *Red Flag* once again consulted the Central Committee, this time about an article by Tan Zhenlin. The editors feared that the contents of this article could be understood as a defense of practice as the criterion of truth and that if they published the article, the *Red Flag* would find itself dragged into the controversy. Deng Xiaoping then gave his opinion:

> I think that Tan's article is a good article in that it does not in the least contain any mistakes. I myself have amended it. If the *Red Flag* is unwilling to publish it, send it to the *People's Daily*. How come the *Red Flag* won't get involved in the debate? It should get involved and publish articles with different views. It seems that noninvolvement itself is a form of involvement.

Li Xiannian also commented: "If the *Red Flag* does not publish it, it will be in a very passive situation. In fact, its situation now is already passive." After reading these comments, Xiong Fu went to ask for Wang Dongxing's instructions and then informed the staff at the *Red Flag*: "Vice Chairman Wang says that we will have to follow the tide." Thus, eventually, Tan's article was published in the *Red Flag*, Number 12.

And what was going on over at the Academy of Social Sciences, which at that time was under the thumb of Hu Qiaomu and Deng Liqun? At a Beijing symposium, members of the academy expressed their support for practice as the sole criterion of truth, which was immediately reported to the public. Many of the theory workers of the academy were also actively involved in the debate by publishing articles, this despite the fact that the leaders of the academy did not express their own attitudes. Later, driven by a strong and intense demand among theory workers from all over the country, a symposium on theory and practice was finally held July 17–24, 1978. Right at the start, Deng Liqun announced that the symposium would be "purely academic."

In the course of this meeting, Zhou Yang, then a consultant to the academy, declared: "Personally, I think the question of the criterion of truth is a problem at once ideological and political. This debate touches on the fate and the future of our Party and our nation." Zhou Yang's speech, warmly applauded by those present, was leaked to the public and had a great impact all over the country. When he learned about it, Hu Qiaomu went into a rage. At the closing session, he announced to the surprise of all: "I'm taking the responsibility of making the following point: On the issue of the criterion of truth, there isn't any diverging ideological line. The Central Committee is unanimous."

The second task to which Hu Yaobang devoted himself while he was at the Central Party School was to carry out the rehabilitation of victims of trumped-up charges and injustices going back to the "Cultural Revolution" and even earlier. It was imperative to emancipate a great number of old cadres and intellectuals in order to prepare for the political opening to the outside world. Most of the rehabilitation work was done under the guidance of Hu, who from December 1977 onward, directed the Party Organization Department. He discovered that the total number of people affected by phony accusations in all of China, including family members and relatives of those accused during the various periods, approached about one hundred million.

At that time, only Wang Dongxing had the power as director of the Central Office of the Special Cases Investigation Group [*Zhongyang Zhuan'an Banggongshi*] to pry into "special cases." But Hu came up with his principle of the "two no matters," an ironic allusion to the "two whatevers": "All false accusations and unfair punishments, no matter who on what level made them, must be corrected." Someone asked: "What about cases personally approved by Chairman Mao?" to which Hu replied: "Likewise!" Hu also sent special groups to investigate important cases personally finalized by Mao. He not only rehabilitated victims of Mao's false judgments, but those condemned by Hua Guofeng and Deng Xiaoping as well.

The rehabilitation of the cases of rightists from 1957, involving several tens of thousands of intellectuals, met with a lot of resistance because those specifically responsible for this affair were Deng Xiaoping and Peng Zhen. Jiang Nanxiang and others, who under the guidance of Deng Xiaoping and Peng Zhen had condemned many people as "rightists" in the 1950s, tried in every way to hinder the rehabilitation process. Thumbing his nose at these pressures, Hu Yaobang succeeded in rehabilitating most of the rightists. For symbolic reasons he had to admit that a few "outstanding figures" were not rehabilitatable, for Deng Xiaoping persistently reiterated: "It was necessary to implement the anti-rightist campaign and the only mistake is that it was pushed too far." This was a concession that unfortunately left the door open to future "anti-rightist" battles.

It's necessary to recognize Hu Yaobang's incontestable accomplishment in freeing all the intellectuals and cadres and reversing the phony verdicts and remedying these inequities. But he committed one error when, undoubtedly with the idea of reinforcing his own influence, he returned power to conservative cadres. Old cadres like Bo Yibo, Peng Zhen, and Yang Shangkun who had committed certain mistakes in the past but who were now rehabilitated showed great gratitude to Hu Yaobang at the time. Soon after the 1978 Third Plenum, I bumped into Yang Shangkun and his wife, Li Bozhao, at Hu's house, where we were having a meeting to discuss a document. Having just been rehabilitated, gratitude permeated their conversation with Hu Yaobang beyond belief. However, I personally think that it would have been a better idea to appoint the rehabilitated cadres to honorary positions. The excessive power that was restored to them after their rehabilitation allowed them to enlarge their overall power. These old men formed the kernel of the antireformist forces that never stopped swelling. They ended by forming the irresistible force that ultimately would overturn Hu Yaobang and destroy Zhao Ziyang and suppress the democratic movement.

During his time at the Central Party School Hu prepared for the historic turning point of the 1978 Third Plenum. Hu created the preliminary conditions for Deng Xiaoping's subsequent return to power. That is the historical reason why later Deng chose Hu as his "successor." It was not exactly Deng's choice; rather, it was the choice of history. Deng later admitted in effect that he had at the time no other alternatives.

Notes

1. It was General He Long who issued the order to execute Wang Shiwei.

2. The Anti-Bolshevik League was a counterrevolutionary, underground spy organization set up by the Nationalists throughout the Red areas, largely in Jiangxi province.

3. Mao Zedong, "Serve the People," "In Memory of Norman Bethune," and "The Foolish Old Man Who Removed the Mountain," in *Selected Works of Mao Zedong* (*Mao Zedong Xuanji*) (Beijing: People's Publishing House, 1977), vols. 2, 3.

4. Mao Zedong, "On Practice," "On Contradiction," "Problems of Strategy in China's Revolutionary War," "Problems of Strategy in Guerrilla War Against Japan," and "On Protracted War," in *Selected Works*, vols. 1, 2.

5. Chen Yun said this many times. The first time was to Deng Xiaoping on March 24, 1981. Three days later (March 27, 1981) Deng Xiaoping mentioned the struggle against bourgeois liberalism for the first time. See Deng Xiaoping, *Selected Works of Deng Xiaoping: 1975–1982 (Deng Xiaoping Wenxuan: 1975–1982)* (Beijing: People's Publishing House, 1983), p. 336. After the June 4, 1989, slaughter, Chen Yun spouted the same words again.

6. *Reference Materials* is a bulletin of articles translated from the foreign press, newspapers and journals compiled by the Xinhua News Agency.

7. This theory worker was Li Honglin. Later, due to Deng Liqun's slanders, the Party Organization Department did not agree to send Li on this work assignment.

8. Karl Marx, "Introduction to *A Contribution to the Critique of Hegel's 'Philosophy of Right,'*" in *Critique of Hegel's "Philosophy of Right"* (Cambridge, UK: Cambridge University Press, 1970), p. 142.

9. Hu Yaobang, "Speech Delivered at the [Politburo] Standing Committee Meeting on the Issue of Eliminating the Influences of Feudalism," June 10, 1980.

10. Deng Xiaoping, "The 'Two Whatevers' Do Not Accord with Marxism," in *Selected Works*, p. 36.

11. Li Xin was a secretary to Kang Sheng who after the smashing of the "Gang of Four" was given enormous responsibilities by Hua Guofeng and Wang Dongxing. Within the space of a few days, the Central Committee announced his appointment to five separate positions: vice director of the General Office of the Central Committee (Wang Dongxing, director); vice director of the Central Office of the Special Cases Investigation Group (Wang Dongxing, director); vice director of the Office of the Committee on Mao Zedong Works (Wang Dongxing, director); director of the Theoretical Group of the General Office of the Central Committee; and director of the Office of the Chairman Mao Memorial Hall. Therefore, Li Xin suddenly became a prominent figure under Hua Guofeng and Wang Dongxing.

12. Deng Xiaoping, "The 'Two Whatevers' Do Not Accord with Marxism," *Selected Works,* p. 35.

13. Deng Xiaoping, "Mao Zedong Thought Must Be Correctly Understood as an Integral Whole" (September 21, 1977), in *Selected Works,* p. 39.

14. At that time, Wu Jiang concurrently held the positions of vice president and director of theory research at the Central Party School.

15. At that time, Luo Ruiqing was concurrently secretary in chief of the Central Military Commission and PLA chief of staff. He firmly supported Hu Yaobang's campaign for ideological emancipation and the reversal of phony verdicts. During the "Cultural Revolution," Luo was paralyzed in the lower limbs as a result of torture by Red Guards. He said: "I must walk again." Therefore he was sent for treatment to West Germany, where he received an artificial leg. On August 3, 1978, he died from a heart attack in a West German hospital. His death was an important event in China's political development, for if Luo had lived it would have been possible following Hua Guofeng's resignation from the Party chairmanship and the chairmanship of the Central Military Commission for Hu Yaobang to assume the Party chairmanship and for Luo Ruiqing to assume the chairmanship of the Central Military Commission. Together they could have carried out the reform and dealt effectively with the antireform forces.

3

Deng First Joins and Then Breaks with the Democracy Wall Movement

not in this chapter

Deng Xiaoping's return to power involved quite a twisted process. After the elimination of the "Gang of Four," his followers demanded both a political reinterpretation of the 1976 Tiananmen incident and his return. Neither Hua Guofeng nor Wang Dongxing wanted Deng Xiaoping to take back the reins of power, but the only weapon at their disposal was the barely cold corpse of Mao. The February 7, 1977, editorial emphasizing the "two whatevers" was not sufficient to suppress the calls for Deng's restoration.

In March 1977, Hua Guofeng insisted on the need to "brandish the banner of Mao Zedong Thought" and abide by the "two whatevers" before addressing the problem of Deng Xiaoping. Hua specifically addressed the issue of Deng by saying that the immediate restoration of Deng to work would damage Mao Zedong's banner. But at the same time he made two minor concessions on the matter of Tiananmen and Deng. He admitted: "It was completely natural for the masses to go to Tiananmen Square to mourn Premier Zhou," and he agreed that Deng Xiaoping "had nothing to do with the Tiananmen incident." Hua also promised to create conditions to "allow Comrade Deng to resume work at the appropriate time."

As soon as Deng heard this, he seized the initiative.

On April 10, he wrote to Hua Guofeng, expressing first of all his joy and gratitude for Hua's proposals in March to the Central Committee. He next admitted that during his time at the State Council in 1975, despite "some beneficial work," he had "committed mistakes and had willingly accepted instructions and criticisms from Chairman Mao." Then Deng proposed, "We should use genuine Mao Zedong Thought taken as an integral whole to guide our Party, our military, our nation, our people, and the socialist enterprise over succeeding generations in order to promote the victory of the international communist movement." And last but not least, Deng stated that "the time of his resumption of work and the position to which he would be appointed all depends on the decision of the Party Central Committee."[1]

Thus did Deng "create the conditions" for his own return to power.

Hua was very pleased with Deng's letter. He circulated it throughout the Party along with a copy of another letter by Deng (written on October 10, 1976, four days after the smashing of the "Gang of Four"). This first letter was very simple. Deng expressed his happiness over the smashing of the "gang"; he praised Hua as a man of "wisdom" and noted that Hua's age would "guarantee at least fifteen to twenty years of stability in China and allow for a smooth and peaceful entrance to the twenty-first century." Deng added that "he put body and soul behind Hua Guofeng as the leader of the Party and nation."[2]

Deng's two letters aroused favorable reactions, and it was clear that "the appropriate time" would not be delayed. In July 1977, the Third Plenum of the Tenth Party Congress restored to Deng the functions he had lost after the Tiananmen incident in April 1976. His disgrace had lasted one year and three months. At this 1977 Third Plenum, which restored his functions, Deng gave a universally popular speech in three parts consisting respectively of "Chairman Mao," "Chairman Hua," and "myself." He first forcibly reaffirmed the thought of Mao: "We must acquire a correct understanding of Mao Zedong Thought taken as an integral whole." He next declared that Hua Guofeng possessed the historical attributes that made him worthy of his role as leader. And then he revealed that his own mission would be to become, along with Ye Jianying, Chairman Hua's mentor.[3]

Although Deng successfully regained his functions, his influence and power were limited relative to those of Hua Guofeng. Hua Guofeng was after all at the time the head of the Party and the government, and the all-powerful head of the military. He held supreme power and he also had two powerful allies on the military side: Ye Jianying, with whom he was in complete accord, was his right-hand man (in effect, having at heart respect for the last wishes of the late chairman, Ye supported Mao's "dauphin"); and Wang Dongxing supported Hua on the Party and ideological side. Wang had successfully shepherded an army of "scholars," including some "big scholars" who had stood by Deng Xiaoping in 1975, such as Wu Lengxi, Hu Sheng, and Xiong Fu. These men had also rallied to the side of Hua Guofeng and Wang, as had the former secretary of Kang Sheng, Li Xin, who served as the head of the group. Wang Dongxing and Li Xin now found themselves at the head of propaganda and ideology. And in the government, there was also Li Xiannian, a slippery and changeable customer, who visibly disliked Deng Xiaoping. Li Xiannian had actually attacked Deng in a speech after the smashing of the "Gang of Four": "Whoever thinks he is big stuff is bound to topple one way or another: Lin Biao considered himself big stuff, the 'Gang of Four' considered themselves big stuff, and Deng Xiaoping also thinks he's big stuff."

So, although Deng regained his positions in 1977 as Party vice chairman, vice premier, and PLA chief of staff, he did not retrieve his former power and influence. For when Deng had regained his power for the second time in 1974, Zhou Enlai being seriously ill, Mao actually granted the substantial power of controlling the Party, government, and military to Deng. At that time, Deng was also in control of the routine work of the Politburo, the State Council, and the Central Military Commission. Matters were different now. This time Hua Guofeng concentrated the real power over these three areas in his own hands. In the administration of the Party, government, and military, his assistants Ye Jianying, Li Xiannian, and Wang Dongxing were all close to Hua. Deng had no choice but to "put body and soul behind Hua Guofeng as the leader of the Party and nation."

Immediately following the 1977 Third Plenum came the Eleventh Congress of the Chinese Communist Party in August 1977. Besides reelecting Hua Guofeng as Party chairman, the Chinese Communist Party added two vice chairmen to the Party, raising the number to four. They were, in order of seniority, Ye Jianying, Deng Xiaoping, Li Xiannian, and Wang Dongxing. Deng succeeded in reinforcing neither his power nor his influence at this congress. The line and various policies proposed by Hua Guofeng in his political report were a continuation of Mao Zedong's "leftist" cant: pursuing the revolution under proletarian dictatorship and reaffirming the "Cultural Revolution." To quote a passage from the Party Constitution passed at that congress:

> Our nation's Great Proletarian Cultural Revolution was a big political revolution in which under the conditions of socialism, the proletariat opposed the bourgeoisie and all exploiting classes, consolidated the proletarian dictatorship, and prevented the restoration of capitalism. Such cultural revolutions should be carried out over and over again in the future.[4]

The Eleventh Party Congress did not rule on any problem that would have changed the political line and policies of the Mao Zedong empire. Deng Xiaoping gave a brief speech at the closing session that contained no new opinions, but merely repeated the theme of "three big work styles" that Mao had developed in his political report titled "On Coalition Government" delivered at the 1945 Seventh Party Congress. This particular speech by Deng would later not be included in his *Selected Works*.

No democratic movement existed in society at that time, and reformers were isolated from the bosom of the Party. Only a small number of delegates to the Eleventh Congress voiced different opinions on some of the "leftist" errors contained in both Hua's report and the Party Constitution, but to no effect. Everyone decided to "abide by past policies" [*zhao guoqude fangzhen ban*].[5] From summer 1977 to summer 1978, Hua Guofeng still commanded the leading role on the historical stage of China. Deng Xiaoping played only a secondary role, contenting himself by giving advice in the areas of science and education, domains in which he had secured some authority.

If China wanted to embark on a new path, it was going to have to change its political and ideological line. It was going to have to transform this dogmatism of Mao that was being promoted by the theory squad of men like Hua Guofeng and Wang Dongxing. Hu Yaobang alone, then responsible for the Central Party School, was struggling to reinvigorate the ideology. After he had returned to business for the third time, Deng formed his own theory squad. He reestablished the Policy Research Office of the State Council that he had set up after his second return in 1974. But he also put Hu Qiaomu back in charge of this department.

Hu Qiaomu once again was a kind of intellectual flunky. In character and moral comportment he was totally at odds with Hu Yaobang. Since he played an important role in shaping Deng's later political ideology, it is essential to dwell briefly on this personage.

Hu Qiaomu became Mao Zedong's secretary during the Yan'an era. Originally, he was a student at Qinghua University. When he arrived in Yan'an he worked at the Central Committee with the Communist Youth League, but Mao, who had been much impressed by one of Hu's articles, switched Hu to his own secretariat. Hu Qiaomu knew how to second-guess his master's intentions and molded his tastes to those of Mao. When Mao proposed that intellectuals should reform their way of thinking, Hu forthwith made a self-criticism: He confessed the error of his ways and wept hot tears. He thus purified his soul. Mao once eulogized Hu Qiaomu in Yan'an, declaring that he was the most spotless intellectual, whose soul was the most pure. As the historian Li Shu puts it, Mao's approach to reforming intellectuals was the best way to create hypocrites. The example of Hu Qiaomu is eloquent testimony. Almost all of Mao's important secretaries came to a rather pathetic end. Tian Jiaying committed suicide because he found himself at ideological odds with Mao. As for Chen Boda, who had always closely followed Mao, he was arrested as a scapegoat for Lin Biao in 1970. Hu Qiaomu is the only one who had the good luck to survive. Mao in his later years was quite bored with Hu, but he put up with him.

In 1974, when Deng resumed work for a second time, Hu Qiaomu worked for him. At that time, Deng was vice premier of the State Council. He set up the Policy Research Office and made Hu Qiaomu the head of it, backing him up with directors like Li Xin, Hu Sheng, Deng Liqun, Yu Guangyuan, and Xiong Fu. But later, when the campaign to criticize Deng was launched, Hu Qiaomu threw himself once again into self-criticism with hot tears and wrote letters to Jiang Qing wherein to prove his support he denounced Deng. Jiang Qing used Hu's materials as "heavy artillery" against Deng and distributed them throughout the Party. The other directors of the Policy Research Office split into two groups, among whom one would meet once again Wu Lengxi,

Hu Sheng, and Xiong Fu. Li Xin headed the opponents of Hu Qiaomu, whereas Deng Liqun and Yu Guangyuan recognized the errors of their respective ways and stood by Hu Qiaomu's side.

When Mao died and the "Gang of Four" was arrested, Li Xin suddenly, very briefly, became a celebrity. Over the course of several days the Central Committee issued notifications announcing new posts for him along with Wang Dongxing in such sensitive central positions as deputy director of the Special Cases Investigation Group and the Office of the Committee on Mao Zedong Works. This series of hasty and spectacular appointments attracted people's attention to the way Wang Dongxing and Li Xin were cornering the power formerly held by Kang Sheng and the "Gang of Four," notably the power over two key sectors: special cases and theory.

Li Xin appointed Wu Lengxi, Hu Sheng, and Xiong Fu to positions in the Office of the Committee on Mao Zedong Works and in the theory squad of the General Office of the Central Committee (in reality, the squad was under the control of Hua Guofeng). Li Xin next concentrated his forces against Hu Qiaomu, accusing him of rallying to the side of Jiang Qing during the campaign against Deng. Li tried very hard to prevent Hu Qiaomu from resuming work. Hu had no choice but to beg with hot tears for forgiveness by Deng and plead for his help. Hu also asked Wang Zhen and Deng Liqun to intercede on his behalf with the old man. Deng Xiaoping, who was in the process of preparing for his own third reentry, needed these "scholars"; thus, he forgave Hu Qiaomu, whom he characterized as a "soft bone,"* but not a traitor, and whom he reinstated: Hu found himself at the head of the reestablished Policy Research Office of the State Council with Deng Liqun, Yu Guangyuan, and Lin Jianqing as deputy directors.

After this third return to the political scene, Deng's most significant political speech was the one he gave at the All-Military Conference on Political Work on June 2, 1978. This was the era when Hu Yaobang launched the debate over the criterion of truth and suffered harassment from Wang Dongxing, Wu Lengxi, and company. Deng supported his aide, noting:

> Many comrades in our Party are persistent in their study of Marxism-Leninism and Mao Zedong Thought. ... There are other comrades, however, who talk about Mao Zedong Thought every day, but who often forget, abandon, or even oppose Comrade Mao's fundamental Marxist viewpoint and his method of seeking truth from facts, of always proceeding from reality, and of integrating theory with practice. Some people even go further: They maintain that those who persist in seeking truth from facts, proceeding from reality, and integrating theory with practice are guilty of a heinous crime.[6]

---

*A term of opprobrium first used by Wang Shiwei during the 1942–1944 Rectification campaign to criticize weak-kneed and generally gutless cadres in the CCP.

Deng's speech was obviously a criticism of Wang Dongxing and Wu Lengxi. It was warmly received by the masses, but of course it triggered a dreadful outburst of rage from Wang Dongxing. Not daring to respond directly to Deng's speech, he violently attacked the *People's Daily* for the title of the article that reported the speech: "Vice Chairman Deng Makes a Brilliant and Penetrating Analysis of Chairman Mao's Glorious Thought of Seeking Truth from Facts." Wang accused the *People's Daily* of "purposefully degrading Chairman Hua Guofeng and Vice Chairman Ye Jianying." He further questioned the *People's Daily*: "How come you never speak of speeches by Chairman Hua and Vice Chairman Ye as 'brilliant and penetrating analysis'? Does that mean Chairman Hua and Vice Chairman Ye are incapable of profound and penetrating analysis? The title is not ingenuous." The following issue of the *Red Flag* published an article about the All-Military Conference on Political Work that was more respectful of the hierarchy: Chairman Hua made a "brilliant and penetrating analysis"; Vice Chairman Ye "gave an important speech"; and finally, Vice Chairman Deng "stressed in his speech. ..."

The debate over the criterion of truth was not only an important ideological debate that laid a theoretical foundation for the watershed 1978 Third Plenum. It also aroused the masses and lit the fire under the democratic movement of the Xidan Democracy Wall. At the Third Plenum, it was the close alliance of the democratic reform force within the Party and the people's democratic movement that would enable the victory over the "whatevers," until then the holders of supreme ideological power. And thanks to the support of this alliance, Deng Xiaoping's political influence expanded and his bases of power consolidated.

The watershed Third Plenum was held in Beijing December 18–22, 1978. It followed a central work conference, in which the Central Committee, provincial Party leaders, the government, and the military all participated for more than a month, from November 10 to December 15. The main documents submitted at the meeting included speeches by Party Chairman Hua Guofeng and Vice Chairman Ye Jianying and a resolution. These three documents were concocted by the theory squad of the Central Committee under the direction of Wang Dongxing.

The initial intention of those who presided over this group was: first, uphold Mao's theory of "continuing the revolution under proletarian dictatorship" and Hua Guofeng's Eleventh Party Congress line of "taking class struggle as the key link and bringing about great order across the land," and second, shift the focus of the Party's work to modernization of the country.

The two objectives were inherently contradictory. The "Gang of Four" had been eliminated in reality more than two years earlier, and in those more than two years, most of Hua Guofeng's speeches and articles—written by Wang Dongxing's theory squad—were aimed at the theme of adhering to "continuing the revolution under proletarian dictatorship." They had successfully linked this theory with Hua Guofeng's name by employing the following logic: Mao Zedong's greatest contribution to Marxism was his theory of "continuing the revolution under proletarian dictatorship" and what qualified Hua to be Mao's successor was that Hua persisted in and supported this theory.[7] Yet Hua Guofeng himself reflected neither Wang Dongxing nor Wang's theory squad. Hua had practical experience and understood that after the smashing of the "Gang of Four," centering the political life of the country on modernization was an incontestable requirement of the people. That's why he was willing to combine the two objectives that the past twenty years of history had proven to be irreconcilable. His defeat was thus unavoidable, and fatal. It is unfair to accuse Hua of being unwilling to engage in modernization, but it's true that he could not renounce the magical value that the slogan "continuing the revolution under proletarian dictatorship" had acquired. This is what blocked the opening to new policies, and this was his tragedy.

In theory, Hua Guofeng's two objectives did not essentially differ from the line proposed later by Zhao Ziyang at the 1987 Thirteenth Party Congress or from the "two basic points" that to this day Deng Xiaoping still defends. The only difference is that Zhao and Deng merely replaced the concepts of "continuing the revolution under proletarian dictatorship" and "opposing the power holders taking the capitalist road" with the "struggle against bourgeois liberalism."

As for old crew members like Wang Zhen, they did not even possess an iota of Hua's thoughts about modernization, except perhaps the modernization of their own homes. In any case at that time none of the old crew members supported Hua, from whom they differed on one point: Their power had weakened during the "Cultural Revolution," and they could not stand the fact that Hua had climbed over their heads in the hierarchy. They wanted the Party chairman to concede part of his power to them and let them expand their influence. To Hua they now preferred Hu Yaobang, who had put a lot of effort into their rehabilitation. They were even to some extent willing to support the Democracy Wall movement in Beijing. At the preparatory conference of the Third Plenum when Feng Wenbin reported the contents of big-character posters on the Democracy Wall that advocated urging rehabilitation of the cadres who were victims of false accusations and phony verdicts, not to mention the suppression of the Special Cases Investigation Group directed by Wang Dongxing, the majority present cheered.[8]

In November and December 1978, a powerful coalition emerged, consisting of the Democracy Wall movement and the democratic reform forces in the Party who wanted to put an end to the Mao Zedong empire in China. The debate over the criterion of truth gave birth in society and in the Party to new waves of thought in the name of which the movement called for the end of dictatorship and the realization of democracy (the later so-called ideological wave of liberalization [*ziyouhua sichao*]). The battle against the "two whatev-

ers," for freedom of expression and freedom of the press, for realizing political democracy and establishing a legal system, and thoroughly reversing the
phony verdicts reached under the despotic system—these were the subjects
that henceforth aroused intellectuals, students, young workers, cadres, and
the masses to passion.

It was in this context that the recently restored journal *China Youth*
[*Zhongguo qingnian*] published poems from the 1976 April Fifth movement
on Tiananmen Square as well as articles by Han Zhixiong and others demanding a political reinterpretation of this demonstration. Wang Dongxing ordered the journal to cease publication. His reasons were many: Mao Zedong
himself decreed that the Tiananmen incident was counterrevolutionary and
there could be no question of rehabilitation; *China Youth* did not publish the
newly released poems by Mao Zedong; and *China Youth* did not carry Chairman Hua's calligraphy. But staff members at *China Youth* refused to yield; instead, they posted, sheet by sheet, the page proofs of the review onto Democracy Wall. The crowd reacted with support, and on the same wall, they
attacked Wang Dongxing in big-character posters.

That was the real inauguration of Xidan Democracy Wall. Once it was
started, it could not be stopped. Big-character posters flourished at Xidan in
greater and greater numbers. Some demanded rehabilitation; others discussed
politics and democracy, or better yet, denounced the bureaucracy and corruption of Party cadres. These protests pasted on the wall were mentioned at the
Central Work Conference prior to the Third Plenum and played a driving role
in the forward momentum of the meeting.

At about the same time, some of the young workers' organizations from
outside Beijing, such as the "Enlightenment Society" from Guiyang in
Guizhou province came to Beijing. They posted big-character posters in front
of Tiananmen Square criticizing Mao Zedong, pointing out that Mao had
committed a number of errors and that the ratio between Mao's contributions and defects should be seven to three. They also opposed the "two whatevers."

Those posters aroused great interest among important Chinese and foreigners in Beijing. On November 28, the *People's Daily* published statements
made by Deng Xiaoping to Sasaki Ryo, chairman of the Japanese Socialist
Party: "It's perfectly normal for people to put up posters. It's a sign of the stability in our country. We do not have the right to deny or criticize the blossoming of democracy and the posters. If the people are angry, we have to let
them blow off steam."[9]

A statement like that was tantamount to legalizing the use of big-character
posters to criticize high-level leaders. From the end of 1978 to the beginning
of 1979, Democracy Wall was the political center of the capital, attracting
people from all over the country, including cadres, not to mention journalists,
foreign and local. It was a common practice for cadres attending conferences

in Beijing to go take a look at Democracy Wall to "inhale the air of democracy in Beijing."

On December 13, 1978, Ye Jianying declared at the Central Work Conference: "The Party's Third Plenum is yet another model of democracy within the Party, and the Xidan Democracy Wall is yet another model of people's democracy."[10]

Under the influence of Democracy Wall, the Central Work Conference completely deviated from the route mapped out by Hua Guofeng and Wang Dongxing. In his opening speech, Hua Guofeng had demanded a debate on the issue of shifting the focus of work, but the delegates debated the topics proposed on Democracy Wall: the 1976 Tiananmen incident; the 1959 Lushan Conference and the purging of Peng Dehuai;[11] the death of Tao Zhu and the affair of the Central Propaganda Department he directed;[12] and the issue of the sixty-one traitors, among whom figured Peng Zhen, Bo Yibo, and others[13] plus the question of whether to simply pardon the "rightists" or to rehabilitate them;[14] and finally, the issue of Liu Shaoqi. As head of the Party Organization Department, Hu Yaobang had already conducted investigations into these great matters and the false convictions that Mao had approved, but, owing to obstacles raised by partisans of the "two whatevers," he had not been able to rehabilitate victims. The offensive of the forces of democracy suddenly provided a unique opportunity to rule on these problems. Hu Yaobang now decided to arrange the various documents and hold discussions about the cases at the conference. Most of the victims were rehabilitated right on the spot, with the exception of Liu Shaoqi, who had formally been "permanently purged from the Party" at the 1968 Twelfth Plenum of the Eighth Party Congress. Hu Yaobang thus decided to handle this particular case at the upcoming Fifth Plenum of the Eleventh Congress.

At the outset, this Central Work Conference did not concern itself with ideological or theoretical debates, but the "two whatevers" faction provoked them. Hu Sheng had launched the initial attack on the criterion of truth. He concentrated his fire on Zhou Yang:

> Some comrades are pretending in public speeches (thereby unavoidably ending up in the newspapers) that there exist differences within the Party on this subject and that such differences are not only ideological, but also involve an issue of political line that relates to the destiny and future of our nation. I find this kind of declaration irresponsible, and although expressed in "eight-legged platitudes," [*bagu laodiao*]* such announcements are rather indiscreet because they arouse anxieties among people both at home and abroad about our country's stability. Their effect is mischievous.

---

*A literary composition originally prescribed for the imperial civil service examinations, known for rigidity of form and absence of ideas.

Hu Sheng's challenge to Zhou Yang triggered an ideological free-for-all at the session. The propagandists and intellectuals who attended the meeting, Zhou Yang, Yu Guangyuan, Hu Jiwei, Qin Chuan, Yang Xiguang, Li Chang, and others explained to the participants the history of the debate and attacked in their turn Wang Dongxing, Li Xin, Hu Sheng, Xiong Fu, and Wu Lengxi for all the damage they had done: persisting in the "two whatevers," the personality cult, hindering the emancipation of ideology, suppressing democracy, refusing to overturn phony verdicts, and so forth. The majority of leaders present conceded that the reformers were right and made the decision to relieve Wang Dongxing of his duties in the propaganda and ideology sections. The Third Plenum finally put an end to the ideological and cultural despotism of the "two whatevers" and China experienced a short period of free thought.

In a statement to this same plenum, a statement that later came to be seen as the plenum's principal document, Deng Xiaoping, using the same language and tone as Zhou Yang, confirmed the significance of the debate over the criterion of truth:

> The current debate about whether practice is the sole criterion for testing truth is also a debate about whether people's minds need to be emancipated. Everybody has recognized that this debate is highly important and necessary. Its importance is becoming clearer all the time. When everything has to be done by the book, when thinking turns rigid and blind faith is the fashion, it is impossible for a party or a nation to make progress. Its life will cease and that party or nation will perish. ... In this sense, the debate about the criterion for testing truth is really a debate about ideological line, about politics, about the future and the destiny of our Party and nation.[15]

The contribution to history of the Third Plenum was that it put an end to the despotic empire founded by Mao Zedong. During the two years that followed the smashing of the "Gang of Four," the alliance between Wang Dongxing and Hua Guofeng concentrated on advancing the "two whatevers," and propagated the personality cult. They tried to impose the dictatorship of a "wise" leader, without hesitating to execute young people who were accused of "viciously attacking" leaders of the Central Committee. Their purpose was to maintain the continuation of this despotic empire in their own hands. But the refutation of the "two whatevers" and the rehabilitation of persons on whose cases from the 1976 Tiananmen incident Mao had personally ruled wiped out the legal foundation of the empire. True, the plenum did permit Hua Guofeng to hang on to the title of supreme leader, but Wang Dongxing's loss of power in the ideological arena and the appointment of Hu Yaobang as secretary in chief of the Party and as head of the Propaganda Department greatly weakened Hua's status. Moreover, Hua's absolute authority in the ideological arena was already lost with the negation of the "two whatevers" and of the theory of "continuing the revolution under proletarian dictatorship." By insisting on the necessity of free thought and the realization of democracy, the Third Plenum put China on the road to modernization and promised to rid it forever of poverty and despotism. For the first time, the forces of reform in the Party and society were united and had happily married.

A new core, one that was later labeled the "second generation of leaders," appeared in the person of Deng Xiaoping. The Mao Zedong empire was over, and Hua's attempt to build a new Mao-like dynasty had foundered. The fate of China fell into the hands of Deng Xiaoping, a pragmatic politician seventy-four years old. He had been kicked off the stage three times as a rightist opportunist and a revisionist. Despite all that, he had been trusted and liked by Mao. What would his third return to the political scene portend for China and the world?

Notes

1. "Letter by Deng Xiaoping to Chairman Hua Guofeng and the Party Central Committee," April 10, 1977. See Central Document Number Fifteen, May 3, 1977.

2. Ibid.

3. The paragraph mentioning "understanding Mao Zedong Thought taken as an integral whole" in the first section of this speech by Deng Xiaoping was the only part included in Deng Xiaoping, *Selected Works of Deng Xiaoping: 1975–1982 (Deng Xiaoping Wenxuan: 1975–1982)* (Beijing: People's Publishing House, 1983), pp. 39–44. The other two parts, discussing "Chairman Hua" and "myself," were dropped.

4. *Chinese Communist Party Constitution*. Approved at the Eleventh Party Congress held in August 1977.

5. "Abide by past policies" was contained in a note written to Hua Guofeng by Mao Zedong not long before Mao died. The "Gang of Four" changed this to read "abide by policies laid down" [*an jiding fangzhen ban*]. Hua Guofeng took this as an unauthorized alteration. Later, this was considered a major crime committed by the "Gang of Four."

6. Deng Xiaoping, "Speech at the All-Military Conference on Political Work" (June 2, 1978), in *Selected Works*, p. 109.

7. The so-called theory of continuing the revolution under proletarian dictatorship was first proposed in an article titled "Celebrating the Fiftieth Anniversary of the October Revolution," jointly published in the *People's Daily*, the *Liberation Army Daily*, and the *Red Flag*, November 6, 1967. It was originally drafted by editors of those papers and was approved by Chen Boda and Yao Wenyuan. Later, it was considered the greatest contribution to Marxism by Mao Zedong. At the time of the publication of volume 5 of the *Selected Works of Mao Zedong*, the entire volume was judged to be a compendium of the theory of "continuing the revolution under proletarian dictatorship." Hua Guofeng naturally became the successor of that theory.

8. At that time, Feng Wenbin was vice president of the Central Party School and an assistant to Hu Yaobang. In Yan'an Feng Wenbin was vice secretary of the Communist Youth League and was well connected to Ye Jianying and Chen Yun. Feng played a

very important role in passing on information from Democracy Wall to these leaders during the 1978 Third Plenum.

9. *People's Daily,* November 28, 1978.

10. These two sentences from Ye Jianying's speech delivered at the Central Work Conference were later deleted by Hu Qiaomu when the central document was formally transmitted to the rest of the Party.

11. Peng Dehuai was a most courageous general with the greatest military ability in the CCP. Mao once complimented him in a poem: "Who dares swing the sword on the horse? Only my great general Peng." In 1959, Peng's letter to Mao Zedong criticizing the 1958 "Great Leap Forward" was correct, whereas Mao's accusation against him was erroneous. [For a review of this titanic struggle see Roderick MacFarquhar, *The Origins of the Cultural Revolution 2: The Great Leap Forward, 1958–1960* (New York: Columbia University Press, 1983), Part 3.]

12. Tao Zhu was once the Number Four leader in the ranking of the Standing Committee of the Politburo, just below Mao Zedong, Lin Biao, and Zhou Enlai. Because of his conflict with Chen Boda and Jiang Qing during the "Cultural Revolution," Tao was removed from his position in January 1967, and later, after being accused of treason, he was persecuted to death.

13. The clique of sixty-one traitors refers to the sixty-one CCP members who were arrested by the Nationalists just prior to the anti-Japanese War. They were released in 1936 from prison after writing formal confessions. But this was not an individual act, rather it was a way to gain release from prison approved by the CCP because of the crying need for cadres during the anti-Japanese War. Peng Zhen, Bo Yibo, and others, after being released from prison, held important positions, and so accusations concerning their disloyalty were incorrect.

14. The so-called accusation in 1957 of "rightist bourgeois" was removed just prior to the 1978 Third Plenum. But these people were not completely rehabilitated as they were still referred to as "rightists whose labels have been removed" and were still discriminated against politically. After the Third Plenum, however, the majority were totally rehabilitated.

15. Deng Xiaoping, "Emancipate the Mind, Seek Truth from Facts, and Unite as One in Looking to the Future" (December 13, 1978), in *Selected Works,* p. 133.

4

The War to Punish Vietnam
Lays the Foundation of
Deng's Power

Three incidents greatly influenced the evolution of the political situation in China after the 1978 Third Plenum: First, Hu Qiaomu joined in an alliance with the "two whatevers" faction to propagate a new "anti-rightist" campaign; second, on his return from the United States Deng Xiaoping launched a punitive war against Vietnam that he called "a defensive retaliation"; and third, Deng became very concerned with his "deeply felt belief in his military genius" [*junshi tiancai qingjie*] when Hua Guofeng made a surprise inspection of military units.

Once the "two whatevers" theory was criticized at the Third Plenum, neither Wang Dongxing nor Li Xin could continue to lead the theory and propaganda sectors. And so Hu Yaobang was appointed secretary in chief [*mishuzhang*] of the Party and head of the Propaganda Department. Hu Qiaomu had himself been appointed deputy secretary in chief [*fu mishuzhang*] and director of the Office of the Committee for the Editing and Publication of the Works of Mao Zedong, thereby taking charge of theory work. Soon after his appointment, Hu Qiaomu did three unexpected things. A Chinese proverb says, "A new official possesses three torches." That's why people now spoke of "Hu Qiaomu's three torches."

The first torch thrown by Hu Qiaomu was aimed at the *People's Daily*, which under the byline "special commentator" had published an article called "Long Live the People—On the Movement of the Revolutionary Masses on Tiananmen Square." The article underlined an important point:

> How is it that in a country under a proletarian dictatorship a few thieves like those in the "Gang of Four" could seize so much power and act according to their own will and ignore the law, causing immense loss to the Party and the nation? How could they maintain their status for ten years? And then collapse only after the

awakening of the masses, who fought so hard and sacrificed so much in the battle against them? How can we prevent such a tragedy from happening again? The Tiananmen incident tells us that the key factor is to give true power to the masses. If the people had truly been able to choose leaders at different levels of government according to their hopes and interests, if the people had the right to supervise the leaders and to dismiss those proven unqualified, the "Gang of Four" would never have been able to rise to a position of such importance and stay there so long. If the people were really able to practice their democratic rights as described in the constitution, the "Gang of Four" could never have used counter-revolutionary violence against the people on the square and shed blood.[1]

The article added that despite the victory of the democratic revolution in our country in 1949, antipeople and antidemocratic forces remained. China remained a workers' state poisoned by the "bureaucracy," as Lenin had already described it, with a "modern bureaucracy 'embodied by Communist Party members.'" In such a context, the people's democratic rights were very often flouted. That's why the main political task over the long haul for Party comrades and the people was to continue to fight for and protect the people's democracy.

As soon as Hu Qiaomu got wind of this article, he rang up Hu Jiwei, editor in chief of the *People's Daily*, and criticized its contents. He accused the author of "Long Live the People" of "only praising the people, and not the Party and the leadership, and of advocating bourgeois democracy and attempting to establish a democratic party in order to reform the Communist Party."

Next, Hu Qiaomu hurled his second torch. As the newly appointed director of the Office of the Committee on Mao Zedong Works, he went over to Maojiawan [the location of Lin Biao's old residence in Beijing] to demand that Li Xin, Wu Lengxi, Hu Sheng, and Xiong Fu be assigned to the Policy Research Office of the State Council. The staff members of this office accused Hu of "surrendering to the partisans of the 'two whatevers.'" Such a criticism was not altogether justified. Hu Qiaomu had in effect decided to block the move toward democracy and reform, and to pull this off he needed an army of dogmatic theoreticians and dyed-in-the-wool totalitarians. With Wang Dongxing and Li Xin's "two whatevers" theory squad already in existence, naturally he wanted to throw his lot in with them. But after the strong objections of the Policy Research Office, the Central Committee did not approve Hu's plan for the Office of the Committee on Mao Zedong Works to swallow up the Policy Research Office. It was Deng Liqun who later on and by other means helped Hu Qiaomu organize the theory squad of despotic dogmatists. Deng Liqun not only recruited Kang Sheng and Wang Dongxing's old troops, he also recruited old "rebel faction" [*zaofanpai*]*

---

*This was the most radical leftist faction during the Cultural Revolution.

forces that had been cultivated during the "Cultural Revolution" at the *Red Flag* by Chen Boda, Wang Li, Guan Feng, Qin Benyu, and Yao Wenyuan. He was thus able to form a theory squad consisting of flunkies who doubled as henchmen, devoted body and soul to Hu Qiaomu and Deng Xiaoping—the "commander in chief and deputy commander in chief of the ideological arena." They did not cease to stir up trouble on the theory front, lying, attacking, and squeezing out any independent spirits who didn't want to submit to the domination of their band of ideologues.

The third torch was intended to provoke a new "anti-rightist" campaign. At the close of the Third Plenum, Hu Qiaomu immediately claimed that three winds blew through society, the "anti–Communist Party wind," the "anti-socialist" wind and the "anti–Marxist-Leninist-Maoist" wind. He warned anyone who wanted to hear it: "The situation at present is very similar to the first half of 1957 when the anti-rightist campaign began. Don't force Chairman Hua to launch another anti-rightist campaign." In fact, it was Hu Qiaomu himself who attempted to provoke Hua to start another anti-rightist movement after the Third Plenum. But Hua Guofeng did not endorse Hu Qiaomu's analysis of the situation. Hu Yaobang later told me that Hu Qiaomu then appeared to make a vague self-criticism for throwing his three torches, although behind the scenes he refused to abandon his original plans. He was simply waiting for the opportune moment, which was not long in coming. After the "defensive retaliation" against Vietnam, Deng Xiaoping accepted Hu Qiaomu's estimation of the situation and pronounced before the January to April, 1979, Conference on Guidelines in Theory Work a discourse in anti-rightist tones on the subject of "upholding the Four Cardinal Principles" and "anti-rightism," a discourse that came from the pen of Hu Qiaomu.

The initial goal of this conference on theory work was to provide a new theoretical foundation for the emancipation of ideology and democratic progress initiated by the Third Plenum. Its origin can be traced back to the debate before the Third Plenum over the criterion of truth.

Xiong Fu, the editor in chief of the *Red Flag* and a proponent of the "two whatevers," prohibited all discussion of the theme in his review and sent a long article prepared for the *Red Flag* titled "Reviewing 'On Practice'"[2] to the Standing Committee of the Politburo. In the article he wrote of the need to struggle against erroneous ideological trends such as "skepticism and uncertainty, and so forth." This was nothing more than an expansion of the contents of Wu Lengxi's famous telephone call. When the article was delivered to the Politburo Standing Committee, Ye Jianying suggested that a conference on guidelines in theory work be held to resolve major theoretical issues. The Third Plenum had upheld the partisans of "practice is the sole criterion of truth," but given that it was such an important issue, the Central Committee had to create this conference suggested by Ye Jianying. Presiding over the

November-December 1978 Central Work Conference, Hua Guofeng announced in his closing speech: "We have dealt with a number of topics at this
conference, and since time was limited, we haven't been able to give enough
time to these theoretical issues. Comrades of the Politburo have decided to
adopt Marshal Ye's suggestion and hold a special conference devoted to this
matter right after the Third Plenum."[3]

The first session of this theory conference, which lasted from January 18 to
February 15, concentrated mainly on two big questions: democracy and freedom of thought. It also came up with a series of important proposals for
eliminating the personality cult, abolishing the lifetime tenure of leaders, and
negating the theory of "continuing the revolution under proletarian dictatorship," along with issues regarding economic reform. Hua Guofeng, Ye
Jianying, and Deng Xiaoping all followed the conference closely by reading
briefs and listening to reports, all of which they found highly satisfactory.
Deng gave a speech on January 27 (two days prior to his visit to the United
States) in which he urged the delegates to talk about democracy and to prepare a document to be published on May Fourth.[4] But during the hiatus that
followed this first session, the situation in China abruptly changed.

Before the end of February, Deng Xiaoping launched a war against Vietnam. Military strategy vis-à-vis Vietnam, the Soviet Union, and Taiwan, and
the Chinese-U.S. relationship were some of the closely linked issues Deng had
in his head before he left for the United States. His visit reinforced his decision for war against Vietnam. The Carter administration viewed this war as an
important element of the anti-Soviet strategy the United States and China
had in common. For Deng, this offensive had three objectives: First, to assist
Cambodia; second, to counteract the Soviet Union strategically; and finally,
to gain the trust of the Americans so that they would support modernization
in China.

The war broke out on February 17. Chinese troops entered Vietnamese
territory from Guangxi and Yunnan provinces. Deng Xiaoping believed that
this offensive would be as easy as the one Mao launched against India in the
1960s, unfolding as planned and winning the approval of all Chinese people.
But Chinese troops ran up against surprising Vietnamese resistance. The command structure and communications of the Chinese army were mediocre, so
that in this mountainous terrain with only jungle paths, operations were very
difficult. Chinese troops didn't reach Liangshan [Lao-Kay, Vietnam] until
March 5, more than fifteen days after hostilities began. The order to retreat
was made immediately thereafter. Withdrawal was completed by March 16.
The war had lasted exactly one month. Originally Deng had said that once the
Chinese were there, it would be essential to really smash the Vietnamese. That
goal absolutely was not attained. The prestige of Vietnam was not impaired,
and the Khmer Rouge were not relieved. Moreover, the war revealed some of

the internal weaknesses of the Chinese army that made it unfit for modern warfare.*

The relative defeat of the entire enterprise provoked public unrest in China. Some people started to criticize Deng on Democracy Wall. Wei Jingsheng pasted a big-character poster on the wall titled "Democracy or the New Autocracy?" that directly criticized Deng Xiaoping, asserting that he was in danger of becoming a new despot.

Deng Xiaoping was furious. He could tolerate Democracy Wall when criticism was directed at Mao Zedong, but certainly not when it was aimed at himself. Above all, he couldn't stand criticism of his war of "defensive retaliation." Such an attack severely wounded Deng's deeply felt belief in his own military genius. Deng had always been very proud. In 1954, when military ranks were distributed, Mao had awarded none to himself, but he had wanted to make a marshal of Deng. Deng declined the offer, not because he didn't appreciate the promotion, but because he thought he could hang on to a bigger margin of maneuver by remaining without rank. At that time, he had no position in the military, but in the Party he was secretary in chief (*mishuzhang*), charged with assisting the Party chairman. Mao also made him vice-chairman of the National Defense Council. Among the twelve-member Central Military Commission, only Mao and Deng did not carry military rank while the other ten members were all marshals. And of the sixteen chairmen and vice chairmen of the National Defense Council, again only Mao and Deng alone did not carry military rank. The rest of the fourteen members, except for those ten marshals, were four former outstanding Nationalist generals, including Fu Zuoyi, Cheng Qian, Zhang Zhizhong, and Long Yun who all received the rank of general in the People's Republic. Mao and Deng were the only two holding supreme military positions without military rank. Zhou Enlai, a longtime member of the Central Military Commission and a former commander during the war, was excluded from these two supreme positions.[5]

Later, when Mao Zedong criticized the military rank system, he praised Deng for having the foresight to refuse all rank. Twenty years later, when he had eliminated his two designated successors, Liu Shaoqi and Lin Biao, Mao criticized the way Zhou Enlai ran the Politburo and Central Military Commission, maintaining that he "debated neither military nor political problems." And so once again, at an enlarged meeting of the Central Military Commission, Mao nominated Deng as the secretary in chief of both the Politburo and the Central Military Commission. But since there was no such posi-

---

*An example of the Chinese military's ineptitude was the firing by scattered Chinese units at the "enemy" during the night only to discover in morning light that they had fired on their own men.

tion in either the Politburo or the commission, the Central Committee nominated Deng to be vice chairman of the Central Military Commission and PLA chief of staff. What this meant in reality was that Deng took over all military power on behalf of Mao. Deep down, Deng was convinced that after Mao's, his own military genius knew no equal. With a touch of disdain, he once told Lin Biao: "You, you won the battles of Liaoshen and Pingjin, and of Beijing-Tianjin. But I, I won the Huaihai and the Yangtze River Crossing battles!" The message was clear: My two battles were more significant and decisive.

Especially now that Mao was dead, Deng couldn't tolerate any challenge to his military authority. Perhaps down deep, he himself was dissatisfied by the way his punitive attack on Vietnam turned out. This could be one more reason why he reacted violently when this sore was touched—and why Hu Qiaomu and Deng Liqun chose this moment to intervene.

After the complete withdrawal of Chinese troops on March 16, 1979, Deng turned his attention to domestic affairs. Hu Qiaomu and Deng Liqun made it their business to report on the Democracy Wall attacks on the war and Deng personally. They advanced their own interests by coming out again with the same analysis they had made after the Third Plenum, that the situation was worse than it was prior to the 1957 anti-rightist struggle. This time, they addressed themselves not to Hua Guofeng, but to Deng Xiaoping, in order to incite a new campaign against the right. This was the origin of the speech delivered by Deng Xiaoping at the end of March before the Conference on Guidelines in Theory Work, where he spoke on "upholding the Four Cardinal Principles." In the draft prepared by Hu Qiaomu, it was expressly stated: "The right is the main danger, and the Party should concentrate its energy against the right." But this formula encountered opposition from the participants, who argued that its direction was inconsistent with that designated by the recent plenum, and in the end it did not appear in Deng Xiaoping's official speech. Nevertheless, it was a general order of mobilization in anti-rightist tones given before an audience of more than six thousand people, including not only theory personnel but also leading cadres of the Party, of the military, of the central government, and of the municipality of Beijing.

Deng confirmed in this speech the complete rupture of his alliance with the democracy movement in society. Deng also mentioned the names of a number of students and workers active in the Democracy Wall movement and condemned them for collaborating with political forces in Taiwan and abroad—with hooligan organizations in society and remnants of the "Gang of Four"—and accused them of "openly opposing the proletarian dictatorship."[6]

Hardly two months had gone by since Deng, on January 27, had declared: "Democracy Wall, what energy!"[7] And now he was claiming that "these counterrevolutionaries and bad elements ... must be dealt with sternly and according to the law!"[8]

Deng Xiaoping also tossed a warning to the reformers in the Party: "These counterrevolutionaries do all they can to use as a pretext—or a shield—indiscreet statements of one sort or another made by some of our comrades."[9]

Just four months earlier, during his talk with the Japanese Socialist Party chairman, had not Deng Xiaoping affirmed the big-character posters as "a sign of the stability in our country"? Did these proposals, officially published in the *People's Daily,* constitute "a shield"? To be sure, Deng Xiaoping was not criticizing himself; he was referring to those "indiscreet statements" by Hu Yaobang and the intellectuals denounced by Hu Qiaomu. This speech ("Uphold the Four Cardinal Principles") drafted by Hu Qiaomu now furnished Deng Xiaoping with the political program that allowed him to build his future despotic empire; it was a major historical step backward from the Third Plenum.

Mar '79

But what about Hua Guofeng? During this entire time he was nowhere to be seen. He probably had not expected such a spectacular turnabout. Of course, Hu Yaobang did not expect it either. He dared not invite Hua to give a speech at the Conference on Guidelines in Theory Work, although prior to the conference Hua had mentioned that both he and Deng Xiaoping would give speeches and that a group to draft his speech had already been formed.[10] After Deng's announcement of his new political guideline (it was merely a shallow reprint of Mao's Six Criteria for doing a good job in the Socialist Education movement in the early 1960s), the Conference on Guidelines pitiably ended its work. But Deng's sudden about-face aroused strong political reactions throughout the country.

First, the alliance between the reform elements within the Party and the democratic elements in society forged at the Third Plenum was terminated. That was Deng's first betrayal of the democratic movement. Democracy Wall, activists in the democracy movement, and their organizations and journals, so recently flattered by Deng, now became his targets. It was now forbidden to post posters on Xidan wall. The initial move called for removing all the posters to the remote Yuetan Park in northwestern Beijing. After that, a complete ban was placed on all posters. Organizations and journals that had appeared in the democratic movement were now declared illegal. Totally unprepared both ideologically and organizationally for Deng's first betrayal, the democratic elements in society withdrew temporarily without retaliating.

Second, the reform elements within the Party, which had been no better prepared for Deng's turnabout than the people, dared not directly express their disagreement. They tried to slow the historic retreat provoked in Deng's speech by putting a different spin on his words. On April 3, Hu Yaobang furnished the following explanation:

Nowadays some people say: It's a recurring illness, it's a new battle against the right. When the man in the street says this, we can understand it. But cadres who say that would be considered naive. In two and a half years we have drawn so many lessons from history! We have rehabilitated so many people mistakenly accused of "rightism." How can we hastily and in total confusion start attacks all over again on the "right"? Recurring illness and the battle against the right are not the order of the day.[11]

Third, the political elements in the Party resisting the reform line of the Third Plenum became active again and put on a full show at the Central Work Conference on April 5–28, 1979. Normally, this kind of conference was held to discuss economic issues, but as soon as it began, quite a few high-level cadres expressed their discontent about the Third Plenum. They attributed responsibility for the troubles and demonstrations, otherwise rare at that time, to the emphasis on ideological emancipation and promotion of democracy at the Third Plenum. Those who had supported the "two whatevers" and been silent for the three months following the Third Plenum began to talk again:

> The Third Plenum was rightist, and the Conference on Guidelines in Theory Work was also rightist. Political reinterpretation of the Tiananmen incident provoked demonstrations all over China. Reversing historical cases caused a negation of Chairman Mao. Now that the Four Cardinal Principles have been advocated, that means we were correct after all. It was wrong for the Third Plenum to criticize the "two whatevers."

Three months had passed since the Third Plenum. The fact of the matter was that the call for "ideological emancipation and seeking truth from facts" had not had time to spread very extensively over China. It was apparent that Deng's "Four Cardinal Principles" had aided the antireform force. The budding process of ideological emancipation was seriously hobbled.

Another incident then occurred that intensified the conflict between Deng Xiaoping and Hua Guofeng. After the war in Vietnam, Hua had made a tour of the military. When he traveled to China's northeast and east to review the troops, he was warmly welcomed. Guards of honor above all wished him welcome. I personally had no idea why Hua suddenly had an interest in inspecting troops. Had he perhaps felt abandoned by Deng during the period of the Sino-Vietnamese War—he who was chairman of the Central Military Affairs Commission? And did he want to prove he still existed? Or more likely, did he figure that Deng's expression of power was a threat to himself and want to find support in the military? Perhaps none of these surmises are correct. It may simply have been that his friends in the military, fearing that he was feeling lonely, invited him for a tour.

Deng, however, always showed himself to be very vigilant, very attentive. Combined with the fact that the Vietnam war had revealed problems in the military, pictures of the troops welcoming Hua obviously cut him to the quick. But the most important thing without question was to prevent the military from rallying behind Hua Guofeng. Without the slightest hesitation, "policy" contingent upon "power"

Deng decided as vice chairman of the Central Military Commission to mobilize a campaign to "review the debate over the criterion of truth." In effect he was simply pursuing a criticism of Hua's "two whatevers" in the military. Later this review spread from the military to the entire country.

Thus, the year 1979 witnessed two contradictory developments: On the one hand, in the country, the attack on the Democracy Wall movement was launched; on the other hand, at every level of the Party and the military, in the name of "reviewing the debate over the criterion of truth," there evolved a measured and veiled criticism of Hua Guofeng. At the time, Hua was still officially Party chairman, chairman of the Central Military Commission, and premier. But from the moment he observed the welcome Hua received in the barracks, Deng made up his mind to change this state of affairs. Such is the explanation for the halt of the new anti-rightist campaign in the military and the Party and the revving up of the anti-"leftist" movement.

By choosing anti-leftism after a brief anti-rightist detour, Deng was not going against the historical current or the common desire of the Chinese people. Despite his betrayal of his allies in the Democracy Wall movement, he did not lose his large popular support. Despite everything, China once again seemed to be stepping into an era of hope, moving toward reform and opening up to the outside world.

Notes

1. Special commentator, "Long Live the People," *People's Daily*, December 1978. [Crowds gathered in Tiananmen Square on April 5, 1976, shouted "Long live the people" (*renmin wansui*)—a democratic twist on the chant "Long live Chairman Mao" spouted by Red Guards during the Cultural Revolution.]

2. This article was never published in the *Red Flag*, though it was submitted to the Conference on Guidelines in Theory Work for discussion.

3. "Comments by Hua Guofeng at the December 13, 1978 Central Work Conference Preceding the Third Plenum of the Eleventh Party Congress."

4. Hu Qiaomu didn't pay the slightest attention to Deng Xiaoping's speech, for he knew that Deng would soon travel to the United States where he would have important consultations. Hu also realized that Deng would launch the war to punish Vietnam upon his return. Perhaps Deng estimated that in the future when democracy was no longer practiced, dictatorship would reign and therefore he was preparing for the political program of the new empire.

5. From September 15 to 18, 1954, the First Session of the First National People's Congress held in Beijing set up the National Defense Council and appointed Mao Zedong as the council chairman. Following the suggestion of appointing Mao as state chairman, the congress also appointed the vice chairmen of the council and other members. Zhu De, Peng Dehuai, Lin Biao, Liu Bocheng, He Long, Chen Yi, Deng Xiaoping, Luo Ruiqing, Xu Xiangqian, Nie Rongzhen, Ye Jianying, Fu Zuoyi, Cheng Qian, Zhang Zhizhong, and Long Yun were all appointed vice chairmen. On Septem-

ber 28 the CCP Politburo set up the Central Military Commission consisting of Mao Zedong, Zhu De, Peng Dehuai, Lin Biao, Liu Bocheng, He Long, Chen Yi, Deng Xiaoping, Luo Ruiqing, Xu Xiangqian, Nie Rongzhen, and Ye Jianying. See People's Liberation Army, *Sixty-Year Chronology* (*Liushi nian dashiji*) (Beijing: Military Science Publishing House, 1988), pp. 538–539.

6. Deng Xiaoping, "Uphold the Four Cardinal Principles" (March 30, 1979), in *Selected Works of Deng Xiaoping: 1975–1982 (Deng Xiaoping Wenxuam: 1975–1982)* (Beijing: People's Publishing House, 1983), p. 160.

7. Deng Xiaoping, "Speech on Hearing Reports from the Conference on Guidelines in Theory Work," January 27, 1979.

8. Deng Xiaoping, "Uphold the Four Cardinal Principles," p. 161.

9. Ibid.

10. Just before the first session of the Conference on Guidelines in Theory Work came to an end, a drafting group was established consisting of seven people: Hu Yaobang, Hu Qiaomu, Yu Guangyuan, Wu Jiang, Ruan Ming, Lin Jianqing, and Li Honglin. However, they only met once. In discussions of the speeches to be made during the second session of the conference by the Party chairman and vice chairman, the drafting group discussed the outline of Hua Guofeng's speech. Hu Yaobang came up with a proposal that was not discussed; rather it was decided that Hu Qiaomu would come up with a more complete outline that would be discussed by the group, which would then begin the actual writing of the speech. However, no further meetings were ever held.

11. "Speech by Hu Yaobang at the Closing Session of the Conference on Guidelines in Theory Work," April 3, 1979.

PART II

The Critical Element in Deng Xiaoping's Reform (1979–1986)

In 1979, ten years before he mobilized several tens of thousands of troops to surround Beijing and ordered tanks into Tiananmen Square, thus aborting China's reform, Deng Xiaoping had an unprecedented historical opportunity to carry out reform. It was one of the rare moments in modern Chinese history when the common people were united with the Communist Party. Hu Yaobang once commented that this constituted a spiritual emancipation unseen anywhere in the nation since the proposal to establish a "free and democratic China" at the Seventh Party Congress in 1945.

In fact, the historical opportunity offered to Deng Xiaoping following the Third Plenum was even better than the one that presented itself to Mao Zedong. For in that earlier era, fully half of China was occupied by the Japanese invaders and Chiang K'ai-shek. But now an optimistic spirit toward the future and fate of the nation permeated China.

Second, consider the situation in the Communist Party. From the central to the local levels, a tremendous reform force had evolved, along with the emergence of large numbers of Party and governmental leaders possessed of strategic insight and rich practical experience. Hu Yaobang, Wan Li, Zhao Ziyang, Xi Zhongxun, Li Chang, Zhou Yang, Hu Jiwei, Ren Zhongyi, Xiang Nan, and Zhou Hui were among the most notable of these. There were also quite a few intellectual pillars in the areas of economics, politics, ideology, culture, and theory. The leading force determined to implement the reform was full of hope and confidence about its goals. Its members relied on persuasion to get their case across, rather than the usual practice of purging cadres who held different views. Hence, although the "two whatevers" and Mao and Hua's personality cults came in for a fair share of criticism, it was accompanied neither by "ruthless struggles" nor "cruel attacks." Indeed, Hua Guofeng remained in his leading position as Party chairman and showed considerable progress after the Third Plenum, for instance, refusing to endorse the proposal by Hu Qiaomu for another "anti-rightist" campaign. Hua also supported the proposal by Hu Yaobang to hold the Conference on Guidelines in Theory Work that was scheduled in order to prepare the theoretical groundwork for overall reform. As a result of Hua's change of heart, Wang Dongxing, Wu De, Ji Dengkui, Chen Xilian, Li Xin, and Guo Yufeng, who were opponents of reform in the main sectors of the Party, government, and the military, surrendered without a fight. At the same time, new antireform forces had not yet formed.

Third, let's consider the international situation. The changes announced at the Third Plenum were supported by countries from all over the world, the exceptions being the Soviet Union, which was then ruled by Brezhnev, and its client state Vietnam. New developments occurred in the relationship between China and the major Western countries, including the United States, and also Japan. Following his visit to the United States, Deng Xiaoping won the support of the U.S. government for himself and his policies. Although the Soviet Union under Brezhnev appeared on the surface to be strong, internally its economy was stagnating and its military expansion was in its terminal phase. Soon it would be trapped, mired in the swamp of the Afghanistan war. Further, the Carter administration was confronted with problems like Iran and needed support from China against Brezhnev's apparently expanding empire. By comparison, China had just recovered from the disaster of the "Cultural Revolution" and was rapidly changing its reputation among socialist countries from one of despotism to that of a pioneer in democracy, reform, and opening up to the outside world. It was also a rising star in international politics.

Such advantageous conditions both at home and abroad provided Deng Xiaoping with a historic chance to alter China's fate. His room for maneuver to implement reform was far wider than Gorbachev's six years later. But the question remains: Did Deng Xiaoping adequately and effectively utilize this historic initiative?

The answer is clearly no. At one time, Deng Xiaoping captured the forces of reform in China and seemed ready to march forward. But he was a pragmatic politician without profound insight. He lacked a fixed target and too frequently altered his judgment and changed his decisions in reaction to the immediate situation, making one concession after another to the Chen Yun *focus on failure of single person* (handwritten)

clique (*Chen Yun jituan*).* At critical junctures, he made the wrong decision with sudden changes in direction away from reform, and thus squandered the best opportunity for meaningful reform in China. The critical element in all of this was political reform, on which Deng Xiaoping and Chen Yun had major differences. Ultimately, Deng completely caved in to the Chen Yun clique, discarding political reform and maintaining despotism. This was the political basis for his joint action with Chen Yun in crushing the democratic movement in China on June 4, 1989.

On the issue of political reform, there were three advances and accompanying retreats by Deng Xiaoping. In his report at the Third Plenum given on December 13, 1978, he proposed that "to protect the people's democratic rights, [we] must institutionalize democracy." This was the first time Deng Xiaoping had ever spoken out on the vital point of institutionalizing political reform. He stated: "To ensure people's democracy, we must strengthen our legal system. Democracy has to be institutionalized and written into law, so as to make sure that institutions and laws do not change whenever the leadership changes, or whenever the leaders change their views or shift the focus of their attention."[1]

I drafted that part of Deng's speech on the basis of comments he had made during a talk with his speech writers on December 2. On that occasion he said: "The reality of democracy must be stabilized in legal form. It must be institutionalized so that it is protected by the system."[2] Of course, since I was concerned with history and the reality of the situation, I was given free rein to write what I wanted. Deng's report continued: "The trouble now is that our legal system is incomplete, with many laws yet to be enacted. Very often, what leaders say is taken as the law and anyone who disagrees is called a law breaker. That kind of law changes whenever a leader's views change."[3]

I personally think that this was the key issue in the transition from the despotic, totalitarian rule of the Mao Zedong empire to democratic politics. The Third Plenum negated the "two whatevers" and the old- and new-style versions of individual worship for Mao and Hua. This created the historical premise for terminating totalitarian rule by the despot. But the only way to consolidate the democratic fruits gained by the alliance between Party reform forces and the social democratic movement in the transitional period was to institutionalize and legalize democracy, that is, to achieve the fundamental reform of the political system and to prevent present and future leaders from returning to the old system of despotic, totalitarian rule.

Deng Xiaoping's spiritual state at the time indicated that he took this transition very seriously. It wasn't a hoax or some temporary strategy. Prior to the

---

*According to Ruan Ming, this powerful clique of top conservative leaders around Chen Yun consisted of Wang Zhen, Deng Liqun, Hu Qiaomu, Yao Yilin, and Song Ping. See Glossary.

Conference on Guidelines in Theory Work he had also proposed that a study be conducted to determine why an even better democracy than that existing in capitalist democracies had not been established in the Soviet Union in the sixty years since the October Revolution. Clearly, moving the political system toward democracy was one of the earliest issues Deng Xiaoping considered. Unconcerned with becoming the "emperor" or "the backstage ruler" [*taishang huangdi*], he was able to ponder the historical lessons of Mao and Stalin's autocracy and to limit as well Hua Guofeng's power as a leader.

However, Deng is a pragmatist [*shiyongzhuyizhe*] at heart, and his views and concerns change in accord with immediate political needs. Just as he was consolidating his position after the war against Vietnam, he was bombarded with criticisms both from Democracy Wall and from within the Party. This led him to retreat from the position of institutionalizing and legalizing democracy and to accept Hu Qiaomu's proposal for a new "anti-rightist" campaign. He also announced the "Four Cardinal Principles."

But that was not the end of Deng Xiaoping's political reform. He would make another change in direction—again in accord with his political needs. As for his first retreat, this came in his grand speech on March 30, 1979, "Uphold the Four Cardinal Principles," drafted by Hu Qiaomu. This was actually a negation of his speech entitled "Emancipate the Mind, Seek Truth From Facts, and Unite as One in Looking to the Future." But the alliance between Party reform elements and the social democratic movement was by that time already severed, even though Deng had launched the campaign to "review the debate over the criterion of truth." With the ebbing of the Xidan Democracy Wall movement, it was impossible for a strong political force to form in urban areas to counteract the incredible resistance to reform emanating from the bureaucratic, autocratic system. The center of reform in China would inevitably shift to the vast rural areas where the influence of the bureaucracy is relatively weaker.

Notes

1. Deng Xiaoping, "Emancipate the Mind, Seek Truth From Facts, and Unite as One in Looking to the Future," in *Selected Works of Deng Xiaoping: 1975–1982 (Deng Xiaoping Wenxuan: 1975–1982)* (Beijing: People's Publishing House, 1983), p. 136.

2. See Introduction to this book.

3. Deng Xiaoping, "Emancipate the Mind," p. 136. [Equating the leader's words with the "law" was also a central feature of Stalinism and Hitler's Germany. See Ian Grey, *Stalin: Man of History* (London: Abacus, 1979), p. 259; and Ian Kershaw, *The Hitler Myth: Image and Reality in the Third Reich* (Oxford, UK: Oxford University Press, 1989), p. 255.]

5

The Apotheosis of Chinese Reform: The Countryside Overwhelms the Cities

Most people entertain a false idea about the history of reform in China. They believe that reform was conceived by Deng Xiaoping, or by the 1978 Third Plenum, and applied according to a well-conceived process, orchestrated by higher authorities to move from the countryside toward the cities and from the economic sphere toward the political. The reality was quite otherwise. To be sure, Hu Qiaomu had drafted a document on agriculture for the Third Plenum, but this was a proposal that actually opposed the household contract system [*baochan daohu*]. This plenum had also affirmed the famous slogan according to which practice is the sole criterion of truth. But the first people to put this maxim to the test were China's peasants, who by their own "practice" won control of their land and the fruits of their labor. That was China's first step toward freedom and democracy, its first step toward reform and openness to the outside world.

The foundation of democracy is the autonomy of the individual in matters at once ethical and economic. The progress achieved by Chinese peasants in this direction constituted the essential element of the ten-year reform that China has experienced. The tanks on Tiananmen Square in 1989 could crush the bodies of students and workers longing for freedom, but they could not destroy the acquisitions of the emancipated peasants. We can say that all the reform measures of the last ten years—the individual contracts [*lianchan chengbao*] and the rural enterprises—were instigated by the creativity of the peasants, all in the countryside. The special economic zones were first created in Shenzhen and Zhuhai, not Beijing and Shanghai, and that was no accident. Reform in China burst forth in rural areas where dogmatism, bureaucratism, and totalitarian controls were less crushing. The real brains behind rural reform in the countryside were not Deng Xiaoping, nor Zhao Ziyang or Wan Li, but the Chinese peasants themselves.

In fact, the very first reformers were the members of the eighteen farming households of the Xiaogang production team in Anhui province's Fengyang county, at that time, one of China's poorest. They wrote down their decision to contract output to family households in a document that stipulated that if in the course of putting this system into practice the production team leader was imprisoned, everyone would take turns bringing food to him. That if he was executed, the entire village would undertake the responsibility for raising his children until they reached the age of eighteen. And the eighteen farming families signed this document with their fingerprints. This is how rural reform in China began.

Just why was the household contract system in rural China, or as it was later called, "the individual household responsibility system" [*jiating lianchan chengbao zerenzhi*], so significant? The answer lies in the fact that it was the very first step taken by Chinese peasants since liberation in 1949 toward establishing an independent personality [*dulide renge*] of their own. The switch from the system of agricultural cooperatives to that of the People's Communes in 1958, which appeared to be spontaneous, was superficially the choice of the majority of China's rural inhabitants. But a deeper look at the causes show that it in fact was the upshot of an unhappy choice imposed by force.

Toward the end of the 1940s, China's rural population had supported the Chinese Communist Party because it represented their fundamental interests. "Land to the tiller," Mao had declared in 1945.[1] Mao also stated that the future of the Chinese countryside was industrialization. "Tens of millions of peasants would enter the cities and factories" and "build many great modern cities" and "rural inhabitants would become urban."[2] But this process, which responded to the common desire of China's peasantry and was aimed toward the development of productive forces, was interrupted by the Korean War in 1950. The blockade organized by the West forced China to draw closer to the Soviet Union. Korean War weapons were purchased from the Soviet Union. The defense and construction industries depended heavily on Soviet aid. The 156 major projects realized thanks to this aid consisted essentially of arms factories (airplanes, tanks, artillery) or heavy industry. The USSR sent a large number of experts to "Sovietize" government organs, factories, schools, and research institutes, resulting in the annihilation of the New Democracy and the disappearance of ideas like "land to the tiller."

What happened was that the adoption of the Soviet path of heavy industrial development and arms buildup rapidly expanded the demand of industrial and mining enterprises for grain and various industrial materials. To pay for the military and economic assistance furnished by the USSR in the Korean War and defense-related industrial machinery and equipment, it was necessary to ship great quantities of agricultural by-products to the Soviet Union. And finally, the Korean War itself demanded great quantities of grain for the military and for storage.

Thus it was that conflicts between the peasantry and the state began to expand. The year 1950 brought a good harvest. Chen Yun, who was then in charge of the economy, raised the matter of the use of all grains. He said:

> What should be done with surplus grain after the harvest in places like the northeast and Hubei, Hunan, and Jiangxi provinces? I think we can shift some to other areas of economic production and in the interim rely on the three hundred million peasants living near railway lines to store grain. If each peasant stores seventeen or eighteen *jin* [one *jin* = one-half kilogram], then the total will be fifty billion. This fifty billion [*jin*] along with another fifty billion in the hands of trading companies will play a very important role in our country's politics. Grain is our strategic material. If we are in constant control of 100 billion *jin* of grain, then Truman or Syngman Rhee won't concern us. If in disastrous years millions of people are in need of grain, the country can make up the supply. No problem.[3]

Then hardly two years later, the grain situation was completely changed. Chen Yun proposed on October 10, 1953, replacing the grain market with a state monopoly for purchasing and marketing of grain [*tonggou tongxiao*]. The Central Committee made a decision to create such a monopoly on October 16 and the State Council announced it on October 23 exactly as Chen Yun had proposed it. This monopoly originally applied only to grain, but it rapidly extended to cooking oil and other basic products. Knowing that this policy would enflame tensions between the state and the peasants, Chen Yun himself declared beforehand:

> Purchasing and rationing refer to purchasing in rural areas and rationing in the cities. Other methods don't work. If everyone agrees with this policy, then we should think it through and anticipate possible problems and outbreaks of chaos. In total there are 26,000 townships [*xiang*] and a million natural villages [*cun*]. If chaos breaks out in one out of every ten natural villages, that means altogether there will be chaos in 100,000 villages. There could be cases of people being beaten to death all over and even riots. This may affect the production incentives of the peasantry, for even though they are paid by us, they can no longer sell at a good price and will lose control of their grain. Therefore, if we want to affect their incentives, along with cash, we must also provide them with other materials. But as of now we are unable to provide all the materials, for thirty percent of what they want is consumer goods and seventy percent is draft animals and agricultural implements. There may also be other problems that we cannot anticipate, for we have no experience at all in this matter. Two choices confront us now: one is to carry out the requisition, and the other is to hold back. If we follow the second choice, there would be big problems with grain supply and the market; if we follow the first, there would be small or even big problems in the villages.[4]

Chen Yun's invention was nothing surprising. Along with Wang Ming and Kang Sheng he was once one of the three representatives from the CCP residing in Moscow during the period of the Wang Ming line. He was perfectly well aware of the consequences of the exploitation of peasants in the Soviet Union. Now, in the course of following the Soviet model of heavy industrial and military development, China was forced into following the Soviet method of exploiting the peasants' grain and raw materials. Mao Zedong, who was apparently not very familiar with these problems, allowed himself to be ruled by Chen Yun's ideas on the state monopoly and planned purchase and supply.

The establishment of a state monopoly on grain destroyed the grain markets that had been born in the countryside following land reform. Chen Yun pursued his work, and the monopoly on cooking oil was in turn established on November 13, 1953.[5] That amounted to all but suppressing the basic liberties of the peasants in order to slip the chain of the state around their necks. Thus, the winter of 1953 marked a historic turning point for the peasants, who now that they had just been freed from bondage, fell once again under the yoke of the state.

Enslavement to the state was the foundation of the Stalinist empire. Stalin exploited the peasants in order to accumulate the capital and grain indispensable to building his heavy industrial base and thus created a form of enslavement that was not exactly socialist. Originally, Mao did not want to copy Stalin, but ultimately he failed for the simple reason that he had no other choice: Once the state monopoly on the sale of grain was in place, China inevitably found itself committed to this path.

The first step in the erection of this system was therefore the progressive application of the politics of planning. But it was no easy thing to apply to hundreds of millions of peasants who were immediately opposed to it. In Chen Yun's opinion, there were two reasons for the difficulties. First, "as small individualized producers, who after paying rent and taxes were accustomed to holding on to their surplus, the peasantry had not yet adjusted to the new method." Second, "the problems were caused by the fact that former landlords and rich peasants spread rumors by taking advantage of the selfish state of mind of the peasants and some of the defects in our work."[6] Thus, the next step was the establishment of agricultural cooperatives. Chen Yun argued:

> It is much easier and more rational to recruit the 110 million peasant households in the production cooperatives and assign the state monopoly of purchase and sale work to the cooperatives. Yes, we are confronted with many difficulties in terms of the state monopoly, but these are caused by two reasons: First, we lack experience; second, the number of peasants engaged in individual production is such that it is extremely difficult to make accurate estimations of production and to clarify whose is more and whose is less.[7]

Therefore it would be unfair to attribute responsibility for the accelerated cooperatives solely to the arbitrary decisions of Mao Zedong. True, Mao himself criticized those who "worried too much" on the subject of cooperatives and who were "nothing other than conservative rightists advancing as slowly as women with bound feet."* But Chen Yun's criticisms were far more vicious:

This spring, peasants in some places yelled about the lack of grain and along with that there appeared some erroneous opinions holding to the view that the management of grain and cooperative production work had not been conducted well. We have countered such erroneous opinions.

The backgrounds of those making such statements are complex. Some chose the standpoint of the former landlords and rich peasants and only focused on the bad part and ignored the good part. Some are representatives of the landlord class holding a revenge mentality: They intentionally invented things and spread them. Some are counterrevolutionaries opposing the people and the people's government, attempting to make use of every error in our work to conduct conspiratorial activities. The majority, however, have a different background. They consist of Party members, non–Party members, workers, petty bourgeois intellectuals, personalities from various social strata. Their idea is considered a good one in that they really hope the government does everything well. Their errors are that they started yelling without first making rational analysis.[8]

In short, from the start of the Korean War, China was constrained to adopt the methods of Stalinist states, which plunder their peasants as cannon fodder for building heavy industry and armaments factories. Inevitably, state enslavement emerged in China. The establishment of a monopoly over the sale of foodstuffs, the agricultural cooperatives, and then the People's Communes were all part of a gradual process that led to enslavement to the state. It can be summarized as follows:

First, the peasants were no longer their own masters, having neither the right to dispose of their land nor the right to control their work. The state decided for them what they ought to grow, when, how, and in what quantity. The peasants completely lost the right to plow their fields and became passive instruments taking orders from blind bureaucrats.

Further, the peasants had no right to dispose of the fruits of their labor. Production quotas depended on the will of the state. There was no relation between the peasants' labor and their share of the product. How much was to be requisitioned, how much retained as seeds, and how much distributed to the family were all blindly determined by state authority.

---

*Mao Zedong, "The Question of Agricultural Cooperation," July 3, 1955.

Finally, the peasants were bound to one piece of land, to which they were assigned for life; they could never change their status. This was referred to as the "rural residency registration" [*nongcun hukou*] and was virtually impossible to alter. Effectively it was the total confiscation of the individual freedom of the peasant by the state.

Since the 1950s, the enslavement by the state that spread throughout China has had two consequences. On the one hand, at the price of the sweat and blood of the peasants, this system accumulated the necessary capital for the construction of heavy industry and armaments and the manufacture of the atomic bomb, the hydrogen bomb, rockets, satellites, and so forth. On the other hand, such a system had a completely devastating impact on the peasants' spirit of initiative or creativity in agricultural production and obstructed the implementation of modern scientific methods in the Chinese countryside, which was thereby left to stagnate.

By the end of the 1970s, the rural economy was on the verge of collapse. From 1976 to 1978, the state imported over 13 million tons of grain, which along with a few billion *jin* of grain from the state storehouses was an inadequate supply for the entire country. In 1977 the average amount of grain per capita was less than that in 1957 and resulted in starvation conditions among a hundred million peasants. It was clear that the state-controlled enslavement could not maintain itself in the countryside any longer.

In 1978, Anhui province once again experienced a severe drought. In the past, natural disasters such as droughts and floods had usually provided peasants with the opportunity to break the system of enslavement to the state. In fact, peasants in Anhui had already, in 1956, 1960, and 1964, tested out the practice of "household contracts," a system according to which the state partially restores to the peasants the right to dispose of their land and production. The biggest opportunity came in spring 1961, when fully 40 percent of peasant households in Anhui* adopted this practice. Each time, this system stimulated the ambition of the peasants to produce and so gave them the confidence to overcome their difficulties. But each time, when it was all over, these peasants were criticized.

Mao Zedong was particularly severe about the household contract system that was practiced on a grand scale in Anhui between 1961 and 1962:

> The household contract system touched forty percent of Anhui province. It was a self-described competition between collective and individual production, but in reality the latter prevailed. Even Khrushchev dared not dismantle the collective farms. Which road should we follow: the socialist one or the capitalist one? Do we

----

*This undoubtedly reflected the especially devastating impact in the early 1960s on Anhui of the starvation conditions that followed the ill-conceived Great Leap Forward.

want, yes or no, collectivization of the countryside? The household contract system or collectivism? It's a matter of the conflict between the proletariat and the rich peasants. Neither landlords nor rich peasants dared to speak up, but the moderately rich peasants were free of constraints. Nor should we neglect the influence of certain peasant leaders. Some Party secretaries at the district and provincial levels such as Zeng Xisheng (Anhui province's first Party secretary) spoke on behalf of those well-to-do peasants. Bourgeois thinking will continue to exist for decades, for centuries. In the Soviet Union, revisionism continues to exist decades after the October Revolution, and it serves international capitalism. In effect, it's a counterrevolution. It would be wiser to call this opportunism of the right "Chinese revisionism."[9]

The reality was that in the summer of 1962 the household contract system was practiced not only by 40 percent of the villages in Anhui, but by more than 20 percent of the villages in all of China. This state of affairs was already approved of by the majority of Chinese leaders at the time, including Deng Xiaoping and Chen Yun, who once when Mao was away from Beijing, proposed to legalize the "household contract system." But as soon as Mao returned, he provoked a veritable storm of criticism of the quota system as "revisionism" before taking the proposals already cited to the leadership's summer retreat at Beidaihe in August 1962.

Once Mao had died, there was no longer anyone to counter this current of rural reform. In Anhui, Wan Li, the provincial first Party secretary, not only did not search out resistance, but took the initiative to designate pilot projects in Fengyang and Chu counties, and the Liuan prefecture. These were areas for testing the "household contract system" and "household contracts with fixed levies" [*baogan daohu*],* together commonly known as the "dual contracts." Thus took form the responsibility system of the union of many families for a single production contract that subsequently spread throughout the entire country. In the language of the peasants, this meant "one gives a quota to the state and a quota to the collective and hangs on to everything else for oneself." That is to say, each household was responsible for paying the agricultural tax, meeting the state requisition, providing for the public and welfare funds of the production team, and retaining whatever was left.

The peasants called this reform the "second liberation," a reference to the land reform in the early 1950s. Henceforth, they felt independent and truly masters of their own lands, on which they could begin to live with dignity. That brought about a great emancipation of agricultural production forces in

---

*In this system, land is divided among households that contract to meet obligations previously fulfilled by the collective. See David Zweig, "Context and Content in Policy Implementation: Household Contracts and Decollectivization, 1977–1983," in *Policy Implementation in Post-Mao China,* ed. David M. Lampton (Berkeley: University of California Press, 1987), p. 282.

China. If one takes Fengyang as an example, by 1980 95 percent of the households had implemented the "dual contracts" system. The total output of the entire county was 14.2 percent higher than it had been in 1978, the year when the county's output had been the highest. Thus in 1980 the county provided 101 million *jin* to the state purchase, which actually surpassed the total amount of grain output from the twenty-six years that had passed since the beginning of the state monopoly policy in 1953. Thus this famous native place of the Ming dynasty founder Emperor Zhu Yuanzhang, celebrated for "having agricultural catastrophes every nine years out of ten," changed utterly. Now one can no longer keep count of the number of families or villages in which the situation was "considerably improved within a year, even one season."

Now the peasants had finally realized their complete transformation [*fanshen*]. And along with that, the People's Communes, those massive yokes so indispensable to the upkeep of state enslavement, were dismantled. Zhao Ziyang, who was then Party secretary in Sichuan province, experimented in Guanghan county, Sichuan, with the separation between the People's Communes and government administration, which came down to eliminating the People's Communes as basic administrative power was given to the local government at the township [*xiang*] level.

The establishment of the People's Communes, those structures that harness political and civil powers at the local level, marked the extreme of Chinese totalitarianism. These communes possessed in effect an unlimited power in the economic and political realms, not to mention those of education and culture. With impunity they violated the family life of peasants and at the same time the intimate life of each individual. Lacking any real protection of their basic human freedoms, the peasants were treated as slaves. In the revolutionary past, Mao Zedong had called on the peasants to overthrow "political, clan, and religious authority," as well as the "masculine authority of husbands," and to end the "cruel corporal and capital punishments" in ancestral temples, such as "flogging," "drowning," and "burying people alive."[10] The irony is that soon these practices made their appearance under the new despotic system of the "People's Communes." During the "Cultural Revolution," on market days in certain communes in Guangxi province, people gathered to consume the flesh of one or two human targets of criticism in a public place.* Mao Zedong was certainly not ignorant of this. Year after year he launched "rectification of work style in the People's Communes" [*zhengfeng zhengshe*], the "Socialist Education movement," or the "Four Cleans,"

---

*These events are graphically described by Zheng Yi. See *Hongse jinianbei* (Red Memorial) (Taipei, Taiwan: Huashi wenhua, 1993).

as it is known, pushing the peasants to use "class struggle" to banish the authority of the "bad elements" that held power. Yet, the result of these efforts was that the communes went from bad to worse. What caused it all was that this totalitarian system inevitably corrupted the "victors" who gained power in these "class struggle" campaigns and inevitably turned them into "bad elements": Whosoever refused to be turned into a "bad element" was sure to be eaten up by the system.

Once the "dual contracts" policy totally dismantled the economic foundation of the People's Communes and returned economic power to the peasants, naturally the peasants wanted to make a clean sweep in demanding the return of their basic rights in every area. Rural economic reforms thus perforce encouraged reform in the political realm. The experience in Guanghan county, Sichuan, spread through the country. People's Communes were dismantled all over China. The tanks on Tiananmen Square were indeed able to drive the students back to school, but Deng Xiaoping, despite his military genius, couldn't drive hundreds of millions of Chinese peasants back to the "People's Communes." Besides, the soldiers themselves were none other than armed peasants and had not the least desire to return to slavery.

The rapid spread of the family responsibility system in the countryside and disappearance of the People's Communes emancipated the peasants and the forces of agricultural production. The outlook of the rural population was fundamentally changed. As a first consequence, harvests were bountiful four years in a row, from 1980 to 1984. In five years' time, the total output of grain increased by 100 billion kilograms and cotton production by 3.8 million tons. The old problem of the nourishment and basic clothing of the Chinese peasants was at last resolved. After 1984, stagnant agricultural production had a lot to do with the stagnation in the guiding ideology of reform. But we will be returning to this matter later in this book.

The second consequence of the rural reform was that the market economy made great strides in the countryside. The most profound economic change induced by reform was that it put an end to the combination of the self-reliant and semi–self-reliant natural economy that has dominated China for thousands of years and that was joined after 1953 to a barter economy under the protection of the state. But the Chinese economy was nevertheless entering a new era. Despite the many frustrations of the ten-year reform, the development of the rural commercial economy is irreversible. More than 65 percent of the rural economy was converted into a market economy. More than one hundred million people formed rural enterprises that produced one trillion *yuan* worth of merchandise. The production value of Chinese rural industries surpassed that of rural agricultural production and so brought an end to the old view of Chinese villages as places where "eight hundred million shift for themselves to feed themselves." Not only do they now shift for themselves to feed themselves, but they throw themselves into animal husbandry, forestry, and fishing; they are entrepreneurs in industry, commerce, and transportation or other service sectors. This great upheaval has made altogether impossible a return to the old economy based on People's Communes and the state grain monopoly.

Finally, the third consequence of rural reform: The farmers [*nongmin*]* constitute the greatest force of reform in China and a powerful new independent force. Land reform in the early 1950s freed them the first time, as a class, from the landlords. In theory they were the masters of the country, but in reality they lived as prisoners of the People's Communes and state planning. This time, now that they are emancipated, they truly want to influence the nation's destiny.

Their power is first of all manifested in the economic realm: Rural merchandise has flooded the Chinese market, and some has even penetrated the global economy. The independent economic status of China's farmers has truly increased. At the same time, the emancipation of agricultural production forces has led more and more free rural people to quit the land to enter industry, commerce, and service areas or to install themselves in the cities, where they have become the motivating factor behind urban reforms. That was the big picture of the great reform carried out from 1979 to 1980: The countryside had overwhelmed the cities.

The great strides of the market economy in the countryside and the motivating role that the farmers play characterize the Chinese reform. There reside its advantages (compared to Gorbachev's reforms in the USSR). There also reside its weaknesses. The market has no coherence, and its mechanisms are incomplete. The coexistence of two systems of price setting—by the market and by the state—allows an abuse of power and a sabotage of market mechanisms. Cultural and technical backwardness of rural enterprise has created a huge waste of natural resources and labor as well as environmental pollution. The reform launched in the countryside must be relieved. It needs the support of workers and intellectuals from the cities to help the farmers transform this rural market economy, backward and partially developed, into an advanced and fully developed one. But this second phase has not been realized. And that is the source of the tragic fate of reform in China.

------

*From this point on in the text, the Chinese term *nongmin* is translated as "farmers" instead of "peasants." This, the translators believe, is in accordance with Ruan Ming's characterization of the promarket and entrepreneurial skills displayed by China's cultivators from the late 1970s onward that defy the connotations of backwardness, economic subsistence, and obsequious obedience to the state implied in the word "peasant."

Notes

1. Mao Zedong, *Selected Works of Mao Zedong* (*Mao Zedong Xuanji*) (Beijing: People's Publishing House, 1977), pp. 1075–1076.

2. Ibid., p. 1078.

3. Chen Yun, "Important Points Involving Financial Work in 1951, 1954," in *Selected Works of Chen Yun: 1949–1956* (*Chen Yun Wenxuan: 1949–1956)* (Beijing: People's Publishing House, 1984), p. 130.

4. Chen Yun, "Implement the State Monopoly for the Purchasing and Marketing of Grain" (October 10, 1953), in *Selected Works,* pp. 209–210.

5. Chen Yun, "How to Handle the Situation Involving the Production and Marketing of Cooking Oil" (November 13, 1953), in *Selected Works,* p. 217.

6. Chen Yun, "Support and Improve the State Monopoly for the Purchasing and Marketing of Grain" (July 21, 1955), in *Selected Works,* p. 273.

7. Ibid., p. 276.

8. Ibid., pp. 278–279.

9. "Speech to the Central Small Group Meeting by Mao Zedong at the Central Work Conference in Beidaihe," August 9, 1962.

10. Mao Zedong, "Report on an Investigation of the Peasant Movement in Hunan," in *Selected Works of Mao Zedong* (Beijing: Foreign Languages Press, 1967), vol. 1, p. 44.

6

From "Promoting Proletarian Ideology and Eliminating Bourgeois Ideas" to Reforming the Political System

The reformist experience in "household contracts" that began in 1978 in Fengyang, Anhui, spread through all of China in less than two years. On the threshold of spring 1980, the excellent results of grain and agricultural production in general constituted a veritable challenge to the cities.

But the cities did not budge. Once Deng Xiaoping had launched his "Four Cardinal Principles" he never ceased to vacillate between opposing the "left" and the right. To those who questioned him, he replied in an ambiguous manner: "If there are errors on the right we must attack them; if there are errors on the 'left,' we must also attack them."

Not long after Deng delivered his speech "Uphold the Four Cardinal Principles," on March 30, 1979, all over the place, partisans of the "two whatevers" criticized the Third Plenum and the Conference on Guidelines in Theory Work as "rightist" and asserted that only the "whatever" policy was correct.

After Hua Guofeng's tour of the barracks, Deng Xiaoping endeavored to start up a "review of the debate on the criterion of truth" in the military in order to continue criticism of Hua Guofeng's "two whatevers." But dogmatists in the military dug in behind the "Four Cardinal Principles" in order to shut the door on this debate.

In spring 1980, these dogmatists in the military got together with like-minded allies in the Party to launch an attack on the wave of reforms that were now approaching the cities. Their slogan: "Promote proletarian ideology and eliminate bourgeois ideas" [*xing wuchanjieji sixiang, mie zichanjieji sixiang*]. The principal performers in this campaign were Hu Qiaomu and Wei Guoqing.

On April 1, 1980, Hu Qiaomu launched his first attack on the Central Propaganda Department. On that day, this department held a forum to discuss the problem of the intellectuals. Hu Yaobang had requested I write an article, to be entitled "Policy Toward Intellectuals," that he wanted to have published in the *People's Daily* under the byline "special commentator." But in the face of Hu Qiaomu's opposition, the *People's Daily* refused. That's why Hu Yaobang suggested that Zhu Muzhi invite Hu Qiaomu to join the discussion at the Central Propaganda Department forum. Hu Qiaomu seized the opportunity to cry out: "The time has come to launch an attack on liberalism: The Propaganda Department must behave like police and stop this trend!" Hu Qiaomu added:

> The object of this debate escapes me, and I know very little about the issue of intellectuals. The real issue now is to struggle against liberal ideas and policies. Bao Tong [an assistant to Zhao Ziyang] is not very precise in his speech as to these targets [Bao Tong's speech dealt with noticeable leftist tendencies in the policies toward intellectuals]. This could lead to a messy battle! Bao Tong is in favor of publishing Ruan Ming's article. I don't oppose that. But I think it would be better to stop talking about the problem of the intellectuals.
>
> The problem now is to launch an attack on liberalism. We must show a militant spirit [*jingongde jingshen*]. Propaganda constitutes a battlefront. The Propaganda Department must behave like police to ferret out the targets for attack. For example, I am personally acquainted with all sorts of bad movies, foreign literature, publishing, and music, but the Propaganda Department has to go out and find these targets. As soon as they've found them, they have to attack them. I was shocked to discover that a certain publishing house is in the process of issuing the *Collected Essays of Hu Shi*.* Why do this? I firmly oppose it and I am ready to wage a war without mercy! This kind of thing, like the publication of *Gone With the Wind* or detective stories, shows that the ideological front must establish whether it's Marxism or liberalism that guides us.
>
> The same goes for music: Hong Kong songs have swamped us. That singer, Deng Lijun, has become a veritable red singing star, and our own. They say that we have to know how to put up with it, but we can't put up with it forever. We have to get out of this situation and launch an attack.
>
> Just why are the *Collected Essays of Hu Shi* being published? I posed this question to the publishing house, which explained that it was part of the movement for the teaching of new literature. I dare not share in such an opinion. If you want to talk about the history of China, it would be much better to publish the *Complete Works of Zhuxi [Chu Hsi]*,† who had a hundred times more influence on Chinese history than Hu Shi. Where are we headed if our bookstores are selling the *Collected Essays of Hu Shi*? Just where the hell is China headed? And our socialist culture? The Propaganda Department ought to intervene to stop this!

---

*Hu Shi was a liberal, intensely anticommunist intellectual in the May Fourth period.

†Chu Hsi was the founder of the neo-Confucian school of philosophy in twelfth-century China.

These particular examples prove that we can't reduce our political culture to that of the "Hundred Flowers." These cultural and ideological principles aren't those of the "Hundred Flowers." This would be too easy, the Propaganda Department could sleep all day! To revive a "Hundred Flowers" coup after the "Gang of Four," that was possible, but if one had idled away one's time talking one would have risked losing one's way and crossed the line into liberalism.[1]

If "the cultural and ideological principles aren't those of the 'Hundred Flowers'" then what were they? The answer came quickly. On April 18, 1980, at the All-Military Conference on Political Work that he chaired, Wei Guoqing flung forth the slogan "promote proletarian ideology and eliminate bourgeois ideas."[2]

The origin of the slogan can be traced back to 1956, when Deng Xiaoping had formulated it in a speech to Communist Youth League cadres. After the anti-rightist campaign of 1957, this expression became one of the principal slogans in the campaign to "implement the overall dictatorship against the bourgeois class in the realm of ideology and culture." This time it wasn't Mao Zedong's "whatevers" but Deng Xiaoping's "whatevers" that Wei Guoqing inserted into a speech given by Chairman Hua Guofeng at the military conference after Deng Xiaoping approved it. This was a very smart move.

The attack that Hu Qiaomu had launched at the Central Propaganda Department forum was of an internal nature, and very few people knew of it. To make up for this, the speech at the military conference was publicized and immediately aroused strong reactions throughout the nation and abroad. Was the absolute cultural and ideological despotism that had reigned in China in the second half of the 1950s going to reemerge? It was at this point that a completely unexpected character, Li Weihan, addressed himself directly to Deng Xiaoping.

Li Weihan was a veteran Communist Party leader with special ties to Deng Xiaoping. In 1934, persecuted in the name of Wang Ming dogmatism, Deng Xiaoping was forced to get a divorce from his [first] wife, whom Li Weihan then married in order to protect her.* In late May 1980, Li had a two-hour talk with Deng that played a key role, since it was then that Li persuaded Deng to drop the slogan to "promote proletarian ideology and eliminate bourgeois ideas" and direct himself instead to the reform of the political system first mentioned at the 1978 Third Plenum.

A few days after his talk with Li Weihan, on May 31, 1980, Deng gave an important speech. It addressed three major themes: rural politics, the elimination of the influence of feudalism, and the problems of the international com-

---

*Li Weihan, also known as Luo Mai, was a longtime critic of Mao Zedong and of feudalism in the CCP.

munist movement. The speech in fact concentrated on the second subject, that of feudalism, which was a special topic of discussion at a meeting among Politburo members. But what's amusing about this is that in the *Selected Works of Deng Xiaoping*, Hu Qiaomu and Deng Liqun pared down the speech in order to suppress precisely this second part, including parts one and three only as two separate articles discreetly titled "On Questions of Rural Policy" (May 31, 1980) and "An Important Principle for Handling Relations Between Fraternal [Communist] Parties" (May 31, 1980).[3] Not a trace, then, of the core of his speech.

But here is the following original passage on feudalism, printed by the Propaganda Department, which I preserved:

II. The Elimination of the Influence of Feudalism

A few days ago, Comrade Li Weihan came to see me to discuss the slogan "promote proletarian ideology and eliminate bourgeois ideas." We had a two-hour discussion. In my opinion, this slogan has some drawbacks and it is not complete. I myself am not involved with this meeting of the PLA's General Political Department. I have asked Comrade Deng Liqun to tell Comrade Hua Nan of the General Political Department not to overpropagandize this slogan. It's important to interpret its contents correctly and apply it accordingly. The *People's Daily* and the *Enlightenment Daily* can circulate it.

Comrade Li Weihan insisted on one thing: Our main task on the ideological front is not to go on criticizing bourgeois ideas, but instead to first eliminate the influence of feudalism.

Li estimates that feudalism has long persisted in our society. Feudalism is a system anchored in the life of society and close to the masses. Its influence is considerable, even in the bosom of the Party. It should not be underestimated.

By its victory, the democratic revolution has eliminated the system of exploitation. But the antifeudal mission has not been fully accomplished.

Neither Mao, nor Liu Shaoqi, nor Zhou Enlai completed it. Our people and our Party have been influenced quite severely by the plague of feudalism, because we have never really considered its elimination as one of our main tasks.

Why in our time, in the bosom of the Party, do certain people appropriate privileges to themselves? The reason has a lot to do with the influence of feudalism. And what are all these memorials, to the memory of Chairman Mao, Premier Zhou Enlai, and now Liu Shaoqi? But worst of all is the patriarchal system [*jiazhang zhi*] that has severely disturbed normal Party life. Comrade Li Weihan hopes that the current Central Committee can carry out this antifeudal mission to its conclusion.

The idea of Comrade Li Weihan is excellent and deserves to be taken into consideration. Let's take the case of the patriarchal system, a tradition anchored in our Party. Chen Duxiu, in his later years, severely practiced the patriarchal system. At this time, in the 1920s, eight major secretaries were elected but only "I" [Chen Duxiu] receive reports. Whenever central meetings were convened, it didn't matter what others said, only Chen Duxiu's ideas were accepted and that was that. Some comrades in the Party at that time told me "Chen is the 'old man' [*lao touzi*]. What the 'old man' says goes."

Comrade Qu Qiubai was once in the same position as the Party leader. His attitude was much milder. However, this situation only lasted a short while.

Later, in the 1930s, came Xiang Zhongfa's turn, but in reality it was Li Lisan who ran things for him. The patriarchal system was very severe.

We must absolutely abolish within our lifetime the system of life tenure of leaders, that is to say, the post of chairman for life. We must eliminate feudalism from the life of the Party and from the life of society. To reform them, we have to examine the whole work from the perspective of whether the influence of feudalism has been purged.

Comrade Li Weihan first of all suggested that I specifically emphasize this problem at the Party's upcoming Twelfth Congress. But in my opinion, this idea of Li's ought to be first brought out in the "Resolution on Certain Questions in the History of Our Party."[4]

Following Deng Xiaoping's speech, the Politburo Standing Committee got together especially to discuss the issue of eliminating the influence of feudalism. As for this concept of "feudalism," it is certainly vague, especially in view of the differences between Chinese and Western feudal society. In a general way, when one speaks of Chinese feudalism, one is referring to an imperial autocratic system that goes back to the time of Qin Shihuang in the third century B.C. and ideological despotism (of both thought and culture). This combination of the traditional despotic system of a great centralized feudal empire and the Stalinist type of communist totalitarian system constitutes the particular political and cultural characteristics of the empire of Mao Zedong (especially after the start of the Korean War in 1950). One can go back to the expression of Mao himself: "Marx plus Qin Shihuang," but it would be more exact to speak of "Stalin plus Qin Shihuang." Thus, in 1980, talking about the elimination of the influence of feudalism meant reforming ideology and totalitarian and despotic political systems of the "Stalin plus Qin Shihuang" type. Hu Yaobang made very clear declarations on this point when he reported the contents of the Politburo Standing Committee discussion:

> On June 10, 1980, a special meeting of the Politburo Standing Committee debated the issue of eliminating the influence of feudalism. The advice of the Standing Committee is that two fundamental issues should be taken into consideration: first, the political system, and second, ideology.
>
> In terms of political system, world socialist revolutions don't date from today; the Russian Revolution is already sixty-three years old, ours is already thirty. After the revolutionary victories, the parties developed imperfections, as did the state systems. Powers are excessively concentrated, positions are occupied for life and represent the "iron rice bowl." This has created a situation where cadres can only be promoted, never removed. In all these respects, we didn't do as good a job as the bourgeoisie. Everything had to be approved by the supreme leader, and without his approval, nothing could be done. Since he spent his lifetime at the top, if

those beneath him gave the wrong advice, they risked being nipped from one day to the next and suffering reprisals. This problem must be solved without delay on a system [*zhidu*] level.

Another issue connected to system is that of social consciousness. We haven't been baptized into bourgeois democracy, though this democracy represents a very great advance over feudal despotism. Since our revolution we have, without making ourselves accountable, promoted certain feudal things. According to Comrade Xiaoping, in sixty years, among the top leaders of our Party, general secretary or Party chairman, Qu Qiubai was perhaps the only one who did not run things according to "what I say goes" [*yiyantang*] or practice the patriarchal system. Nowadays, our propaganda must not promote feudal ideas because if it does it would endanger the Party, the nation, and our own lives. Why are those who engage in corruption so bold? Because they rely on feudalism to act like Mandarins and make mischief under the protection of this umbrella. Let's destroy this umbrella! Let's take the necessary time! In my opinion it can't be done in six months, it will take three years or even longer.[5]

During summer 1980, the debate between "promoting proletarian ideology and eliminating bourgeois ideas" and "eliminating the influence of feudalism" seemed to evolve in a direction favorable to the reformers. Deng Xiaoping seemed to be even more willing than he had been at the 1978 Third Plenum to resolve the main obstacles blocking reform in China, namely, the issue of the political system. He adopted the proposals of Li Weihan to "eliminate the influence of feudalism" and discarded his own slogan of "promoting proletarian ideas and eliminating bourgeois ideas," and that was an important change in direction—a change very closely tied to the overall situation in China and not the result of happenstance.

The speedy development of reform in the countryside forced the cities to react, but urban reform was much more complicated. In the countryside, the family responsibility system sufficed to free the rural economy from the commune system, whereas in the cities, reform required breaking innumerable shackles that in the old system yoked productive forces together from the level of the Central Committee all the way down to factories and enterprises. Though partial and sometimes spectacular successes were possible in the countryside without changing the fundamental arrangement of the political system, it was not possible to take this route in the cities.

The reform forces understood this point. They took the reform of the political system as the starting point for China to enter an epoch of even greater reform. They therefore threw themselves into discussion, devoting themselves to overall research in areas of system reform, including politics, economy, culture, science and technology, and education.

On the other side, antireform forces showed themselves to be more sensitive to this key issue. They understood perfectly well that if the reformers managed to weaken the political system, it would hasten the total collapse of the old edifice. They had no choice other than to quickly "put on the brakes." Therefore, soon after that June 10 discussion was held in the Politburo, the two sides entered into veritable hand-to-hand combat.

On June 11, the Propaganda Department held a forum to transmit the content of the discussion by Politburo members over the issue of eliminating the influence of feudalism. Beijing theory circles considered this issue to be even more important than that of "the criterion of truth" ideological emancipation and preparation for the epoch of great reform. It was necessary to quickly get started on theory research and propose concrete reforms in different institutions.* By mid-June, the entire country was aware of this great reform policy, which aroused lively reactions in all walks of life. The majority of opinions were supportive, but of course there was also some resistance and fear. It was in this context that Li Weihan on June 22 wrote a letter to Hu Yaobang and Hu Qiaomu:

> Comrades Yaobang and Qiaomu:
>
> Regarding the issue of feudalism, I have suggested to Comrade Xiaoping that this topic be added to the scientific system of Mao Zedong Thought. I also thought that we could carry that out at the Twelfth Party Congress.
>
> Due to the fact that this issue has already become a matter of public debate, I wonder if it wouldn't profit the August session of the National People's Congress [NPC] and the Chinese People's Political Consultative Conference [CPPCC]† to invite Comrade Xiaoping to give a speech at the closing session of the CPPCC. After the discussion at the two conferences and being set down in a central document, the issue might activate debates and function as the ideological preparation for a thorough examination of this issue at the Twelfth Party Congress. (I think that the report on these Party statutes that will be undertaken at the Twelfth Congress must necessarily address this subject.)
>
> With respect,
> Salute!   **Li Weihan**, June 22 [1980][6]

That was a very good suggestion. The fact that the NPC and the CPPCC would be the first to debate reform of the political system and elaborate on central documents in itself constituted a reform of great historical signifi-

---

*This included substantial work by Chinese historians supporting political reform who now reinterpreted China's long history of despotism in terms more conducive to a transformation toward democracy, though not without opposition from more traditional prodespot interpretations. See Lawrence R. Sullivan, "The Controversy Over 'Feudal Despotism': Politics and Historiography in China, 1978–82," in *Using the Past to Serve the Present: Historiography and Politics in Contemporary China*, ed. Jonathan Unger (Armonk, N.Y.: M. E. Sharpe, 1993), pp. 174–204.

†A largely ceremonial body composed of many noncommunists whose ostensible role is to advise the CCP, but in reality just rubber-stamps Party decisions.

cance. Li Weihan won Hu Yaobang's support, but was opposed by Hu Qiaomu.

On June 25, Hu Qiaomu wrote a letter to Hu Yaobang in which he circuitously expressed his opposition:

Comrade Yaobang:

It's necessary to make a detailed preparation of the critique of the remnants of feudal thought in the Party, government, and society. What should be reformed? It's necessary to specify these points to avoid precipitating action that might result in chaos in ideology, politics, and even organization. In addition, one such criticism will hardly help to resolve issues concretely. Nowadays it seems adequate to attack only feudalism and forget about the battle against decadent capitalist behavior like greed and egotism. That's why it would be preferable to appoint a few people to first do research and then come up with a proposal that can be submitted for discussion within the Party Secretariat before deciding whether or not to raise the problem at the CPPCC.

Hu Qiaomu[7]

A few points about Hu Qiaomu's letter need to be noted here: First, he completely discarded the key issue in the elimination of the influence of feudalism as stated in the speech by Deng Xiaoping and in the Politburo Standing Committee discussions, namely reform of the political system. He reduced everything to an issue of mere ideology. Then he reduced the ideological issue to the single question of "remnants of feudal thought." And even those little "remnants" were to his mind untouchable, because to get started on them might create "chaos in ideology, politics, and even organization"—that is, the Party might break apart and the nation founder in chaos. In addition, he used a strategy of intimidation to shift his target back to his own objective, that of the "critique of capitalism," and thus came back to the line of the slogan to "promote proletarian ideology and eliminate bourgeois ideas."

And finally, he employed a stalling tactic—"appoint a few people to first do research and then come up with a proposal." No such project ever saw the light of day. Six months later, in December 1980, at the Central Work Conference, he finally realized his objective in launching the "struggle against bourgeois liberalism," a struggle not fundamentally different from "promoting proletarian ideology and eliminating bourgeois ideas."

At the time, however, Hu Qiaomu had not begun to realize the objectives that he had bared in his letter. True, the Propaganda Department circulated his letter, invited him to come to a special meeting to give a discourse, and ordered that prior to his so-called proposal no mention should be made of the elimination of the influence of feudalism and political system reform. But public opinion and the media did not respond to the wishes of Hu Qiaomu. China, which was profiting from the reforms under way, found it easier to accept the strategy of Deng Xiaoping and the Politburo Standing Committee for a reform of the political system than Hu Qiaomu's old tunes on the "critique of capitalism."

In addition, Deng Xiaoping and Hu Yaobang weren't about to yield just yet.

Right at that moment, I personally was beginning to edit an article entitled "The Most Important Strategic Task on the Ideological Front." The major part of this article had been written during winter 1977, when Hu Yaobang had just started work at the Central Party School. At that time, he had a lot of spare time in the evenings and often invited me over to discuss certain issues. The subject that preoccupied us the most was that involving the social and historical causes for the emergence of the "Gang of Four." Neither of us agreed with the decision of the Central Committee that had described the gang as "power holders responsible for taking the capitalist road." We both agreed that the social base of the "Gang of Four" was not the bourgeoisie, but rather the corrupt feudal bureaucratic class and the thug proletarians.

Hu Yaobang suggested that I formulate an outline based on our discussions. Once he read it, he suggested that I expand it into an article. At that time, the article was entitled "The Total Collapse of the 'Gang of Four' and the Strategic Task on the Ideological Front." In it I proposed the elimination of feudal influences in China and stressed the importance of reform in various realms, including politics, economy, ideology, and culture. Hu Yaobang once asked some leaders to read the draft and give their opinions. Only Luo Ruiqing insisted that it had to be published. He phoned Hu Yaobang to tell him that he wanted to distribute it to the military so that the soldiers could look through it. But Hu Qiaomu, Deng Liqun, and certain members of the Central Party School were against it. The article was put aside.

After Hu Yaobang had reported to us the contents of the discussion of the June 10 meeting of the Politburo Standing Committee regarding the issue of eliminating the influence of feudalism, I decided to further edit my article and add new aspects. Essentially I altered the part in which I analyzed the "Gang of Four" and instead focused more on the current situation in China. Inspired by the conversation between Li Weihan and Deng Xiaoping, I changed the title, which became "The Most Important Strategic Task on the Ideological Front." But because the letter and speech given by Hu Qiaomu were already known, the journal *Theory Trends* of the Central Party School and other newspapers and journals in the capital did not dare to publish this article. Therefore I sent it to Hu Yaobang and the journal on theory called *Theory and Practice*,

---

*Publication of controversial articles and books in relatively obscure journals and publishing houses outside Beijing and the major cities became a common practice after 1978 and continues

which was then under the Liaoning provincial {Party} committee.* After reading it, Ren Zhongyi, first Party secretary in Liaoning, gave the journal the okay to publish it. Hu Yaobang sent a letter to the leaders of the Central Party School who had opposed publishing my article:

> TO: Comrades [Song] Zhenting, Wu Jiang, [Sang] Zizhen, July 22:
>
> I have read both Comrade Ruan Ming's letter and the attached article.
>
> I made some changes in the first sixteen pages of his long article. I asked him to consider these. I suggested that before page sixteen, issues regarding policy should be added of the sort that might enable readers to distinguish issues of a different nature without confusing them. I have no time to make the changes myself. Consider this further with him. All told, it's not a bad article, and I think that it can be published in *Theory Trends*.
>
> **Hu Yaobang**[8]

The changes Hu Yaobang had suggested for the article essentially concerned the tone, which he softened. He dulled the edge that had upset certain people. The title was now changed to "An Important Task on the Ideological Front." Yet, despite all the changes, the leaders of the Central Party School, who were afraid of making an enemy of Hu Qiaomu, didn't publish it.

The political climate that prevailed in July and August 1980 was similar to that of July and August 1978. Two years earlier, it was Wang Dongxing who had suppressed the debate on the criterion of truth; this time it was Hu Qiaomu who suppressed opinions on the subject of political system reform and elimination of the influence of feudalism. It was exactly the same suffocating situation. And Deng Xiaoping, for his part, remained silent for two months.[9]

During that period the situation involving Polish Solidarity held the attention of China and the world. Reform in the rural areas continued to go forward, whereas in the cities, after great clamor, it was stuck in a wait-and-see standstill.

At this crucial moment, Deng Xiaoping proposed an enlarged meeting of the Politburo. On August 18, 1980, he gave a speech at the meeting entitled "On the Reform of the System of Party and State Leadership," in which he reiterated and further developed the basic points of his speech of May 31, 1980. In two and a half months Deng Xiaoping indeed was able to draw up a balance sheet of Chinese history and the international communist movement. He had seriously thought about the key problem of reform and no longer

———

to the present. See for instance, Dai Qing, *Yangtze! Yangtze!: Debate over the Three Gorges Project*, a collection of interviews and articles by scientists and journalists opposed to the construction of the Three Gorges dam that was originally published by the Guizhou People's Publishing House and later banned. English translation published in 1994 by Probe International, Canada, and Earthscan, U.K.

wanted to abandon it. His speech at the enlarged Politburo meeting and his reply to the Italian journalist Oriana Fallaci during an interview reflected the major consequence of his thinking during that period.

First, he clearly realized that from the Soviet October Revolution to the Chinese Cultural Revolution the reason that both the international communist movement and the CCP committed major mistakes was because of defects in the political system. It was thus necessary to initiate reform to avoid repeating these historical mistakes. Deng explained that

> Stalin gravely damaged socialist legality, doing things that Comrade Mao Zedong once said would have been impossible in Western countries like Great Britain, France, and the United States. Yet although Comrade Mao was aware of this, he did not in practice solve the problems in our system of leadership. Together with other factors, this led to the decade of catastrophe known as the "Cultural Revolution." There is a most profound lesson to be learned from this. I do not mean that the individuals concerned should not bear their responsibility, but rather that the problems in the leadership and organizational systems are more fundamental, widespread, and long-lasting, and that they have a greater effect on the overall interests of our country.[10]

Second, Deng analyzed the historical reasons for the existence, at the heart of the Party and in China's state structure, of "bureaucracy, over-concentration of power, patriarchal methods, life tenure in leading posts, and privileges of various kinds." He identified three: (1) the long historical tradition in China of feudal despotism; (2) the tradition of concentrating power in Party leaders from the time of the Communist International; and (3) the highly centralized system of planning and management in areas of the economy, politics, culture, and society imported from the Soviet Union during the period of "socialist construction" in the 1950s. Deng made clear that without changing the system the economic reform could never progress, and the same went for the other sectors.[11]

Third, he specified that

> the goal of political reform was to ensure that through various effective forms all the people truly enjoy the right to manage state affairs, particularly state organs at the grass roots level, and to run enterprises and institutions; and that they truly enjoy all the other rights of citizens. [The objective] was to create a higher level of democracy with more substance than that of capitalist countries.[12]

Finally, Deng completely rejected the system by which the leaders selected their own successors. He explicitly said: "For a leader to pick his own successor is a feudal practice."[13]

Such, ten years ago, were the new political thoughts of Deng Xiaoping at the age of seventy-six. This was also probably the zenith of Deng Xiaoping's thoughts on political reform. After that time this pragmatic politician began a rapid downhill slide and never again did one catch a glimpse of his radiant wisdom.

These ideas of Deng Xiaoping on the reform of the political system were not, to my mind, so far removed from those that much later, in 1989, animated the demonstrators of the democracy movement on Tiananmen Square. When Deng thought that he could no longer retreat and had no other choice but to mobilize several tens of thousands of "People's Liberation Army" soldiers to encircle the capital, I myself thought that in reality Deng Xiaoping neither had to retreat nor did he have to mobilize the troops—that it would have sufficed for him to return to his political positions of August 1980. He could have held a dialogue with the students by again bringing out two of his speeches, long since published, that deserved to be called "Deng Xiaoping's contributions to reform," although he had never acted on them. Thus he could have proved that unlike Mao, who merely acknowledged the problems inherent to the system but did nothing about them, he, Deng Xiaoping, wanted to resolve them in a practical way. If that had been the case, the history of the twentieth century would have been rewritten. Then the man of the hour that pioneered the democratic reform of the socialist system in the 1990s would not have been Mikhail Gorbachev, but Deng Xiaoping. In reality, the problems confronted by Deng Xiaoping in China were much easier to solve than those faced by Gorbachev in the USSR or leaders in Eastern Europe.

But Deng Xiaoping chose to commit the same wrong move that Mao Zedong had also made in 1976, in strangling in blood the democracy movement of Tiananmen Square. How would he react today if his entourage read back to him, in his right ear the one that is not yet completely deaf—his speech of ten years ago? Every historical lesson drawn by Deng Xiaoping from the tragedies of Stalin and Mao Zedong years before is now actually reflected in the contemporary tragedy of Deng Xiaoping. The lessons that he drew at this time were not only historical judgments on Stalin and Mao, but predictions of his own future destiny.

Ten years ago those words of Deng Xiaoping's shook China and the entire world. The great reform seemed truly to begin, and we felt ourselves called upon to build a modern and democratic China, in which a market economy was on the verge of being created. People were full of hope and confidence, and optimism reigned throughout the country. The whole world took China seriously. Businesspeople from all over the world came there to search for opportunities in what was potentially the largest market on earth. Even I, a common Chinese citizen, benefited from this spirit. On August 19, the day after Deng's speech "On the Reform of the System of Party and State Leadership" to the {enlarged] Politburo, the Central Party School circulated the contents of his proposals among its members. On August 20, my article "An Important Task on the Ideological Front," amended by Hu Yaobang but tucked away just out of sight, was published by *Theory Trends*. It was simultaneously reprinted in the *People's Daily* and the *Enlightenment Daily*.[14]

On August 31, 1980, Deng Xiaoping's speech on reform of the leadership system was formally approved by the Politburo. It had an immediate impact on events:

First, the Third Session of the Fifth National People's Congress [NPC] was held from August 30 to September 21, 1980, immediately after the enlarged meeting of the Politburo. It remains in the history of the NPC as the first "democratic and reform-oriented meeting." The delegates not only engaged in intense debate on the issue of reforming the political system, but also put this into immediate practice by enlarging and expanding the democratic power of the NPC itself. They demanded that the principal leaders of the government present themselves before the congress to listen to criticisms, questions, and suggestions regarding the government's work—and to respond. The NPC also elected a committee to revise the state constitution. This group prepared to modify the constitution according to the principles of reform of the political system adopted by the Politburo, so that it would accord with the needs of progress toward democracy.

There followed elections for delegates to the local People's Congresses. These were the most democratic elections in the history of local elections in post-1949 China. Candidacies could be made outside the official lists, and the people could freely nominate candidates. In some regions open primaries were organized.* In many localities, candidates chosen by the local Party committees were defeated by candidates freely chosen by the masses. These newly elected delegates to the local People's Congresses represented more the people's real aspirations.

The pace of reform and opening up to the outside world quickened. On September 23 and 24, 1980, Hu Yaobang presided over a session of the Central Committee Secretariat, a meeting in the course of which it was decided to apply specifically flexible political measures in Guangdong and Fujian provinces. Their aim was to use the winning hands that these two provinces had at their disposal to favor their great enrichment, to test the effect of systemic reforms on the economy, and to train cadres and accumulate experience that would benefit the rest of China. The Central Committee demanded that these two provinces open themselves up more to the unknown, look far and wide, more speedily animate economic life, become intermediaries for contacts with the outside world, and unlock the situation by deploying a great creative ardor on the basis of mature reflection and prudent calculation.

―――――

*Liu Shaoqi's son ran as a candidate in a campaign that became the topic of a popular novel in China.

One witnessed a fresh outbreak of studies and research on political and cultural reform. Conferences and meetings on these subjects were held at all levels of the Party. Associations and study groups designated some of their members to examine reforms in different areas and to conduct investigations or research. To be sure, certain sensitive issues, such as that of the multiparty system, were not explicitly mentioned, but in the course of meetings held by the Legal Committee [*Fazhi Weiyuanhui*] of the NPC on reforming the present system of the People's Congresses in which I myself participated, negative opinions were voiced about the Chinese Communist Party as a legal [*fading*] and permanent "party in power" and were in the process of being turned into amendments to be submitted to the Committee on Constitutional Amendments [*Xianfa Xiugai Weiyuanhui*] of the NPC.

All in all, when China entered the 1980s, a faint glow of light seemed to dawn, and it was permissible to believe in a fundamental change in the political system. But just as Deng Xiaoping himself had stated in his criticism of Mao, to verify and acknowledge the blemishes of the political system was one thing, to actually find a concrete cure for them was another. Deng Xiaoping probably did not imagine when he pronounced those words that he would follow the same old route as Mao and that he would never succeed in making that decisive leap of actually changing the system. The poor Chinese people never suspected that just when everyone was enthusiastic about reform of the political system and at last getting ready to take the plunge, antireform forces waiting on the sidelines for the opportune moment were now ready to launch their attack!

The opponents to reform focused on two points: the "Polish crisis" and the Chinese budget predicament. They reckoned that these two problems could serve them by opening a breach in the reform strategy worked out by the August 1980 [enlarged] Politburo meeting. Only four months after that meeting, in December 1980, the offensive against reform began. It was led by Chen Yun.

Notes

1. Author's recorded notes.

2. "Speech by Wei Guoqing at the All-Military Conference on Political Work," *People's Daily*, May 9, 1980.

3. Deng Xiaoping, *Selected Works of Deng Xiaoping: 1975–1982 (Deng Xiaoping Wenxuan: 1975–1982)* (Beijing: People's Publishing House, 1983), pp. 275–279.

4. "Draft Record of Deng Xiaoping's May 31, 1980, Speech," CCP Propaganda Department Reprint. [The "Historical Resolution" in which Mao's role as leader was evaluated would be completed in 1981, as discussed below.]

5. "Hu Yaobang's Transmission of the Draft Record of the June 10, 1980, Meeting of the Politburo Standing Committee."

6. "Reprint of Li Weihan's June 22, 1980, Letter to Hu Yaobang and Hu Qiaomu," CCP Propaganda Department.

7. "Reprint of Hu Qiaomu's June 25, 1980, Letter to Hu Yaobang," CCP Propaganda Department.

8. "Transcript of Hu Yaobang's Letter to Song Zhenting, Wu Jiang, and Sang Zizhen."

9. According to rumors at the Central Party School at that time, Deng Xiaoping, in talking about eliminating the influence of feudalism and carrying out reform of the political system, had fallen into the trap set by Li Weihan.

10. Deng Xiaoping, "On the Reform of the System of Party and State Leadership" (August 18, 1980), in *Selected Works,* p. 293.

11. Ibid., pp. 287, 289.

12. Ibid., pp. 282, 296.

13. Deng Xiaoping, "Answers to the Italian Journalist Oriana Fallaci" (August 21 and 23, 1980), in *Selected Works,* pp. 305–306.

14. Prior to Deng's August 18 speech, the journal *Theory and Practice,* under the Liaoning provincial [Party] committee, was the sole publisher of my article. Therefore, I demanded that in reprinting my article, the *People's Daily* and the *Enlightenment Daily* give a full citation to the Liaoning journal and not to *Theory Trends* of the Central Party School.

7

The Situation in Poland
and Deng's Second Break
with the Democratic Reformers

The Polish crisis exploded in July 1980, six months after Brezhnev ordered Soviet troops into Afghanistan. At that time, all the Chinese leaders, including Deng Xiaoping, supported the struggle of the Polish people, who they figured constituted an important challenge to Soviet hegemony. In their speeches for internal distribution, Deng Xiaoping and Hu Yaobang expressed in a four-point analysis how they evaluated the Polish events and the influence these had on China:

First, they said the struggle carried out by the Polish people was justified. The Polish people had a long, historic tradition of resisting invasions from two big empires—the Russian and the German. The Polish Communist Party had earned the confidence of its people in the struggle against fascism. But once in power, it had turned its back on the people, and renouncing sovereignty and the country's independence, it had folded before Soviet hegemony. Twice, in 1956 and 1970, the Polish people had risen up, and twice the people had succeeded in changing the leaders of the government and Party, but this failed to stop their leaders from betraying them. Now for a third time, the Polish people began again to struggle.

Deng and Hu's second point was the lesson the Chinese could draw from the Polish situation: that it was not possible in any case to restrain the efforts to achieve total reform. After each revolt, the new Polish leaders addressed themselves to the work of reform. But at the least difficulty or obstacle, they set the machine back. They neither dared to offend the Soviet Union nor to call into question the Stalinist system, which resulted in constant crisis.

Third, from the perspective of the situation at the time, it appeared that the Soviet Union dared not launch an armed attack as easily as it had done in 1956 when it invaded Hungary, and in 1968, Czechoslovakia. As it was, with troops already trapped in Afghanistan, the Soviet military encountered severe condemnation in world opinion. If the Soviet Union had invaded Poland, it would have run up against a major resistance from the entire Polish nation—the Poles made that fact loud and clear at the time. The Polish army would have fought the invading Soviet troops shoulder-to-shoulder with the people, united against the Soviet invader.

Fourth, Deng Xiaoping and Hu Yaobang were confident that such things could never happen in China. Having analyzed the domestic and international factors that had caused the Polish crisis, they pointed out two fundamental differences between China and Poland: China had always been independent and self-reliant, unwilling to submit to any hegemony, whereas the Polish Communist Party had given up the national banner; and the line of the 1978 Third Plenum on reform had wide popular support in China, whereas the Polish Communist Party had betrayed the interests of the people. This Polish crisis thus strengthened the idea that Chinese reform could be carried on to its conclusion. It must be pointed out that Deng Xiaoping's declarations on reform in the leadership system of the Party and state were formally approved by the enlarged Politburo meeting two months after the strike by Polish workers.

However, at the time when the country was intensely discussing these declarations, on September 24, 1980, Hu Qiaomu wrote Hu Yaobang to express his opinion on the Polish crisis. He reckoned that a similar situation could well "explode" in China and that it would be absolutely necessary to implement a series of protective measures, as Mao Zedong had himself done after the 1956 Polish and Hungarian incidents.

Hu Yaobang did not reply immediately. Then Hu Qiaomu altered the letter twice, on October 1 and 3, and ordered the Central Party Secretariat to distribute it to various central units, government sectors, and finally all mass organizations.

Here are the principal points of the letter:

1. The Polish situation can teach us a lesson. The CCP International Liaison Department [*Zhongyang Lianluobu*], the Central Investigation Department [*Zhongyang Diaochabu*], research units on foreign affairs, social science research units, the State Planning Commission, as well as other relevant financial and economic units, labor unions, the Communist Youth League, the CCP Propaganda Department, the *People's Daily*, the Xinhua News Agency, educational and cultural affairs units, publishing organs, public security and legal affairs units, the Central Discipline Inspection Commission *(Zhonggong Jilu Jiancha Weiuyanhui)* and the CCP United Front Department: all must carry out research and formulate policies, each in its own specific area.
2. The Polish events demonstrate that in a country where the Communist Party is in power, internal contradictions can reach a critical stage where they assume explosive forms.

3. In China also, certain differences that the socialist system has not yet re-solved separate the government and its people or turn them against one another. There are notably conflicts of an economic or political order that also exist in our country. The coalition of minority political dissi-dents and the dissatisfied mass of workers could constitute a gigantic force. There's an important lesson to take from these events.
4. Foreign influence, as much intellectual as economic, political, or cul-tural, constitutes a big problem for us.
5. The labor unions can split up into official and independent syndicates. If we don't find quick solutions, we cannot exclude such a possibility. The same thing could happen with other mass organizations.
6. Religion could also become a serious issue. We must draw urgent les-sons from this.
7. The Polish crisis is not over, it continues to evolve. It can have repercus-sions in neighboring countries and provoke a Soviet intervention.
8. In 1956, after the first Polish and Hungarian incidents, Chairman Mao tried to draw conclusions from them on the right way to resolve internal contradictions among the people. Now the new Polish incident has ex-ploded. I hope that the Party Central Committee of today will consider it a warning and carefully research each issue and put into practice cor-rect and concrete resolutions so that other people's bad luck will be of benefit to us.[1]

These two fundamentally different estimates of the Polish events thus led to opposite conclusions over what measures to take. Indeed, the situation was very similar to that in 1956. At that time, Mao Zedong, who at first thought that no such crisis could occur, had for a time continued his criticism of Stalin-ist dogmatism and implemented his policies of "Let a hundred flowers bloom, let a hundred schools of thought contend." He had then pronounced his discourse "On the Ten Major Relationships." He thus adopted a "liberal" orientation [*ziyouhua*]. But great and sudden revisions occurred in mid-May 1957, when Mao launched his attacks against the rightists and against Tito and Khrushchev's revisionism.

The events of the second half of 1980 were nothing other than a replay of the first half of 1957. Initially, Deng Xiaoping and Hu Yaobang supported the Polish people's resistance against Soviet hegemony and their demands for re-form. In addition, in view of the Polish example, they foresaw the acceleration of the process of reform and opening up to the outside world in China, and notably, got reform of the political system started. But the situation suddenly changed after the publication of Hu Qiaomu's letter in early October.

On October 9, 1980, the Propaganda Department distributed this "Letter on the Polish Situation." Wang Renzhong (head of the Propaganda Depart-ment) stated:

On the basis of Comrade Hu Qiaomu's suggestions, we estimate that the Polish events effectively furnish a subject for discussion and serious thought.

We do have problems in China similar to those in Poland, and if they continue to develop we will have to face the same consequences.

The dissemination of Comrade Xiaoping's speech "On the Reform of the System of Party and State Leadership" should cease.

The Polish situation is not merely an economic problem, but a political one as well. It results from chaos in people's internal thoughts.[2]

Later the Propaganda Department also circulated the views of Chen Yun on propaganda work: "If we don't pay enough attention to propaganda and the economy, China will experience the same kind of events as Poland."[3]

But at the same time, the reform that had begun in the countryside and had spread through the whole nation was literally overwhelming the cities. The reform of the leadership system of the Party and state, proposed by Deng Xiaoping at the August 1980 [enlarged] Politburo meeting, reflected general aspirations. A letter from Hu Qiaomu and a warning from Chen Yun, both circulated by the Propaganda Department, were not enough to stop these things in their tracks. In the days that followed, October 17, 18, and 19, the *Enlightenment Daily* published speeches in two columns of its daily edition on the issue of reform of the political system by theory circles in the capital.[4] These publications aroused a reaction on the national level. If the Chen Yun clique wanted to block reform of the political system, reform so fundamental to the future of China, it would have to create a more important coalition and take more decisive action.

At that same time, three other events punctuated the political life of China. First, Hua Guofeng, Mao's successor, had to be replaced. The Politburo met many times in enlarged session between November 10 and December 5, 1980, to criticize the errors of Hua Guofeng. Three resolutions were passed: A proposal was made that the Party's upcoming Sixth Plenum would accept Comrade Hua Guofeng's resignation from his two posts of Party chairman and chairman of the Central Military Commission. Then the Sixth Plenum would elect Hu Yaobang as Party chairman and Deng Xiaoping as chairman of the Central Military Commission. And finally, prior to the Sixth Plenum, Hu Yaobang should temporarily take charge of the routine work of the Politburo and the Standing Committee, and Deng Xiaoping would temporarily assume the leadership of the Central Military Commission.

The enlarged meetings of the Politburo nevertheless reaffirmed Hua Guofeng's contribution in smashing the "Gang of Four" and gave thanks for the good work he had accomplished over the past four years. The meeting also expressed the wish that Hua Guofeng be elected as a Politburo member and a Party vice chairman.[5]

The second political event was the public trial of the two gangs of Lin Biao and Jiang Qing,* which began on November 20, 1980, at a special court of the Supreme People's Court and involved ten major criminals: Jiang Qing, Zhang Chunqiao, Yao Wenyuan, Wang Hongwen, Chen Boda, Huang Yongsheng, Wu Faxian, Li Zuopeng, Qiu Huizuo, and Jiang Tengjiao. Since Lin Biao, Kang Sheng, Xie Fuzhi, Ye Qun, and Lin Liguo [Lin Biao's wife and son, respectively], and Zhou Yuchi were already dead, the court did not try to establish their penal guilt, although their cases were examined.

The public trial ended on December 23. On January 25, 1981, Jiang Qing and Zhang Chunqiao received death sentences with a two-year suspension, and Wang Hongwen was given life in prison. Yao Wenyuan and the rest were given sentences ranging from sixteen to twenty-five years.[6]

The third major event involved the drafting and discussion of the "Resolution on Certain Questions in the History of Our Party Since the Founding of the People's Republic of China."

These three events finalized the legal transformation from the empire of Mao Zedong to the Deng Xiaoping empire. At first, after the death of Mao, Hua Guofeng had carried out the immediate arrest of the "Gang of Four." The arrest had come in the form of a palace coup d'état, which unquestionably had the support of the population, but that in the absence of a formal conclusion, retained an illegal character. The public trial of the "Gang of Four" effectively served to legitimize this coup d'état.

As the successor appointed by Mao Zedong, Hua Guofeng had decided, in the name of the "two whatevers," to maintain the same program and the same political line. The Third Plenum had in practice abandoned the Mao Zedong–Hua Guofeng political line in favor of the liberal political line of Deng Xiaoping. But this change of orientation had not been clearly established either in a legal plan or an organizational one. The November 1980 enlarged Politburo meeting effectively completed the conversion of all the powers of Hua Guofeng to Hu Yaobang and Deng Xiaoping. Thus, the Sixth Plenum had nothing left to do but to formalize this transfer after the fact.

As for the "Historical Resolution," it at last set forth the ideological and theoretical program that Deng Xiaoping wanted to implement in his empire. However, the resolution was a retreat from "On the Reform of the System of Party and State Leadership" previously passed in August by the Politburo. Whereas the August program announced the radical reform of the totalitarian

---

*These two gangs included Jiang Qing's notorious Gang of Four and the group surrounding Lin Biao in his alleged conspiracy to assassinate Mao in 1971.

system, a fundamental change in the overconcentration of power in the highly despotic Stalinist and Mao Zedong systems, the "Historical Resolution" [drafted primarily by Deng Liqun] reinstated Mao Zedong's political legacy. This resolution was inspired by the fear that Deng Xiaoping was turning out to be "China's Khrushchev."* If he hurried to pass his resolution, it was because he wanted to show the country and the world that he would not conduct a "de-Maoization" similar to Khrushchev's "de-Stalinization."

In any event, these three matters strengthened Deng Xiaoping's political status. He henceforth possessed absolute power, enabling him to master total authority not just politically but also in actual leadership of the Party and the state. Deng Xiaoping's power struggle against Hua Guofeng ended with Deng's absolute victory.

This outcome was not necessarily a victory for China's reform. Henceforth, the politics of reform and opening up to the outside world had to reckon with adversaries much tougher than Hua Guofeng: Chen Yun and his clique. These men would once again force Deng into retreat from his political program of August 1980. They would succeed in breaking the currents of reform and turning the future of China onto their own conservative track.

The first important confrontation took place at the Central Work Conference between December 16 and 25, 1980. The Chen Yun clique had quietly prepared for this meeting both politically and organizationally. On four separate occasions in November and the beginning of December, Deng Liqun came to the Central Party School to deliver speeches that focused on his idea: "Let's follow the example of Comrade Chen Yun to conduct our work in the economic arena." But the content of these speeches went far beyond the sole arena of economics. Three points are worth mentioning:

Deng Liqun severely reprimanded high-level cadres in the Party who had taken so-called liberal positions in opposition to the Four Cardinal Principles during their debate over the "Historical Resolution." In so doing Deng Liqun violated the rules of Party order, since Hu Yaobang had demanded that four thousand high-level Party cadres participate in discussions on this resolution and freely express themselves and propose their amendments. Certain high officials like Fang Yi and Lu Dingyi had formulated extremely harsh criticisms of Mao. Others had hoped that "Mao Zedong Thought" would not figure in the resolution or in future Party constitutions, just as it was excluded at the time of the Eighth Party Congress in 1956. Deng Liqun exaggerated and distorted these opinions, however legitimate, when he reported them to Deng Xiaoping, and finally aroused Deng's anger. Then, when he had at-

---

*This undoubtedly reflected Deng's fear of following in the steps of the deposed and disgraced Liu Shaoqi, whom Mao dubbed "China's Khrushchev" during the Cultural Revolution.

tained this outcome, Deng Liqun returned to the Central Party School, where he hurled himself into a virulent attack against one group of the top reform leaders, enhancing his own position in the process.

Deng Liqun next attempted to establish an image of absolute authority for Chen Yun. His key statement was that as Mao Zedong had been the first leader to master the objective laws in China's stage of democratic revolution, Chen Yun had been the first leader to master the objective laws for the stage of the socialist revolution and socialist construction. It was this statement that was passed on to Deng Xiaoping's ear by a busybody at the meeting, and naturally upset him, so much so that Deng Liqun deleted this sentence from the record of the session.

Lastly, Deng Liqun formally announced the publication of the *Selected Works of Chen Yun* in three volumes. At that time, apart from the five-volume *Selected Works of Mao Zedong*, works by other leaders consisted of only one or two volumes. The selected works of Liu Shaoqi and Zhou Enlai each contain two volumes, for instance, and Zhu De's one volume. Deng Xiaoping's also contained one volume in the first edition and was only later expanded to a second volume. Thus the works of Chen Yun appeared to be the most important after those of Mao. The other collections, including those by Mao Zedong, were put together by the Compilation Committee of Party Literature [*Wenxian Bianji Weiyuanhui*], whereas only Chen Yun's was compiled by the Research Office of the Central Secretariat.

One story made the rounds of the Research Office: When Chen Yun heard that Deng Liqun had decided to compile his three-volume works, Chen Yun had cried out: "If he thinks that just because he compiled my works I'm going to like him any better, he's wrong!" Later Deng Liqun fell ill. But despite a high fever, he pursued his work, all the while exhorting his followers: "Speed up the work because this publication has great importance. Above all don't mention my illness to Chen Yun." Of course, Chen Yun ended up hearing talk of Deng Liqun's fever and his commands of silence, and greatly moved, he finally took a liking to Deng Liqun.

On the organizational side, Chen Yun and his clique set up an alliance with Zhao Ziyang and Li Xiannian before the December 1980 Central Work Conference. On December 16, at the start of the conference, Chen Yun gave the central report, which was followed by speeches by Zhao Ziyang and Li Xiannian.

Chen Yun came up with an economic and political proposal totally at odds with that of the enlarged Politburo meeting in August. He spoke for the first time of a "struggle against bourgeois liberalism," thus returning to Deng Xiaoping's slogan of "promoting proletarian ideology, eliminating bourgeois ideas"—which its author had himself already rejected. As it turned out, Chen Yun's proposal ended the strategy of eliminating the influence of feudalism and reform of the political system.

In the economic realm, Chen Yun came up with the twenty-four–character slogan "curb demand, stabilize prices, curtail development, seek stability, suspend reform, make readjustments, emphasize centralization, and allow few deviations."

The various think tank supporters of the Chen Yun clique advocated a return to measures applied by Chen Yun in the early 1960s: reduce economic growth to zero or even less, install a centralization of total power, and stop all reform to make up the budget deficits and avoid an economic crisis. Deng Xiaoping did not approve all these measures, but he agreed to reduce economic growth to four percent a year.

In their speeches, Zhao Ziyang and Li Xiannian propped up Chen Yun's entire position. Zhao in particular emphasized the "potential danger of the moment" and the possibility of "an economic crisis that runs the risk of exploding" and called for a "high-up centralization of power."

As for Hua Guofeng, who had just resigned from his positions of Party chairman and chairman of the Central Military Commission, he didn't say a word. Hu Yaobang, who was now acting chairman of the Politburo and its Standing Committee, did not himself have anything to add. But Deng Xiaoping, then the future chairman of the Central Military Commission and already in charge of its work, delivered a speech on the last day of the meeting, December 25, titled "Implement the Policy of Readjustment, Ensure Stability and Unity."

Hu Qiaomu and Deng Liqun had jointly drafted this speech. By comparison to the two speeches Deng Xiaoping had given four months earlier, this one was striking for the speed of his retreat! The speech was choked with "I fully agree with Chen Yun and Zhao Ziyang." What a contrast to his totally independent style a short time before! Now he said:

> I fully agree with Comrade Chen Yun's speech. He correctly summed up our experience in handling a series of problems in economic work over the past thirty-one years and the lessons we have drawn from it. His statement will serve as our guide in this field for a long time.
>
> I also fully endorse the speech by Comrade Zhao Ziyang and the arrangements with regard to the plan for 1981 approved by the Leading Group for Financial and Economic Affairs under the Central Committee of the Party.[7]
>
> I fully agree with Comrades Chen Yun and Zhao Ziyang that for a time we should make readjustment our main job, with reform subordinate to readjustment, so as to serve it and not impede it. The pace of reform should be slowed a little, but that doesn't mean a change in direction.
>
> We should continue to implement the decision to establish several special economic zones in Guangdong and Fujian provinces, but the steps taken and methods used should be subordinated to the current readjustment and the pace should perhaps be slowed somewhat.[8]

Comrade Chen Yun has said that our economic work and our propaganda have an important bearing on whether our economic and political situation can steadily improve. He mentioned propaganda because he wants us to make a sober appraisal of our achievements and shortcomings in that work and to ensure that in the future it is adapted to the requirements of the economic and political situation so that it helps rather than hinders the readjustment.

We must point out that there are still serious shortcomings in our propaganda work. Chief among these is our failure to propagate the Four Cardinal Principles actively, confidently, and with good results and to combat effectively the fallacious ideas opposed to them.

We should criticize and oppose the tendency to worship capitalism and to advocate bourgeois liberalism. We should criticize and oppose the decadent bourgeois ideas of doing everything solely for profit, seeking advantages at the expense of others, and always putting money first. We should criticize and oppose anarchism and ultraindividualism.[9]

It has come to our attention that in some places a handful of troublemakers are using methods employed during the "Cultural Revolution" to carry on agitation and create disturbances. ... A few ringleaders who control illegal organizations and publications are working hand in glove with each other. Anti-Party and anti-socialist statements have been published, reactionary leaflets have been distributed, and political rumors have been spread. ... We must never cease to be on the alert against all such practices. ... Depending on their nature, some may be categorized as contradictions between ourselves and the enemy, and others are a form of class struggle reflected in varying degrees among the people.

Therefore, we must strengthen the state apparatus of the people's democratic dictatorship. We must attack and split up those forces that are inimical to political stability and unity.

To ensure stability and unity, I suggest that state organizations adopt appropriate laws and decrees calling for mediation to avoid strikes by workers and students. These documents should also rule out marches and demonstrations unless they are held by permission and at a designated time and place, forbid different units and localities from clubbing together for harmful purposes, and proscribe the activities of illegal organizations and the printing and distribution of illegal publications.[10]

The December 1980 Central Work Conference thus marked a retreat all down the line for Deng Xiaoping. But it was also a turning point for Chen Yun and his clique, expanding their power and their influence on the two fronts of the economy and ideology.

From that point onward, all the tentative reforms of Deng Xiaoping were checked by the Chen Yun clique. The reform of the political system was practically halted. On economic reform the Chen Yun clique made some concessions and left Deng Xiaoping's hands free. But these concessions were provisional and the clique was on the lookout for the slightest excuse to launch an attack. For instance, the "case of the bogus medicine" in Jinjiang, Fujian and the "automobile smuggling case" on Hainan Island* were both used to expand the attack against reform forces in general and to inhibit the progress of reform, forcing Deng Xiaoping to make a step-by-step retreat. This strategy was much more clever and the objective far more substantial than had been the case for Hua Guofeng with his "two whatevers."

The attack on the reform forces was well planned and methodical, isolating them in order to break them one by one. After the first action against Hu Yaobang, who advocated total reform as much economic as political, the attackers took advantage of the disagreements that existed between Zhao and Hu, allying with one against the other. After eliminating Hu Yaobang, they then concentrated their forces against Zhao Ziyang. Little by little, they gradually eliminated the reform forces around Deng Xiaoping, finally isolating him and forcing him to rely on their power when it became necessary to face the dissatisfaction and anger of the people.

Of course, the reason why Chen Yun and his clique were able to apply their strategy and attain their goal is inseparable from their perfect understanding of the thought and character of Deng Xiaoping. Deng Xiaoping's reform ideology itself was full of profound contradictions. Deng was sincere; when meditating on the historical lessons of the Stalin-Mao epoch, he advocated complete reform, of a liberal and democratic tendency. But as soon as he got the feeling that the move to democracy and liberalism risked diminishing his personal power, immediately his political pragmatism of an antidemocratic and antiliberal tendency revealed itself, as did his character as an authoritarian tyrant. In this respect, Deng was heir to Mao's political legacy. But because he was not animated by the romantic imagination of Mao, his political pragmatism always overwhelmed his long-term strategy. Chen Yun and his clique exploited this character trait with regularity in order to practice opposing Deng with a "strategy of encirclement." They made sure to whisper in his good ear that the reform forces could become a danger to his own political power. They told him, for example, that if Hu Yaobang had approved the publication of the article "Eliminate the Personality Cult" by Guo Luoji it was because this article "directed a spearhead at Deng Xiaoping," and so forth. Such a "strategy of encirclement" was a very effective tool against an isolated dictator like Deng Xiaoping. That was the secret of the successive victories of the

---

*Both occurred in 1985. The first case involved the sale of bogus medicine on the open market. In the second case, 89,000 automobiles were reportedly illegally imported and then sold throughout China for huge profits. The latter allegedly involved nearly the entire top echelon of the Hainan Administrative Region. See Hsi-Cheng Ch'i, *Politics of Disillusionment: The Chinese Communist Party Under Deng Xiaoping, 1978–1989* (Armonk, N.Y.: M. E. Sharpe, 1991), p. 215.

Chen Yun clique that led Deng to retreat after retreat and to destroying with his own hands the reforms that he himself had initiated.

The victory of the Chen Yun clique at the December 1980 Central Work Conference put a stop to the newly born process of urban reform. But the policy of "curb demand, stabilize prices, curtail development, seek stability, suspend reform," and so forth was hard to apply to the countryside. Because of the dismantling of the People's Communes, the planned economic system of Chen Yun could no longer control the direction of the rural economy, of which the basic unit was henceforth the farm family.

In the political and ideological realms, class struggle began again. The slogan of "promote proletarian ideology, eliminate bourgeois ideas," which Deng Xiaoping had renounced at the suggestion of Li Weihan, was revived now in a new call to arms: "struggle against bourgeois liberalism."

This was easily explained at the outset by a ruthless crackdown on the social democratic forces at the heart of civil society: the arrest and imprisonment of social democratic activists, the elimination of the so-called illegal organizations and illegal publications. In December 1980, at the Central Work Conference, Deng had proposed that "the competent state organs establish laws and decrees" for the purpose of controlling "underground journals," to "register" these in advance with the authorities. But a little later, Deng Liqun gave a speech at the Propaganda Department:

> As far as a law on publications is concerned, I have referred it to Comrade Chen Yun. According to him, we have not developed any law on publication. In the past, during our struggles against Chiang K'ai-shek, we took advantage of the loopholes in the law on publications established by the Nationalist government to advance our legal struggle. At present, we must avoid allowing others to take similar advantage in turning what's illegal into legal and employing their legal struggle against us. So that they can't have any place to register their publications we must outlaw all of them.[11]

In addition, the democratic reform forces in the Party were also violently attacked. Following the December conference, Deng Liqun used his power over the Research Office of the Central Secretariat to compile political data on bourgeois liberalism and "violations of the Four Cardinal Principles" ranging from speeches given by Party leaders on the draft of the "Historical Resolution" to the officially published articles in periodicals by sympathizers of reform among intellectuals in areas of ideology, theory, art, journalism, publications, education, and science and technology. He also adopted the method of quoting out of context and twisting and distorting so as to make false reports to the Central Committee. People working under Deng Liqun had let it be understood that they had already formulated two hundred topics and were in the process of composing two hundred articles to conduct a "decisive battle" in this political and ideological war. Later, thanks to Hu Yaobang's efforts at reconciliation, the Chen Yun clique was not able to completely achieve its ends. Nevertheless, in that struggle, Deng Xiaoping basically stood with the Chen Yun clique and thus committed himself to a road well removed from the forces of democratic reform in the Party.

In two of his speeches, given in March and July 1981, Deng reiterated that the anti-rightist campaign in 1957 "was necessary" and that "presently some people have the same murderous look on their face!" Moreover, he criticized by name certain well-known intellectuals, such as Bai Hua, Wang Ruoshui, and Guo Luoji, whom he knew had taken up the cause of reform. After his July speech, Zhou Yang and Hu Jiwei expressed their different opinions on the spot in defense of Wang Ruoshui and Guo Luoji, and later both Zhou and Hu Jiwei were themselves severely criticized.[12]

The Chen Yun clique had already endeavored to conquer systematically the political and ideological fronts. Chen Yun sent Wang Zhen to the Central Party School to create a sort of "Whampoa Military Academy"* where they could train their own cadres. Deng Liqun, in addition to holding the position of director of the Research Office of the Central Secretariat, grabbed the position of director of the Propaganda Department from Wang Renzhong. After that, Chen Yun and his clique employed their power in a number of ideological sectors—academic, editorial, journalistic, artistic, and educational—to eliminate their adversaries and the reformers. In all areas of the intellectual domain they applied a dictatorial domination more vicious than that of Wang Dongxing. Hu Qiaomu and Deng Liqun became the new self-appointed popes of Chinese "Marxism."

This, then, was the second time Deng Xiaoping broke with the democratic reform forces after the Third Plenum, a rupture far more profound than his distancing himself from the Xidan Democracy Wall movement in March 1979. Because this time, Deng not only split from the social democratic movement but also began to cut himself off from the democratic reform forces more fixed within the Party.

If before December 1980, the Chinese reform seemed to be in a state of dazzling health, after this Central Work Conference, the blow against bourgeois liberalism left it a paraplegic.

Notes

1. "Reprint of Hu Qiaomu's October 3, 1980, Letter on the Polish Situation," Central Secretariat.

---

*Named after the military academy in Canton where the Nationalists trained its military officers in the 1920s.

2. "Draft Record of Wang Renzhong's Transmission of the Central Propaganda Department Meeting Discussing Hu Qiaomu's 'Letter on the Polish Situation.'"

3. "Draft Record of Chen Yun's Comments on Propaganda Work as Conveyed by Wang Renzhong."

4. *Enlightenment Daily*, October 17, 18, and 19, 1980.

5. This is according to the "Circular of the Central Politburo Meeting." This circular was formally conveyed to the entire Party on January 9, 1981.

6. See *Chronology of the Party Since the Third Plenum of the Eleventh Party Congress* (*Dangde shiyijie sanzhong quanhui yilai dashiji*), compiled by the Research Office of the Central Secretariat.

7. Deng Xiaoping, "Implement the Policy of Readjustment, Ensure Stability and Unity" (December 25, 1980), in *Selected Works of Deng Xiaoping: 1975–1982 (Deng Xiaoping Wenxuan: 1975–1982)* (Beijing: People's Publishing House, 1983), p. 313.

8. Ibid., pp. 321–322.

9. Ibid., pp. 322–323, 328.

10. Ibid., pp. 329–330.

11. "Draft record of Deng Liqun's speech at the Propaganda Department."

12. For Deng Xiaoping's two speeches, "On Opposing Wrong Ideological Tendencies" and "Concerning Problems on the Ideological Battle Front," see *Selected Works*, pp. 334 and 344, respectively. Part of the debate between Zhou Yang and Hu Jiwei with Deng was deleted.

8

The Chen Yun Clique
and the First Alliance Against
Hu Yaobang

In December 1973, after Deng Xiaoping's second return to the center of action, Mao Zedong had a curious conversation with him. Mao criticized the Politburo and the Central Military Commission because they wouldn't discuss either politics or military affairs; he proposed to appoint Deng Xiaoping secretary in chief of these two outfits.[1] He said to him on this occasion: "I offer you this pair of sayings: 'A hand of iron in a velvet glove, steel needles in a pincushion.'" Then he added: "You should consult more frequently with others, they are all afraid of you!"

Mao's comments were full of implications. Mao was not satisfied with the way that Zhou Enlai was running the Politburo and the Central Military Commission. Mao had recently denounced the Ministry of Foreign Affairs in these terms: "They don't ever discuss big issues; on the contrary, they submit everyday minor problems to me. If this zany behavior persists, sooner or later they will become revisionists." These comments were aimed at Zhou Enlai. The latter was already dying of bladder cancer, and Mao planned to replace him with Deng Xiaoping, who he wanted to direct the assorted activities of the Central Committee.* Moreover, Mao knew very well that Jiang Qing, Zhang Chunqiao, Wang Hongwen, and Yao Wenyuan feared Deng, but he

---

*Mao's motives toward Zhou Enlai may have been even more nefarious than Ruan Ming suggests. The chairman allegedly withheld medical care from Zhou at a critical stage in his terminal bout with cancer, perhaps to ensure that Zhou would not outlive him. See the account of Zhou's doctor, Dr. Dong Fengchong, cited in Ross Terrill, *China in Our Time: The People of China from the Communist Victory to Tiananmen Square and Beyond* (New York: Simon & Schuster, 1992), p. 139.

hoped that Deng would cooperate with them to restore the stability that had been rocked by the 1971 Lin Biao incident.*

However, Deng Xiaoping did not fully grasp the import of Mao's words of advice for him. Right after he had taken up his public duties the "Gang of Four" attempted to co-opt him. In April 1974, when Deng was leaving for New York to attend a special session of the United Nations General Assembly, Jiang Qing accompanied him to the Beijing airport, where she performed a great scene of impassioned farewell. But shortly after that, the two were at each other's throats. Mao at first supported Deng Xiaoping and told him to convene the Politburo to criticize the "Gang of Four," though he ended by recommending moderation. "In my opinion this is not a serious problem, so don't make a mountain out of a molehill." He intended thus to show Deng that he wanted him at the same time to cooperate with the "gang." But as their confrontation only hardened, Mao launched a global criticism of all of them (earlier he had said "they are acting too strong") declaring that Deng and Jiang Qing were both "patrons of the steelworks." Mao had long since taken to speaking ironically of Jiang Qing, accusing her of "running two factories: one for forging iron and steel and the other for sticking labels on people." In making the same reproach to Deng, Mao wanted to remind him of the double advice about the hand of iron and the steel needles that he had bestowed upon Deng a little earlier in the game. But once again Deng didn't pay the slightest attention, and so the "Gang of Four" began to really intrigue against him. They painstakingly selected from Deng's pronouncements a tendentious batch of verbiage that they delivered to Mao via Mao Yuanxin (Mao's nephew, that is the son of Mao Zedong's brother, Mao Zemin, who at the time was serving as Mao's liaison). By this devious method, the Four accused Deng of attempting to reverse verdicts on the "Cultural Revolution." Their accusation had its desired effect: Deng had initially regained Mao's trust by promising "never to reverse verdicts." But reading Deng's comments passed along to him by Mao Yuanxin, Mao now quipped: "Never reverse verdicts? I don't buy it." Consequently Mao decided in 1976 to launch a campaign to "criticize Deng and carry out counterattacks against rightists who try to reverse verdicts."

When Deng Xiaoping was restored to the leadership for a third time in July 1977, he commented on the historical lesson to be drawn from his setbacks. He acknowledged that he had never truly understood Mao's intentions and had shown himself to be maladroit in the struggle against the Four and conse-

---

*This refers to the ill-fated attempt to assassinate the chairman by Mao's designated successor and closest "comrade in arms" Lin Biao, who then allegedly attempted to flee China only to die in a plane crash.

quently run aground. Well then, what of his struggle against Hua Guofeng after this third restoration?

It's important to remember that the strategy enacted by Deng Xiaoping to wrest the empire of Mao Zedong from the hands of Hua Guofeng worked perfectly at first. This time he would not have disappointed Mao, because he seemed to have grasped the advice contained in the famous double saying. Renouncing his old way of doing things, he did not seek out a systematic confrontation with Hua. Instead of attacking the "two whatevers," he showed himself to be a good tactician in training his fire on Wang Dongxing and his scribblers and avoiding a direct confrontation with Hua. He didn't hesitate to repeat many times over that on the contrary, he was ready to serve under the leadership of Hua Guofeng. In December 1980, when the Politburo made the decision to remove Hua from his leadership positions, certain people, Wang Zhen among them, made a great display of insisting that Deng play the role of the "trinity," holding supreme power over the Party, the government, and the military. Deng turned it down. He was of the opinion, he said, that younger leaders should be chosen to take on the jobs and that powers should be separated.

This was a good idea. The Politburo therefore compared the relative merits of Hu Yaobang, Zhao Ziyang, and Yao Yilin, all three of whom belonged to the generation of the sixty-year-olds. For the title of Party chairman, the choice was Hu Yaobang, who would hold this job along with that of general secretary. Zhao Ziyang already ran the government. As for the Central Military Commission, Deng Xiaoping agreed to assume the chairmanship, because there was no adequate candidate in the next generation (Luo Ruiqing would certainly have been the most appropriate candidate if he had not already died). The redistribution of power was a sign of a new deal: Despite his refusal to hold all the powers held up till then by Hua Guofeng (a refusal moreover not completely hypocritical, given Deng's historical status and his past relationships with Hu Yaobang and Zhao Ziyang and considering his own personality), once he took the position in the military, he gained not only the highest power. His presence at the head of the military commission made possible the supremacy of the military over the Party and the government and so left the field free for an eventual military dictatorship.

In hindsight, one can say that the dismissal of Hua Guofeng at the end of 1980 and the accompanying discussion on the draft of the "Resolution on Certain Questions in the History of Our Party" were two less-than-beneficial influences on the economic and political reforms in progress: on the one hand, an enlargement and reinforcement not truly indispensable to Deng's power base; on the other, the ascension of the Chen Yun clique, a development that was not beneficial to economic and political reform.

In fact, ever since the Fifth Plenum in February 1980, Hua Guofeng's power had been weakened and undermined. The collective dismissal of four members of the Politburo, Wang Dongxing, Ji Dengkui, Wu De, and Chen Xilian having been ratified, Hua Guofeng had lost his main supporters, and his position at the heart of the Politburo was considerably weakened. This same plenum had decided to reestablish the Central Secretariat and elected Hu Yaobang to the post of general secretary, which also undermined Hua's real power as Party chairman. Finally, the plenum decided that Hua could no longer hold the job of premier with that of Party chairman given that the Third Session of the Fifth National People's Congress had on the recommendation of the Central Committee named Zhao Ziyang as premier. In this way, Hua lost his power in the government. Even if Hua had retained his position as Party chairman, he would not have been able to establish himself as a dictator; he would on the contrary only have been able to play the role of power mediator. Between the 1978 Third Plenum and the December 1980 Politburo meeting, China had known two years of exceptional political and ideological gentility, largely because of this absence of excessive concentration of powers at the center. The presence of Hua Guofeng would have presented another advantage in the inevitable conflict between reformers and conservative forces: Because of the defeat of his political line of the "two whatevers" Hua undoubtedly would not have given his support to dogmatic conservatism or despotism, but would very probably have adopted a neutral position. The reform forces would then have disposed of one large area of maneuver in the economic and political domains, and the conservatives would have had more trouble quickly gathering their forces.

The discussion over the draft "Resolution on Certain Questions in the History of Our Party Since the Founding of the People's Republic of China" had consequences similar to those of the dismissal of Hua Guofeng. In the course of the discussion, many people had advanced the notion that it was not necessary to issue such a resolution so quickly. In and outside the Party, they said, there exist very different opinions on many historical issues, notably the historical role of Mao Zedong. A more just appreciation required deeper research and long examination. The adoption of a resolution, one that Party members were required to abide by, would prohibit research and further discussion.

But history followed its course. The Chen Yun clique, which during the years of tentative reforms opposed the march of China toward a market economy and democracy, had profited from circumstances at the end of 1980 to set up a veritable army placed at the service of dogmatism and despotism. Key people of this clique were Wang Zhen, Deng Liqun, Hu Qiaomu, Yao Yilin, and Song Ping. After Hua Guofeng lost his power, the Chen Yun clique alone was in a position to challenge the new power structure created by Deng Xiaoping, Hu Yaobang, and Zhao Ziyang. Benefiting from the power vacuum left by the old Party chairman, they adopted an "orthodox" [*zhengtong*] Stalinist position, dogmatic and totalitarian, and threw themselves into a violent offensive against the modernization and the democratization of China.

Chen Yun and Wang Zhen were veterans sprung from the working class. They were the "perpetuals" of the Chinese Communist Party. Ever since the first purges at the heart of the Party, that is to say, of "A.B. elements" (Anti-Bolshevik League) in Fujian during the 1930s, their victims were always independent-minded intellectuals or humanistic idealists. Whereas the arrivistes endowed with a "good class origin" succeeded in placing themselves on the side of the accusers, Chen Yun and Wang Zhen were of this last species. Above all Chen Yun. He was a typographer at the Shanghai Commercial Press. Being both educated and a worker, he moved up through the Party ranks very quickly at a time when the Communist International gave priority to labor. Chosen as one of the three representatives of the Chinese Communist Party to the Communist International, he benefited from having Stalin on his side. He made his way to Moscow in the company of Wang Ming and Kang Sheng, pure Stalinist dogmatists both. As for Chen Yun himself, he not only had an understanding of dogma but also possessed practical experience, and thus was far more vicious. In the middle of the 1940s, after the "rectification" campaign in Yan'an in which Wang Ming was criticized, Mao called Chen Yun and Kang Sheng to his side and gave them substantial powers. As director of the CCP Central Organization Department, Chen Yun had the upper hand in appointments, dismissals, and assignments of cadres throughout the Party. Director of the Central Social Affairs Department, Kang Sheng controlled the system of public security and purges.

Numerous are those who in China and abroad believe that Chen Yun was allied with the right wing and liberal side of the Chinese Communist Party. Nothing could be farther from the truth. Of course, there were examples of Chen Yun opposing "leftism." For instance, he resisted the focus on high production targets during the Great Leap Forward, and more recently, he also opposed Hua Guofeng's "too high targets" and the "modern-day leap forward" [*yangyuejin*].* However, if one considers his entire career, one discovers that Chen Yun was essentially a Stalinist dogmatist crossbred with a Chinese pragmatist. Chen Yun's power base lies mainly in the Party's organizational and financial sectors, which have long been under his control

---

*Hua Guofeng's ambitious plans, announced in February 1978, included setting annual production targets of 60 million tons of steel, 400 million tons of grain, eighty-five percent mechanization of all farmwork, ten new oil fields, and 120 large-scale industrial projects to be completed by 1985. He also announced that state revenues during the years 1978 to 1985 would be equivalent to the last twenty-eight years combined! See Lowell Dittmer, *China's Continuous Revolution: The Post-Liberation Epoch, 1949–1981* (Berkeley: University of California Press, 1987), p. 224.

and have always implemented the Stalinist system of centralizing state power. In these two domains, he consistently practiced a very Stalinist centralization.

After the Communist Party took power in 1949, Mao brought Chen Yun from the Northeast to Beijing to the Central Committee, where he occupied himself with the economy. The industrial and agricultural policies adopted by Chen were inspired fundamentally by the Soviet model, and secondarily, by some of the experiences accumulated during the Yan'an era. By establishing a monopoly over the sale of grain for purchase and marketing and by adopting the First Five-Year Plan, Chen Yun effectively copied the entire Soviet model of exploiting the peasants to develop heavy industries and the military that to this day he believes is the only true "socialism." Thus, he saw ten years of reform as a challenge to the socialism that he had fought for in the 1950s; from this derives his visceral hatred for reforms.

As for Wang Zhen, Deng Liqun, Hu Qiaomu, Yao Yilin, and Song Ping, they represent Chen Yun's backers in the military, the Party, and the propaganda and economic sectors. A cunning man, Chen Yun has always been very good at employing strategies. He is very sharp-witted in dangerous situations, having avoided direct confrontations with the major leaders, such as Mao Zedong and Deng Xiaoping. He would never play the part of "patron of the steelworks." He has always known how to escape criticism, test the wind, and wait for the right occasion to stage a political comeback—in such a way that neither Mao nor later Deng Xiaoping, could do anything about him. Mao once said of Chen Yun that he was not a man to give himself over to factionalism. To succeed in attaining such a reputation with Mao was in itself a sign of Chen Yun's intelligence. At the 1953 National Conference on Financial and Economic Work, when Gao Gang came to persuade him to join an alliance with Liu Shaoqi, Chen Yun discussed it with Deng Xiaoping, then both denounced Gao Gang to Mao. The truth is that Chen Yun did indeed have his own faction, but it did nothing, or more exactly, its activities were very discreet. At the 1959 conference at Lushan, and then during the "adverse current" of February 1967, a man as true blue as Zhu De was classified by Mao Zedong among the malcontents and criticized. But from Chen Yun, in the most crucial moments of internal struggles, not a peep. When he does speak up, generally it's when he's certain of victory. That's why Mao's formula, "A hand of iron in a velvet glove, steel needles in a pincushion" applies better to Chen Yun than to Deng. As for the principal members of the Chen Yun clique, these people are often thought of as supporters of Deng Xiaoping!

Isn't Wang Zhen, the knife-wielding "Zhou Cang," guarding the temple of Deng Xiaoping?

Isn't Hu Qiaomu Deng's "Number One pen"?

That's how vicious Chen Yun is. He is a master at using people around Deng Xiaoping to imperceptibly achieve his own goals. And that's the key difference between the Chen Yun clique and the other groups. And that's the reason why it has never yet known failure.

When Hu Yaobang threw himself into the ideological struggle against Hua Guofeng and Wang Dongxing as he began to reverse the verdicts of unjust prosecution, the Chen Yun clique adopted a "wait-and-see" virtually neutral position. Hu Qiaomu even once tried to persuade Hu Yaobang to give up his effort at promoting the debate over the criterion of truth. Overestimating the forces of Hua Guofeng, the Chen Yun clique wanted to frighten Hu Yaobang in letting it be understood that continuing the debate would only cause further divisions in the Party. After the February 1980 Fifth Plenum, recognizing that Hua Guofeng's power had cracked and weakened, the members of the clique at once changed into active critical agents. However, instead of focusing on Hua's "two whatevers" and his new version of the personality cult, they attacked Hua's "unrealistic" economic targets and his "modern-day leap forward," which they ironically characterized as a "leap into the unknown." They hoped to kill two birds with one stone.

In 1978 to accelerate the pace of modernization in China, Hua decided to import large-scale turnkey plants for the transformation of metals and the manufacture of chemical fibers. These decisions had already received the approval of the Central Committee, including that of Ye Jianying and Deng Xiaoping. Hu Yaobang was not opposed either. After the Fifth Plenum of 1980, they discovered that the budget was excessive and that the budget deficit had exceeded several million *yuan*. The Chen Yun clique, seeing this argument as a godsend, immediately denounced the "too-high targets" and the "leap into the unknown." Not realizing that he was scratching away at the memory of Mao Zedong, Deng Liqun even made the sensational statement that this was worse than the "Great Leap Forward" of 1958. Happily for him, Chen Yun put a stop to this dangerous comparison, advancing his policy of readjustment: "curtail development, suspend reform." In this way, behind an apparent critique of Hua Guofeng, the clique concealed a real hostility to the politics of reform and opening launched by Deng Xiaoping after the 1978 Third Plenum.

To expand their power, Chen Yun and his clique tried to modify the redistribution of power that had been decided by the Fifth Plenum. They had a three-step plan: First, align with Deng to dethrone Hua; second, align with Zhao Ziyang to destroy Hu Yaobang; third, align with Deng Xiaoping to get rid of Zhao Ziyang. And thus isolate Deng Xiaoping, who would be forced to abide by their will.

The problem of Hua Guofeng would have to be dealt with differently from the past practice of outright purge. It was possible to let him hang on to his rank in the Party. If he stayed on as Party chairman, he wouldn't be able to make a single decision of importance. Not only were the powers redistributed between the general secretary of the Party, who managed current affairs, the premier, and the chairman of the National People's Congress, but in addition, the Politburo at its August 1980 meeting had okayed in its grand design the system of reform of the leadership of the Party and state, precisely to avoid an excessive concentration of powers. Further, even at the heart of the Party, the opponents of Hua Guofeng weren't overzealous, because they didn't think of him as dangerous. From what I know, neither Hu Yaobang nor Deng Xiaoping really wanted to replace him in the Party chairmanship.

Those who were the most outspoken critics of Hua Guofeng in the Politburo meetings were Chen Yun's men, especially Deng Liqun. At that time, Deng Liqun was not even a Central Committee member. He attended meetings of the Central Secretariat in his capacity as director of the Research Department of the Central Secretariat, and in the same capacity he participated in Politburo meetings consecrated to the criticism of Hua Guofeng. In the course of these meetings he gave flowing discourses, posing as a hero who had been struggling against Hua Guofeng since time began. The desires of the Chen Yun clique notwithstanding, most of the Politburo members preferred to keep Hua in one of the posts of Party vice chairman and in the Politburo. A little later, in 1981, at the Sixth Plenum of the Eleventh Congress, the Party elected Hu Yaobang Party chairman and concurrently general secretary of the Party. Both Zhao Ziyang and Hua Guofeng were appointed as Party vice chairmen. But after this plenum, the Chen Yun clique continued to oppose the appointment of Hua Guofeng to leadership positions in the Party.

Deng Liqun traveled all over the place to discuss Hua Guofeng's errors and described how he himself, Chen Yun, Wang Zhen, and Hu Qiaomu had struggled against Hua. Some of these stories were quite silly. Deng Liqun recounted, for example, how once when Chen Yun wanted to talk to Hua Guofeng on the phone, Chen got a secretary who told him that Chairman Hua was in the midst of reading documents and that he'd have to call back later. Deng Liqun turned this totally insignificant incident into a crime against Chen. At the opening of the Twelfth Party Congress in 1982, Chen Yun addressed the chiefs of delegations, clasping his hands on his chest in the ancient manner: "I count on you, don't vote for Hua Guofeng," he said. At the end of the Congress, Hua Guofeng was no more than a mere member of the Central Committee, just like Wang Ming after the Seventh Congress in 1945.

In reality, Chen Yun and his clique opposed Hua Guofeng, apart from personal reasons, because only the elimination of Hua allowed them to move on to their next objective: Hu Yaobang. Everyone knew that Hu Yaobang had played an important role in the solution of the two crucial problems posed by the "two whatevers" and reversing the phony verdicts and that he had put all his weight behind the struggle against Hua Guofeng and Wang Dongxing. No matter how much effort Deng Liqun put into his own self-promotion, there was no way to change that historical fact: It seemed unthinkable that the Chen Yun clique could rally Hua Guofeng to its cause against Hu Yaobang.

Moreover, the clique's attempt to reverse the decisions of the Third Plenum would not have been convincing. In reality, prior to the Twelfth Congress in 1982, the Chen Yun clique, while taking action to chase Hua Guofeng out of the Politburo, was already mobilizing its energy against Hu Yaobang.

Taking advantage of the modification of the Party constitution, Hu Qiaomu acted to eliminate the position of Party chairman. He also reduced the responsibilities of the general secretary to that of merely overseeing routine work, which effectively denied him the authority to run Central Committee meetings. Undoubtedly fearing that his foxiness would not be explicitly understood, Hu Qiaomu also gave the Xinhua News Agency an interview in which he declared: "These modifications of the constitution introduce new rules, the general secretary can only call meetings of the Central Committee, he can't preside over them." From that point on, people observed a weird phenomenon: The communiqués issued after each Central Committee meeting described the meetings as having been presided over by the entire Politburo. But the real reason, kept secret, for the modifications introduced by Hu Qiaomu—a reason that did not appear in an explicit way either in the Party constitution or in the Xinhua interview—is that when all was said and done the Central Committee and the Politburo, outside the elected leaders, had to obey one or two very powerful patriarchs. This hidden reason was not revealed until after the fall of Hu Yaobang in 1987, when in the course of the "Party life meeting" [*shenghuo huiyi*] held from January 10 to 15, 1987, at which Hu Yaobang's "errors" were described to top Party cadres, Hu Qiaomu publicly emphasized one of Hu Yaobang's "crimes": He did not obey the representative of the collegial leadership of the Politburo, Deng Xiaoping.

In reality, the primary reason that Hu Qiaomu amended the Party constitution was to make sure that legally elected Party leaders would not be able to take charge of the Party's leading organizations, a way of erecting a godhead situated above the people, the Party, and the country who could decide everything without being subject to laws, institutions, or procedures. That was a masterpiece: Hu Qiaomu anticipated the desires of Deng Xiaoping, who refused the formal leadership positions, but wished—for the purpose of political effectiveness—for a cult to develop around his personality.

Next, the Chen Yun clique turned the "struggle against bourgeois liberalism" on Hu Yaobang. During the more than one-year period from the end of the Sixth Plenum in June 1981 to just prior to the Twelfth Party Congress in September 1982, the clique launched several campaigns against "bourgeois liberalism" and restarted "the class struggle on all fronts and throughout the country" [*quanguo quanmian jieji douzheng*]. They used every means, including slanders against Hu Yaobang aimed at molding public opinion and instigating attacks against him in secret.

Recall that in the period following the Sixth Plenum held from June 27 to 29, 1981, Hu Yaobang held the positions of Party chairman and general secretary of the Party; Zhao Ziyang and Hua Guofeng were elected vice chairmen of the Central Committee, and Deng Xiaoping chairman of the Central Military Commission. Soon after the meeting, Deng Liqun and Hu Qiaomu conveyed a set of "materials" to Deng Xiaoping that they had compiled with the intention of denouncing Hu Yaobang's excessive tolerance of "bourgeois liberalism" in theoretical and artistic circles. They claimed that certain articles slyly attacked Deng Xiaoping. They also told him that certain people supported Hua Guofeng in order to overthrow Deng. Thus they tried to provoke Deng's rage. In his speech "Concerning Problems on the Ideological Battlefront," which he gave on July 17 to heads of the propaganda organs, Deng Xiaoping seriously criticized intellectuals like Guo Luoji, Wang Ruoshui, and Bai Hua, as well as Ye Wenfu. But what he said about the "going to pot and weakness" of the leadership on this front was in fact aimed at Hu Yaobang.

Guo Luoji was a philosophy teacher at Beida (Peking University) who had written three articles that were denounced by Hu Qiaomu and Deng Liqun. The first article, "Who's the Guilty One?" celebrated the memory of Zhang Zhixin, who had been executed during the Cultural Revolution. In this article, which was published by the *Enlightenment Daily,* one sentence had mentioned the "extreme leftist" trend at the end of March 1979. Hu Qiaomu singled out this sentence and added his own elaborations, saying that Guo Luoji had used that article to make indirect attacks on Deng Xiaoping for his speech "Uphold the Four Cardinal Principles," published on March 30, 1979. The second article written by Guo Luoji, titled "Political Issues Should Be Freely Discussed," was published in the *People's Daily.* Hu Qiaomu accused Guo of using that article to attack Deng Xiaoping's decision to terminate Xidan Democracy Wall and to arrest Wei Jingsheng. The third article was titled "Eliminate the Personality Cult." Prior to its publication, Guo had sent it to Hu Yaobang, who agreed with its contents and wrote a return letter suggesting that he have it published after the Sixth Plenum. What Hu Yaobang meant was that when Mao Zedong was still alive, Lin Biao had engaged in promoting personal worship of Mao Zedong, and then after Mao died this was continued by Wang Dongxing and others who wanted to develop a new personality cult around Hua Guofeng. But all that was in the past. Since it was he himself who would become Party chairman after the Sixth Plenum, Hu Yaobang figured that the moment had perhaps come to talk about the elimination of the personality cult.

Hu Yaobang had also expressed this view to some of the leaders of the media. But Hu Qiaomu and Deng Liqun insisted that Guo Luoji's article, to which Hu Yaobang had given a green light for publication, was directed at Deng Xiaoping. They maintained that this eradication of the personality cult proposed by Guo opposed Deng Xiaoping's proposal to "reduce propaganda around personalities." If Hu Yaobang supported Guo Luoji in his struggle against the cult of Deng Xiaoping, this was, they said, done with the idea of establishing another cult, around his own personality.

As for Wang Ruoshui, the deputy editor in chief of the *People's Daily,* Deng Liqun and Hu Qiaomu accused him not only of promoting articles favoring "bourgeois liberalism" but also of maintaining relations with "illegal organizations" and "illegal journals."*

The writer Bai Hua had received numerous letters of support after his film script *Bitter Love* was attacked. Deng Liqun and Hu Qiaomu insisted that the reason for the support was because Hu Yaobang was in fact hostile to criticism of this writer's works. Ye Wenfu, finally, was warmly applauded when he let it be known in front of students that he was not a Party member. This was immediately reported to Deng Xiaoping by Hu Qiaomu and Deng Liqun as proof that Hu Yaobang was doing nothing about "bourgeois liberalism."

During a speech given by Deng Xiaoping, Zhou Yang and Hu Jiwei, who happened to be in the audience, expressed their opposition. Zhou came to the defense of Guo. He said that he hadn't known Guo Luoji for a long time, but they had worked in the same group during the 1979 Conference on Guidelines in Theory Work. He found the critique Guo had made of Wu De excellent and affirmed that contrary to the opinions of Deng Liqun and Hu Qiaomu, Guo Luoji was anything but anti-socialist or anti-Party. Zhou Yang opposed the practice of rashly attaching political labels of "anti-Party" and "anti-socialism" on some of the articles. Hu Jiwei also defended Wang Ruoshui by saying that there were no connections between Wang and those "illegal" organs and "illegal" journals.[2] The comments of Zhou Yang and Hu Jiwei were not so much an expression of differences with the notions of Deng Xiaoping as attempts to reveal the intrigues fomented by Deng Liqun and Hu Qiaomu on the basis of trumped-up documents. It's for that reason that Deng Liqun and Hu Qiaomu next incited Deng Xiaoping to make both Zhou Yang and Hu Jiwei targets of the campaign against "spiritual pollution."

Armed with "Concerning Problems on the Ideological Battlefront," Hu Qiaomu took immediate action. From August 3 to 8, 1981, in the course of the Forum on Problems on the Ideological Battlefront, he staged a veritable "antiliberal" comedy. This forum normally would have been presided over by the director of the Central Propaganda Department, Wang Renzhong. But

---

*Wang Ruoshui had himself authored the article "The Greatest Lesson of the Cultural Revolution Is That the Personality Cult Should Be Opposed." *Mingbao Monthly* (*Mingbao Yuekan*), February 1, 1980, pp. 2–15. This accusation referred to contacts between Wang and Xu Wenli, a democratic activist and member of the April Fifth Forum, during the Democracy Wall Movement.

Wang hadn't shown any enthusiasm, and claiming illness, failed to even appear. In reality, he left with Deng Xiaoping on August 10 for an inspection tour of Xinjiang Province. Hu Yaobang also left Beijing after giving a speech on the first day of the forum. That left five days to unfurl under the direction of Zhu Muzhi, the deputy director of the Propaganda Department. Deng Liqun had dispatched his bully boys to each commission of the forum to attack Zhou Yang and Xia Yan, but this turned out to be a fiasco. On the sixth and last day, August 8, the master of ceremonies had to come out from behind the stage and put on his own show.

That morning it was the turn of Xia Yan, Zhou Yang, and Yu Guangyuan to give their speeches. These were the first targets of Deng Liqun's and Hu Qiaomu's "struggle against bourgeois liberalism" campaign. The ultimate target was Hu Yaobang. Deng Liqun's henchmen repeated to anyone who would listen that Zhou Yang and Xia Yan were the éminences grises of bourgeois liberalism in literary and artistic circles. As for Yu Guangyuan, according to them he was guilty of "doing everything solely for profit" and advocating "always putting money first." But the forum did not turn out to be an attack on Zhou and Xia, because to the great surprise of Deng Liqun's henchmen, the spectators applauded their speeches.

Zhou Yang said: "What's better for China? To be like stagnant water in a dead pond or to become a roaring river like the Yangtze, which carries mud and sand? Which road to choose? That's a question that contains the destiny of the nation." And he added:

> My choice is clear. I prefer the Yellow River or the Yangtze. I'm not afraid of a little sediment. Do you think our great country can settle for being like little mountain streams? The politics of a Hundred Flowers is being subjected right now to tests, but it mustn't flinch. The peasants fear sudden political change. The intellectuals do too. Does one want to launch initiatives in the spiritual domain? In this domain, enthusiasm is fragile; we must protect it and take care, encourage it and not kill it. It's important to protect two kinds of freedom, free academic debate and the free development of art. Don't be afraid of talking about freedom. Forbidding people to talk is not Party policy. It's easy to forbid people to talk, but it is also very dangerous.

I personally twice had occasion to hear Zhou Yang speak of China's destiny. The first time was around the time of the debate on the criterion of truth in 1978, when Zhou Yang assured the premier that these discussions concerned the future of the Party and country. Zhou Yang's statement was later adopted by the Third Plenum and included in that meeting's historical documents. The second time was at a crucial moment of history, when Hu Qiaomu launched the struggle against bourgeois liberalism and assailed freedom of thought. But this time Zhou Yang was stranded. China turned its back on freedom. The courage and wisdom that Zhou Yang put at the service of the struggle for liberty nevertheless deserve respect. Personally, I think the words he spoke that day are of great historical significance and must not be forgotten. I mention them here above all because for ten years nobody has alluded to them.[3]

Xia Yan's speech put all the rumors to rest. He gave a very lively talk, which was followed by the accusation hurled at him: "Xia Yan is engaging in bourgeois liberalism." This smear was based on all sorts of gossip and notably, on remarks he had made at a forum held by the Guangzhou [Canton] Drama Association: "There should be no forbidden zones in anything concerning subject matter, but authors must have a forbidden zone in their heart," Xia had suggested. Later Xia Yan recalled with humor that he had recently been accused of wanting to increase the forbidden zones and that he did not expect to be taxed as a tenant of bourgeois liberalism who encouraged youth down this path. Xia Yan said that he hoped that criticisms could one day be based on more serious investigation.

Yu Guangyuan declared that as far as he was concerned the methods used for criticism were at their heart problematical. He recalled the historical lessons one could draw from events since the establishment of the People's Republic, notably in the realm of natural science: All the criticisms, from those against Thomas Hunt Morgan to those against Albert Einstein's theory of relativity, have led to fiascos. This kind of "criticism" resulted in casualties for science and the perpetuation of superstition. It led to mind reading, communicating with spirits, making objects move without actually touching them, going through walls, and seeing ghosts in broad daylight.

On this morning of August 8, the brief speeches by Zhou Yang, Xia Yan, and Yu Guangyuan thoroughly exposed the absurdity of the comedy directed by Hu Qiaomu and Deng Liqun. Therefore, that afternoon, Hu Qiaomu himself appeared on the scene and indulged in a number of "crocodile tears" to win over the audience. He talked for more than three hours in a tremulous voice, mopping up torrents of tears. I still remember it very well. Later, his discourse was modified and published in a much tamer form in a pamphlet entitled "Several Problems Relating to the Contemporary Ideological Battlefront." When he appeared on the scene at Huairen Hall, his speech was devoted to reading central documents issued since the Third Plenum to try to establish a "legal" basis for his opposition to bourgeois liberalism. But unfortunately for him, nobody heard him once mention "bourgeois liberalism." Then he proceeded to the second part of his speech, "Criticize What?" The greatest number of his tears sprouted in the course of that dissertation. Perhaps he finally grasped that the present situation was no longer the same as that of summer 1957 and that his opposition to liberalism could not arouse much support. How many people sitting in Huairen Hall were willing to follow him in lambasting his "comrades in arms," who were present in the same chamber? He lost his self-assurance and blurted out the following remarks:

There are a lot of differences among quite a few comrades at this meeting. Given this situation, how can we carry out the struggle shoulder-to-shoulder against bourgeois liberalism or against our enemies both at home and abroad just as Mao Zedong once described it at the 1945 Seventh Party Congress when he called for uniting as one person or as a tightly knit family? Not only do we now lack that kind of unity but I am also doubtful whether we can even unite like two people or two tightly knit families. We will be unable to carry out any struggles if we have numerous debates over small issues and are unable to come out with a unanimous opinion. If this happens, how can our Party be the core of the unity of people all over the country? How can our Party be the supporting pole in the construction of socialist spiritual civilization [his crying interrupted the speech].[4]

Did the sobs signify Hu Qiaomu had lost confidence before the defeat of his antiliberal comedy or were they the "crocodile tears" that he shed to give himself a good conscience before abandoning himself to the blandishments of comrades in arms like Zhou Yang? Perhaps they were both at the same time.

Hu Qiaomu could not go on because of his sobbing, and the meeting was adjourned. Even though it was a summer day with sweltering heat, Hu Qiaomu indicated that he felt cold and needed to put on more clothes. He put on a sweater that somebody brought him, then he sobbed: "I'm old and ailing like a candle fluttering in the wind."

This was a lovely artistic performance. Many people who weren't even in agreement with his ideas, but didn't know his true nature, came to tell me in effect: "Apparently the 'leftism' of Hu Qiaomu comes from the bottom of his heart." That's why, although his long-winded speech on the struggle against bourgeois liberalism failed in its ideological appeal, he did win the "hearts" of some in the audience in an emotional sense: "This Hu Qiaomu, he is a brave man," some people were heard to say.

After some uproar, the curtain fell on this antiliberal comedy, which resembled those botched Peking opera productions at which one hears the gong but not the drum.

The rural reform continued to progress. Contrary to the predictions of the Chen Yun clique, the rural economy did not "collapse" or experience "negative growth." In reality, in 1981 it grew by 5.7 percent more than it had in the year just prior to the year of "rash advance" to collective agriculture in 1958 and surpassed the growth rate of industry. The production of staples like cottons and oils progressed faster than ever, like all enterprises in the rural zones. Apparently, opening up and reform were not being suffocated by the sacrifice of development and the retreat from reform proposed by Chen Yun. But with his partisans, he was on the lookout for the right moment.

The opportunity came in early 1982. Illegal and criminal activities, smuggling, and corruption or abuse of social charities multiplied in the process of opening in the special economic zones of coastal Guangdong, Fujian, and Zhejiang, as well as on the approaches to the Yunnan frontier. Normally, these irregularities ought to be dealt with by the law. But the Chen Yun clique decided to make a mountain out of a molehill and spoke of a "grave class struggle throughout the country," a "fourth great ideological struggle in the Party's history."

Hu Qiaomu declared at an open forum on Guangdong and Fujian provinces held by the Central Secretariat in February 1982:

> We must not view this struggle in isolation, but as a serious class struggle on the national level.
>
> Smuggling is not only an economic phenomenon, but also involves the spreading of different waves of ideological thought.
>
> We are confronted with our fourth serious ideological struggle. The first involved the rightist errors of Chen Duxiu during the CCP-KMT First United Front [1924–1927]. The second was Wang Ming's rightist errors during the Second United Front [1937–1945]. The third was during the national liberation when we resisted the sugar-coated bullets from the bourgeoisie and unarmed enemies. Now is the fourth struggle to resist bourgeois liberalism. Many phenomena unprecedented since liberation have cropped up: Young people are reluctant to join the Party; one youth after withdrawing from the Communist Youth League invited people over for a celebration. His copies of the *Collected Works of Zhou Enlai* totaled only a few, whereas he had a collection of more than a hundred copies of *Tales of the Knight Errants.**
>
> Problems keep mounting. The truth is only one foot high—the evil is ten feet [*daogao yizhi, mogao yizhang*]. This is class struggle. Even after the elimination of classes, there will still be class struggle. The influence of the exploiting classes is still with us. Hong Kong and Macao are in daily contact with us and Taiwan is on our periphery. It's impossible to eliminate class struggle right away and it's very difficult to say when it will be eliminated in the future. We should not view these phenomena only as class struggle in the realm of ideology, for bourgeois liberalism also involves economics. Thus the struggle against liberalism is a common task in all walks of life. To carry out a serious battle we must have a clear understanding, otherwise neither the rectification of the Party's style of work nor the creation of spiritual civilization will occur.
>
> The situation today can be compared not only to that in 1937–1938, but also to that in 1952 when during our Party's cooperation with the bourgeoisie we were attacked by sugar-coated bullets, and the three- and five-antis campaigns† rescued large numbers of people. At present, inadequate attention is being given to class struggle. In the past, we were able to control the capitalists, but not now.

---

*This refers to the common practice in China, especially during the Cultural Revolution, of demonstrating one's political fealty by possessing multiple copies of published works by great leaders.

†Two early campaigns of mass mobilization in 1951–1952 ostensibly aimed at eliminating corruption, waste, and bureaucratism, but that involved vicious attacks through "struggle meetings" and arbitrary arrests and persecutions of people summarily designated as "bourgeois."

The struggle is a long term one. Soon after Lenin implemented the New Economic Policy [NEP] in the Soviet Union in the 1920s, NEP-men appeared.

Our work in political structure and ideology has failed to catch up with the change in policy. Blatant attacks by bourgeois ideology have occurred and among some people there is the problem of the two-line struggle. A street in one local area is given the name Officials' Fortune. In those places, rectification of the Party must be implemented and the Party branches must be dismantled and we should send down cadres to carry out the rectification.

In the past, we accused Khrushchev of being blinded by lust for gain and nowadays in our Party there is indeed blindness by lust for gain.[5]

Hu Qiaomu used the issue of smuggling to expand and enlarge the "struggle against bourgeois liberalism" and turned it into a "serious overall class struggle on the national level and on every front." The political proposals that were recommended on his insistence were partially written into a document entitled "Memorandum of the Forum on Guangdong and Fujian," distributed by the Central Committee on March 1, 1982. The "memorandum" reads as follows:

For several years, the implementation of our policy of opening up to the outside and stimulating the domestic economy has outpaced our ideological work and the necessary management system. The influence in China of decadent capitalist ideologies and bourgeois lifestyles has grown. In many realms of social life serious tendencies toward bourgeois liberalism have appeared. In the economic domain, smuggling and speculation, fraud, corruption and influence peddling, abuses against the state and the collectives, and other illegal acts are far more serious than in the time of the "three antis" and the "five antis" of 1952. Outside of Taiwan, the islands of Quemoy and Matsu, the Pescadores, Hong Kong, and Macao, the exploiting classes have ceased to exist as much as all the classes in China. But because of its internal factors and external pressure, class struggle will persist in certain realms in the long run and might well, in certain conditions, increase. The current struggle against bourgeois liberal tendencies and the attacks on illegal criminal conduct in the economic realm form an important component of this class struggle. The issue of this struggle will decide the success or failure of socialism in our country and of our modernization; it will determine the greatness of our Party and our country. We can't be bystanders. In addition, due to certain special historical conditions, this struggle is bound to be long term and persistent, and there will be ups and downs. Thus the entire Party must fully understand and maintain high vigilance. Not for a moment must it weaken.[6]

Hu Qiaomu's speech and the document of the Central Committee thus spoke all over again about class struggle—"serious overall class struggle on the national level." This return to an old song quickly aroused hostile reactions throughout the country. Hu Yaobang tried to ease the blow by softening the rhetoric, declaring that the expression "class struggle" would very easily arouse sensitivities and therefore did not make a desirable propaganda theme. In the end, this class struggle on all fronts and throughout the country never got off the ground.

Chen Yun and his clique never attained their ends in open ideological debates, but they were more successful at intrigue. Since their "struggle against liberalism" in 1981, thanks to plotting they had little by little taken over the Central Party School, the Central Propaganda Department, and other key instruments of the ideology apparatus, steadily enlarging the base of their power in order to launch a decisive offensive against forces within the Party.

A weird event occurred in summer 1981. A certain Mr. Wang, deputy director of the Research Office of the Central Secretariat under the command of Deng Liqun, and at the same time Chen Yun's secretary, came to see Feng Wenbin, vice president of the Central Party School and deputy director of the General Office of the Central Committee. This Mr. Wang explained to Feng that in general people didn't properly understand the root of the problem posed by Hua Guofeng, that they found him to be a person who was both modest and prudent, and therefore it was necessary to prepare theoretical groundwork for Hua's formal resignation after the upcoming Sixth Plenum. Stating that he was acting on a wish of Chen Yun, Wang demanded that the Central Party School's journal *Theory Trends* publish an article to this effect. Feng Wenbin, who hadn't recognized the fine Italian hand of Deng Liqun in all this, fell into the trap. He immediately assigned this task to Wu Jiang, who then asked Sun Changjiang to write an article entitled "Modesty, Prudence, and the Spirit of Hard Work," which was published in *Theory Trends* (Number 282, June 10, 1981) on the eve of the Sixth Plenum.

Deng Liqun immediately got his hands on a copy of the review to show Chen Yun, claiming that it was alluding to him, Chen Yun. Deng Liqun added that Hu Yaobang had used a whole bunch of bad hats at the Central Party School to oppose Chen Yun. Chen Yun then upbraided Hu Yaobang in the presence of Deng Xiaoping: "I'm one of your supporters, so don't amuse yourself by turning people from the Central Party School against me." This event provided the impetus for sending Wang Zhen to the Central Party School at the behest of Chen Yun in 1982.

Consequently Feng Wenbin sought to explain himself on this "modesty and prudence" affair in a report he made on the entire matter, but those who had set the trap denied the whole thing. A little later, it was Song Renqiong who discovered the following phrase in an article entitled "Escape from the Trap and Think" published in ₁*Theory Trends* (Number 296): "When they consider the modernization of today, some comrades parrot in words and acts 'the First Five-Year Plan' and make of the experience of that epoch an iron collar that restricts all research on new problems."

Song Renqiong claimed that this phrase was also aimed at Chen Yun, because he had once talked about the experience of the First Five-Year Plan.

In August 1981, the Central Organization Department again sent an "inspection team" to the Central Party School to investigate three members of the school: Wu Jiang, Ruan Ming, and Sun Changjiang. It was Deng Liqun who pulled these strings. He it was who had appointed the two members of the team, Zhou Yutian and Tang Lianjie. On August 22, with Deng Liqun, they planned the steps for falsifying documents for the prosecution.

It was at this moment that Hua Guofeng expressed his desire to resign from his position as president of the Central Party School. This was a job that he had acquired along with the Party chairmanship. Now that he was only a vice chairman of the Party, he offered to turn the post over to Hu Yaobang. But Hu refused the offer and in addition asked that he be allowed to resign from his current position of vice president. Therefore, Deng Liqun, at a meeting of the Central Secretariat, three times nominated Wang Zhen to be president. Hu Yaobang began by resisting this proposal, because he thought Wang Zhen was too old. His choice fell on a much younger candidate, as it happened, Xiang Nan. But as Chen Yun was categorically opposed to Xiang, and Deng Liqun insisted on Wang Zhen, Hu Yaobang finally gave in. Initially, Wang Zhen projected an air of modesty, suggesting that his feeble level of theory made it impossible for him to accept this post. Nevertheless, as Chen Yun personally spurred him on to make the Central Party School into a "Whampoa Military Academy," Wang Zhen charged into battle.

As soon as he arrived at the school, he called the enrolled students together for a conference. (The students were from Party organizations throughout the country.) Banging the floor with his walking stick he shouted: "Do you know that here in this school is a 'Hu Yaobang think tank'? I'm here to root it out!" Then he barked: "Do you know that there's a certain person named Ruan Ming in this school? I've never seen him, but I'd like to pit myself against him!" Hearing this, the students were puzzled, because they didn't have the slightest idea what the new president was talking about.

I was on Hainan Island off China's south coast carrying out an investigation when I received a phone call from Zhang Hanqing, who was then secretary in charge of the Guangdong provincial [Party] committee, informing me that Wang Zhen's office had ordered me to return to Beijing immediately and had already reserved a seat for me on the plane.

When I returned to the Central Party School, I felt as though I had been swept back into the period of military supervision during the Cultural Revolution. Tension filled the air to the point that even my oldest friends didn't dare say a word to me. As I entered my office, a friend secretly came in and informed me: "Wang Zhen has sent out a work team. You are under surveillance and it's forbidden to have contacts with you. Right now there's a Party branch meeting going on. Wang Zhen has announced that within three days you will be kicked out of the Party. The secretary of the Party School, Wang Jieshan, is also haranguing everyone to call for a denunciation, even if what comes up risks involving Hu Yaobang!" When I was told that the Party cell was meeting to discuss my expulsion, which was to follow in three days, I decided to go hear what was being said. As I arrived at the meeting hall, I saw that the door was closed and well guarded. I wanted to enter. The guard wouldn't let me in. I pointed out that according to the Party constitution I had a right as a Party member to participate in Party meetings. He still refused to let me enter. Later, someone went inside to find Wu Jiang. He left the meeting and took me to an office, where he advised me to "deal with the issue directly."

I said I was in the midst of an investigation in Hainan Island when I was called back by Wang Zhen's office. Now I'm about to be kicked out of the Party and I don't even know what crime I've committed. According to the Party constitution, a member has a right to challenge any accusations.

Wu Jiang told me, "I will transmit your observations, but Wang Zhen has given the order to forbid you access to your file. That's why you can't participate in any of the meetings."

Later I discovered that this alleged file contained two essential pieces. They had been prepared by Deng Liqun and then delivered to Wang Zhen. If these had been shown to me, I would have been able to reveal the nature of their conspiracy right away.

One version of the materials was an alleged "anticommunist article composed by Ruan Ming." This was in fact the exposé I had composed at the time of a debate organized in October 1980 by the *Enlightenment Daily* on the topic of Deng Xiaoping's speech given at the Forum on Reform of the System of Party and State Leadership. My exposé had been originally published in the paper on October 19, 1980. In April 1982, a Chinese review in New York, *Overseas Chinese Voice* [*Haineiwai*], reprinted it, after which Taiwan *Central News* [*Zhongyang Ri Bao*] published a news report on that article.

Throughout this whole sordid affair involving the compilation of materials, Deng Liqun had mounted a conspiracy. In the name of the Research Office of the Central Secretariat he had prepared an exhibit that he'd entitled "An Anticommunist Article by Ruan Ming." Deng Liqun also added his two cents' worth: "A communist wrote an anticommunist article. Take a look." Later, Deng Liqun felt that it wasn't a good strategy to issue the material in his own name and that of the Research Office. Therefore, the material was put into my dossier and was never reported to the Central Committee. A few days later, he nevertheless sent the material to Zhang Chengxian of the Ministry of Education and asked Zhang to convey it to Wang Zhen. Thus, the source of this "anticommunist article by Ruan Ming" distributed to the Central Party School by Wang Zhen was not, to all appearances, Deng Liqun, but the Ministry of Education.

The other part of the dossier consisted of a so-called inspection report also drafted at the instigation of Deng Liqun. This report contained a document entitled "Comrade Deng Liqun Speaks Out About Ruan Ming" (August 22, 1981), which set the tone of the entire "report." Deng Liqun thus saddled me with two crimes.

I was first accused of "bourgeois liberalism." Deng Liqun said:

Ruan Ming wrote several articles in which he advocated unconditional freedom of speech. He pretends that we must "be vigilant to make sure the leaders aren't isolated from the masses by a small minority of people" and that "once one leader falls, this minority immediately quits the fallen tree to attach itself to another power holder." Ruan Ming practices political allusion and attacks by ricochet. This was reported to me by Comrade Hu Qiaomu who discovered it. I showed these materials of Ruan Ming to Comrade Feng Wenbin. But Ruan Ming always forgets to make his self-criticism. He accuses the Secretariat of compiling defamatory files on him. Once, at a meeting, Ruan openly expressed discontent to Comrade Yaobang's face. There you have a problem of political ethics.[7]

The second crime concerned my past alleged membership in the "rebel faction" [*zaofanpai*]. According to Deng Liqun: "Ruan Ming was very red during the Cultural Revolution and thus was not attacked until later. It's not an exaggeration to call him a member of the *zaofanpai*."[8]

Wang Zhen's commentary on both batches of materials went as follows: "Ruan Ming wrote anticommunist articles, plus there's the fact that he's an old rebel faction member. He should be booted out of the Party in three days' time." Originally, Wang Zhen had added a note that, "Ruan Ming himself should get a copy of the materials." But since Deng Liqun didn't think that this was necessary, Wang Zhen now changed his mind: "Ruan Ming cannot get a copy." All the same, since Wang Zhen had distributed many copies throughout the school, I read them. A little later, having heard that Wang Zhen was persecuting me, Zhou Yang phoned me. I told him that among the articles was one entitled "Comrade Zhou Yang's Comment on Ruan Ming" (September 10, 1981). Zhou said that he knew nothing about it and that he would like to take a look. After reading the article, he invited me over and told me that he had never held the views that pertained to this "conversation," of which the date and content were fictitious. He also told me that he had written a letter to Wang Zhen providing an explanation of the nature of the article along with my behavior at the Central Propaganda Department during the "Cultural Revolution" together with his own personal view of me. Wang Zhen called Zhou Yang and his wife over to his place and told them that they did not know what was going on and that they should clam up. Zhou Yang said that he tried to reason with Wang, saying that he might try to get to know me better.

Exposed to the methods of Wang Zhen, I appealed to the Central Discipline Inspection Commission* about Wang Zhen's actions and sent a copy of my appeal to Hu Yaobang. A few days later, Li Chang, secretary of the commission, met with me and said that Hu Yaobang had instructed the Standing Committee of the commission to hold a meeting to discuss the entire affair. The Standing Committee decided to set up a joint investigation group formed by the five divisions under the Central Committee while all of the materials collected by Wang Zhen were submitted to the Inspection Commission. Li Chang headed the investigation group. He said very clearly: "Henceforth, we can't allow any fabricated documents or unjust accusations."

Hardly had the investigation begun when Deng Liqun, seeing that things could turn out badly for him, asked Wang Zhen to intervene with Chen Yun to halt everything. Wang Zhen received a three-line comment on the matter from Chen Yun: "Ruan Ming can no longer stay at the Party school; Ruan Ming can no longer remain in the Party; and Ruan Ming's articles can no longer be published in any newspaper or journal." Wang Zhen immediately passed it on to the Party school and added: "Whoever does not agree with these three lines is not in accord with the Central Committee."

Thus I was kicked out of the Party.

Immediately after that, Wang Zhen dismantled the Theory Research Office set up by Hu Yaobang at the Party school and kicked the following people out of the Party school: two other directors, deputy directors Wu Jiang and Sun Changjiang, and vice president Feng Wenbin. At the same time, he invited Jiang Nanxiang to be the deputy director of the Party school and promoted crooks working under Deng Liqun who had carried out attacks, such as Zhou Yutian. He also altered the General Affairs Committee and the Academic Affairs Committee of the Party school so that from that point on the Central Party School would become a "Whampoa Military Academy" training "family troops" for the Chen Yun clique.

At the same time that the Chen Yun clique gained control of the Party school, Deng Liqun staged another sort of "coup d'état with the suddenness of a thunderbolt" and simultaneously seized power over the Central Propaganda Department from Wang Renzhong.

This happened in March 1982. Wang Renzhong, director of the Central Propaganda Department, had ascertained that the work of theory research

---

*The Party body formally charged with investigating corruption and other violations of discipline in the Communist Party, but which under the direct influence of Chen Yun, became an apparatus for rooting out proponents of reform and liberalism in the CCP. Rank-and-file Party members live in constant fear of the arbitrary methods of the Central Inspection Commission for determining Party member "corruption." These include bringing charges against suspected Party members on the basis of calculating the difference between their salaries and the value of their property that commission inspectors arbitrarily seize and appraise.

had stagnated for more than a year because of the "struggle against bourgeois liberalism" and that it wasn't responsive to the needs of reform and opening up. After consulting with Deng Xiaoping and Hu Yaobang, he decided to hold a theory forum. This forum opened on March 16, 1982, in Beijing, with the participation of over three hundred theory workers, who worked in eight small groups.

In his opening discourse, Wang Renzhong said: "The major problem in the realm of theory work is it has not adapted to reform and the open door policy, it's too remote." He also came up with what he called the two most important measures to alter the situation: first, to arm ourselves with courage, continue to liberate thought, dare to think, dare to speak, and dare to write; and second, to relate theory to reality. "It's necessary," Wang said, "to investigate new circumstances, research new problems, and advance new points of view." Wang also said that the word "inconsistent" was first mentioned by Comrade Hu Yaobang and that indeed the theory work had lagged behind reality. Wang also emphasized that the forum should follow the principle of the "three don'ts," namely, to refuse to trap people, to refuse to put labels on them, and to refuse to punish their authoritativeness. He also said everyone should "speak one's mind freely" and insisted that "We must take the position that everyone is equal before the truth and never follow the practice of the minority going along with the majority in the realm of theory work and obeying whoever thinks he has the truth. We must create a lively atmosphere; otherwise theory work will remain stale and will not develop."

On the fifth day of the forum, the heads of the small groups held a meeting at which Wang Renzhong once again laid emphasis on the "three don'ts," on "never engaging in settling accounts after the autumn harvest." He reiterated that the purpose of the seminar was not to criticize anyone, but to encourage everyone to speak out. He counted on the comrade leaders of the intellectual world to set an example and create a new situation.

It was on this day, March 20, 1982, that Deng Liqun participated in a meeting of the heads of the small groups where he announced his "suggestions to the forum":

> The participants present at this meeting are all communists and also theory workers. Nowadays, in society as well as the Party, we hear people speak less and less about communism. We Party members, especially those in the field of theory work, should use communist thought to guide our words. We must think not only of the present but also of the future of the Party. We must loudly proclaim our slogans to preserve the purity of communism and brandish the communist banner and spread communist propaganda to the masses.[9]

Deng Liqun also wanted the forum to print and distribute an article by Hu Qiaomu entitled "Sticking to the Socialist Road." He also demanded that Hu Qiaomu's speech in which Hu insisted on confronting "serious class struggle on the national level," presented at the forum on Guangdong and Fujian, be presented to each small group.

At that time no one perceived Deng Liqun's real intentions. The head of each small group simply followed his orders in presenting Hu Qiaomu's article and speech. In fact, Deng Liqun had already chosen as his target a speech given by Ma Peiwen from the third small group that Deng would use to remove Wang Renzhong from his post.

The former deputy editor in chief of the *Enlightenment Daily*, Feng Wenbin, had lost this position at the newspaper because of his love affair with a woman named Yu Luojin. But in Feng's speech to the third small group at the forum, he had defended the article by Guo Luoji, "Who's the Guilty One?" in the *Enlightenment Daily*, expressing his opposition to the unfair treatment Guo had received in being forced to leave Beijing. Deng Liqun showed Feng's speech to Deng Xiaoping and maintained in his presence that Wang Renzhong had convened this forum of theory workers only to attack the Central Committee. Deng Liqun asserted that Feng Wenbin had to know that Guo's article had slyly alluded to Deng Xiaoping himself, and that Feng not only didn't investigate why the *Enlightenment Daily* had committed the error of publishing Guo's article, but even went so far as to defend Guo and criticize the decision of exile taken by the Central Committee. Deng Liqun also said that Feng's actions had not been refuted at the Propaganda Department forum, so that the word was spread all over about attacks on the Central Committee, and Wang Renzhong again had dared to insist that he had acted simply to allow Feng to express himself without reservation and to defend his ideas. If the forum was allowed to continue like this, it would result in uncontrollable ideological chaos!

Deng Liqun hit Deng Xiaoping's raw nerve. Deng Xiaoping lost his temper and decided on the spot that Deng Liqun would replace Wang Renzhong as head of the Central Propaganda Department and take over from him the theory forum in progress. What's more, he left to Deng Liqun the pleasure of instructing Hu Yaobang to implement this decision immediately. Hu Yaobang immediately convened a crisis meeting of the Central Secretariat, and conforming with Deng Xiaoping's order, he named Deng Liqun chief of the Central Propaganda Department—a man who was not even an alternate member of the Central Committee. All heads of Propaganda had either been members of the Central Committee, members of the Standing Committee of the Politburo, members of the Politburo, secretaries in the Central Secretariat, or members of the Standing Committee of the Central Secretariat. Their appointments were always made the object of an official document approved first by the Politburo and then the Central Committee. Even during the exceptional period of the Cultural Revolution, when on June 6, 1966, the Central Committee appointed Tao Zhu to head the Central Propaganda Department, this parachute jump was first discussed and then approved by the

Politburo, and then a document was issued. It wasn't until after all this that Tao Zhu was able to take up his functions. That an intrigue such as Deng Liqun had used to arouse the fury of Deng Xiaoping had succeeded in one day in getting him the position of chief of the Propaganda Department truly constituted an event unprecedented in the history of the Chinese Communist Party.

On March 22, 1982, the day before Deng Liqun took over his new position, the Central Propaganda Department had already met again to discuss the issue of the passage of power from one generation to the next. Wang Renzhong had said: "The Central Committee has decided that it would no longer be possible to hold concurrently the positions of secretary of the Central Committee and chief of the Central Propaganda Department. Therefore, I will relinquish my position as head of the Propaganda Department. The Secretariat has also investigated the possibility of appointing Zhu Muzhi to take the position as Propaganda head." Relatively young, Zhu Muzhi was a former deputy head of the Propaganda Department and was also a member of the Central Committee. Apparently Deng Liqun, who sat in on the meetings of the Secretariat and was thus aware of this eventuality, decided to act quickly. Imagine the surprise of Zhu Muzhi and Zhou Shouyi when Deng Liqun and the gangsters he assembled at the last minute—bully boys among whom one found Yu Wen—arrived to take over the department! Why now this Deng Liqun, who was not even a member of the Central Committee, and who was older than Wang Renzhong?

March 23, 1982, was a very hectic day for Deng Liqun.

In the morning as soon as he received his appointment from the Secretariat, he hurried to the meeting of the first small group of the ongoing theory forum, which consisted essentially of members of the Central Secretariat, to give a long speech on the theme, "Our Banner is Communism." Taking the first small group as his base, Deng Liqun launched his attack on the whole forum and particularly on the former leaders of the Propaganda Department. Those who immediately responded with great favor to Deng Liqun included the following: the first small group (led by Wang Li, who was a member of the Research Office of the Secretariat); the fifth small group, controlled by Zhao Yiya (from the military); the seventh small group, composed of people from higher education in Beijing; and the fourth small group, made up of some members of the *Red Flag* under the control of Xiong Fu. The other four small groups were turned off by Deng Liqun's "Communist Manifesto."

That afternoon, Deng Liqun burst into the Propaganda Department to take up his duties. In an inaugural address, he announced that the most important thing was to be "consistent" with the Central Committee. He said, "Even if their level is low and their work capacities are reduced, those who can support these principles can stay at work. As for those who can't, they can get the word at any moment. We will take them to the door with joy, we don't have to hang on to them." Thus those whom Deng Liqun wanted to get rid of were accused of not wanting to be "consistent with the Central Committee." The director and deputy directors of the Theory Bureau [*Lilunju*] in the Central Propaganda Department, Hong Yu, Li Honglin, and Li Fu, were thus accompanied to the exit by Deng Liqun—with joy.

Between the Sixth Plenum of June 1981, in the course of which Hu Yaobang was appointed Party chairman, and the opening of the Twelfth Party Congress in September 1982, Chen Yun and his clique had seized power over a great part of the central organs of power, including the Central Party School, the Central Propaganda Department, the Central Organization Department, the Research Office of the Central Secretariat, and the Central Discipline Inspection Commission. Deng Liqun and Hu Qiaomu were jubilant. They now held in their hands the reins of ideological power and were ready to initiate a retreat from China's national and international policies: Hu Qiaomu made a series of "important proposals," including cessation of sending students to study in Western countries, lowering the institutional level of U.S.-Chinese relations to that of a liaison office, and reinforcing the country's ties with Brezhnev's Soviet Union. Alas for Hu Qiaomu, the joint "August Seventh" Sino-American pact was signed with President Reagan, making the best of the bad job of Brezhnev's refusal to accept Chinese advances. So despite his strategies, Hu Qiaomu failed to regain the upper hand.

Then, in the suffocating atmosphere created before the Twelfth Party Congress, Chen Yun and his clique seemed to hesitate: Should they, before this congress, openly take aim at Hu Yaobang?

Zhao Yiya, who was the hit man for Deng Liqun and Hu Qiaomu in the military, published under his own name an article criticizing bourgeois liberalism. He claimed that if the failure to oppose bourgeois liberalism posed grave problems that had to be solved in the theoretical realm, in journalism, and in literature, it was because an orchestra director pulled strings backstage. The target of that article was very obvious, and although Zhao didn't mention any names, everyone knew to whom the comment was directed, just as during the "Cultural Revolution" everyone knew who was designated by the expression "the biggest capitalist roader in the Party" [Liu Shaoqi]. People like Zhou Yang, Xia Yan, Hu Jiwei, and Yu Guangyuan were some of the important personages in the fields of literature, journalism, and theory, but none among them had the necessary competence to be this all-powerful "orchestra director" in all these areas at the same time. The "backstage supporter" [*zong houtai*] could be none other than Hu Yaobang. He was the only one taking charge of the three areas. A wild public uproar rocked the whole country, and Deng Xiaoping was angry again: Why raise such an issue prior to the Twelfth Congress? And just who was this Zhao Yiya?

It seemed that the climate was not quite right. Deng Liqun and Hu Qiaomu withdrew that trial balloon. They held a criticism meeting at which

Hu Qiaomu, stern in voice and countenance, criticized Zhao Yiya as being "unworthy of his trust" in that he "published an erroneous article without asking Hu Qiaomu's permission." But everyone understood that he was acting out a comedy, because Zhao Ziya was not a man who dared to act on his own.

Anyway, Hu Yaobang went through the Twelfth Congress unscathed. Conforming to the new Party constitution, he lost his title of Party chairman, keeping that of general secretary, though now possessing only the power to convene and not to preside over Central Committee meetings.

Following the Twelfth Congress, Hua Guofeng was retained as a member of the Central Committee in name only; in reality, he quit the stage of Chinese history. The so-called Deng-Hu Zhao triumvirate was a fragile structure, inconsistent both in ideology and action, and under challenge by the Chen Yun clique, in which ideology and action were tightly unified.

Chen Yun and his clique quickly consolidated the terrain conquered prior to the Twelfth Congress, then embarked on their second-phase strategy: ally with Zhao Ziyang to get rid of Hu Yaobang. Zhao Ziyang was then premier and head of the State Council. He was mainly in charge of economic work. Thus, the Chen Yun clique chose the economy as the terrain of its alliance with Zhao Ziyang. Chen Yun and his people had observed that since Zhao had quit his provincial responsibilities to enter the Central Committee, he had changed his line; now he insisted on centralization and the necessity of expanding the power of the premier. Such a position happened to be consistent with the Chen Yun clique's economic ideology and would now become the basis of the anti–Hu Yaobang alliance: allying with Zhao to get rid of Hu.

But how to relate economic issues to Hu Yaobang? That was certainly difficult, because Hu Yaobang was not in charge of the economy, and the economic situation itself in 1982 in China was not bad. Thanks to the rural reform, agriculture continued to produce excellent results. Total output increased by 11.2 percent over and above the increases of the previous year; grain output increased 8.7 percent, cotton 21.3 percent, and oilseed 15.8 percent. The predictions of the Chen Yun clique about the impending collapse of the rural economy and negative growth fell by the wayside. Industrial growth increased 7.7 percent in 1982, far exceeding the planned 4 percent increase. But far from recognizing their error, Chen Yun and his clique attempted to hold Hu Yaobang accountable by focusing on the issue of fixed investment exceeding the national plan. This was really very strange, because Zhao Ziyang and Yao Yilin were in charge of economic planning, and so it was impossible to see how the overinvestment could possibly concern Hu Yaobang.

Deng Liqun tried to gather together from correspondents of the *Red Flag* all of Hu Yaobang's many talks with local cadres during his ubiquitous investigation work throughout various parts of the country. Deng made a report to Chen Yun to prove to him that the overheating of the economy, the troubles

of excessive capital construction, and the tendency of so-called fixed investment to exceed the original economic plan all resulted from Hu Yaobang's
talk about "quadrupling" the economy by the end of the twentieth century.
Deng Liqun also told Zhao Ziyang: "During your visits abroad, Hu Yaobang
spread the idea of 'quadrupling' all over the country, sowing disorder in your
well-laid plans." Once Chen Yun and Zhao Ziyang were in cahoots, Hu
Yaobang's crime of disrupting the economy was finalized.

Chen Yun proposed holding a meeting of the Politburo Standing Committee to criticize Hu Yaobang. He and Zhao Ziyang both gave talks. Chen Yun
brought up ten criticisms, all of which accused Hu Yaobang of sowing disorder in the economy. Zhao went one better in saying that he had planned the
economy perfectly the preceding December, just prior to his visit to the
eleven African countries, and Hu's investigations had disrupted these careful
plans for economic work. Deng Xiaoping remained silent. Chen Yun then
made a further proposal to convene a meeting of the first Party secretaries on
the provincial, municipal, and autonomous region levels to further criticize
Hu's mistakes and settle his hash.

But Deng Liqun became overstimulated and made a rash move. In his haste
to mold opinion before this meeting, he decided to gather together all the
correspondents of the *Red Flag* to give them a complete account of the criticisms of Hu Yaobang voiced by Chen Yun and Zhao Ziyang at the meeting of
the Politburo Standing Committee. His goal was to return with them to inform leaders of the provincial, municipal, and autonomous region levels. But
the result was not exactly what he'd intended. Some of the leaders wanted to
know just what was going on in the Party center. Would Hu Yaobang be
dropped as Party leader right after Hua Guofeng's removal? And what of the
policy of "engaging in the four modernizations with one heart and one
mind"?

Informed of the reactions of these local leaders, Deng Xiaoping consulted
with Marshal Ye Jianying, who was then in Guangdong. Ye opposed the idea
of criticizing Hu Yaobang. Deng decided to cancel the meeting of first Party
secretaries. Furious, Chen Yun set off in a huff to Hangzhou to "recuperate."
Deng Xiaoping sent Wang Zhen along to console him.

The first anti–Hu Yaobang alliance had failed.

Notes

1. This proposal was changed somewhat later, as Mao decided to appoint Deng to
the positions of vice chairman of the Military Commission, first vice premier of the
State Council, and chief of staff of the People's Liberation Army.

2. When Deng Xiaoping's July 17, 1981, speech, "Concerning Problems on the
Ideological Battlefront" was finally made public, the comments on Guo Luoji, Wang

Ruoshui, and others were excised along with the additional remarks by Hu Jiwei and Zhou Yang.

3. These quotations are from the "Original Draft Summary of Zhou Yang's Speech Based on His Talk at the August 8, 1981, Forum on Problems on the Ideological Battlefront."

4. Based on the original draft summary of Hu Qiaomu's speech at Huairen Hall on the afternoon of August 8, 1981, and the small pamphlet titled "Several Problems Relating to the Contemporary Ideological Battlefront," in which there are numerous differences from the original speech.

5. "Draft Summary of Hu Qiaomu's February 1982 Speech at the Open Forum of the Central Secretariat on Guangdong and Fujian." This speech was never published, but was transmitted internally in the Party.

6. Central Committee, "Memorandum of the Forum on Guangdong and Fujian," March 1, 1982.

7. Excerpts from "Investigation Report on Ruan Ming" and "Comrade Deng Liqun Speaks Out About Ruan Ming."

8. Ibid.

9. "Draft Summary of the March 20, 1982, Speech by Deng Liqun to Various Participants in the Open Forum on Theory by the Central Propaganda Department."

9

Deng Counterattacks on the Economic Reform Front

In the beginning of 1983, after the failure of the first anti–Hu Yaobang alliance, the Chen Yun clique changed tactics to recapture the offensive in the ideological realm. The critique of "humanism" [*rendaozhuyi*] and "alienation" [*yihua*] resuscitated by two of its members, Hu Qiaomu and Deng Liqun, which appeared to be aimed at Zhou Yang and Wang Ruoshui, constituted in fact a whole new and important attempt to unseat Hu Yaobang.

In March 1983, at an academic forum organized by the Central Party School to commemorate the one-hundredth anniversary of Marx's death, Zhou Yang gave a speech titled "A Few Issues Regarding Marxism" in which he raised the issues of humanism and alienation. Zhou Yang's speech was warmly welcomed. After his speech, Wang Zhen, the president of the Party school, who presided over the forum, went up to the speaker and said to him: "Comrade Zhou Yang, you gave an excellent speech from which I learned a great deal. I have only one question: How do you write the characters '*yihua*.'" As Zhou Yang wrote down the two characters for him on a piece of paper, Wang nodded his head and walked away. However, that evening, Hu Qiaomu, who had not shown up at the forum, made an urgent phone call to the Central Party School in which he claimed that Zhou Yang's speech contained certain political errors and that the forum should not conclude, but should be continued for three more days so criticism could be leveled at Zhou Yang. However, the four speeches that Hu Qiaomu concocted to criticize Zhou Yang were of a quality so low and contained so many incoherences that they appeared deplorable. The *People's Daily* reprinted Zhou Yang's speech along with the four speeches criticizing him, and readers could easily spot the difference in quality between Zhou's speech and the others.

This made a fool of Hu Qiaomu. Infuriated, he accused the *People's Daily* of "turning up its nose at organization and discipline" in publishing an article by Zhou Yang without first seeking Hu's approval. But the funniest thing happened afterward, when one day while presiding over an orientation meeting at the Central Party School, Wang Zhen declared that bourgeois liberalism and agitation by students had originated with the utterance of the word "alienation" by Zhou Yang. Wang Zhen also attacked Hu Yaobang for being too soft on Zhou Yang, carefully forgetting to recall that he had congratulated Zhou at the time.

Some months later, Hu Qiaomu and Deng Liqun drafted the speeches Deng Xiaoping and Chen Yun would give at the October 1983 Second Plenum of the Twelfth Party Congress before announcing the campaign to "clean up spiritual pollution." They also continued their criticism of Zhou Yang and Wang Ruoshui's concepts of humanism and alienation. They wanted, too, to unsettle Hu Yaobang, who was scheduled to speak at this plenary session on Party rectification. But once again Deng Liqun made a mistake: Once the "clean up spiritual pollution" campaign was launched, he overstepped his position as head of the Propaganda Department in expanding the campaign from the realm of ideology and politics to those of economics, science and technology, and policy in the vast rural areas. He immediately collided with the collective opposition of Zhao Ziyang, Fang Yi, and Wan Li, so much so that Deng Liqun's campaign against spiritual pollution was arrested after a mere twenty-eight days of "cleaning up."

Deng Xiaoping ultimately realized that when he made his speech on "Spiritual Pollution" before the Second Plenum, he'd fallen into a trap set by Deng Liqun and Hu Qiaomu. He expressly ordered that this speech not be included in his *Selected Works* and at the same time decided to remove Deng Liqun as head of the Propaganda Department.[1] Beijing's citizenry were ready to raise a cheer of "bottoms up" to celebrate the occasion when they heard the news on Voice of America. But right away, unwilling to let anyone think he was going to be bossed around by foreigners, Deng Xiaoping suspended the removal of Deng Liqun.

It was at that time that Hu Yaobang's hands were freed once again. This was the period when Deng Xiaoping announced to his foreign friends: "If the sky falls down, we have Hu Yaobang and Zhao Ziyang to hold it up." And he turned all his attention to opening up and economic reform.

Because the campaign against "spiritual pollution" was terminated very quickly, the economic situation of 1983 didn't suffer. The rural economy, in particular, followed its irresistible course. Grain and cotton output showed nationwide increases of 33,700,000 tons and 1,039,000 tons, respectively. This enabled the total output of grain and cotton to reach a level of 387,300,000 tons and 4,637,000 tons, respectively. These were records! This increase, which indicated the great impact of the rural reform on emancipating production, was unprecedented. Largely because of constant interruptions from political campaigns against liberalism, against humanism, and against spiritual pollution, the urban reform was still stagnating. There was barely a scintilla of improvement in economic efficiency. Deng Xiaoping seemed to indicate awareness of this state of things when he commented: "Apparently there were too many concessions on the economic plan at the December 1980 Work Conference." Therefore, Deng was prepared to counterattack on the economic reform front in the cities.

On January 24, 1984, Deng Xiaoping went on an inspection tour to the Shenzhen Special Economic Zone in Guangdong. On January 29, he visited the Zhuhai zone in the same area. Then, from February 1 to 10, he inspected the Xiamen (Amoy) Special Economic Zone in Fujian province. Upon returning to Beijing, he had published, on February 24, 1984, "Questions on the Special Economic Zones and on Increasing the Number of Cities Open to the Outside World." In it he said:

> Recently, I paid a special visit to three special economic zones in Guangdong and Fujian provinces. Today, I would like to discuss issues regarding the policy on establishing the special economic zones and how to further their opening. When we create the special economic zones and practice the opening-up policy, the direction of our thought ought to be clear: We cannot curl up on ourselves, we have to go on opening up. My impression of Shenzhen was that it is prosperous and developed. The speed of construction was quite rapid, especially in Shekou. Why? Because they were given authority over expenditures that did not exceed $500 million. Their slogan is "time is money, efficiency is livelihood." In buildings undergoing construction, one floor is finished every day and the entire building is completed within a couple of weeks or so. The construction teams are composed of laborers from the hinterland, and the reason for the great efficiency stems from the contract system and explicit guidelines for rewards and punishments.*
>
> Special economic zones are a window to technology, management, knowledge, and foreign policies. Through the zones, we can import technology, acquire knowledge, and learn about management, which is also a form of knowledge. The special zones will become a foundation for opening up to the outside world. We will not only benefit in economics and personnel training, but also extend the positive impact of our country on the world.
>
> The Xiamen Special Economic Zone is too small. We must turn the entire Xiamen Island into a zone to attract investment from overseas Chinese and foreigners so as to mobilize the surrounding areas to provide services to the special economic zones. All this aims at enlivening the economy of Fujian province. Although we won't refer to the Xiamen zone as a free port, we can certainly implement such policies there. Such a practice is not unprecedented in the world. As long as there is a free flow of capital, foreign businessmen and overseas Chinese will come and invest. As far as I am concerned, it's not going to fail, but is bound to bring great benefits.

---

*Contrast Deng's description of efficiency of construction in these zones with the situation in Beijing and most other cities in the mid-1980s when construction of residential and commercial buildings was notoriously slow and/or of very low quality.

Apart from the current special economic zones, we can also consider opening up more of them and setting up port cities such as Dalian in Liaoning province and Qingdao in Shandong province. We will not refer to them as special economic zones, but we can certainly implement the same policies there and gain great benefits. We will also develop Hainan Island. If the economic development there is successful, that will certainly be a great victory.[2]

That talk marked a real turning point in Deng Xiaoping's thinking on reform. Deng is a political pragmatist. Throughout most of his political career, he had fundamentally conformed to the thought of Mao Zedong. It's enough to read volume 1 of his *Selected Works: 1938–1965* to see that he hardly had any ideas or personal opinions. Even in July 1962, when he had first used his famous theory of cats—borrowed from Liu Bocheng—that night he telephoned Hu Yaobang to ask him to cut it. In my opinion, the time when Deng was able to come up with his most independent and innovative views was from 1977 to 1980 when he was in the midst of his struggle with Hua Guofeng, Mao's successor, who was even less independent and innovative. Deng's personal contribution resides in his guidelines on the two aspects of economic and political reform: Opening up and reform signify for him, in economy, the liberalization of the economy and the introduction of markets, and in politics, his own liberalization and democratization.

Of course, Deng did not come up with such concise concepts as I have summarized here. However, rich and legitimate though his thought is in many ways, it doesn't always seem very consistent and lacks constancy. After the Polish events of winter 1980, he performed a political turnabout of 180 degrees, just as Mao had done in 1957. After advocating democracy, he decided to crack down on the democrats, and under pressure from the Chen Yun clique, for three years he renounced his policies of economic reform. During those three years from 1980 to 1983, he was basically used as an instrument of the Chen Yun clique in its campaign against liberalism and in "cleaning up spiritual pollution." What's more, Deng was in profound accord with himself (in contrast to the time when Mao had forced him to criticize himself and to promise to "never reverse verdicts"). But the twenty-eight–day campaign against "spiritual pollution" following the Second Plenum in October 1983 aroused very serious fears: Was China going to retreat to the closed door and resume the class struggle of the Mao era? The uneasiness in China and abroad was so widespread that Deng was compelled to take it into account. Besides, since the economic situation was far better in 1983 than the dire predictions made by the Chen Yun clique, Deng decided to put his economic reform back in the saddle when he set out on his trip to the special economic zones.

The establishment of the special economic zones has been a persistent bone of contention between the reform forces and the Chen Yun clique. Hu Yaobang was the first one to support "implementing special policies" and "flexible measures" [*linghuo cuoshi*] in the provinces of Guangdong and

Fujian and in establishing the special economic zones in Shenzhen, Zhuhai, and Xiamen.

More than three years earlier, from September 23 to 24, 1980, he had presided at the fifty-second meeting of the Central Secretariat, where it was decided to implement "special policies" and "flexible measures" in Guangdong and Fujian. After this meeting, Hu Yaobang proposed to utilize the advantages of the two provinces and allow them to "become rich first," which would then make it possible for them to explore new roads, gain experiences, and train cadres in the fields of economic construction and structural reform. Hu also said that these two provinces must have a long-term vision and be more open to both the entire country and the outside world in order to enliven the economy, carve out new roads, and become the entrepôt for contact with the outside world.[3]

After that meeting, I myself went on an inspection tour in December 1980 in Guangdong province to visit the newly established Shenzhen zone. I was able to talk to Wu Nansheng and Huang Shimin, the directors of the special zone, and visited the Shekou zone, which was the first place to be developed. I was particularly impressed by Shenzhen, where the politics of reform and opening up were in full swing, taking advantage of foreign investment so as to accelerate our modernization. Upon returning to Beijing, I read the documents from the December 1980 Work Conference, which because of the 1980 budget deficit had decided to slow down the construction of special economic zones. I personally thought that the document might have a negative impact on the development of the zones. But in fact, most of the investment slated for the special economic zones was from foreign sources. At a time when the domestic financial capacity was inadequate, introducing foreign investments would only bring benefits, not defects, to the entire national economy. Therefore I immediately wrote an investigation report titled "The Speed of Construction in the Special Economic Zones Should be Accelerated." Hu Yaobang immediately ordered that my report be transmitted to leading organs in Guangdong and Fujian. Fujian's first Party secretary, Xiang Nan, told me afterward that this report had been very helpful to Fujian. The situation there was that since the Xiamen Special Economic Zone had been started relatively late, conservative forces in the Fujian provincial Party committee had wanted to slow down construction in the zones after the December 1980 Work Conference. It almost caused a complete halt to development. But with the report transmitted by Hu Yaobang, Xiang Nan said that he could continue to move forward.

In April 1981, I made another inspection tour to the Xiamen Special Economic Zone and exchanged ideas with Xiang Nan. Upon returning to Beijing, I wrote a second investigation report, titled "On the Construction of the Special Economic Zone in Fujian Province," in which I came up with a theoretical perspective on the developmental strategy of this zone, as well as theoretical problems tied to economic zones in general. That report was the one used in the attack launched against me by Chen Yun, Wang Zhen, Deng Liqun, and Hu Qiaomu as "proof" to demonstrate that I was guilty of the crime of "bourgeois liberalism." In it, I proposed the expansion of the Xiamen Special Economic Zone from the 2.1 square kilometers in the Huli area to the 123 square kilometers of the entire Xiamen island; the practice of open door policies and favorable treatment of foreign capital throughout the island, such as is employed in Singapore and Hong Kong; and turning the island of Xiamen into an international free port. Utilization of the land, personnel resources, and such installations as existed, with recourse to foreign investment and modern technology and modern management methods would permit the building of an international city advanced in all aspects of the economy, culture, science, education, and municipal administration. Thanks to the international level attained by the economy, the culture, and social relations, this area would rival Singapore and Hong Kong and stimulate the economic development of Fujian province and the entire country.

I attached a theoretical analysis to my report in which I noted that the modernization of our country could and must utilize resources and capital of the Americans and other Westerners, as well as their knowledge, experience, and skills. I sent both the report and its theoretical analysis to Hu Yaobang. He sent the report to Gu Mu, then vice premier, with the following accompanying note:

Comment on the report:

To: Comrade Gu Mu: May 25 [1981]

Apparently the views expressed herein are not without basis. I beg you to ask the comrades in charge of this area to pluck up their courage and quickly carry out this work in a better way.

As for the theoretical text, Hu Yaobang returned it to me first with the following note:

Comment on the analysis:

To: Comrade Ruan Ming: May 25

I passed on your report to Comrade Gu Mu and asked him to inform the comrades in charge of that area to concentrate on what they're doing. As for your analysis, please send me the complete article when finished, for I will recommend it to comrades of the Politburo and the Secretariat. This analysis is very helpful to the Center in its reflection on theoretical questions and on questions of direction.

Hu Yaobang

When the analysis was completed I sent it to Hu Yaobang, who made the following comment on May 29, 1981:

This article contains rich materials and the viewpoints are also acceptable. I recommend that it be sent to Comrades Xiaoping, Chen Yun, Li Xiannian, Zhao Ziyang, and the Party Secretariat along with the vice premiers in the relevant fields.

I also sent my report, along with the analysis and the three comments by Hu Yaobang, to Xiang Nan. Xiang was very happy and replied:

Comrade Ruan Ming:

I have received both letters and the materials. I finished reading the materials in one sitting. Regarding the special economic zones, about which there are different understandings and debates, they especially need to be explored and tested out in terms of theory and practice. It wouldn't be an exaggeration to say that these two sets of materials are actually more important than an investment of money.

Due to the above-mentioned reasons, I took the liberty of copying them. I don't think this is a matter of "revealing secrets," nor do I think it shows disrespect for the author. I don't lay much hope on the conference that will be held in Beijing, for implementing these policies can only occur step by step. I am looking forward to what happens after the meeting. Any retreat will be intolerable and impossible. First of all, the people will not allow such a move. Are we willing to remain perpetually behind Taiwan? If we don't begin to develop the economy, we can't pretend in any way to the superiority of our system. You guys yelling and shouting there in Beijing will make it helpful to the growth of newly emergent things.

I hope that in the future you will keep in frequent touch with us. Of course, this should not be limited just to matters involving special economic zones.

With warm regards,
Xiang Nan, June 2 [1981]

The State Council was holding at precisely that time a work conference on special economic zones (the Beijing conference mentioned by Xiang Nan); Gu Mu presided over the meeting, but he mentioned neither my report or analysis nor Hu Yaobang's comments that accompanied them. That's because the Chen Yun clique was in a hurry to blackball the policy of establishing the special economic zones. Knowing their negative opinions about the zones, Zhao Ziyang clammed up. As for Gu Mu, he resigned himself to a low profile at the meeting. The proposition launched by Hu Yaobang to promote the special economic zones failed.

At the instigation of Chen Yun, between June and July 1981, Hu Qiaomu and Deng Liqun attacked two aspects of Hu Yaobang's proposals for establishing the special economic zones. First, they carefully compiled a whole series of documents on the old foreign "concessions" [*zujie*] in Chinese history and denounced the current special economic zones as replicas of the "concessions" from China's semicolonial past; creating such zones amounted to "selling out the country." At the same time, they spread the rumor that "leaders of the Central Committee [read Chen Yun] have advised suppressing these zones."

Next, on July 5, 1981, in the "Memorandum of the Work Conference Convened by the Central Secretariat on the Special Economic Zones," Hu Qiaomu and Deng Liqun inserted a passage regarding my report and analysis along with Hu Yaobang's comments:

> Today, following the transitional period that has spanned thirty years from the New Democracy to Socialism, there are still people who blatantly speak of state capitalism, and what's more, the kind of state capitalism that employs foreign funds. Also, they incorrectly associate the special policies and flexible measures in the two provinces with state capitalism. This is bound to cause ideological chaos.[4]

In the course of this summer of 1981, Deng Xiaoping did not support Hu Yaobang's efforts toward economic reform in the special economic zones. He didn't utter a word on the subject of the zones. He was content to silently watch the Chen Yun clique attack from the sidelines. At the very time that Hu Qiaomu and Deng Liqun launched their attacks on the special zones on the economic battlefront, they wildly exaggerated the so-called flood of bourgeois liberalism on the ideological front as a way of shifting Deng Xiaoping's attention to the struggle against liberalism. Indeed, it was Hu Qiaomu and Deng Liqun's effort that led Deng Xiaoping to give his speech "Concerning Problems on the Ideological Battlefront" on July 17, 1981. In the course of the second half of 1981, both economic and political reform met with reverses in the economic domain as well as in the domains of politics and ideology.

The establishment of the special economic zones and the application of "flexible measures" in Guangdong and Fujian was suspended. In December 1981, in a speech at a forum of party secretaries from the municipal and provincial levels, Chen Yun stated that no further special economic zones should be permitted beyond the current areas in Shenzhen, Zhuhai, Shantou in Guangdong, and Xiamen (the 2.1-square-kilometer Huli area) and the national economy must proceed in a unified order and closely adhere to the five-year economic plan. Although Chen Yun did not expressly state that he wanted to suppress the special economic zones, under his insistence on "the national economy proceeding in unified order," the various central ministries withdrew the autonomy previously granted to Guangdong and Fujian provinces and the special economic zones, thus making the pursuit of economic reform and opening up impracticable.

Hu Yaobang tried to save the store on January 14, 1982, with a speech at a meeting of the Central Secretariat, "On the Issue of Foreign Economic Relations." In this ten-point speech he proposed the utilization of two investment sources: domestic and foreign. Hu Yaobang also proposed that we open markets, both domestic and international, and master two sets of skills: those that would enable us to organize the interior economic construction and those that would permit the conduct of foreign economic relations. But without the support of Zhao Ziyang and the State Council, Hu Yaobang's effort did not produce any results. Deng Xiaoping was still sitting on the sidelines watching. That's why, in 1982 and 1983, Guangdong and Fujian provinces, along with the special economic zones, were in a very difficult situation. Even Xiang Nan—that eternal optimist—in 1982 no longer glowed with the same confidence he had exuded in 1981. In one letter he wrote:

> Comrade Ruan Ming:
>
> I have read both your letter and the speech.
> Recently, we have been inundated with floods of regulations coming out of the relevant ministries in Beijing. If this continues, the special policies and the "flexible measures," not to mention the special economic zones, will be, practically speaking, null and void; these instructions and regulations are contrary to the ten points of Comrade Hu Yaobang, and they are also contrary to the Central Committee's orders of two years ago. With these instructions and regulations, the scanty progress accomplished after the 1978 Third Plenum has been swept away.
> Attached to this letter, I have sent three documents for you to read if you have the time. Thus, you will be well up on the situation. One set was sent to me by the grandnephew of Chen Jiageng [Hong Kong man of affairs].
> But please do not quote from them.
> Salute.
>
> **Xiang Nan,** May 17 [1982]

This letter well demonstrates that without having decreed the "suppression" of the special economic zones or the particular political measures applied in Guangdong and Fujian, Chen Yun had for all practical purposes vetoed them. It was in these circumstances that at the end of 1983, when the "cleaning up spiritual pollution" campaign had raised considerable doubts both domestically and abroad about the continuation of China's reform and open-door policies, that Deng Xiaoping was forced to come out and respond with vigor.

He took advantage of the period of the Spring Festival [Chinese New Year] to undertake a tour of inspection. He chose to travel to the three special economic zones in Guangdong and Fujian provinces, and to the Baoshan Iron and Steel plant in Shanghai—all of them sources of debate among high-level leaders. Deng Xiaoping asked Wang Zhen to accompany him, for although the latter was a key figure in the Chen Yun clique, he also had close personal relations with Deng Xiaoping.

In the course of his trips through the special economic zones, Deng showed great vigor. He stayed in Xiamen for ten days and had extensive discussions with the first Party secretary of Fujian province. Xiang Nan was the most thorough reformer among all provincial first Party secretaries. He told me that

Deng Xiaoping had known him for many years, and when he—Xiang—was a young man, Deng used to call him "Little Xiang" [*xiao Xiang*], a phrase of endearment that Deng still sometimes uttered. On this occasion, time and again Deng referred to Xiang as "Little Xiang," each time exclaiming: "Oh! Little Xiang, you've reached such an old age." Xiang Nan spoke to Deng Xiaoping of the proposal transmitted to him in 1981 by Gu Mu to make Xiamen Island a free port. Deng Xiaoping expressed his full support and added that it should be more open and that a series of coastal cities should be established in order to mobilize urban reform on the national level.

Xiang Nan also explained his views about Taiwan and Tibet to Deng Xiaoping. He suggested that to put Chiang Ching-kuo and the Dalai Lama at ease, Taiwan should be allowed to develop Fujian with Chiang Ching-kuo in charge, and the Dalai Lama should run Tibet. Such a policy would eliminate any temptation for Taiwanese and Tibetan independence by the indigenous populations and would be beneficial both to the process of reunification and to further development. Deng Xiaoping, of course, made no explicit comments on these very audacious ideas of Xiang Nan's.

Upon returning to Beijing from Fujian, Deng gave a talk on February 24 on the issue of the special economic zones and increasing the number of cities open for foreign trade. Hu Yaobang showed his immediate support and in no time began to prepare for a conference to further research those issues. This time Zhao Ziyang also responded to Deng's call. In March 1984, the Central Secretariat and the State Council held a joint meeting on the issue of opening up fourteen coastal cities, to wit: Dalian, Qinhuang island, Tianjin, Yantai, Qingdao, Lianyungang and Nantong [Jiangsu province], Shanghai, Ningbo, Wenzhou, Fuzhou, Guangzhou [Canton], Zhanjiang [Guangdong province], and Beihai. At the meeting, it was also suggested that the authority to engage in economic relations with foreign nations be expanded to the fourteen coastal port cities. These areas would also develop policies for favorable treatment of foreign personnel and overseas Chinese, as well as fellow countrymen from Hong Kong, Macao, and Taiwan and their companies.[5]

Except for Chen Yun, all the members of the Standing Committee of the Politburo, notably Hu Yaobang, Deng Xiaoping, Zhao Ziyang, and Li Xiannian, participated in the meeting. Chen Yun opted out and vowed that he would never go to the special economic zones, and indeed he is the only high-level central leader who has never visited there. His absence from the meeting was glaring, and Deng Xiaoping made a pointed comment at the time: "Yao Yilin is requested to make a special report to Chen Yun on the decisions of this meeting."

Wang Zhen, who had accompanied Deng on his tour of the special economic zones, was at the top of his form and very happy. He played the role of an active supporter of the reforms. This was interesting, because before he took this trip with Deng, from October to December of 1983, he had never ceased to give speeches everywhere from Beijing to Nanjing against "spiritual pollution." In his speech at the Central Party School, he had singled out my suggestion of turning Xiamen into a free port as one of the crimes that supplied the proof of my "bourgeois liberalism." However, upon returning to Beijing from his little joyride with Deng, he immediately returned to give a speech at the Central Party School in which he said: "Comrade Xiaoping has said that Xiamen must be turned into a free port. I support this with both hands."

Deng Xiaoping made three leaps toward reform, in 1978, 1980, and 1984. After each leap, however, he retreated. Nevertheless, each leap was higher than the previous one. But after 1985 he seemed crippled.

Deng's leap in 1984 was different from his previous leaps in that he completely avoided the key issue of the reform of the political system [*zhengzhi zhidu*]. That's why, although the reform program of Deng Xiaoping reached a high point between February 1984 when he spoke of the opening of coastal cities, and October 1984, when the Third Plenum of the Twelfth Congress approved the "Central Committee Resolution on the Structural Reform of the Economy," the fall was nevertheless unavoidable. Without the protection of political system reform, the leap toward economic reform was bound to falter. When much later, in 1986, Deng once again raised the issue of political reform, the moment of opportunity had passed. The antireform forces had made ample preparation, and Deng could never summon enough enthusiasm for a fourth leap.

Nevertheless, in 1984, Deng's last leap toward economic reform assured him of a reputation both at home and abroad. On October 1, 1984, for the thirty-fifth anniversary celebration of the People's Republic of China, an impressive military review was staged, followed by a mass rally. About half a million military personnel and civilians took part in this demonstration. That day was the pinnacle of Deng's political career. As chairman of the Central Military Commission, he reviewed elements of the three military branches. Leaving Cambodia's Prince Sihanouk standing atop the Gate of Heavenly Peace, he climbed aboard a military jeep and traveled from Tiananmen to Dongdan just east of the square, and then after being applauded by the three military branches, returned to the gate. A military ceremony exuding such power and prestige was unknown of, even for Mao Zedong. When Mao inspected troops, he merely stood in the jeep, passed the troops in review, and returned to the gate to observe their parade.

The mass rallies at this time were also unique. The presence of pennants inscribed with spontaneous slogans such as "Xiaoping, how are you" showed the enthusiasm that united this crowd and the energetic reformer. How popular Deng Xiaoping was at that time! In 1984, his reform gained support from almost everyone in China, a level of support Gorbachev never matched. That's why the failure of reform can't be imputed to any opposition from the people, or from their influence. If Deng had known how to rely on the masses, he certainly would have defeated the opposition with one stroke. Deng's failure is due to him alone. Little by little he turned his back on a people who were truly supportive to move step by step to the other side. In the end, he behaved like Mao Zedong.

Following the National Day celebration, the Third Plenum of the Twelfth Congress on October 20 unanimously approved its resolution on reform of the economic structure.

The major breakthrough in this decision was the proposal for the concept of a "planned commodity economy" [*you jihuade shangpin jingji*], which carried a certain strategic significance. In fact, it provided a theoretical basis for the evolution of the Chinese economy toward a market economy. To ensure the approval of this resolution by the Central Committee, one had to avoid using concepts more precise than the general notions of "market" and "economy."

In 1984, given the favorable situation for reform, the Chen Yun clique could not mount any opposition to this decision. But Chen Yun submitted a written speech to the Central Committee Plenum in which he emphasized that in the process of economic reform there would appear "problems difficult to predict at the moment." In fact, less than a year later, in September 1985, at the National Party Conference Chen Yun once again proposed Stalin's so-called socialist economic laws based on plans and material balances [*bili*] in order to inhibit the Chinese economy from continuing on the road toward a market economy.

Despite the fact that Deng's last leap toward economic reform avoided the key issue of political reform, the economic situation in 1984, from an objective perspective, influenced the development of the political situation. The political campaigns engaged in by Chen Yun over the past three years, such as the "struggle against bourgeois liberalism," "renewing class struggle," and "cleaning up spiritual pollution," lost any support in the eyes of the Chinese people and became the butt of after-dinner jokes. This change in political atmosphere was most obvious at the Fourth Congress of the All-China Writers' Association held in December 1984. Deng Liqun and Hu Qiaomu, who still controlled the Central Propaganda Department (Deng Liqun remained the head), prepared a list of nominees to the association's council, but they met with strong opposition from the delegates. Hu Yaobang, who supported the opinion of the delegates, approved two decisions at a conference of the Central Secretariat: first, an explicit proposal for freedom of literary creativity before the congress of the writers' association. Hu Qili was designated to give a speech on behalf of the Central Committee dealing with the topic of freedom of creativity. Second, the leaders of mass organizations such as the writers' association were not to be determined by the Communist Party. The list of nominees prepared by Deng Liqun and Hu Qiaomu should be negated; the leading committee of the writers' association should be freely elected by the membership.

These two decisions allowed the congress of the writers' association to unfold in a free and democratic—and very lively—atmosphere. The result of the election was that the famous liberal writer Liu Binyan gained the second highest number of votes, just slightly below the old writer Ba Jin. Liu Binyan was also elected vice chairman of the association.

Deng's last leap toward reform had now borne ample fruit. Of the ten years of reform, 1984 was the most brilliant: Industrial and agricultural output (based on 1980 prices) reached over one trillion *yuan*, 14.2 percent higher than the previous year, with agricultural output reaching over 330 billion *yuan*, an increase of 19.5 percent over the previous year.* Grain and cotton output saw a breakthrough, as grain production reached 407 million tons, 19 million tons higher than the previous year. Average grain per capita was now 395 kilograms per year, which for the first time was in line with international standards. Cotton output reached over 6 million tons, an increase of 1.5 million tons in one year with a per capita figure of 5.9 kilograms, also up to international standards. Industrial output reached over 701 billion *yuan*, 14 percent higher than the previous year. Of this, light industrial production was 13.9 percent higher and heavy industry was 14.2 percent higher. Both the urban and rural markets were prospering. The general retail output reached over 300 billion *yuan*, 18.5 percent higher than in the previous year.

The breadth of the economic development in 1984 and the evolution of the political atmosphere proved that the decision to set China on the course of a market economy and on the democratic road was in accord with the popular will of the Chinese people. The market economy and democracy were not at odds with Chinese culture and the national character of the Chinese people. But we would soon discover that there nevertheless was resistance, which didn't come from the people, but from certain corrupt and privileged bureaucrats in the Communist Party, along with a "clique of intellectual elites" [*zhishi jingying jituan*] who were utterly under their influence.

Notes

1. Deng Xiaoping's speech at the Second Plenum (Twelfth Party Congress) "On Spiritual Pollution" was not formally issued until after the fall of Hu Yaobang.

2. This is the talk given by Deng Xiaoping to various central leaders on February 24, 1984, after return to Beijing from his inspection tour of Guangdong and Fujian and other areas. It was reprinted in *Comrade Deng Xiaoping on Reform and the Open Door*

---

*These figures are approximately $147 billion and $42 billion at current exchange rates.

(*Deng Xiaoping tongzhi lun gaige kaifang*) (Beijing: People's Publishing House, August 1989), pp. 75–77. There are some discrepancies in this version. Originally, Deng had said: "Xiamen should become a free port," but this was changed to: "Although we won't refer to the Xiamen zone as a free port, we can certainly implement such policies there."

3. "Memorandum of the Fifty-Second Meeting of the Central Secretariat," September 23–24, 1980.

4. "Memorandum of the Work Conference Convened by the Central Secretariat on the Special Economic Zones," July 5, 1981.

5. The conference proposed the following favorable policies: (1) reduce the limit on utilizing foreign capital in financing construction projects, (2) expand the foreign exchange quota and loans in foreign exchange, (3) actively support the utilization of foreign capital to import advanced technology in order to reform obsolete domestic enterprises, (4) provide favorable treatment to joint ventures, cooperative management enterprises, and enterprises financed exclusively with foreign capital, (5) establish zones of economic and technological development, (6) develop processing work for exports utilizing imported materials, (7) readjust the rules governing the opening up of cities, (8) consolidate capital construction, (9) strengthen guidelines and rules in the plans for utilizing foreign capital, and (10) be the vanguard of reform.

10

Deng Breaks with the Democratic Forces for the Last Time and Hu Yaobang Falls

From January 10 to 15, 1987, at the "Party life meeting" called to criticize Hu Yaobang, Hu Qiaomu and Deng Liqun put on a splendid show. Hu Qiaomu labeled Hu Yaobang's mistake "a typical example of violating the collegial leadership of the Politburo." This was a brand-new accusation personally concocted by Hu Qiaomu.

During the era of the Mao Zedong empire, Lin Biao once proclaimed: "Down with anyone who opposes our great leader Chairman Mao!" That slogan was easier to comprehend, for Mao Zedong was the Party chairman and the highest leader, whose "every line contains the truth—with one line worth ten thousand lines." Thus, it was clear that whoever opposed Chairman Mao "opposes the Party, socialism, and Mao Zedong Thought" and also "opposes Chairman Mao's revolutionary line." Lin Biao accused Liu Shaoqi, who held the second position in the leadership, of opposing Mao, and then Mao placed Lin in the power structure in the Number Two spot. The practice of denouncing Mao's critics for self-advancement was in tune with the logic of a totalitarian empire.

The Deng Xiaoping empire, however, is different from Mao's. Deng has never held the position of Party chairman and has not served as state premier. His highest position was vice chairman of the Party when Hua Guofeng served as chairman, and what's more, Deng's position was no higher than the other vice chairman at the time, Ye Jianying. In June 1981, the Sixth Plenum of the Eleventh Party Congress accepted Hua Guofeng's resignation as Party chairman, elected Hu Yaobang as chairman, Zhao Ziyang and Hua Guofeng as vice chairmen, and retained in their positions of vice chairmen Ye Jianying, Deng Xiaoping, Li Xiannian, and Chen Yun. The subsequent Twelfth Party Congress passed the modified version of the Party constitution proposed by

Hu Qiaomu in which the positions of chairman and vice chairmen were eliminated, thereby leaving in place only the Politburo Standing Committee with six positions filled by the former chairman [Hu Yaobang] and the vice chairmen—Hua Guofeng was kicked out. The line of authority among the six standing committee members was in the following order: Hu Yaobang, Ye Jianying, Deng Xiaoping, Zhao Ziyang, Li Xiannian, and Chen Yun. Hu Yaobang's name came first and Hu also concurrently held the position of the Party's general secretary.

Thus, the person holding the highest position in the empire of Deng Xiaoping lacked any legal standing. In his speech on December 30, 1986, forcing Hu Yaobang's resignation, Deng criticized Hu for failing to obey Deng's orders: "Shanghai's Wang Ruowang," Deng said, "had been acting in a rather reckless way. I ordered him kicked out of the Party a long time ago. How is it that this order hasn't been followed?" Deng also pointed out that lately rumors had been flying all over the place about a protective umbrella in the Central Committee, and that there were two conflicting voices on whether to oppose bourgeois liberalism.[1]

The story has it that in a 1986 article on the issue of "the third echelon" [*disan tidui*], published in the Hong Kong monthly *The Mirror*, Wang Ruowang claimed that this method of appointing the new generation of leaders to the Party and state was a completely inappropriate, feudal practice.* Hu Qiaomu and Deng Liqun showed the article to Deng Xiaoping and made an accusation: "Wang Ruowang opposes you!" Outraged, Deng Xiaoping threatened to boot Wang out of the Party, but Hu Yaobang merely ordered the Shanghai Party Committee to deal with the issue, which it did by delivering a report to Hu pointing out that any rash and oversimplified approach would have a bad impact. And thus the matter of Wang Ruowang's dismissal was postponed. Now it became the fuse that triggered Hu Yaobang's ultimate dismissal. Three days after Deng's speech, on January 2, 1987, Hu Yaobang submitted a letter of resignation, admitting that he had not listened to Deng Xiaoping's words and that "some villainous fellows use me as their protective umbrella."

Hu Yaobang's crime was allegedly that of "violating the collegial leadership of the Politburo." But to accuse Hu Yaobang of this was in itself absurd, because Deng Xiaoping had decided to kick Wang Ruowang out of the Party without ever consulting the Politburo. And it was simply illogical to say that Hu Yaobang had committed certain heinous crimes for violating Deng's

---

*For Wang Ruowang's account of his turbulent life in China under both the Nationalist and communist regimes see Wang Ruowang, *Hunger Trilogy*, trans. by Kyna Rubin (Armonk, N.Y.: M. E. Sharpe, 1991).

words. And how is it that Hu Yaobang, the highest ranking member of the Politburo Standing Committee and the general secretary of the Party, had to follow orders from Deng Xiaoping, who was officially ranked third in the Standing Committee? (After Ye Jianying resigned all his positions in the Party on September 16, 1986, Deng placed second).

Thus, Hu Qiaomu had to invent a new crown for Deng Xiaoping. It was none other than Hu Qiaomu who created this new title, "representative of the collegial leadership of the Politburo." Once that neat piece of sorcery was accomplished, Hu Yaobang's crime was clear to see. He had violated the orders of the "representative of the collegial leadership of the Party."

After Hu Qiaomu laid out the nature of Hu Yaobang's mistakes at the "Party life meeting," Deng Liqun gave a five-hour speech exposing Hu Yaobang. This long-winded tale described how Deng Liqun had himself always willingly followed instructions from "the representative of the collegial leadership of the Politburo" ever since 1978 and how he had struggled against Hu Yaobang's promotion of bourgeois liberalism. Deng Liqun craftily summarized the past ten years as a titanic struggle between the forces of bourgeois liberalism and anti–bourgeois liberalism and described how it had almost come to a nearly final conclusion with the spread of liberalism in even-numbered years countered by an anti–bourgeois liberalism counterattack in odd-numbered years. In accord with this conclusion, Deng Liqun described his so-called theory of five rounds of struggles in the preceding ten years.

Round One: 1978–1979

The year 1978 was an even-numbered year. In 1978, Hu Yaobang launched the debate over the criterion of truth and criticized the "two whatevers." The social democratic movement, represented by the Beijing Xidan Democracy Wall, spread throughout the entire nation. The CCP held a Central Work Conference and the Third Plenum at which the reform forces within the Party, supported by the social democratic movement in Beijing, took the lead and rectified Hua Guofeng's "two whatevers" and rehabilitated the many victims of phony verdicts reached by Mao Zedong during the Cultural Revolution. In addition, the policy of implementing reform and the open door were also inaugurated. This was, indeed, an important historical turning point for China to march forward toward liberation.

The year 1979 was an odd-numbered year. That year, Deng Xiaoping betrayed his alliance with the social democratic forces. With his speech "Uphold the Four Cardinal Principles" on March 30, 1979, he retreated from his proreform position and put obstacles in the way of the achievements already accomplished by reform in China.

Round Two: 1980–1981

The year 1980 was an even-numbered year, and reform in China was renewed as Hu Yaobang was elected Party general secretary and a member of the Politburo Standing Committee at the February 1980 Fifth Plenum. The same meeting also approved the document "Guiding Principles for Political Life in the Party," which effectively set the stage for the Party to progress in a democratic direction.* In May 1980, Deng Xiaoping accepted Li Weihan's suggestion and discarded the slogan to "promote proletarian ideology and eliminate bourgeois ideas." Deng Xiaoping also proposed sweeping away the feudal remnants in the Party and state and in society. In August 1980, an enlarged Politburo meeting decided to carry out institutional reforms in the Party and state, by all means an important decision in synchronizing political and economic reforms.

The odd-numbered year 1981 actually began with the Central Work Conference held in December 1980, when the Chen Yun clique launched an all-out attack on both the economic and political fronts against the policies of reform and the open door. The Chen Yun clique also proposed the policy to oppose bourgeois liberalism in politics and "curb demand, curtail development, and suspend reform" in the economic realm. Deng Xiaoping caved in and accepted Chen Yun's proposal, which effectively brought a halt to economic reform and progress toward democracy in the Party. The first wave of anti–bourgeois liberalism rose in 1981.

Round Three: 1982–1983

The year 1982 was an even-numbered year, but one that did not exactly favor reform. Although the anti–bourgeois liberalism campaign launched by Chen Yun and his clique in 1981 did not have much effect until the first half of 1982, they were still in an attack mode. Deng Liqun and Wang Zhen gained power over the theory realm in the Central Propaganda Department and the Central Party School, respectively. However, prior to the Twelfth Party Congress held in September 1982, when the Chen Yun clique launched its attacks against Hu Yaobang, Deng Xiaoping came to Hu's rescue. Hu Yaobang's goal of "building our country into a highly civilized and highly democratic social-

---

*This meeting also rehabilitated Liu Shaoqi; removed Wang Dongxing, Ji Dengkui, Wu De, and Chen Xilian from all Party posts; and discussed the proposal to eliminate lifelong tenure for Party leaders. It also eliminated the right to "speak out freely, air views fully, hold great debates, and write big-character posters," ostensibly as principles held over from the Cultural Revolution.

ist country" was enunciated in the course of a speech in which he ensured the continuation of reform and the open door.

The year 1983 was an odd-numbered year. The Chen Yun clique launched its criticism of Zhou Yang and Wang Ruoshui's theories of humanism and alienation at a meeting celebrating the one-hundredth anniversary of Marx's death. Next, the Chen Yun clique launched its campaign to "clean up spiritual pollution" at the Second Plenum in October of the same year. Deng Xiaoping initially supported Chen Yun's criticism of Zhou Yang and Wang Ruoshui and the "cleaning up spiritual pollution campaign." But he changed his mind after noting that people at home and abroad were losing confidence in China's commitment to reform. Thus he turned 180 degrees and supported Hu Yaobang, Zhao Ziyang, Wan Li, and Fang Yi's suggestion to halt the campaign.

Round Four: 1984–1985

The year 1984 was an even-numbred year. Deng Xiaoping counterattacked on the economic front. He decided on his guiding principle of further opening instead of retreat after touring the special economic zones in Shenzhen, Zhuhai, and Xiamen. In March 1984, the CCP and the State Council jointly held a forum on the issue of the further opening up of fourteen coastal cities. In October of the same year, at the Third Plenum of the Twelfth Party Congress, the "Resolution on the Structural Reform of the Economy" was approved and the concept of a "planned commodity economy" was proposed, thereby providing the theoretical basis for China to march forward toward commercialization and a market economy.

But in the odd-numbered year of 1985, the Chen Yun clique zeroed in on some of the specific problems that had popped up in the economies of Fujian and Guangdong—the two provinces at the forefront of reform. One was "the case of the bogus medicine" in Jinjiang, Fujian, and the other the "automobile smuggling case" on Hainan Island. As a result of the great efforts by Chen Yun and his clique to exaggerate the two cases, they eventually succeeded in removing to other positions Xiang Nan and Ren Zhongyi, the first Party secretaries of these provinces, who were two of the most committed reformers in China. Thus, the Chen Yun clique achieved its purpose of reversing the trend toward nationwide reform instituted at the 1978 Third Plenum.

Round Five: 1986–1987

The year 1986 was an even-numbered year in which Deng Xiaoping evidently realized that the economic reform that he had designed could no longer move forward as long as two organizations—the State Planning Commission and the Central Discipline Inspection Commission [both controlled by Chen

Yun]—not only were able to exploit their privileged positions of power to interfere in just about any economic activity, including the special economic zones, but also were able to subject cadres at all levels to arbitrary treatment. The Central Discipline Inspection Commission not only had the power to punish party members in various ways, it could also issue orders to arrest and even execute non–Party members. The abuse of power by these two organs reached its peak in 1985 when the State Planning Commission and the Inspection Commission not only prevented the reform from moving forward by removing reformers from power, but also had a great many persons arrested and incarcerated. All this provoked Deng Xiaoping to once again put political reform back on the agenda in 1986—but for the last time.

Yet in the odd-numbered year 1987, the Chen Yun clique forced Deng Xiaoping into another struggle campaign against bourgeois liberalism and forced Hu Yaobang's resignation by using the student democratic movement at the end of 1986 for its own purposes.

Deng Liqun's conclusion that over the previous ten years even-numbered years were adverse and odd-numbered years were advantageous was simply a ploy to prove that he had always held the correct standpoint. That is to say that in the five rounds Hu Yaobang promoted bourgeois liberalism in even-numbered years while Deng Xiaoping launched anti–bourgeois liberalism in odd-numbered years. As for Deng Liqun himself, he had always stood with Deng Xiaoping, and thus the rationale was that Deng Liqun should be appointed to replace Hu Yaobang as the general secretary. Deng Liqun even asked Wang Zhen to ask Deng Xiaoping to appoint him, but Deng Xiaoping turned him down.

Although Deng Liqun's generalization about the ten years to some extent accurately depicted the ups and downs of reform in China, it is basically inaccurate, for the history of those ten years was a conflict within Deng Xiaoping himself over liberalism versus antiliberalism, rather than a conflict between Hu Yaobang's proliberalism and Deng's antiliberalism. It was Deng Xiaoping who separated himself from the democratic forces both within and outside the Party. That's what brought an end to his enterprise of reform for China. To borrow Deng Liqun's concept, Deng Xiaoping favored the reform forces and pushed them forward in the even-numbered years, but in the odd-numbered years, Deng turned around and supported the antireform forces, time and again launching antiliberalism campaigns that greatly frustrated the reform enterprise. Or perhaps we can put it this way: Deng held two cats with different colors, releasing the yellow cat in even-numbered years to catch mice who obstructed reform, and releasing the black cat in odd-numbered years to chase the "liberal" mice who were pushing forward the political reform, thereby enabling mice hindering the reform to carry out their blatant acts. Such an inner conflict in Deng Xiaoping's mind made him incapable of carrying out thoroughgoing reform.

As for Hu Yaobang, in his personal political views, he was indeed a more thorough reformer and democrat. However, the support Hu gained and his influence both domestically and internationally were far weaker than Deng's. Even though Hu was Party chairman for a short while and general secretary for an extended period, and both functions granted him a high legal status, Hu never placed himself above the Party and state, as did Mao Zedong and Deng Xiaoping. In China's reform process, Hu usually appeared as a follower of the Deng Xiaoping line. However, despite Hu's effort to follow Deng, he was still accused of violating Deng's orders, for instead of following Deng blindly, Hu discarded those orders that were adverse to implementing reform in China.

I would like to provide a slightly different version of those ten years in China than Deng Liqun's. My version will provide the basic contours of the formation and development of the Deng Xiaoping empire.

In Deng's political ideology development, he did not consistently polarize political and economic reform, nor did he advocate a coexistence between economic freedom and political dictatorship. Twice—at the 1978 Third Plenum and the August 1980 enlarged Central Politburo meeting—he made proposals for democratizing China and political system [*zhidu*] reform. However, right after each proposal, Deng reversed his position.

How can we explain Deng's ups and downs?

First, his proposals for carrying out political reform at the aforementioned two meetings were not hypocritical; they were, instead, genuine political proposals at the time. These proposals were not simply off the cuff. They were the product of serious meditation, in the course of which Deng came up with a rather earnest consideration of the origins and historical lessons of the structural errors committed by Stalin and Mao. Only after serious consideration did Deng come up with his own design for democracy and political system reform. In the two years from the end of 1978 to the end of 1980, Hua Guofeng still held supreme power over the Party, the government, and the military, a concentration of power that was a legacy of the Mao Zedong empire. Hua failed to make good use of those powers. Deng Xiaoping attempted to change that situation. At that time, there were indeed some people who believed that if Deng replaced Hua Guofeng everything would be okay. But Deng didn't approach the question from that perspective. Even though he could have done so, at the time, Deng did not want to replace Hua and establish a Deng Xiaoping empire to replace the Mao Zedong empire. The reason is that Deng had once planned to terminate the totalitarian system of the Mao Zedong empire and turn China into a democratic republic [*minzhu gonghe-guo*]. What Deng was contemplating was a fundamental institutional reform of that empire, not just in the economy but also in the political system.

Second, Deng gave primary emphasis to political system reform. This was the real situation.

Third, Deng's proposals were not isolated and impractical utopian ideals. At that time, the democratic reform forces in the Party represented by Hu Yaobang firmly supported Deng's proposals for democracy and political reform. Also the veteran leader of the Party and army, Ye Jianying, supported Deng, along with other democratic reform forces in the Party. With the wave of reform in the rural areas washing over into the cities, Deng's political reform proposal could gain the most extensive support from intellectuals, students, and democratic parties as well as farmers and workers. If Deng Xiaoping had relied on the democratic reform forces in both the Party and society, his political reform proposals could have been gradually implemented.

Fourth, Deng's political system reform proposals indeed met with great resistance in the Party, especially from Chen Yun and his clique, who were pretty good at exploiting the international environment and the problems and difficulties in the domestic situation to resist and halt the reform, along with crimes such as "violating the Four Cardinal Principles" and "bourgeois liberal tendencies" that Deng himself would use in his attacks on the democratic reform forces. In addition, there was another school of thought both within the Party and outside, represented by Zhao Ziyang and his "power elite" [*quanli jingying jituan*] who on the point of opposing democratic forces both in and outside the Party effectively allied with Chen Yun's conservative clique.

Fifth, throughout the entire process of reform, Deng Xiaoping was confronted with two choices. The first was to rely on democratic forces in and outside the Party, along with support from the masses, to overcome the privileged class within the Party and to promote overall reform in the realms of politics, economics, and culture. The second choice was to make a concession to the privileged class in the Party and its beneficiaries and betray the democratic forces by reducing the target of reform solely to the economic realm. Deng's capricious acts resulted from his switching back and forth between those two choices. But his political vision increasingly narrowed as he was overcome by concern that growing democratic forces in and outside the Party would threaten the CCP and his own monopoly of power. That's why he gradually separated himself from the democratic forces, until ultimately he had no choice but to seek an alliance with the conservative forces.

Deng's retaliation on the economic front in 1984 was more or less maintained until the first half of 1985:

On January 1, 1985, the CCP and the State Council jointly issued "Ten Policies on Further Enlivening the Rural Economy" [*Guanyu jinyibu huoyue nongcun jingjide shixiangzhengce*] based on the decision to reform the economic structure adopted by the Third Plenum of the Twelfth Party Congress, which called for expanding the freedom of the rural economy. It stipulated among other things that starting from 1985, the state would no longer impose quotas on farmers for the delivery of agricultural products. The state monopoly on the sale of grain and cotton would be replaced by contractual purchase. That decision put an end to the system of state monopoly that had ruled the Chinese farmers for over thirty years. Dismantling the People's Communes, it finished off the system of state slavery in the Chinese country-side and proclaimed freedom.

Meeting January 25–31, 1985, the State Council held a forum on the issue of developing the Yangtze River and Pearl River deltas and the three-corner area in southern Fujian composed of Xiamen, Zhangzhou, and Quanzhou. A suggestion was made that the three-corner area be developed into the first free, open, and modern economic zone along the coast, where there would be interchange between the domestic and international economies and an inter-face between the rural and urban economies.

Then, on March 2–7, 1985, the State Council held an open national forum on science and technology in Beijing at which the issue of reform in science and technology was discussed. On March 13, the CCP issued its "Decision on Reform of the Science and Technology System," in which it was decided to open up a nationwide market for technology to enable science and technol-ogy to meet the needs of a free market economy.

Meeting March 27–April 10 of the same year, the Third Session of the Sixth National People's Congress affirmed that it was essential to take the first im-portant step toward price reform.

May 23–June 6, 1985, the Central Military Commission held an enlarged session at which Deng Xiaoping announced that the Chinese government had decided to demobilize one million PLA soldiers.

On June 29, 1985, the State Council officially approved Fujian province's "Report on the Proposal on the Xiamen Special Economic Zone" and for-mally gave its approval to the proposal to enlarge the Xiamen Special Eco-nomic Zone to the entire Xiamen Island and the entire Gulangyu Island. And in that zone the policy for a free port would be gradually implemented.

Thus, from 1984 to the first half of 1985, dazzling victories had been won on the economic reform front, but not being accompanied by political re-forms, they were soon destroyed by the corrupt bureaucrats within the CCP and the "power elite" group. From the second half of 1985 the situation be-gan to deteriorate. The operations of sabotage were of two kinds. First came direct attacks on reform and reformers, in which the State Planning Commis-sion and the Central Discipline Inspection Commission, both controlled by the Chen Yun clique, played an important role. At every level the State Plan-ning Commission resisted resolutions of the Third Plenum of the Twelfth Party Congress on reform of the economic structure—decisions to streamline government organizations, loosen up power, and reduce administrative inter-ference in the economic activities of enterprises and on policies such as em-ploying economic means to carry out macroeconomic management. Refusing to accept a reduction in their power, the planning commission also continued to interfere in the implementation of the resolution in order to prevent decisions of the Central Committee from being acted on. As for the Central Discipline Inspection Commission, at all levels its members used the alibi of attacking economic crimes to launch accusations—in disregard of all legal procedures about "evidence of criminal acts." These "affairs," which formed a basis for attacking liberal reformers, occurred all over the country. In July 1985, the Central Discipline Inspection Commission advanced "the case of the bogus medicine" in Fujian, as well as the "automobile smuggling case" of Hainan Island (Guangdong province), to launch an assault on these two provinces that were at the forefront of reform. The whole thing was planned by Chen Yun himself, who was bound and determined to remove Xiang Nan and Ren Zhongyi from their positions in Fujian and Guangdong provinces. He also insisted on giving Xiang Nan an "inner-Party administrative warning" [*dangnei jinggao chufen*].

Further, the opponents of reform used their bureaucratic privileges to gain, in the name of reform and the open door, personal benefits. In that respect, the fishy bureaucrats who opposed reform and some of the "power elite" clique who draped themselves in reform were actually quite similar. Family members of those high-level officials competed in setting up their own "companies," and thanks to their family connections, obtained capital, raw materials, foreign exchange reserves, and licenses for import and export, including the export of weaponry. And by taking advantage of the dual price system and double foreign exchange system, they engaged in speculation on a grand scale both at home and abroad and made astronomical profits; thus they realized their stated goal of letting "some people get rich ahead of others." Hu Yaobang, prior to his resignation as general secretary, attempted to put a halt to such bureaucratic corruption, but ran into concerted resistance from the bureaucrats and the "power elite." Zhao Ziyang flowed along with the corrupt trend. In a document that he distributed in 1987 after Hu Yaobang's downfall, Zhao spoke of official speculation by functionaries as a remedy utilized by the Central Committee to "accelerate" the development of the market economy. This document also proposed that those children of high-level cadres who were engaged in official profiteering [*guandao*] should not be "discriminated against"*; and their enrichment should not arouse "jealousy." This document gave bureaucrats the green light to expand the monstrous corruption and aroused public wrath.

At the Party Conference held in September 1985, at which the seventh Five-Year Plan was discussed, Chen Yun formally challenged the resolution on

---

*Zhao Ziyang's and Wang Zhen's sons were included in this group of offspring of high-level cadres who used their parents' official position to reap enormous rewards.

economic structure reform approved by the Third Plenum of the Twelfth Party Congress. In his speech, he also emphasized "socialist economic laws based on plans and material balances"; in reality he was in effect requesting a return to the Stalinist system.

All this took the economic reform to a new impasse in 1986. At that time, except for those who started to turn toward "new authoritarianism" and a "power elite," the majority of intellectuals realized that to push the economic reform further, political reform must be carried out. This issue was raised on the occasion of the Thirtieth Anniversary of the 1957 "Hundred Flowers Campaign." Calls for democratization were not only immediately supported by some of the leaders of the Central Committee like Hu Yaobang and Wan Li, but they even stimulated Deng Xiaoping to recall his idea of reforming the leadership system of the Party and state, a project that he had proposed six years earlier and subsequently discarded. Between the beginning of June and mid-September 1986, Deng Xiaoping gave four consecutive speeches on the issue of political reform. On June 10, 1986, he said upon hearing a report of economic conditions:

> Now it seems that without engaging in political structure [*tizhi*] reform we cannot deal with the present situation. Reform should include political structure reform. In addition, political structure reform should be taken as a mark of the overall reform. We must have better troops and simpler administration* and truly release power in order to enlarge socialist democracy and mobilize incentives among the masses and local organizations. However, the situation now is that far from diminishing, the number of state bureaucracies has actually grown. You liberate power on the one side and on the other side they take it right back. Also, many companies have been established that in reality are official organizations. With the proliferation of organizations and so many people, they have to look for things to do and hold fast to power. As a result, the work on local levels has not been enlivened. The proposal for political structure reform was first made in 1980, but it has not been elaborated in detail. Now it's time to put this on the agenda.[2]

On June 28, 1986, Deng Xiaoping gave a speech at the meeting of the Politburo Standing Committee, "Reform the Political Structure, Strengthen Legal Consciousness," in which he criticized the Central Discipline Inspection Commission and the State Planning Commission. He said:

> Some comrades have raised the issue of distinguishing between squaring the Party's style of work and rectifying incorrect trends. In reality, it is not a matter of

---

*A phrase from the Yan'an era that called for avoiding excessive bureaucracy and personnel in the wartime CCP, but hardly suggestive of true democratic reform.

distinguishing between the two, but an issue involving the relationship between the Party and the state. It is inappropriate for the Party to involve itself in legal matters and affairs. Too much interference from the Party hinders the establishment of legal concepts among the population. The Party should be in charge of issues involving Party discipline whereas issues involving law and legality should be managed by the state. This issue of the relationship between Party and state involves the issue of the structure of the political system.[3]

In the following paragraph, Deng criticized the interference by the Discipline Inspection Commission of the Party in legal affairs:

The success of our overall reform rests on the issue of political structure reform. This is because things must be conducted by people, but what's to be done when "you" advocate liberating power but "he over there" calls for limiting power to a few hands. There are other issues involving other aspects. Political and economic reform should be interdependent and mutually supportive. If we only engage in economic reform without political reform, we won't be able to carry out the economic reform. Every aspect of reform relates to many people and things. It is so profound that it touches many people's interests and it will meet with many obstacles.[4]

The next part of the speech criticized the State Planning Commission. When it was published, however, there was no explicit reference to either the Central Discipline Inspection Commission or the State Planning Commission.

On September 3, 1986, Deng said when meeting with the president of the Komeito Party from Japan:

Although some opposition exists within the Party and the state to reform, it's not great. The important issue is that the political structure cannot meet the demands of reform in the economy. Thus, without engaging in reform of the political structure, we can neither guarantee results for economic reform nor enable the economic reform to continue.

The reform we propose includes reform in the political structure. At present, after each step that the economic structure reform goes forward we feel the necessity to carry out a reform of the political structure, without which the development of productivity and the success of the four modernizations will be hindered. As for the content of political structure reform, it is still being discussed because this issue is too complex. Each aspect of reform involves many people and things. It is profound and touches the interests of many people and therefore it will meet with many obstacles. That's why great caution and prudence should be shown. We must first of all specify the scope of political structure reform and make clear where it should begin. It is best to focus on just one or two things to begin with, instead of trying to take on too much, which will inevitably bring about chaos. Since this issue is so difficult and complex, we haven't made up our minds yet where to begin.[5]

We can envision the evolution in political ideology of this historical figure by comparing Deng's thoughts on political reform in 1986 with those he advanced in 1980.

When Deng Xiaoping first proposed reform of the leadership system [*zhidu*] of the Party and state in 1980, he viewed political system reform as an important target of reform in China. At that time he set himself three objectives: to catch up economically with developed capitalist countries, to create an even more democratic and realistic democracy than already existed in capitalist countries, and to train more outstanding personnel than existed in those capitalist countries. He dared to assault dictatorship of the Stalinist or Maoist kind. He launched a powerful attack against bureaucracy, overconcentration of power, the patriarchal system, and the lifelong tenure of leaders, along with various kinds of special privileges. Deng also emphasized that the system must guarantee three democratizations: democratization of the political life of the Party and state, of economic management, and of overall social life. He also advocated a "profound and serious study," which is to say, a "comparative study of different experiences of many countries that would call on the widest possible thinking in order to come up with practical plans and measures."[6]

But when in 1986, Deng proposed political reform for the last time he had already lost the spirit of a reformer that he had possessed in 1980. This time around he avoided using the term "system" [*zhidu*] and instead referred only to "structure" [*tizhi*]. Moreover, he only talked about political structural reform as a means of protecting economic reform. It seemed that now he was more acutely aware of the resistance to political reform than he was six years before. "Each aspect of reform involves many people and things. It is profound and touches the interests of many people and therefore it will meet with many obstacles." And he appeared this time to be indecisive when confronting any resistance.

An even greater difference was that Deng no longer emphasized democracy—the fundamental target of political reform—but instead he subordinated reform of the political structure to solving concrete issues involving the relationship of the Party and state and emphasized that "the Party's leadership is unshakable."[7] He no longer dared to alter the Stalinist–Mao Zedong style of autocracy and instead was fearful of shaking his own autocratic, totalitarian system. This attitude condemned to failure the political reform proposed by Deng in 1986, and much later would lead to the paradoxical development of strengthening his own autocratic, totalitarian system.

It was on September 13, 1986, when listening to reports from the Central Financial and Economic Leading Group [*Zhongyang Caijing Lingdao Xiaozu*], that Deng came up with his basic conception of political reform. He said:

> As for the substance of reform of the political structure, what can it be? We have to talk about this. As far as I'm concerned, the purpose of reform of the political

structure is to mobilize incentives for the masses, increase efficiency, and overcome bureaucracy.

The substance of reform is first, separation of the Party and state and solving the problem of how the Party should lead and be good at leadership. That's the key. Second, it is to liberate power to solve the relationship between the central and local governments; at the same time the various leaders at the local level also must face the issue of how to liberate power. A third essential thing is to simplify organizations, and this is also related to liberating power. Additionally, there is the need to increase efficiency. Just what should be included in political structure reform needs to be worked out by someone. There's a time limit for the reform in that it cannot be delayed too long. There should be a blueprint presented at next year's Party Congress. As far as I am concerned, the issue of separating the Party and the state must be put in first place, and in our reform we should not blindly follow the West, and we should not engage in liberalism. Our leadership system in the past had some advantages, namely, decisions could be made rapidly. To insist too much on a system of mutual control can cause other problems.[8]

Deng Xiaoping's train of thought is clearly expressed in this passage. His blueprint for reform of the political structure was designed to not bring into question the basis of his empire. He also reaffirmed the Stalinist–Mao Zedong structure of concentrating authority in the hands of an individual that he himself had opposed in 1980. And he praised a totalitarian and dictatorial system that enables decisions to be made "rapidly." He said not a word about democracy, and he no longer spoke of the need to study the political systems of other countries. Indeed, he rejected the Western system of checks and balances, viewing it as a "return to bourgeois liberalism."

The interesting thing here was that Deng Xiaoping proposed to find someone to work out the reform of the political structure. And who did he find? Zhao Ziyang.

In the division of labor within the Politburo Standing Committee, Zhao Ziyang was in charge of the government and the economy. As general secretary, Hu Yaobang, in addition to being in charge of the overall work of the Standing Committee, was also in charge of the Party, politics, theory, and ideology sectors. Hu Yaobang had organized the leadership reform of the Party and state in 1980. This had been halted by the Central Work Conference that had launched the campaign against liberalism in December 1980. The designation by Deng Xiaoping of Zhao Ziyang, and not Hu Yaobang, clearly reflected the difference in nature between the reform of the political structure proposed in 1986 and the reform of the political system proposed in 1980. By renouncing democracy, Deng Xiaoping parted company with Hu Yaobang. Zhao Ziyang, who was opposed to democratization, was closer to the new political line of Deng Xiaoping.

Zhao Ziyang accepted the mission with pleasure and established an "Office of Political Reform" [*Zhenggaiban*] and began to carry out political reform in accordance with Deng's blueprint. "The new authoritarianism" in China was a child of the joint political needs of Deng Xiaoping and Zhao Ziyang. This issue will be discussed in greater detail in Part III of this book.

What was Hu Yaobang doing during this period? He was in charge of drafting the "Resolution on the Guiding Principles for Construction of Socialist Spiritual Civilization" that would soon be discussed at the September 1986 Sixth Plenum of the Twelfth Party Congress. This was the last thing Hu Yaobang did in his political career. He attempted to pour all the enthusiasm of his idealism, and the experiences and lessons he had accumulated in practice, into this last document. Little did he know that the debate provoked by this document would terminate his political career and bring new disasters to China.

The draft of the document was completed by summer 1986 and was prepared for discussions and modifications at the enlarged Politburo meeting at Beidaihe before final approval by the Sixth Plenum. Under the historical conditions of the time, this project by Hu Yaobang, who had consecrated all his skill to drafting it, was more than honorable.

First, the document discarded any mention of the despicable phrases "Uphold the Four Cardinal Principles" and the "struggle against bourgeois liberalism" in the section outlining general objectives. He substituted "one axis and three resolute actions": "Taking the structure of the economy as an axis, we carry out reform of the economic structure, reform of political structure, and the development of the new culture."[9]

Second, the document emphasized the necessarily open character of the process of the whole development of a new culture, stating that "it's impossible for any nation or race to develop and make progress without accepting advanced foreign science and culture. A closed-door policy can only bring about stagnation and backwardness." The document also stated:

> We must be determined to energetically learn about advanced science and technology and applicable experiences of economic and administrative management, and to learn about other cultures—from all the countries in the world, including capitalist countries—all that could be used to our own profit. At the same time we have to put these techniques and experiences to the test of practice and develop them. If we don't, we will remain ignorant and we won't be able to realize our modernization. The policy of opening up to the outside world must be considered fundamental and unbreakable, as a policy that is applicable not only to the building of a material civilization but also to the development of a new culture.[10]

That wording in effect negated the campaign against spiritual pollution.

Third, the document gave some emphasis to the idea of moving toward political democracy. In it Hu Yaobang declared that "to achieve a high degree of democracy is one of the great objectives of socialism; democracy is an important demonstration of socialist spiritual civilization in the life of both the state and society." The document affirmed that "in human history, the appearance in the course of the struggle of the newly emergent bourgeois class and working people against the feudal totalitarian system of the concepts of democracy, freedom, equality, and benevolence were a great spiritual emancipation for humankind." The document also struck the following balance: "The history of socialism in China shows that first of all, there has been a lack of concentration of forces for developing the economy, and that second, there is a lack of serious construction of democratic politics."

The document also affirmed the idea emphasized since the 1978 Third Plenum that "without democracy, there is no modernization ... , democracy must be institutionalized and legalized ... , the Party must carry out its work within the scope of the constitution and law ... , and effectively promote the democratization of the political life of the Party and state, democratization of economic management, and democratization of all aspects of social life." The document also established that it was "necessary to begin to teach respect for laws and democracy starting in elementary school and to popularize knowledge about the law and strengthen the legal conscience of the citizens." The document further stated, "All persons are equal before the law; it is thus forbidden for particular individuals to put themselves above the law or regulations. This must become a firm principle as much in the political life as in the Chinese social life."[11]

Fourth, the document also stated the importance of popularizing and increasing the level of education, science, and culture. The document also pointed out that

> in the present world science has become more and more the revolutionary force of initiating historical progress and it has become an important standard of a nation's proficiency. To proceed with our construction of modernization, we must rely more on science; advocate the spirit of respecting science and pursuit of knowledge; and try our best to popularize and increase the level of education, science, and culture of our entire nation.

The document also placed emphasis on the importance of dealing with academic and artistic issues and stated, "we must abide by the principle of our constitution in carrying out freedom in academics, artistic creativity, debate, criticism, and countercriticism."[12]

Prior to the enlarged Politburo meeting at Beidaihe, this document had been sent to the members of the Politburo Standing Committee and the Secretariat. The first to criticize it were Deng Liqun and Hu Qiaomu. They worked out their own modified version, which they sent to Deng Xiaoping and Chen Yun. The modified version completely negated the draft by Hu Yaobang and replayed the old tunes of cleaning up spiritual pollution and struggling against bourgeois liberalism. Chen Yun approved the modified version; in revenge, Deng Xiaoping supported Hu Yaobang's version and rejected that of Deng Liqun and Hu Qiaomu. This was the first round. Hu Yaobang took a temporary lead.

The battlefield quickly shifted to Beidaihe. The antidemocrats Wang Zhen, Peng Zhen, Bo Yibo, Hu Qiaomu, and Deng Liqun and all the antidemocracy forces teamed up against the draft of the resolution proposed by Hu Yaobang, and they insisted on adding a paragraph on the struggle against liberalism. The debate raged. Hu Yaobang then made a concession by adding the following paragraph to the fifth section of the draft: "Bourgeois liberalism negates the socialist system and advocates the capitalist system, it fundamentally violates the people's interest and the historical trend, and therefore it is firmly opposed by the common people."[13]

That paragraph, however, met with fierce opposition from Lu Dingyi, who made three speeches at the Beidaihe conference in which he demanded deletion of this paragraph from the final draft. He showed how, in historical hindsight, this kind of talk against liberalism seemed dangerous and absurd. He pointed out that the notion of antiliberalism had been used, in 1956, by the Soviet dogmatists hostile to the Chinese policy of the "Hundred Flowers." Later, during the Cultural Revolution, Lin Biao and the "Gang of Four" both returned to the same concept in criticizing Lu Dingyi, Zhou Yang, and Deng Xiaoping. Therefore, even a vague reference to a struggle against bourgeois liberalism showed not only a violation in principle of the basic rights of freedom of the people, namely freedom of speech and academic and artistic creativity protected by the state constitution, but it would also have grave historical consequences. It was harmful to the blossoming of the sciences and culture and detrimental to the democratization of political life.

In the end, the debate at Beidaihe did not yield any real results. Hu Yaobang wanted to reach a compromise, but Lu Dingyi refused. The battle continued in Beijing.

In September 1986, in the small group discussion at the Sixth Plenum of the Twelfth Congress, Lu Dingyi reiterated his proposal to delete the paragraph on anti–bourgeois liberalism. His view was not adopted. At the closing session of the meeting on September 28, just prior to the vote, Lu Dingyi stood up to restate, with the same fierceness, his position. Wan Li spoke in support of Lu Dingyi, and Peng Zhen, Bo Yibo, and Wang Zhen spoke in opposition. In his desire for conciliation, Hu Yaobang tried to mediate the conflict by taking a middle position that accepted the paragraph on anti–bourgeois liberalism. Deng Xiaoping made a very stern speech:

> I'm the one who has spoken out most about anti–bourgeois liberalism and who has been most persistent. Why? First, because among the masses, especially the young people, there is a trend in favor of liberalism. Second, there are also those who stand on the sidelines beating the drums of support—the speechifiers of Taiwan and Hong Kong who are all opposed to our fundamental principles. They

want us to adopt capitalism whole hog, as if it were the only way to realize our Four Modernizations.

What is this liberalism? It actually aims at directing our present policies onto the capitalist road, and the representatives of this ideological trend are pushing us onto the capitalist road.

Liberalism is in itself bourgeois and there is no such thing as proletarian or socialist liberalism. Liberalism itself is antagonistic to our present system and policies. Call it opposition or revisionism. The fact of the matter is that engaging in liberalism would direct us to the road of capitalism, and that's why we adopted the expression "struggle against bourgeois liberalism." Little does it matter where or how it was used. For the present political situation requires that we incorporate it into the resolution and I myself agree with this.

It seems that antiliberalism must be emphasized at the present and for the next ten or twenty years. If we don't fight against this ideological trend and oppose all the messy stuff that is entering the nation as a result of our open-door policy, these two things could destroy our socialist Four Modernizations, and that's something we shouldn't underestimate. You pay attention to some of the statements in Hong Kong and some of the foreign bourgeois scholars: The majority want us to practice bourgeois liberalism and accuse us of violating human rights.[14]

The meeting ended with great tension.

When Hu Yaobang organized the distribution of the contents of the meeting to the entire Party, he suggested transmitting only the resolution adopted by the meeting without the discussions that had preceded it, which would avoid divulging the disagreements awakened by Lu Dingyi's position. His purpose was to avoid the differences expressed at the plenum from expanding and deepening, so that all discussion would remain focused on the resolution itself.

Naturally, Wang Zhen, Peng Zhen, Bo Yibo, Deng Liqun, and Hu Qiaomu didn't want to leave it at that. They saw a golden opportunity to stimulate Deng Xiaoping's anger toward Hu Yaobang. They selected Wang Zhen to lead the way. At the Central Party School, Wang Zhen had Deng Xiaoping's speech at the plenum reprinted with copies provided to each person. Then he himself gave a speech to the entire school:

The anti–bourgeois liberalism spirit at the Sixth Plenum was embodied in Comrade Deng Xiaoping's speech. Someone tried to cover up this speech and prevent its distribution throughout the Party. Comrades Liqun and Qiaomu reported this to Comrade Xiaoping, who then noted that "my proposal for anti–bourgeois liberalism at the Sixth Plenum called for opposing liberalism for the next twenty years. So someone didn't like it? Okay, let's add on fifty years or more, seventy years altogether, so that now we'll oppose liberalism until the middle of the next century."

In this way Deng Xiaoping firmly stood on the side of antiliberalism and discarded his earlier proposals for political reform. The incessant capriciousness of Deng Xiaoping on political matters aroused considerable discontent among students. Student democratic movements began to spread all over the country. But by this time, the various forces arrayed against Hu Yaobang in the Party had already forged their alliance. The internal struggles within the Party and the social democratic movement in civil society combined to create an unstable political situation, which aroused unrest in all of China in winter 1986.

The debate over the issue of antiliberalism at the Sixth Plenum and the emergence of the student democratic movement at the end of the year were really only superficial reasons for Hu Yaobang's resignation. In reality, the coalition that formed against him was based on other, more profound factors, tied to internal party struggles.

In the first place, Hu Yaobang opposed worship of the personality cult and personal autocracy within the Party and completely agreed with Deng Xiaoping's proposal that he fully retire. Following the Sixth Plenum, Hu Yaobang and Deng Xiaoping had a personal conversation in which Deng said the following to Hu:

> I myself will withdraw completely and will give up all positions, including the chairmanship of the Central Military Commission. You should also withdraw somewhat, by giving up your position as general secretary of the Party to a younger person while taking over my former position as chairman of the Central Military Commission. Zhao Ziyang will also withdraw somewhat by giving up his position as premier and handing it over to a younger person as he assumes the presidency. In such a way we can convince a number of senior leaders to withdraw from their positions and lower the average age of the corps of Party cadres.

Hearing this, Hu Yaobang expressed his agreement wholeheartedly and responded by saying that this abolition of lifelong tenure would constitute a political legacy to bequeath to the next generation.

After that, Hu Yaobang passed on the content of this conversation to Zhao Ziyang and also mentioned it to some of the first Party secretaries of a few provinces. The broadcasting of this news had intense repercussions in the Party. Wang Zhen immediately dashed to the Central Party School to speak to the students. He said: "Someone has expressed a view calling on Comrade Xiaoping to retire. All of us old cadres oppose this. It's okay for other comrades to retire, but not Comrade Xiaoping! Whoever agrees with the idea of his retirement belongs to the "three categories. [*sanzhongren*]!"

The "three categories" refers to the little chiefs of the rebel faction of the "Cultural Revolution," those who had launched scuffles, giving themselves up to degradation, or to smashing and looting and serious sectarianism. Those three categories of people were targeted for elimination during the anti–Gang of Four campaign. In Wang Zhen's discourse, members of the three categories were all those Wang Zhen didn't like. This time it was Hu Yaobang who earned the right to be called this.

After Hu Yaobang was elected Party chairman at the 1981 Sixth Plenum of the Eleventh Party Congress and then reelected general secretary of the Party at the Twelfth Party Congress, time and again he let the Propaganda Department know that he was opposed to personality worship and to the dictatorship of a single person in the Party, and he demanded that attention be given to these issues in propaganda work. These views, along with his agreement to the idea of Deng's retirement, were taken as criminal evidence of his disloyalty by Wang Zhen, Deng Liqun, and Hu Qiaomu. In reality, however, if Wang Zhen and his pals opposed Deng's total retreat, it was because they wanted to be assured of the protection of their own power and position.

In addition, Hu Yaobang also opposed official profiteering and corruption in the Party. He proposed that attempts be made to rectify the Party's style of work within three years' time and also supported the idea of punishing illegal acts by the children of high-level cadres. He also supported the judiciary organs of the state, which according to the law and on irrefutable proof had arrested the son of Hu Qiaomu, Hu Shiying, who had embezzled three million *yuan*. This had provoked the collective hostility of corrupt bureaucrats and their delinquent offspring.

Then there was the conflict of Zhao Ziyang and his "power elite" group with Hu Yaobang. From 1980, when Zhao Ziyang had entered Beijing to take charge of the State Council to the Party Conference in 1985, Zhao Ziyang shared more common ground with Chen Yun than with Hu Yaobang in the realm of economic work. In the struggle between the Chen Yun clique and Hu Yaobang, Zhao Ziyang usually agreed with Chen's support for centralization and opposed Hu Yaobang, who was in favor of decentralization. In his critiques in regard to Hu Yaobang, Chen often said: "Ziyang and I, we speak the Beijingese of the capital. You, you prefer local dialects." Up until the end of 1984, Zhao Ziyang still wrote letters to Chen Yun and Deng Xiaoping saying that he could not get along with Hu Yaobang and requesting that the Central Committee resolve the Hu Yaobang issue, that is, remove Hu as general secretary. Both Chen Yun and Zhao Ziyang advocated early retirement for Hu Yaobang. But Deng Xiaoping ignored Zhao Ziyang's letters, undoubtedly because he wanted to keep Hu Yaobang on as general secretary until the 1987 Thirteenth Party Congress, when he would name him chairman of the Central Military Commission. But Zhao Ziyang and his "power elite" were impatient and also feared that if Hu was only going to become chairman of the Military Commission then Zhao Ziyang would be kicked upstairs to the purely honorific position of state president. After 1985, even when their conflicts with the Chen Yun clique were aggravated, Zhao Ziyang and his "power elite" never envisioned anything like an alliance with Hu Yaobang.

For his part, Hu Yaobang did not seem to be aware of Zhao's attempts to get rid of him; he fully supported Zhao's work and was very open in his criticisms of Zhao. For instance, Hu Yaobang once criticized Zhao Ziyang's "elites" by saying they were "detached from reality and pointed their fingers randomly, tried to please the audience to get favorable attention, paid lip service to things, and randomly prescribed actions based on very little learning."[15] Such candid criticism had no effect, but on the contrary, deepened the suspicions entertained by Zhao Ziyang and his "power elites" of Hu Yaobang. That's why, when the Chen Yun clique wanted to form an alliance to get rid of Hu Yaobang, Zhao Ziyang and his "power elites" voluntarily joined in.

The September 1986 Sixth Plenum of the Twelfth Party Congress marked the beginning of the formation of the anti–Hu Yaobang alliance. The final attack came in December 1986 at the peak of the nationwide student democratic movement. The anti–Hu Yaobang alliance took the view that the best way to force Deng Xiaoping to make up his mind to get rid of Hu Yaobang was to exploit the anger aroused in Deng by the current wave of student demonstrations. They connected the emergence of the student movement to the impact of Fang Lizhi, Liu Binyan, and Wang Ruowang and other liberal intellectuals and also fingered Hu Yaobang as the protector of the liberal intellectuals.

The explosion went off on December 30, 1986. At 10:00 A.M., Deng Xiaoping met with Hu Yaobang, Zhao Ziyang, Wan Li, Hu Qili, Li Peng, and He Dongchang. Zhao played an important role in the course of this meeting, making numerous interruptions—all of them provocative—without doubt because he was clearly aware that he would inherit Hu Yaobang's powers. Deng Xiaoping started off by dressing down Hu Yaobang for dragging his feet about kicking Wang Ruowang out of the Party. Deng also criticized Fang Lizhi by name and threatened to have him kicked out of the Party as well. But he didn't bother to mention Liu Binyan. This is when Zhao Ziyang interrupted and informed Deng Xiaoping that Liu Binyan was going to convene a meeting to commemorate the victims of the anti-rightist campaign of 1957, and these victims were to participate. This information was revealed to Zhao in denunciations by Qian Weichang and Fei Xiaotong. Deng Xiaoping had himself directed the 1957 anti-rightist campaign. He had always insisted that it was necessary and that the only thing wrong with it was that it had gotten out of hand. So he now blazed with fury. He demanded the immediate expulsion from the Party of Liu Binyan, and at the same time he praised Qian Weichang and Fei Xiaotong. In appearance, all Zhao Ziyang was doing was providing information, but in reality his goal was to raise the level of Deng's irritation, which he succeeded in doing, and the tone changed. From kicking Wang Ruowang out of the Party, Deng moved to the adoption of dictatorial measures. He said:

We must adopt dictatorial measures that must not only be talked about, but used when necessary. Of course, caution must be shown when taking such actions and arrests should be minimized. However, when someone attempts to create incidents involving bloodshed, what should be done? First, our method is to expose the conspiracy and avoid bloodshed and be willing to sustain some injuries. Nevertheless, those who are leaders of these chaotic incidents must be dealt with according to the law. If we don't take any measures and if we retreat, we'll only be confronted with more troubles later.

The tone of Deng's talk was no different in principle from the speech he would give prior to June 4, 1989. Deng Xiaoping had prepared to adopt bloody measures to deal with the democratic student movement long before June 4. From the end of 1986 to early 1987, the reason why there was no bloodshed was that both sides—the students and the public security forces—exercised constraint, as provocateurs were not lacking who wanted to make blood flow. For example, Wang Zhen.

On the afternoon of December 31, Wang Zhen convened a meeting at the Central Party School in the banquet hall. His speech was so vehement that he severed the wire of the microphone when he said, "They have three million college students but I, I can marshal three million PLA troops! I'm going to cut off heads! These sons of whores!" Then: "Do you know who I am? I am the knife-wielding Zhou Cang in the Guandi temple. If you don't believe me, just try me!" He also cursed the intellectuals and accused the writer Ba Jin of being "the nation's black sheep and the dregs of society." Many of the students at the Central Party School on hearing Wang's speech became very worried. They immediately made phone calls back to their provincial committees to tell them of the incident and warn them of the turn of events. Some provincial leaders telexed the Central Committee to find out what had really happened. Deng Xiaoping then learned that Wang Zhen had astonished the entire nation with a menacing and bloody speech to the Central Party School. Deng sent Gao Yang to replace Wang Zhen as head of the Central Party School.

From the end of 1986 to early 1987, Deng Xiaoping's approach to suppressing the student democratic movement was to order public security units to arrest students, threatening that "whoever comes to Tiananmen will be arrested and thrown in the jug as soon as they show up." On the morning of January 1, students were arrested on Tiananmen, and that evening students marched to the square in a heavy snowstorm demanding that the other students be released—who in fact were immediately let go by the public security and transported back to their schools in trucks. The whole affair thus ended peacefully. However, the struggle within the Party continued.

On January 2, 1987, Hu Yaobang submitted his resignation. But the wording of his resignation was very ill advised. He admitted himself of serving as a protective umbrella for villainous people, saying:

Some villainous people dare to make me their protective umbrella in order to stir up people's hearts, poison the youth, create chaos, and threaten stability and unity. The consequences of this are serious. Since my mistakes are serious ones, I request that my resignation be accepted so that I can clear up my thoughts and report back to the Party.

I have heard it said that when Hu Yaobang finally recovered his spirits, he regretted the wording of this resignation letter.

From January 2–3, 1987, Deng Xiaoping stayed at home and refused to speak to any family members as he paced the floor saying: "I did not withstand the blows of the Gang of Four just so that Hu Yaobang can trip me up. This time I must make sure that I don't fall down at the feet of Hu Yaobang."

January 4, 1987, was a Sunday. Deng Xiaoping summoned Zhao Ziyang, Peng Zhen, Wang Zhen, Bo Yibo, and Yang Shangkun to his home to make the arrangements to dismiss Hu Yaobang before he could resign.* The upshot was that Zhao Ziyang was named to replace him. Supposedly this was a decision of members of the Politburo Standing Committee residing in Beijing. In reality, Deng Xiaoping and Zhao Ziyang were the only members of the Standing Committee present. Three of the five members were absent: Hu Yaobang was not even invited, Li Xiannian was in Shanghai, and Chen Yun didn't show. It was a palace coup d'état.

Deng Xiaoping's own children disapproved of this coup. Deng forgot that it was a Sunday and urged them to go to work so they wouldn't be around when he convened his secret meeting, but they reminded him that people didn't go to work on Sunday. After the decision on getting rid of Hu Yaobang was made, parent and children engaged in heated debate with neither side able to sway the other.

From January 10 to 15, 1987, at the "Party life meeting" convened by Bo Yibo to criticize Hu Yaobang, Bo read from the letter written by Zhao Ziyang two years earlier to Deng Xiaoping and Chen Yun calling for the dismissal of Hu Yaobang. Hu Yaobang was greatly shocked and almost fainted. At the closing session of the meeting, Hu Yaobang admitted that he had committed serious mistakes of political principle and said he would always admit to those mistakes. Since, in fact, he had nothing bad to confess, when the meeting was over he went to Wang Heshou, secretary of the Discipline Inspection Commission, to personally complain in confidence about the whole affair. But Wang, giving proof of a lovely kind of morality, immediately reported this.

On January 16, 1987, at 7:00 in the evening, CCTV broadcast the news of Hu Yaobang's resignation. It was one of history's ironies: In 1976, Mao

---

*Resignation from the CCP has generally been forbidden for to do so puts the individual above the organization. Instead, it is the Party that decides to expel offending persons.

Zedong, an old man of eighty-two, criticized and removed the seventy-one-year-old Deng Xiaoping. In 1987, Deng Xiaoping, an old man of eighty-two, repeated Mao's act of eleven years earlier and removed the seventy-one-year-old Hu Yaobang. But Mao Zedong died that year, which allowed Deng, after rectifying his faults, to return and correct Mao's mistake. Deng did not die. And so the question remains: Whither Deng's empire?

Notes

1. When this statement was finally publicized, several key points were excised. For Deng's December 30, 1986, statement see *Comrade Deng Xiaoping on Upholding the Four Cardinal Principles and Opposing Bourgeois Liberalism (Deng Xiaoping tongzhi lun zhichi sixiang jiben yuunze, fandui ziben jieji ziyouhua),* p 139.

2. Deng Xiaoping, "Talk on Hearing Reports on the Economic Situation," in *Comrade Deng Xiaoping on Reform and the Open Door (Deng Xiaoping tongzhi lun gaige kaifang)* (Beijing: People's Publishing House, 1989), p. 101.

3. Deng Xiaoping, "Reform the Political Structure, Strengthen Legal Consciousness," in *Comrade Deng Xiaoping on Reform,* p. 103.

4. Ibid., p. 105.

5. Deng Xiaoping, "Failure to Carry Out Reform of the Political Structure Will Hinder Development of Productivity," in *Comrade Deng Xiaoping on Reform,* pp. 106–110.

6. Deng Xiaoping, "On the Reform of the System of Party and State Leadership," in *Selected Works of Deng Xiaoping: 1975–1982 (Deng Xiaoping wenxuan: 1975—1982)* (Beijing: People's Publishing House, 1983), p. 296.

7. Deng Xiaoping, "Failure to Carry Out Reform," p. 107.

8. Deng Xiaoping, "Reform of the Political Structure Must Have a Blueprint," in *Comrade Deng Xiaoping on Reform,* pp. 108–109.

9. "Resolution of the CCP Central Committee on the Guiding Principles for Construction of Socialist Spiritual Civilization," in *Selection of Important Documents Since the Twelfth Party Congress (Shierdayilai zhongyao wenxian xuanbian)* (Beijing: People's Publishing House, 1986), vol. 3, p. 1173.

10. Ibid., p. 1177.

11. Ibid., pp. 1183–1184.

12. Ibid., pp. 1185–1188.

13. Ibid., p. 1184.

14. Deng Xiaoping, "Talk at the Sixth Plenum of the Twelfth Party Congress," in *Selection of Important Documents,* vol. 3, pp. 1171–1172.

15. Hu Yaobang, "Another Talk with Young Intellectuals on the Issue of the Road to Maturity," in *Selection of Important Documents,* vol. 3, pp. 1108–1109.

PART III

The End of the Empire (1987–1989)

Despotic empires and autocrats alike dig their own graves. It's the inescapable destiny of both. Even a newly born empire can be destroyed by the absence of any constraints on the autocrat's absolute power. His own arbitrary acts can also quickly run an empire into the ground. The empires of Qin Shihuang, Mao Zedong, and Deng Xiaoping all eventually went the way of self-destruction.

The founder of the first unified empire in China, in the third century B.C., Qin Shihuang, made great contributions to China's development. He helped "standardize the width of axles on chariots and created a common written language"; he pushed China's transportation and irrigation systems; he moved culture into a new phase of development and greatly increased the material and spiritual productivity of China's ancient society. Qin was a romantic emperor. He was determined to conquer the seas. On several occasions, he made inspection tours to engrave stones, and he sent Fang Shi to explore the ocean. Unfortunately, when Fang Shi confronted the Pacific Ocean instead of the Mediterranean Sea, he found himself up against the technological limits of the time. Unable to cross the Pacific to reach outer territories, Fang Shi died in great sorrow.

Qin Shihuang also had his ignoble side: consolidating the Great Wall, constructing the Erfang palace and his own tomb, burning books and burying Confucian scholars, criminalizing speech, and "executing defamers of superiors and exiling those who speak out casually." To this day, both the Great Wall and the terra-cotta figurines in Xi'an still attract the awe of the entire world: Were these not accomplishments of great daring? However, his was also a kind of daring that was destructive of both material and spiritual pro-

171

ductivity. Qin Shihuang could neither halt armed invasions nor resist the intrusion of new ideologies over the course of history no matter how hard he tried. In his later years, Qin mobilized over half the entire labor force in the empire to build the Great Wall, the Erfang palace, and his tomb. More than fifty percent of all laborers were sent from their homes to the capital city and its environs or to remote desert areas. This effectively destroyed the economic and cultural foundation of the powerful newly established empire and aroused a nearly nationwide resistance that eventually caused its collapse.

Mao Zedong had a condescending attitude toward Qin Shihuang. Once he exclaimed: "What was so great about him? We have done him over a hundredfold! He buried 460 Confucian scholars, but we buried 46,000!"[1] Mao Zedong also looked down on Stalin and on Chiang K'ai-shek, just as once upon a time they had looked down on him. Mao in 1945 once held aloft the banner of "freedom and democracy" that attracted the masses, including intellectuals, in order to attack the old despotic autocracy in China of "one doctrine, one leader, and one party." And the "People's Republic" established in 1949 had its temporary period of development as a true people's government. Even in the early 1950s, after the Korean War, when China was forced by the Soviet Union into adopting the Stalinist bureaucratic system and interrupted the progression toward democracy expected by the people, the fate of the "republic" was not irreversible. Mao Zedong's last opportunity came in 1956, when he proposed the "On the Ten Major Relationships" and the "Double Hundred Policy," which brought new hope for a real "people's republic." Only a year later, however, he blatantly launched the anti-rightist campaign, and single-handedly destroyed the ideological and cultural elite. After that came the "three red banners," consisting of the "general line" for the realization of socialism and communism, the Great Leap Forward, and the People's Communes, all instruments used by Mao to destroy the material and economic foundations of the country. The Mao Zedong empire, which fundamentally violated basic human freedoms, values, respect, wisdom, and consciousness while dehumanizing the population, was established on the foundation of the absurd anti-rightist campaign and the Great Leap Forward. This empire, which annihilated itself by consuming the spirit of the people, ultimately led Mao Zedong to launch the Cultural Revolution, which he himself referred to as "an overall civil war to destroy everything" [*dadao yiqie, quanmian neizhan*]. After Mao's death, in the hands of Hua Guofeng, the empire only lasted for two years.

Deng Xiaoping's unique experience of losing and then regaining power on three separate occasions,[2] and the importance of his 1978 Third Plenum speech,[3] naturally made him the center of the democratic reform force in China. Indeed, Deng attempted in these first two years to change the political and economic structure of centralized power characteristic of the Maoist and Stalinist totalitarian system. He wanted to modernize China along the lines of political democracy and a free economy. The domestic and international support he gained then was unprecedented, far greater than what Gorbachev and reformers in other countries received. The first stage of the reform—rural reform—was extremely successful, enough to enable Deng to push for reform in the urban economy and politics. That was a favorable opportunity reformers in other countries did not have.

Deng Xiaoping, however, squandered the golden opportunity history had provided for him. He neither relied on forces that supported him, nor took advantage of these favorable conditions to push courageously forward with Chinese reform. On the contrary, he hesitated. Time and again, he suppressed the very democratic and reform forces that had supported him and promoted the corrupt forces encircling him. The Deng Xiaoping empire that he established on the foundation of a corrupt autocracy canceled out his objective of reform and opening up.

The Mao Zedong empire that began in 1949 lasted for thirty years. The life span of Deng Xiaoping's empire has been briefer by far. Hu Yaobang's forced resignation in January 1987 marked the beginning of the destruction of Deng's empire. We shall not have to wait long for the final end.

Notes

1. "Mao Zedong Speech at the Second Session of the Eighth Party Congress," May 1958.

2. Deng Xiaoping was purged on three separate occasions (once by Wang Ming and twice by Mao Zedong). His crimes included right opportunism, counterrevolutionary revisionism, being a power holder responsible for taking the capitalist road, bourgeois liberalism, and a reversal of verdicts on right opportunism. By the latter part of the 1970s, however, the Chinese people had sympathy with these supposedly criminal views. Because of this, when Deng Xiaoping was restored to power, it gave intense hope to the Chinese people and he naturally became the linchpin between Chinese society and the democratic reform force in the Party.

3. Deng Xiaoping, "Emancipate the Mind, Seek Truth from Facts, and Unite as One in Looking to the Future," in *Selected Works of Deng Xiaoping: 1975–1982 (Deng Xiaoping Wenxuan: 1975–1982)* (Beijing: People's Publishing House, 1983), pp. 130–143.

11

Deng Xiaoping and Zhao Ziyang Enjoy a Short Honeymoon

On January 28, 1987, Chinese New Year's Eve, Zhao Ziyang convened a meeting at the leadership compound of Zhongnanhai of over two hundred high-level cadres from various ministries and committees, provinces, cities, and autonomous regions in order to arrange for the struggle against bourgeois liberalism. In the course of his speech Zhao revealed the "process" by which Hu Yaobang had been deposed. Zhao said:

> As far back as 1984, the Central Committee knew of Hu Yaobang's errors and considered removing him. But in light of the fact that the Twelfth Party Congress had just been held, resolving this problem too soon would have upset the relatively stable situation in the country at that time. It seemed easier to hold off until the upcoming Thirteenth Party Congress. Now that the students have been fomenting troubles, Hu Yaobang has been able to realize the severity of his mistakes and with bitter self-reproach has asked to resign. Members of the Politburo Standing Committee then in Beijing decided that under these circumstances it was unthinkable to allow Hu Yaobang to rule on this student problem and thus decided that he should be dismissed from his posts. This does not mean that everything Hu Yaobang has done has been bad. As director of the Party Organization Department, he worked hard to reverse the false prosecutions and phony verdicts, something that many old cadres still acknowledge. But he revealed timidity in the struggle against liberalism. Hu Yaobang himself admitted to serving as the protective umbrella for villainous people, and now he regrets it. On January 2, 1987, he asked to resign, admitting that he had committed serious political mistakes. However, the communiqué issued by the enlarged Politburo meeting showed extreme clemency, only mentioning "mistakes" on important issues of political principle. In the entire history of inner-Party struggles, Hu Yaobang was dealt with in the most perfect way possible.[1]

The next day, January 29, Chinese New Year's Day, Zhao Ziyang said a few words at a New Year's party, and at the end of the speech, he promoted Deng Xiaoping's six "supremes" [zui]:

Comrades and Friends:

It was Comrade Deng Xiaoping who most frequently, profoundly, and at the earliest point in time raised the issues of reform, opening up, and enlivening the economy.

It was also Comrade Deng who spoke earliest and the most often and with great profundity about upholding the Four Cardinal Principles and supporting the struggle against bourgeois liberalism. He came up with his two basic points in the process of a profound study of real conditions in China. Thus, all of us should study well his statements regarding the two basic points. The socialist bible in Chinese colors, they constitute the fundamental political line since the Third Plenum.[2]

These two speeches by Zhao Ziyang laid the basic groundwork for his brief honeymoon with Deng Xiaoping.

Hu Yaobang's dismissal was evidently the outcome of long machinations by Chen Yun, Wang Zhen, Deng Liqun, and Hu Qiaomu. But this dismissal—which by the way provoked the derailment of the empire of Deng Xiaoping—would not have been possible if Deng himself and his favorite disciple Zhao Ziyang had not played a decisive role. That is to say that if either one of them had opposed the idea of removing Hu Yaobang, this outcome could have been avoided. Certain foreign observers interpreted the fall of Hu Yaobang as a concession forced upon Deng and Zhao by the hard-liners. They are wrong.

At the time, on the issue of removing Hu, differences existed among Party members from the Politburo Standing Committee all the way to the provincial and municipal levels of the Party, as well as among members of Deng's own family. Allegations by Zhao Ziyang, which resulted in a decision by the Politburo Standing Committee, were phony. The decision was made, as I've already said, by Zhao Ziyang and Deng Xiaoping. Six members of the Standing Committee had been elected at the 1982 Twelfth Party Congress: Hu Yaobang, Ye Jianying, Deng Xiaoping, Zhao Ziyang, Li Xiannian, and Chen Yun. At the time of the decision on Hu, Ye Jianying had already passed away, in October 1986; Li Xiannian was staying in Shanghai and was away from Beijing. When asked by Deng and Zhao to return to Beijing to solve the Hu Yaobang problem, Li replied: "What's the hurry?" and remained in Shanghai. Just before the decision was announced, Deng sent Yang Shangkun on a special trip to Shanghai (the plane took off in heavy fog) to secure a yes vote from Li. Thus, the only Standing Committee members then in Beijing were Hu Yaobang, Deng Xiaoping, Zhao Ziyang, and Chen Yun.

Hu Yaobang was not invited to the meeting held at Deng's residence on January 4 to decide on Hu's expulsion. Thus, it was a court judgment in absentia. Although Chen Yun had opposed Hu Yaobang, he did not show up for the January 4 meeting. Thus, the only members of the Politburo present were Deng and Zhao. The decision of that meeting was illegal since there wasn't a quorum. Therefore one can say that two members of the Politburo Standing

Committee, Deng Xiaoping and Zhao Ziyang, were able, with the support of Peng Zhen, Wang Zhen, Bo Yibo, and Yang Shangkun who attended the meeting, and with that of other absent characters, Chen Yun, Deng Liqun, and Hu Qiaomu, to launch this palace coup.

The form that this palace coup took was especially amazing. Between January 10 and January 15, Bo Yibo convened a rather nondescript "Party life meeting." The pretext was to "help Hu Yaobang with his self-criticism," whereas in reality the meeting was devoted to denouncing and attacking Hu. A "a group of five" was created composed of Zhao Ziyang, Wan Li, Hu Qili, Bo Yibo, and Yang Shangkun. Hu Qili had been recruited because he'd proved exemplary in his own self-criticism and in the denunciation of Hu. Wang Zhen, Deng Liqun, and Hu Qiaomu, although they were not members of the "group of five," also joined the inquisition. Deng Liqun gave a five-hour speech describing the glorious history of his struggle against Hu Yaobang from the time of the 1979 Conference on Guidelines in Theory Work. Subject to this sudden and withering attack, Hu Yaobang appeared beaten, unsure whether he would be arrested just as the "Gang of Four" had been arrested in its day. That's why he immediately engaged in a panicky self-criticism. Much later, he himself deplored the language he'd used in this self-criticism.

As for the coup d'état, it was highly unpopular. It not only aroused domestic discontent, but foreign reaction was also very strong. After the announcement of Hu Yaobang's dismissal, over two thousand Chinese students studying abroad in the United States signed an open letter in New York addressed to the CCP Central Committee and the State Council expressing their opposition.[3] Some Party leaders from the central, provincial, municipal, and autonomous regions also entertained doubts. Every so often opposition broke into the open. On January 28, 1987, Deng Liqun brought the newly appointed director of the Propaganda Department, Wang Renzhi, to the department to take over from a close associate of Hu Yaobang, Zhu Houze. They were escorted by Hu Qili. Deng Liqun mounted to the stage first to introduce Wang Renzhi and to praise Hu Qili for doing such a good job with his own self-criticism. Zhu Houze spoke briefly: "In the one year that I have served at the Propaganda Department, I did some work. Whether it was good or bad, let history judge!" Upon hearing that, Deng Liqun immediately jumped onto the stage and raged: "We don't need to wait for any historical judgment, let's make a judgment right now! The fall of Hu Yaobang is itself an historical conclusion!" Zhu Houze simply ignored this.

If Zhao Ziyang had reckoned it wise to meet with over two hundred high-level cadres on January 28, it was precisely because he wanted to calm their spirits and respond to their questions about Hu Yaobang's dismissal. When he maintained that "as far back as 1984 the Central Committee knew of Hu Yaobang's errors and considered removing him," Zhao was referring to the letter he wrote to Deng Xiaoping and Chen Yun demanding that they remove Hu Yaobang. One line from the letter goes like this: "If we don't profit now from the presence of the old comrades to rule soon on this problem, no one will be able to control him later." At the time, Deng Xiaoping had not re-acted, but this time the student movement gave Zhao the opportunity to real-ize his desires. At the start, Zhao Ziyang had no way of knowing that Bo Yibo would publicly reveal the existence of the letter in the course of the meeting called to denounce Hu Yaobang. But now that this secret had become public, he in no uncertain terms circulated this letter as a document illustrating the "strategic" intentions of the Central Committee, "which, since 1984, had considered removing Hu."

However, Zhao Ziyang's two speeches delivered on January 28 and 29 weren't appreciated by anyone but Deng Xiaoping. In these speeches, Zhao gave a new twist to Deng Xiaoping's ideology. In that of January 28, in addi-tion to describing the process of Hu's removal, he mainly explained the mean-ing behind Central Document Number Four of the Central Committee, or "Notification of Several Problems Associated with the Present Campaign Against Bourgeois Liberalism." Zhao Ziyang demanded that "all levels of the Party organizations and Party members must earnestly reexamine the series of important statements on upholding the Four Cardinal Principles and the struggle against bourgeois liberalism issued by the Party center and the Polit-buro Standing Committee represented by Comrade Deng Xiaoping since the 1978 Third Plenum." It was also important, he said, to "continue to unify our opinions, to understand the nature and the profound significance of this struggle, and to stand on the front lines."[4] Next, he gave a new explanation of the "political line followed since the Third Plenum":

> These days, the "line since the Third Plenum" [quotation in the original] has be-come the best-known political concept among the people of the entire nation, but that does not mean that everyone fully understands its deepest meaning. So just what is the political line followed since the Third Plenum? The Central Com-mittee considers that this political line consists in part of the construction of so-cialism with Chinese characteristics based on concrete conditions in China. It is characterized by two basic points: Upholding the Four Cardinal Principles is one part, and the other is adhering to the policy of reform, opening up, and enliven-ing the economy. The two are interrelated and interdependent. Without men-tioning the Four Cardinal Principles, the reform and opening up have no direc-tion and no guarantees. And without reform, openness, and enlivening the economy, it is impossible to increase productivity and therefore impossible to build socialism with Chinese characteristics. To mention one but not the other does not comply with the political line since the Third Plenum.[5]

In attributing to Deng Xiaoping the merit of the "elaboration" of these two basic points, Zhao Ziyang wanted to flatter him. On the other hand, for himself, these "two basic points" constituted a double-edged sword—useful at one and the same time against Hu Yaobang and Deng Liqun. Everything was now in the palm of Zhao's hand.

After Hu Yaobang's fall from power, struggles within the CCP evolved. Once the enemy was defeated, the anti–Hu Yaobang alliance collapsed and the conflicts that pitted Zhao Ziyang and Deng Liqun against each other came to the fore. They were immediately faced with the issue of just how to carry out the struggle against bourgeois liberalism. Specifically, their quarrels turned on Central Document Number Four, issued in January 1987.

This document of the Central Committee was, readers will recall, the famous "Notification of Several Problems Associated with the Present Campaign Against Bourgeois Liberalism." From the beginning, Deng Liqun had been in charge of drafting it. Just as in the anti–spiritual pollution campaign of 1983, he wanted to expand the struggle against bourgeois liberalism into the realms of politics, economy, culture, science and technology, and education, as well as both urban and rural social life, and to proceed, through this struggle, to a basic redistribution of power in all sectors. After Hu Qili approved Deng Liqun's rewritten draft, the two of them invited Zhao Ziyang to convene a meeting of the Central Secretariat to approve it. But Zhao Ziyang saw through this. If Zhao had convened the meeting at this point, the document would have been passed easily. But Zhao put this version of the document aside and asked his assistant Bao Tong to write a new version of Document Number Four, a draft radically opposed to Deng Liqun's. Zhao and Bao's version emphasized the following four points:

1. The struggle against bourgeois liberalism will be a long-term affair that essentially will have to be carried out on the basis of education and implies the serious study of articles and statements by Deng Xiaoping since the Third Plenum.
2. The scope of the struggle against bourgeois liberalism should be limited strictly to within the Party, a struggle that ought mainly to be exercised in the ideological and political domains if it is to result in establishing fundamental principles and political direction. This struggle "should not be linked to policies on economic reform, rural policies, scientific research and technology, artistic and literary work, or finally, the everyday life of the people."
3. A "leftward" drift of criticism directed in opposition to the right must be prevented and must not be allowed to form a pretext to hinder the implementation of policies on reform, opening up, and enlivening the economy.
4. Critical articles must be of good quality. Articles too concentrated, repetitive, or empty of content must be avoided. Improper expressions, especially slogans from the Cultural Revolution and other tired movements, also have to be avoided.

All four of these points were aimed at Deng Liqun.

Showing great political aplomb, Zhao did not propose sending the Bao Tong draft right away to the Secretariat for approval, but submitted it first to Deng Xiaoping. Only after Deng Xiaoping had voiced his approval, did Zhao bring it to the Secretariat. As he presented the document, he said, "Comrade Deng Xiaoping has already looked at this and approved it. I invite you to discuss it." Naturally, the Secretariat approved it unanimously. If Deng Liqun and Hu Qiaomu had contemplated expressing oppositional views, now they had to clam up. That was Zhao Ziyang's ingenuity. For if he had allowed the document to be discussed first by the Secretariat, it would not have been approved without at least some alterations.

Central Document Number Four was formally issued on January 28, 1987, the last day of the old Chinese year. On the same day, Zhao Ziyang held a meeting of high-level cadres to issue directives. Showing that he had the upper hand in the campaign against bourgeois liberalism, Zhao Ziyang also ordered Bao Tong, Chen Junsheng, and others to write articles criticizing bourgeois liberalism, ordering them to employ a style that would contrast with the articles packed with jargon but devoid of sense that were Deng Liqun's usual fare. Deng Liqun could not resign himself to a loss of face in front of Zhao Ziyang. He mobilized all his forces at the Central Propaganda Department, the Research Office of the Secretariat, and the Central Party School—wherever he had a dominant or influential position—to break the limitations imposed in Document Number Four and render it null and void.

The first attack came from Wang Renzhi, the newly installed director of the Propaganda Department. At a meeting of the Propaganda Department, Wang had declared: "The significance of this anti–bourgeois liberalism campaign is that it is actually the second time that we have cleared away chaos and set things right since the smashing of the 'Gang of Four.'" The first time that this expression was used was at the 1978 Third Plenum, when the "two whatevers" were negated and Mao Zedong's errors before and during the "Cultural Revolution" were rectified. This time, it was suggested that the time had come to end the chaos that had reigned since the Third Plenum and return to past order. But Zhao Ziyang asked Wang Renzhi: "What do you mean by 'clearing away chaos for a second time'?" Wang Renzhi beat a quick retreat: "I heard it from Hu Qiaomu, and without giving it a second thought, I mentioned it at the Propaganda Department meeting. Now in retrospect, I think it was inappropriate." Zhao Ziyang could tell that after all Wang Renzhi could be docile and decided to retain him as head of the Propaganda Department.

Wang immediately rallied to Zhao's side. He composed an article employing Zhao's two basic points, and Zhao ordered it published in the *People's Daily*. However, when Zhao's power was later reduced, Wang shifted back to Deng Liqun and Hu Qiaomu.

Next came the theory of "the ends and the means" proposed by Jiang Liu, then director of the Education Department at the Central Party School. In Jiang's opinion, the two basic points raised by Zhao Ziyang were a form of the "duality theory" [*eryuan lun*] and one that failed to establish a clear relationship between the Four Cardinal Principles and the struggle against bourgeois liberalism on the one hand, and reform and opening up on the other. Jiang invented the saying, "The Four Cardinal Principles and the struggle against bourgeois liberalism constitute the means, whereas reform and opening up are the ends." Zhao Ziyang, who did not agree with this way of looking at things, charged the new head of the Central Party School, Gao Yang, to find out who was behind it. But Gao Yang protected Jiang Liu.

The Research Office of the Secretariat proposed, for its part, a discourse on "words and acts." Deng Liqun ordered his people at the office to collect material relating to bourgeois liberalism in every domain and classify the material into two large categories of "words" and "acts." The "words" category included articles, statements, and works by intellectuals, scholars, and authors in the realm of ideology and culture. The "acts" category referred to policies and measures implemented in the process of the development of the market economy. Deng Liqun repeated to anyone who wanted to listen: "Nowadays, it is said that only those who talk about bourgeois liberalism are criticized, but never those who actually engage in bourgeois liberalism!" By "those who talk about bourgeois liberalism," he meant Hu Yaobang, whereas "those who actually engage in bourgeois liberalism" referred to Zhao Ziyang. Deng Liqun's attempt was to expand the struggle against bourgeois liberalism beyond the realm of ideology to the economic sector that Zhao had controlled for some time.

Finally, we come to the "discourse on nightmares," which sprang from the brains of Xiong Fu and Lin Mohan. Both of them had been criticized at the 1979 Conference on Guidelines in Theory Work for adhering to the "two whatevers" and for opposing the debate over the criterion of truth. Later, they rallied to the side of Deng Liqun. Although they had held onto their positions, their "Party eight-legged platitudes" were so stale that absolutely no one read them. They truly believed they were the victims of hazing by bourgeois liberals who were encouraged by Hu Yaobang and Zhou Yang. Xiong Fu declared:

> Since the Conference on Guidelines in Theory Work eight years ago, we feel as though we've been living in a nightmare. For eight years, Hu Yaobang closed his eyes on the activities of the liberal elements, those who three times created troubles. The first time, in the debate over the criterion of truth, they wrapped themselves in free thought in order to struggle against the Four Cardinal Principles. The second time was when Zhou Yang spoke of humanism and alienation in order to raise doubt and rattle the socialist system. And the third example of chaos was Lu Dingyi's opposition to the struggle against bourgeois liberalism on the

grounds that it was virtually the same as the anti–bourgeois liberalism promoted by Khrushchev when he opposed Lu's 1956 Double Hundred Policy. Hu Yao-bang's sympathetic attitude in reality constituted support for liberalism and thus inspired the student movement. In the past eight years, Marxism has been trampled. Happily, the bitter taste of the oppression has faded.

And Lin Mohan let fly: "Liberalism is not only an ideological trend, it's also a force. If we fail to eliminate that force today, some day we'll end up being hung on electric poles, as others were in the 1956 Hungarian incident."

In spring 1987, the forces of anti–bourgeois liberalism under Deng Liqun held meetings and gave speeches everywhere to spread their "Marxist" views. Some of the better-known meetings included the Forum on Literature and Arts held by the Propaganda Department in early February 1987; the Theoretical Forum [*Lilun taolunhui*] convened by the editors of the *Red Flag*, the *Journal of Literary and Artistic Theory and Criticism* [*Wenyi Lilun yu Piping*], and the *Enlightenment Daily* in Zhuozhou, Hebei province, in April 1987; and the All-China Meeting of Political and Ideological Workers held in April 1987 in Tianjin. Deng Liqun and his allies also accused Zhao Ziyang's Central Document Number Four of having "poured cold water on the struggle against bourgeois liberalism." He Jingzhi said: "Last time the cleaning up spiritual pollution campaign lasted for only twenty-seven days, but this time the struggle against bourgeois liberalism did not even last that long!"[6]

In dealing with Deng Liqun's attacks, Zhao Ziyang as usual did not submit them for discussion to a meeting of the Secretariat, but instead took them to Deng Xiaoping directly. On April 28, Zhao Ziyang made a solo visit to Deng Xiaoping to give him an oral account of the tendencies of the "left," which in the last three months under the alibi of the struggle against bourgeois liberalism had completely negated the politics of reform and opening up. Zhao cited to Deng Xiaoping all the names of the "second redressing," "the ends and the means," "the words and acts," and, finally, "the discourse on nightmares." He added, "It's impossible for me to work in these conditions, impossible to promote the economy and to continue with the reform." Deng Xiaoping completely supported Zhao Ziyang. He asked him to prepare a speech that would stop this "leftist" ideological wave. Deng also agreed to have his August 1980 speech "On the Reform of the System of Party and State Leadership" re-issued on July 1, the anniversary of the CCP's founding.

With Deng's support secured, Zhao was free of all fears. He asked his assistant Bao Tong to prepare a speech to be titled "Speech for the Meeting of Cadres in the Fields of Propaganda, Theory, Media, and the Party Schools" (delivered on May 13, 1987), in which Zhao embarked on an overall attack against Deng Liqun.[7] In such a way, Zhao successfully retained his power on the economic front and also managed to snatch power from Deng Liqun and Hu Qiaomu on the ideological front. The harmonious relationship that Zhao established with Deng Xiaoping was based on a profound rapport between the two men such as Hu Yaobang had never known.

Indeed, during Zhao and Deng's honeymoon, Deng Liqun clearly had a lot of troubles. First, although Deng Liqun thought he had made great contributions to bringing about the downfall of Hu Yaobang, it had not really enabled him to expand his power. He wanted to win over the staff of the Ministry of Culture and the *People's Daily* for his henchmen, but this was nipped in the bud by Zhao Ziyang, who said: "The Ministry of Culture and the *People's Daily* cannot be touched!"

In addition, Deng Liqun drew up several lists of the names of liberals to criticize, but Deng Xiaoping and Zhao Ziyang stopped him in his tracks. One list included the names of Bao Tong, Yan Jiaqi, and Li Fu, all of whom were "bright scholars" in Zhao Ziyang's political structural reform group [*zhengzhi tizhi gaige banzi*]. Deng Liqun attempted to put pressure on Zhao Ziyang by attacking Zhao's people, a common practice that Deng Liqun had successfully employed against Hu Yaobang in the past. Zhao Ziyang, however, was tougher in this regard than Hu Yaobang: He made sure that not one of his people was removed and that they continued to work as if nothing was wrong, simply ignoring the maneuvers of Deng Liqun, who then came up with another list for Deng Xiaoping. When he saw the name of the economist Yu Guangyuan at the top of the list, Deng Xiaoping guffawed. "Yu Guangyuan is an honest person," Deng declared, and he put the list to one side and paid no further attention to it. Upon learning of this, Deng Liqun turned pale and cried, "What a mistake I've made in classifying these names. I know that if Wang Ruoshui's name had been put first, Deng Xiaoping wouldn't have just dropped the list like that."

Later, Deng Liqun changed his strategy to one of secluding himself in the rear. He no longer put himself on the line. Instead, he spurred Wang Zhen to try to change Deng Xiaoping's mind and ordered Wang Heshou of the Central Discipline Inspection Commission to draft a new list of names from a master list he himself furnished. So Wang Zhen went to Beidaihe to talk to Deng: "According to the original plan, after removing Fang Lizhi, Liu Binyan, and Wang Ruowang, another housecleaning was to be carried out. How come it hasn't been executed?" Deng Xiaoping replied: "That's right. We'll talk about it after you submit another name list." So Deng Liqun told Wang Heshou to submit, in the name of the Discipline Commission, a list of twelve people. Zhao Ziyang then decided to convene two meetings of the Central Secretariat in Beidaihe, which would deal with six names at each meeting.

The first six consisted of Wu Zuguang, Wang Ruoshui, Zhang Xianyang, Su Shaozhi, Li Honglin, and Yu Haocheng. The decision that Wu Zuguang and Wang Ruoshui should be "persuaded to resign from the Party" was passed unanimously. Hu Qiaomu volunteered that "he would personally go and persuade Wu Zuguang to resign from the Party." When the case of Zhang

Xianyang was discussed, Deng Liqun said: "Zhang Xianyang and Sun Changjiang are birds of the same feather. During the Cultural Revolution they were all rebel faction members [*zaofanpai*] from Beijing's People's University who engaged in beating, smashing, and looting. These two people must be kicked out of the Party and should not be merely persuaded to resign!" No one responded, and thus the decision was passed.

Sun Changjiang's name had not been on the original list but was added at the last minute by Deng Liqun. While working at the Central Party School, Sun Changjiang had participated in writing the editorial signed "special commentator" entitled "Practice Is the Sole Criterion of Truth," an article that had played an important role in the emancipation of thought. Although Wang Zhen had kicked him out of the Central Party School, Sun was subsequently appointed the deputy editor of the *Science and Technology Daily*. This time around Deng Liqun was determined to use the opportunity to get rid of him completely. As for the case of Su Shaozhi, Zhao Ziyang put in a word on his behalf, reminding the assembly that Su had written many articles favoring reform and opening up. Zhao recommended that Su should be treated leniently, and Su Shaozhi lost his position as director of the Institute of Marxism–Leninism–Mao Zedong Thought of the Chinese Academy of Social Sciences but hung on to his Party membership.*

At that point, it was time to eat, and Zhao called for a break. The meeting was never reconvened and the eight other people on the list escaped punishment.

In 1987, aside from the anti–bourgeois liberalism campaign and the purge of Fang Lizhi, Liu Binyan, and Wang Ruowang, only the cases of those five listed above were discussed. Later Wu Zuguang withdrew from the Party as a result of Hu Qiaomu's persuasion. As for Wang Ruoshui, since he remained indifferent to "persuasion," his name was struck from the Party. The same for Zhang Xianyang. Su Shaozhi, as mentioned, stayed in the Party, but was stripped of his job. The most interesting case was the one involving Sun Changjiang. The first charge against him was made by Deng Liqun in the name of the Central Discipline Inspection Commission, namely, that "he had slipped through the net and was a member of the three categories" of Cultural Revolution troublemakers. At that time, Sun Changjiang was working at the *Science and Technology Daily,* but his Party organizational relationship was with the Beijing Party organization. Deng Liqun worked frantically behind the scenes to get Xu Weicheng of the Beijing organization to kick him out,

---

*For Su Shaozhi's own account of his experience, see "A Decade of Crises at the Institute of Marxism–Leninism–Mao Zedong Thought," in *The China Quarterly* 134 (June 1993), pp. 335–351.

thinking that Xu would follow his orders and everything would be worked out according to his wishes. Xu Weicheng was the person in charge of eliminating from the Party members of the "three categories." As such he had already ordered the investigation group from the Beijing Party organization to investigate how Sun had slipped through the net, an action that effectively delayed a resolution of Sun's case for a few days. During this period the editor of *Science and Technology Daily*, Lin Zixin, wrote a letter to Nie Rongzhen, an old cadre and military man with considerable authority in the field of science, in which he pointed out that the charges against Sun brought by Deng Liqun were completely trumped up, in no way dovetailed with reality, and should not be used as the basis for a purge of Sun. Sun, he said, was undeserving of the fate that awaited him. Nie Rongzhen passed on the letter to Chen Yun, who then instructed that caution be taken in dealing with high-level intellectuals in the Party, that all the materials must be verified with care, and that rash actions based on hearsay and false evidence should be avoided. Thus, Sun Changjiang waited for the materials to be verified, but since no one bothered to carry out this task, he once again passed through the net and remained as the deputy editor at the *Science and Technology Daily* until 1989.

The last big obstacle that Deng Liqun encountered during the period of the honeymoon between Deng Xiaoping and Zhao Ziyang was the 1987 Thirteenth Party Congress. Soon after Hu Yaobang's dismissal, Deng Liqun dismantled the team recently assembled by Hu Yaobang to draft speeches for the Thirteenth Congress. Deng Liqun was thus in a position to shift the power of drafting the congress reports to his own Research Office of the Central Secretariat. Zhao Ziyang, however, was very vigilant, and he quickly organized a drafting group composed of the original members of Hu's team, plus Bao Tong, and together they became Zhao's own drafting group. Prior to drafting the reports, Zhao Ziyang wrote a letter to Deng Xiaoping in which he provided a rough outline of the main themes in the simplest language and asked Deng Xiaoping to first examine them. This was the letter Zhao Ziyang wrote to Deng on March 21, 1987, that was later given the title "A Tentative Idea for a Draft Outline of the Report to the Thirteenth Party Congress."[8] Deng Xiaoping read it and on March 25, 1987, issued the following instruction: "This project is perfect." Only after that did Zhao Ziyang pass on his letter and Deng's instructions to the Politburo Standing Committee and the Central Secretariat. Deng Liqun could do nothing.

Prior to the Thirteenth Congress, according to Zhao Ziyang and Deng Xiaoping's original plan, Hu Yaobang and Deng Liqun were to be retained as Politburo members. This was a practice that Mao Zedong had also followed. At the 1945 Seventh Party Congress, Mao had suggested that his former political opponent Wang Ming should be retained as a member of the Central Committee. At the 1959 Eighth Plenum of the Eighth Party Congress when Peng Dehuai was criticized, Peng had also been allowed to retain his position as a member of the Politburo. This had indicated that Mao Zedong was able to unite with those who had opposed him while it also provided proof that "the opposition was wrong." Retaining certain representatives of "leftist" and rightist tendencies in the Central Committee also reflected Mao's consistent correctness of remaining in the political "middle."

Zhao Ziyang followed in the same tradition by retaining Hu Yaobang in a leadership position as a "rightist" representative and Deng Liqun as a "leftist" representative. According to Zhao Ziyang, both Hu Yaobang and Deng Liqun could hold in their heads only one basic point whereas he and Deng Xiaoping could entertain two.[9]

However, the election system of the Thirteenth Party Congress had been slightly reformed. Prior to the election of the Central Committee, a preliminary election [*cha'e yuxuan*] was carried out that produced ten more nominees than there were Central Committee seats. Deng Liqun was among one of the ten lowest vote getters, a result that immediately aroused a big debate. Given that the preliminary election was really only an informal poll that carried no legal force, the congress was asked to draw up its formal list of Central Committee names based on that preliminary election and to hold another formal vote. In this formal vote, the number of candidates was to be equal to the number of seats and so three contending opinions emerged on how to handle the situation involving Deng Liqun:

The first opinion, forcefully pushed by Wang Zhen, Bo Yibo, and Song Renqiong, called for listing Deng Liqun's name in the formal election by shifting the name of another candidate who had won more votes to the Central Committee alternates list.

The second opinion favored adding the ten people who had received too few votes to the alternates list. However, Wang Zhen categorically opposed this option, arguing that Deng Liqun was a member of the Central Committee and had been appointed head of the Secretariat at the Twelfth Party Congress. Moreover, if Deng Liqun were not elected to the Central Committee at the Thirteenth Congress, he could not be elected to the Politburo.

Zhao Ziyang himself was considering yet a third option: Since it would be inappropriate to have someone of Deng Liqun's advanced age as an alternate member, why not shift him over to the Central Advisory Commission, which consisted of many old cadres nominally "retired." In this way, Deng Liqun could still be elected to the Standing Committee of the Advisory Commission.

But as there were separate opinions, Zhao Ziyang decided to seek out instructions from Deng Xiaoping by visiting Deng at his home. Zhao delivered a carefully worded report:

> The result of the preliminary election to the Thirteenth Congress indicated that Comrade Xiaoping's two basic points have won the warm admiration of the candidates. Among the ten people receiving the least votes, two are important. One

is Zhu Houze, who had supported only one basic point, and that was reform and opening up, and who as director of the Propaganda Department had resisted the struggle against bourgeois liberalism. The other person is Deng Liqun, who although he grasped the basic point of antiliberalism, had practically nothing to say about reform and opening up. Since Zhu Houze is still young we thought that he could be put on the alternates list along with the other eight people. As for Comrade Deng Liqun, it might be more appropriate for him to become a member of the Standing Committee of the Central Advisory Commission.

Upon hearing that, Deng Xiaoping uttered only four words: "Respect the people's will."

Yet, Deng Liqun had still more rebuffs to fend off. The Central Advisory Commission was composed of two hundred members designated by elections in which the number of candidates equaled the number of those elected. Deng Liqun was thus elected, since every candidate inevitably was. But then came the meeting of advisers to elect the Standing Committee. In this case too the number of candidates equaled the number of seats. In the meeting room, all the chairs were set up for the candidates to be seated. At that time, many of the Advisory Commission members thought that the vote was a mere formality and thus decided not to express any oppositional views. However, one member, Li Chang, demanded that he be allowed to give a speech criticizing Deng Liqun. His criticisms were harsh, ranging from such topics as Deng Liqun's violation of the law and messing up disciplinary matters during the 1936–1945 Yan'an period to the penchant for extreme leftist ideology that he showed during the reform and opening up, contrary to the resolutions taken at the 1978 Third Plenum. Although most of the members of the Central Advisory Commission were quite old, this was the first time that many of them had heard of these charges and they decided to discuss the whole matter among themselves. Wang Zhen, Bo Yibo, and Song Renqiong—all Central Advisory Commission members—spoke up immediately to affirm Deng Liqun's contributions to the struggle against bourgeois liberalism. But Li Chang spoke again, pointing out that the practice of affirming merits in one area so as to cover up serious problems in other areas had long been detrimental to the Party's history. Li Chang's speech was very effective, and as a result Deng Liqun only received eighty-five votes, and therefore did not win a seat on the Standing Committee, because this was less than the required fifty percent.

The electoral defeat of Deng Liqun became the Number One topic at the Thirteenth Congress. Among the masses it was quickly passed about and toasted in celebration, all of which added some real attraction to a congress that originally had generated very little attention. The entire nation followed the closing session of the congress on TV. On the same day, a press conference was held for both Chinese and foreign correspondents and broadcast live on CCTV. Zhao Ziyang was filled with a spring breeze, convinced as he was that his competitors on both the left and right had been balanced off against each other forevermore. Defeated. Although Hu Yaobang was elected to the Politburo with a very large number of votes, he was the only member of the Politburo who did not have any concrete responsibility. That Deng Liqun had been voted out of both the Central Committee and the Standing Committee of the Central Advisory Commission caused his reputation to sink to an all-time low, whereas for Zhao Ziyang it seemed that as long as he continued to maintain his close relationship with Deng Xiaoping he would have no problem in retaining power. It was for this reason that he declared at the First Plenum following the Thirteenth Congress that Deng Xiaoping was the chief architect and "highest authority," who continued to make decisions on important issues.

Such was the tenor of the decision that Zhao revealed to Gorbachev in May 1989 at the peak of the democratic movement in China, the "secret resolution," revelation of which brought about his own downfall. In fact, there was nothing secret about it, because at the press conference on the closing day of the 1987 Thirteenth Congress, Zhao in replying to a question from a correspondent who asked him if henceforth he would take counsel with Deng, had openly declared: "In our Party, Deng Xiaoping is the one who possesses the highest competence and the richest experience. What could be more natural than to ask his advice on important issues!"

The Thirteenth Party Congress marked the climax of Deng Xiaoping and Zhao Ziyang's honeymoon. But at the same time it signaled a retreat of the high tide. The exclusive emphasis on the strategy behind the political report to the congress that so pleased Zhao Ziyang seemed to overwhelm any resolution of the core issues. The so-called primary stage of socialism* was in reality nothing but a modest cover for speaking about what others called "a tutorial on capitalism." Deng Xiaoping's and Zhao Ziyang's courage for theory was even less than Mao Zedong's. Mao was still in the caves of Yan'an when he dared to challenge the orthodox socialism of Stalin and declared that China could not jump over the developmental stage of capitalism. When he attacked "the populist [*mincuizhuyi*] tendency to jump directly from a feudal to a socialist economy" he not only aimed at the populist faction in the CCP but also at Stalin.[10] As for the tortuous history that led Mao Zedong to discard his Yan'an era theoretical views to move from the "right" of Stalin to his "left," that's another story.[11]

By refusing to speak about capitalism, Deng Xiaoping and Zhao Ziyang put themselves between a rock and a hard place. The concept proposed by Zhao Ziyang and his "power elites" on the "primary stage of socialism" was self-contradictory in both theory and practice.

---

*This was Zhao's concept of development for China ostensibly within a Marxist-Leninist perspective that rationalized the use of market forces for economic growth.

Gorbachev in his reform once employed Lenin's New Economic Policy as the legal basis for his own theory. Chinese reform in fact could have referred to a parallel theory that would have given it legitimacy: the theory of New Democracy proposed by Mao, but which he had never put into practice. At the Seventh Party Congress in 1945, Mao Zedong had given an explanation of his theory of capitalism with a New Democracy and the rules of this democracy, which he wanted to realize as "land to the tiller" and "regulation of capital." Yet this "regulation of capital" converged with Sun Yat-sen's Three Principles of the People. The "regulation of capital" was in fact opposed to monopolist and bureaucratic capitalism, but not capitalism in general. If Deng Xiaoping and Zhao Ziyang were reluctant to mention a "tutorial on capitalism," why couldn't they at least have mentioned a tutorial on New Democracy? Instead, they followed the old dogma of Hu Qiaomu and Deng Liqun by insisting on "upholding socialism."

Moreover Deng Xiaoping and Zhao Ziyang each in his heart of hearts was not unaware of just how hypocritical such a notion of "upholding" was. This was made clear at a press conference conducted by a member of Zhao Ziyang's think tank.

Question: Is the Wenzhou* model capitalist or socialist?

Answer: Of course we think that it is socialist. Our logic is that anything that helps promote productivity and is good is socialism. By the same token, anything that is socialist must be good. Following this same logic, the Wenzhou model is socialist and constitutes one of the models of socialism with Chinese characteristics.

We must adhere to this logic and propagandize it, for otherwise the situation will undergo the following transformation: Anything that helps promote productivity would be labeled as "capitalist," and only things adverse to the development of productivity could be called "socialist." Such logic is comparable to automatically admitting that "socialism cannot overtake capitalism." In that case wouldn't "uphold the socialist road," as part of the Four Cardinal Principles, be converted into "upholding the road of backwardness"?

Therefore, our view is consistent with Comrade Ziyang's, and that is, we must protect the Wenzhou model and persistently characterize the Wenzhou model as socialist and see it as a reflection of the superiority of socialism.[12]

Unfortunately, such logic was nothing but a rather unconvincing piece of sophistry in the face of attacks by Stalinist theorists like Chen Yun, Hu Qiaomu, and Deng Liqun.

---

*A city in China's Zhejiang province that has served as a testing ground for the market economy.

When put into practice, the "primary stage of socialism" as devised by Zhao Ziyang did not allow China to absorb such innovations in modern capitalism as new developments in science and technology, advanced management methods, and a role for the state in making adjustments to the economy. Instead, his think tanks were engrossed with the cruel means of exploitation that aimed at pursuit of short-term effects as they were adopted during the early, primitive stage of capitalist accumulation.

In 1983 Deng Xiaoping still advocated "confronting modernization, the world, and the future." And Zhao Ziyang himself spoke of "welcoming the challenge of the world revolution in science and technology." And indeed, at that time, they did aim at learning some advanced things from the outside world. But the situation in 1987 was quite different. Issues regarding education, science, and technology had become the least of their concerns. Zhao Ziyang and his think tanks henceforth proposed such policy lines as "production first and education later" and "pollution first and treatment later." Huge amounts of inefficient and heavily polluting equipment requiring "intensive labor" detrimental to human health were imported from Taiwan, from Hong Kong, and from foreign countries where they had already been shelved, all for the purpose of achieving super profits. These kinds of enterprises often required workers to put in more than ten-hour days in conditions dangerous to workers' health and safety. These workers had no health or safety guarantees or insurance against future insecurity. The unfortunate reality, however, was that the economic income of the workers increased and the overall value of production in the national economy increased, whereas accidents and disasters only afflicted a few. That's why everyone agreed to acknowledge that this search for short-term profit was one of the positive aspects of reform.

But on another plane, that of generalized corruption, the situation was different. This corruption resulted, as I've already suggested, from the parallel development of both a planned and market economy and the dual-price system foretold by the "primary phase of socialism." One crowd of "entrepreneurs of the free economy" were tied to despotic political power. In this system, a bunch of "free economic entrepreneurs" relied on totalitarian political power and their political and economic privileges under the "planned economy" to gain access to raw materials and foreign exchange reserves at the low official rate along with import-export quotas. They became the nouveaux riches by virtue of engaging in the role of middlemen. Theorists working in Zhao Ziyang's system once defended such official corruption by claiming that it was advantageous to the development of a commodity economy in China. But it had also resulted in a huge expansion of the nouveaux riches and produced severe antagonisms between them and the masses. That's why in the early stage of the 1989 democratic movement, the masses took Zhao Ziyang as one of the nouveaux riches, which was not an unreasonable thing, and made him one of their targets.

But the cause of Zhao Ziyang's ultimate defeat was not only this. That is, his failure was not due to the error of his economic strategy, but rather to the errors of his political strategy and the split between him and the anti–Hu Yaobang alliance. According to Zhao himself, Hu Yaobang was supposed to be shelved at the Thirteenth Congress, but because it was decided that he should not deal with the student movement that came at the end of 1986, he was asked to "tender his resignation" much sooner. The period between Hu Yaobang's early stepping down as opposed to his planned later stepping down was only six months, but this was a crucial period of time for Zhao Ziyang. For if Hu Yaobang had not been asked to withdraw earlier, he would have continued to direct preparations for the Thirteenth Congress, which included making the key decisions on appointments and reassignments of cadres to their positions. According to the plan decided upon by Deng Xiaoping and Hu Yaobang, the first generation of old men, headed by Deng Xiaoping, and including Chen Yun, Peng Zhen, Bo Yibo, Wang Zhen, and others, would all step down at the Thirteenth Party Congress. This would constitute a "complete withdrawal" in the sense that they would no longer hold any positions. The second generation of leaders, including Hu Yaobang, Zhao Ziyang, Yao Yilin, and others, would make a "semiwithdrawal." They would withdraw to the "second front" of general policy decisionmaking, leaving positions in the first front of deciding on more concrete policies in the hands of cadres from the young generation. If such an arrangement had been achieved, Zhao Ziyang would not have been able to wield major power following the congress. Therefore, Zhao Ziyang's only opportunity was to have Hu Yaobang replaced before the Thirteenth Congress, something that would effectively put Zhao in charge of the crucial preparatory work, thereby ensuring that his own power would be expanded, not reduced, at the Thirteenth Congress.

This, however, was easier said than done. To replace Hu Yaobang, Zhao Ziyang had to unite with the "first generation" of old men, including Chen Yun, Peng Zhen, Bo Yibo, and Wang Zhen. But as far as these men were concerned, the older they got, the more they loved power. They didn't want to eliminate Hu Yaobang just so that Zhao Ziyang could taste the fruits of victory—they wanted power for themselves. No matter the efforts Zhao Ziyang made to get himself into their good graces, they had no intention of playing the role of supporting committee. They wanted to form their own "senate" to exercise real power. In their struggle against Hu Yaobang, their first act was to create a "cadre group," which seized the power from Hu Yaobang to appoint and dismiss cadres, and they jealously guarded it without ceding anything to Zhao Ziyang. This "cadre group" crossed out more than half the names Zhao Ziyang nominated for the Central Secretariat of the Thirteenth Congress. Zhao Ziyang's victory over Hu Yaobang concealed the germs of his future defeat.

Some argue that Zhao Ziyang did not intend to replace Hu Yaobang as general secretary of the Party. Following Hu's resignation, Zhao Ziyang stated time and again that he would rather continue as the premier instead of assuming the post of general secretary. This contains an element of truth and shouldn't be explained away as merely hypocritical modesty. Indeed, it represented Zhao's true feelings at the time. Zhao Ziyang was sincere. He didn't want to become a general secretary without any real power as Hu had been. Members of his think tanks were very clear on this point in their speeches and articles: "Since the Party rules, its chief ought to form the government and lead it."[13]

Zhao Ziyang's goal was to possess power over both the Communist Party and the government, and of course, he was unwilling to let Premier Li Peng wield power over the government while he himself became a mere figurehead as general secretary.

Originally, Zhao Ziyang believed that once he had tied his fortunes to Deng Xiaoping this would solve virtually everything. And thanks to this tactic he had, prior to the Thirteenth Congress, triumphed over Hu Yaobang and Deng Liqun. But he had undoubtedly not foreseen that this alliance, even if it proved trustworthy in one particular conflict, would founder as soon as the old men no longer turned on Hu Yaobang but acted in concert against Zhao himself. It was under these conditions that Deng Xiaoping's and Zhao Ziyang's alliance began to collapse.

Not long after the Thirteenth Congress, Zhao Ziyang discovered that his allies of yesterday were adversaries far more formidable than Hu Yaobang. The group of old men, including Wang Zhen, Bo Yibo, Peng Zhen, Song Renqiong, and Chen Yun, were all displeased with the defeat of Deng Liqun at the Thirteenth Party Congress and all of them blamed Zhao Ziyang. After the Thirteenth Party Congress, Wang Zhen, on the pretext of taking a cure, left Beijing for Zhuhai. There, in the "presidential suite," he gathered the group of old men to "discuss politics." He was particularly livid over the disgrace of Deng Liqun, to whom he was bound by very old ties, and with whom he had closely collaborated in the more recent period. He said:

> Comrade Deng Liqun has the highest capability in theoretical matters within our Party and is the most staunch opponent of bourgeois liberalism. In addition, Comrade Bo Yibo was a major leader during the era of Mao Zedong and Zhou Enlai and has the highest capability in Marxism-Leninism. Look at what's happened to them. One was voted out and the other failed to receive one-third of the total vote, solely because of the important roles they played in criticizing Hu Yaobang and supporting Premier Zhao. Therefore, it has to be Zhao who alienated the delegates.

Zhao Ziyang got wind of this gathering and immediately sought in every possible way to coax Bo Yibo to his side and frequently went to seek his counsel. But he neglected Deng Liqun.

Zhao's other mistake was to underestimate Li Peng. At the Thirteenth Party Congress, Zhao was elected general secretary while he continued to hold the concurrent position of premier at least temporarily. When he had to choose the next premier, Zhao Ziyang proposed Tian Jiyun, whereas Deng Xiaoping, who wanted to preserve his reputation as a reformer, initially favored Wan Li. However, neither of these candidates had the favor of the old men. If Zhao had allied with Deng to support Wan Li, the appointment of Li Peng could have been avoided. But Zhao stuck stubbornly to Tian Jiyun and as a result neither Tian Jiyun nor Wan Li won the position. Therefore, Deng Xiaoping said: "It seems that only Li Peng is a candidate acceptable to all sides." Believing that Li Peng was not very capable or very quick and that he would be easy to handle, Zhao agreed. He thought with Li Peng as premier and Tian Jiyun as vice premier, he himself would be able to control the overall situation through the latter. Deng Xiaoping initially also thought that Li Peng had a low reputation, and therefore Deng advised Wan Li: "Now that Li Peng has become premier you should support him more in his work," to which Wan Li agreed. In general, Wan Li obeyed whatever Deng willed. Later Wan Li commented that he felt frustrated when at meetings with Li Peng he always felt that the kind of things Li Peng promoted were incorrect. However, they weren't easy to oppose and since he had promised Deng that he would support Li, Wan clammed up.

Zhao Ziyang never thought that his own adversaries could exploit the defects he'd attributed to Li Peng. Although slow witted, Li Peng understood that Tian Jiyun was a faithful ally of Zhao Ziyang's and that to gain power for himself, he had to stand on the side of the Chen Yun clique and ally himself with Yao Yilin. This would counteract the leverage that Zhao Ziyang and Tian Jiyun exercised over him.

After the 1987 Thirteenth Party Congress, Zhao Ziyang's position rapidly declined. The defeat of Deng Liqun and the shock waves that followed galvanized the hard-liners in the CCP. They immediately formed a new alliance with Li Peng. The shock wave of the Thirteenth Party Congress also spread out all over China as the procedure of allowing more candidates than seats resulted in the ousting of hard-liners in elections throughout many Party organizations. The most remarkable case was that of Chen Yuan, the son of Chen Yun, permanent member of the Beijing City Party Committee, who should have been promoted to secretary of the committee on the occasion of the Beijing City Party Congress. Defeated in the primaries, he was not even elected to a post in the Party committee. Zhao Ziyang and Li Peng had no choice but to have him appointed vice governor of the People's Bank of China.

Following the Thirteenth Party Congress, Zhao Ziyang soon began to discover that not only were his powers not strengthened, they were actually weakened. Power over economic work now shifted to Li Peng whereas the power over personnel was now in the hands of the old men from the "cadre group." As far as ideology and the news media were concerned, apart from the *People's Daily* and a few other units, all now conformed with the criteria laid down by Deng Liqun. The partisans of Zhao, who worked in bodies of the "Institute for the Reform of the Economic Structure" [*Tigaisuo*] sort, began to get the feeling that they were in a situation where the "environs were too narrow for heros to demonstrate their prowess": They resigned themselves to "crossing the ocean," which is to say they went abroad.

Notes

1. Summary draft of "Zhao Ziyang's Speech to High-Level Cadres from the Center, Provinces, and Cities" (January 28, 1987), in *Selection of Important Documents Since the Twelfth Party Congress* (*Shierdayilai zhongyao wenxian xuanbian*) (Beijing: People's Publishing House, 1986), vol. 3, p. 1252.

2. Zhao Ziyang, "Talk at a New Year's Gathering," January 29, 1987, in *Selection of Important Documents*, vol. 3, pp. 1265–1266.

3. See *Central News (Zhongyang ribao)* (New York), January 21, 1987.

4. *Selection of Important Documents*, vol. 3, p. 1252.

5. Zhao Ziyang, "Talk at a New Year's Gathering," p. 1261.

6. Only twelve days passed from the time of the acceptance of Hu Yaobang's formal resignation (January 16, 1987) to the issuing of Document Number Four (January 28, 1987).

7. For the complete text of this speech, see *Selection of Important Documents*, vol. 3, pp. 1397–1409.

8. Ibid., pp. 1307–1309.

9. Zhao Ziyang's idea was this: The only thing Hu Yaobang talked about was reform and opening up, never mentioning the struggle against bourgeois liberalism; the only thing Deng Liqun bothered to mention was anti–bourgeois liberalism, whereas he never mentioned reform and opening up. Zhao and Deng Xiaoping, however, talked about both.

10. See "Summary Draft of Mao Zedong's Oral Report to the Seventh Party Congress," April 1945.

11. This topic will be examined in my forthcoming book *The Mao Zedong Empire* as it has so far eluded any analysis.

12. Selected from "Interview with Members of a Zhao Ziyang Think Tank," reprinted in *China Spring (Zhongguo zhichun)*, October 1987.

13. *New Authoritarianism: Debate over the Basic Principles of Reform* (*Xin quanweizhuyi: Dui gaige lilun ganglingde lunzheng*), ed. Liu Jun and Li Lin (Beijing: Jingji Xueyuan Publishing House, 1989), p. 22.

12

The Self-Isolating "New Authoritarians"

An exchange that took place on March 6, 1989, between Deng Xiaoping and Zhao Ziyang is now famous.

> *Zhao Ziyang*: There's a new theory floating around the international arena, now being discussed in theoretical circles in China, called "new authoritarianism." The major point of the theory is that the modernization of backward countries inevitably passes through a phase in which it has to turn to a politics that cannot follow a Western-style democracy, but instead is centered on strong, authoritarian leaders who serve as the motivating force for change.
>
> *Deng Xiaoping*: I quite agree with this notion. But the specific phrasing has to be refined.[1]

In fact, this brief conversation marked the end of the short honeymoon between Deng Xiaoping and Zhao Ziyang. Zhao Ziyang wanted to sell to Deng what he considered to be a new Western theory, but he encountered a rebuff. Deng let him know that this theory didn't hold anything new in it for himself, that he had already practiced it himself, and that he disliked the phrase "new authoritarianism."

Deng Xiaoping was as usual very practical, whereas Zhao Ziyang committed a tactical error. The beating he and his young theorists took on the subject of the "new authoritarianism" was a major factor that led to his self-isolation and his eventual downfall. However, to this day some of Zhao Ziyang's young theorists have still not learned the lessons of this adventure. They have split into two factions. One continues to adhere to the proposal that democracy does not conform with Chinese conditions and that "new authoritarianism" is the panacea that, alone, can save China; the other faction has attempted to forget that at one time it even proposed the "new authoritarianism." It seems necessary therefore to provide a summary here of the history of the "new theory" along with the lessons learned.

As for Deng Xiaoping, his authoritarianism, which did not employ the qualifier "new," was born at the end of China's war with Vietnam in March 1979. However, Deng Xiaoping has always been a pragmatist. He has had no interest in searching in either the West or the East for a theoretical basis for his actions. He figured that he had enough power to dispense with all reference to theories. His own words were themselves gospel. He probably thought that "Dengism" was a more attractive formulation and more typically Chinese than this "new authoritarianism."

Things were different for Zhao Ziyang. He possessed neither the kind of raw authority nor the power wielded by Deng Xiaoping. He needed basic theories to reinforce his own positions. Although Zhao Ziyang had a personal interest in theory, he was not very competent in this field. He was a Deng Xiaoping–style pragmatist, so for theories he had to rely on the brains and pens of other people. Hu Yaobang once said to me that in 1976 when Mao launched the campaign criticizing Deng, Zhao Ziyang commented to Hu Yaobang that he would like to criticize Deng from the perspective of theory and analyze the theoretical origin of the Deng Xiaoping line. Thus it's not hard to see that even back then he had an interest in theory. But he was acting on a basically pragmatic impulse: sticking close to the anti-Deng plan put in place by Mao. Mao's death and Deng's reemergence on the political scene deprived Zhao Ziyang of the opportunity to make his theoretical investigations. Zhao Ziyang's attempts at producing such a theory did not yield any real results.

Zhao Ziyang's passion for theory reemerged on the occasion of the student demonstrations of late 1986 and Hu Yaobang's subsequent fall from power. That was natural, for Zhao would now be replacing Hu as the supreme leader, even though his role as supreme leader would only be temporary and somewhat nominal (there was still the emperor).

Zhao thus needed a theoretical apparatus. He figured that a mastery at the same time both theoretical and strategic would allow him to deal with pressures from both the masses and the higher levels in the Party and help him to avoid following in the footsteps of Hu Yaobang.

Just at that time, the young theorists of the think tank group under Zhao Ziyang delivered up the concept of "new authoritarianism" that they had blindly copied from the West. I won't comment on the differences between the "new authoritarianism" of the Chinese theorists and their Western masters because one can instead directly consult the evaluations of their Chinese students by Western teachers.[2] Instead I will analyze what united or divided Deng Xiaoping and Zhao Ziyang on the issue of "new authoritarianism." Their differences were in effect a major cause of later political changes in China. They came together on the existing idea of "one center, two basic points" [*yige zhongxin, liangge jibendian*] as Zhao Ziyang had declared in his political report at the 1987 Thirteenth Party Congress. This formula delivered the political and economic program of China for the next fifty years. Created by Zhao Ziyang's éminence grise, Bao Tong, it was deeply appreciated by Deng Xiaoping, upon whose fundamental guiding ideology it was based. So much so that even after May 1989, when Zhao Ziyang was dismissed and Bao Tong was arrested, Deng Xiaoping still persisted in his belief that "not a single word could be changed" in Zhao Ziyang's Thirteenth Congress political report. The "one center," we may recall, refers to taking economic construction as the primary goal whereas the "two basic points" refer to adhering to reform and opening up to the outside world while at the same time upholding the Four Cardinal Principles and maintaining opposition to bourgeois liberalism. Opening up thus ruled the economy, an area where liberalism and autonomy were authorized, since "it makes little difference whether a cat is black or white," as long as it can stimulate economic growth. But in politics a dictatorial and despotic system at all times was draped in a coat of lead. Such was the ideological essence of an aging Deng Xiaoping. If the "new authoritarianism" of Zhao Ziyang and his think tanks had not gone beyond this definition, perhaps the honeymoon between Deng and Zhao would not have ended so quickly.

Two great developments occurred after the Thirteenth Congress that rapidly intensified the conflicts among the various cliques in the CCP: the aborted price reform and the alliance between Li Peng and the Chen Yun clique. These two events constituted a challenge to Zhao Ziyang's power. Zhao Ziyang's think tanks responded by deploying their "new authoritarianism" with fanfare. This was a bad idea.

The price reform in 1988 was proposed by Deng Xiaoping himself. Zhao Ziyang had earlier adopted the economic views of Li Yining, who recommended "circumventing" [*raoguo*] price reform. At that time, two opposing points of view divided economists. One school of thought was led by Wu Jinglian, who proposed loosening up prices and tightening control of money markets while carrying out an overall reform in the interrelated areas of prices, property rights, salaries, taxes, finance, and laws. This would lead to a new system in which "the state adjusts the market and the market guides the enterprises" [*guojia tiaojie shichang, shichang yindao qiye*]; it was also a progressive reform agenda for "short-term rather than long-term pain." The other school of thought was represented by Li Yining, who proposed "circumventing" price reform and focusing instead on reform of the "ownership system" [*suoyouzhi*], that is, a reform of property rights. Price reform could not, however, really be "circumvented." Establishing a new system in which "the state adjusts the market and the market guides the enterprises" requires three interdependent conditions:

1. A market must exist allowing for equal competition. That requires in turn a system of reasonable prices.

2. Economic entities must emerge as equally competitive in the market, which is to say that independent enterprises must enjoy property rights and autonomy from the state.
3. A state-run macro control system must be established to employ economic and legal means, including taxation, finance, and laws, to protect the equal and free competition in the market.

By "circumventing" price reform this system of the "market guides the enterprises" could not be realized, for it is prices that constitute the most basic market signal. When the market signal is distorted and chaotic because of the dual-price system, reasonable distribution of resources, equal competition among enterprises, and increasing efficiencies cannot be realized. The failure to form a market with equal competition, moreover, makes "the state adjusting the market" nothing but hollow words. The present dual-price system can only lead to chaos in the economy and enormous waste of resources along with corruption.* Thus, Zhao Ziyang's proposal for "circumventing" price reform did nothing but delay the transition from the old economic system to a new market economy and thereby bungled the opportunity for reform.

In July 1988, in meetings with foreign guests, Deng Xiaoping to the surprise of everyone abruptly proposed to "smash the obstacles to price reform." Time and again he declared that he wanted to "force the five passes and decapitate six generals" [*guo wuguan, zhan liujiang*], that is, go full steam ahead, and "even though there might be errors we will never retreat." He also said, "We cannot avoid risks and these risks cannot be circumvented for we must march forward." Then: "We don't fear big waves, but must march forward against them in order to force our way through."[3]

This resolution took Zhao Ziyang by surprise. Moreover, some of Deng's words were aimed at him personally, notably the expression, "these risks cannot be circumvented for we must march forward." Zhao tried to find out just who had put these ideas in Deng's head and questioned the economist Wu Jinglian. But Wu replied: "Although I had always argued that price reform cannot be circumvented, I dared not suggest such a thing in a year when inflation was going through the roof, for rival forces have already attributed the inflation to the decision to go ahead with price reform." It was perfectly possibly that Deng himself, irritated by reform being restrained by Zhao's evasions, became impatient and decided to talk about "forcing the way." Once the or-

---

*For a scathing exposé by a Chinese scientist of the enormous waste, inefficiencies, and environmental degradation produced by China's planned economy, see He Bochuan, *China on the Edge: The Crisis of Ecology and Development* (*Shan'aoshangde Zhongguo*) (Guiyang: Guizhou People's Publishing House, 1989), trans. by Jenny Holdaway et al. (San Francisco: China Books and Periodicals, 1991).

der was given, Zhao Ziyang didn't dare to "circumvent" the obstacle. He immediately organized various groups among economists and charged them to come up with their own proposals for price reform for discussion at the upcoming summer Beidaihe meetings.

After a month of intense activity, the Politburo met in Beidaihe from August 15 to 17. Here "the preliminary agenda on reform in prices and salaries" was discussed and approved in principle. The major content of the agenda included the following: the necessity of reform in prices and salaries, major principles for guiding the reform, a preliminary outline for reform for 1989–1993, a preliminary agenda for reform in 1989, possible major risks to be encountered in the reform and the basic strategies to deal with them, and ancillary reform measures that must be adopted.

However, prior to the passing down of this preliminary agenda, its content was leaked to the public. This immediately provoked people throughout the nation to engage in panic buying of materials and runs on banks and saving accounts that forced Deng to retreat on the issue before he forced his way through even the first pass.

In reality, that wave of panic buying was nothing unusual. It seemed to me that the consequences of price reform could have been handled much more easily than those of the slaughter carried out on June 4, 1989. In reality, the panic buying and run on banks rapidly reduced the stocks of excess materials gathering dust in warehouses and brought in a hefty amount of cash. In this sense, it was something of a benefit for the economy. Moreover, the panic appeared to be a temporary phenomenon and there was no sign that it had created political instability. If Deng Xiaoping had applied the same determination he showed in carrying out the June 4, 1989, massacre—if he had truly acted on his policy to "force the five passes and decapitate six generals" and carried through on price reform, along with the political reform that he last proposed in 1986—this would have made possible a coordinated development of the political and economic systems toward democracy and a market. Then the situation in China would not be what it is today and China's position as the leader of reform among socialist countries would not have been lost. The crown of the Nobel Peace Prize could have been placed on Deng Xiaoping's head instead of Gorbachev's.

But it was a succession of bungled opportunities. Deng Xiaoping blew the last opportunity in his life by failing to smash the shackles of the old system and move China toward a market economy and democratic politics. He relied instead on despotism and the violence inherent to the old system to push the country toward historical disaster.

Deng Xiaoping's shift from the "helmsman of reform" to a "historical criminal" was itself a historical inevitability. His retreat and weakness shown in the 1988 price reform and his maniacal act of risking everything on a single venture during the June 4, 1989, slaughter were also historical inevitabilities.

Here I will give a brief analysis of the origin of the historical tragedy that he directed, which arose from his guiding ideology and the nature of the foundation of his power.

Deng Xiaoping often said that he could do little with two weak arms, neither the one that worked for reform and opening up nor the one that struggled against bourgeois liberalism. He accused both Hu Yaobang and Zhao Ziyang of weakness in the struggle against liberalism. One such criticism could perhaps be made of Hu Yaobang, for indeed, Hu believed that the struggle against liberalism would have destructive effects on reform and opening up, and therefore he was usually lenient. However, to accuse him of only appearing to obey, of growing lax and weak, would not be justified. As for Zhao Ziyang, he had never been soft in the struggle against liberalism. He had, as I can recall, presided over the expulsion of Fang Lizhi, Liu Binyan, and Wang Ruowang as well as Wu Zuguang, Wang Ruoshui, and Zhang Xianyang. The only one he protected was Su Shaozhi.

Of course, to a great extent, Zhao Ziyang's support for antiliberalism was a strategic move to conform with Deng's guiding ideology. Hu Yaobang's fall from power resulted precisely from his difference with Deng on this issue, so Zhao was forced to go along with Deng on the subject of antiliberalism. Superficially the two "arms" of Deng Xiaoping were in appearance equally strong, but when conflicts became sharper and more intense, he temporarily ignored reform and openness and put all his money on the struggle against liberalism. His comportment in the face of student movements in both 1986 and 1989 testified to this uncertainty. That's why Deng in the end could not become "the helmsman of reform."

In addition, Deng's foundation of power rests primarily on Party cadres. It does not, as some people think, depend on the military, even though the last formal position he held was that of chairman of the Central Military Commission. Indeed, there is great plausibility to this view. The tradition in the CCP is that the Party directly guides the military and the military is dependent on the power of the Party. Even during the "Cultural Revolution," when local Party organizations were paralyzed and a system of military supervision put the PLA at the height of its power, supreme command over the military was still under the authority of the Party Center. Whoever controls the supreme power over the Central Committee is able to command the military. That's why in the late 1960s and early 1970s Lin Biao was never able to gain ultimate authority over the military. At that time a slogan was popularized in the military that went like this: "The People's Liberation Army was founded by Chairman Mao, but it is commanded by Vice Chairman Lin." Upon hearing that, Mao reacted by commenting, "What? The founder cannot be the commander?" During the "Cultural Revolution" actual supreme command over the military was exercised by Zhou Enlai, who was then in charge of the routine work of the Politburo Standing Committee and was not even a member of the Central Military Commission or the National Defense Council.

As for evaluating Deng's authority, it cannot be determined solely from the actual positions he has held. Starting in December 1981, he served as chairman of the Central Military Commission for eight and a half years, but this was partially a matter of chance. After Hua Guofeng resigned as chairman of both the Party and the Central Military Commission, the majority of Party leaders wanted Deng to become the Party chairman. But he refused and instead recommended Hu Yaobang for the post. Initially, Deng Xiaoping also refused the position of chairman of the Central Military Commission, but he could not find an alternative candidate. Allowing Hu Yaobang to take on two leadership posts would have been in contradiction to the principle of dividing power among top leaders that was proposed during the criticism of Hua Guofeng. Deng therefore agreed to serve temporarily as chairman of the Central Military Commission. If Luo Ruiqing had not died in 1978, Deng would certainly have recommended him for the posts. For when Deng had been restored to the position of vice chairman of the Central Military Commission and army chief of staff he had in fact proposed Luo for the post. Deng's plan was to let Luo Ruiqing exercise control over the military. After Luo died, several candidates were available to Deng, among them Geng Biao and Yang Yong, but neither of them quite suited him. Then Yang Yong died, and Deng finally chose Yang Shangkun. But since Yang Shangkun was already quite elderly and not very highly esteemed in the military, he could only hold this post temporarily. Such were the circumstances in which Deng Xiaoping "provisionally" became chairman of the Central Military Commission for eight and a half years.

As for Hu Yaobang, he would only serve as Party chairman for one year (1981–1982). Just prior to the 1982 Twelfth Party Congress, Hu Qiaomu and Deng Liqun got together and altered the Party constitution, eliminating the position of Party chairman. It was at this moment that the role of Party general secretary was limited, so that henceforth he could convene but not preside over Party meetings. This effectively meant that since Deng Xiaoping had been unwilling to serve as Party chairman, no one else could ever assume this post. Thus, the elimination of the chairmanship gave an abstract character to the supreme power at the heart of the Party. The true power did not belong to Hu Yaobang, but needless to say, Deng Xiaoping. Eliminating the Party chairmanship signified that supreme power over the Party was practically speaking conferred on Deng Xiaoping, who had no official positions. Such was the intention with which Hu Qiaomu and Deng Liqun modified the Party constitution, and such was the source of power of Deng Xiaoping, who was consequently able, without striking a blow, to dismiss Hu Yaobang and Zhao Ziyang, his two Party general secretaries.

After the dismissal of Hu Yaobang in January 1987, Deng Xiaoping's power base shrank considerably. On the one hand, he'd attacked and repressed the social democratic movement that had supported his reforms, and on the other, he criticized and dismissed the democratic forces in the Party that had made great contributions to the progress of reform. Henceforth what remained on his political left were the forces of dogmatism and violence of the "power is in the barrel of a gun" school, represented by the Chen Yun and Wang Zhen cliques, respectively, and on his right, the semireformers who like Zhao Ziyang wanted to ally political totalitarianism with economic freedom. Deng himself remained above the two cliques in order to implement the kind of political equilibrium strategy that Mao had also practiced in his later years, ceaselessly swinging back and forth from the antireformers to the semireformers, at times supporting one and at other times supporting the other. In such a deadly political situation, it is difficult to imagine how reform could be pushed ahead in China. After the fall of Hu Yaobang, reform became paralyzed. With the gunfire of June 4, the bells began to toll.

I have already provided an analysis of the Chen Yun, Wang Zhen, Hu Qiaomu, and Deng Liqun cliques. They represent the alliance among hardliners, that is, the dogmatists and the military faction who remain stuck in the Stalinist era of Chinese Communist Party history.* Although they did not have control over major political and military power in the eras of Mao Zedong and Deng Xiaoping, they influenced every major struggle within the CCP and I think they will continue to influence future political developments in China.

As for the Zhao Ziyang partisans, they are a new political force that emerged toward the end of the ten-year reform. They are middle-aged and young intellectuals who see themselves as an elite corps. Most of them have had a series of political and social experiences, including that of "rebellion" and being sent down to the countryside, which they had acquired in the "Cultural Revolution." Quite a few of them have connections with high-level politics and families with superior social standing and are fond of pursuing political power. On returning to the cities following the "Cultural Revolution" the younger ones entered universities, where they majored in the social sciences and liberal arts, and on graduating worked in organizations directly under the Central Committee. Some of the middle-aged people have taken ad-

---

*For an analysis of the ideological and policy position of the Chinese conservatives led by Chen Yun, see Lawrence R. Sullivan, "Reactionary Modernism in China: Cultural Conservatism and Technical Economism in Communist Ideology and Policy Since June 1989," in *The Aftermath of the 1989 Tiananmen Crisis in Mainland China*, ed. Bih-jaw Lin, Maria Hsia Chang, George P. Chen, John F. Cooper, Michael C. Davis, Barry Naughton, W. Gary Vause, and Margaret Y. K. Woo (Boulder: Westview, 1992), pp. 15–38.

vantage of all kinds of contacts they have with middle-echelon leaders to proceed directly behind the scenes of power, where they have formed groups of councillors, or éminences grises. For instance, the Chinese Rural Development Issues Research Group [*Zhongguo Nongcun Fajan Wenti Yanjiuzu*] established in 1980 was founded by Deng Yingtao, who organized his rural "brothers" with the support of his father, Deng Liqun. That was the first such organization to assist high-ranking officials. Deng Yingtao had spent some time in a village and was surrounded by middle-aged and young people interested in politics with whom he had developed close ties. Deng Liqun believed that they constituted a political force that could be used.

In September 1979, Hu Yaobang requested that I help draft a speech to be given by Ye Jianying on the thirtieth anniversary of the People's Republic. Deng Liqun was also a member of that drafting group. At the end of September, at a meeting to discuss the speech project, Deng commented,

> In the future these kinds of drafting tasks will be numerous, and it won't suffice to gather some people together at the last moment to handle them. We must construct a permanent organization. For instance, quite a few young intellectuals are actually ensconced in the countryside, where some of them are Party secretaries of People's Communes. With their rich experience, they should not be left indefinitely in the lower ranks, they should be promoted so that they can play a role. One can provisionally call this structure the "Chinese Rural Development Issues Research Group." Since they are from the rural areas and are familiar with conditions there, it would be better for them to study the situation in the countryside first and then move on to other issues in the future.

When this particular organization was first set up, Deng Liqun was in charge. Later, when Zhao Ziyang was transferred from Sichuan to Beijing to become a vice premier in charge of current affairs and economic reform, some of the people from that group gradually moved over and served as his aides. They worked as a rural development group until 1984, when they established the Institute for the Reform of the Economic Structure [*Tigaisuo*]. At that time, both a committee [*Tigaiwei*] and an association [*Tigaihui*] for structural reform already existed. The former was a state organization in charge of economic structural reform under the State Council and the latter was an academic research organization. But these two organizations were staffed by government officials, experts, and scholars, and they were not well situated to perceive the will of the leaders. Thus they could not be used as councillors in the conception of proposals and projects. Since Zhao Ziyang was fond of a type of politics in which advisers played a major role, opportunists curried his favor by setting up, parallel to the two existing outfits, this Institute for the Reform of the Economic Structure.

This institute was neither an academic outfit nor a state outfit, but purely and simply a private body of personal advisers. The institute faced an immediate crisis, however. Right after the premature defeat of price reform in 1988 and just before the June Fourth slaughter, the elites of the Institute for the Reform of the Economic Structure had begun to call for "the great victorious escape" and left China en masse, thanks to various relatives, in order to "perfect" themselves.

Zhao Ziyang's fondness for adviser politics led him to ignore the necessity of uniting two important forces as possible supporters of his reform: the reformers who found themselves more often in bed with leaders of the Party and government, and the centrists who could have been won over to his side. His opposition to Hu Yaobang surely lost Zhao the trust of many in the reform forces, but if he had paid attention to uniting with this force it would have been possible for him to regain their support. Actually, Zhao gained support from some of them, for instance, Hu Qili and others whom Zhao believed could be swayed. However, he kept his distance from reformers of a character or a spirit too independent, such as Wan Li, Xi Zhongxun, Li Chang, and others and protected himself also from centrists like Wang Renzhong. All of these people were more experimental than he was and of a theory level higher than his, but they lacked much real authority, and therefore, from the point of view of pragmatism, Zhao reckoned it was useless to encumber himself with them. He preferred to expend his energy earning the good graces of hard-line opponents of reform like Bo Yibo, who he thought, since Bo wielded the authority to oppose Hu Yaobang, would certainly be a useful man. But events—notably the final turning against Zhao of Bo Yibo—revealed how vain these efforts really were. It seemed unnecessary to look for trouble.

Zhao equally neglected the reformers who counted among the intellectuals. He mistrusted people like Fang Lizhi and Qian Jiaju, who enjoyed a certain notoriety and who had independent minds along with the courage to come up with opposition views. One day when Qian Jiaju was giving a speech at a meeting of the Chinese People's Political Consultative Conference on the issue of education, his thirty-minute speech was interrupted thirty-one times by applause. After the meeting, Zhao Ziyang paid a visit to Deng Pufang, Deng Xiaoping's son, and asked him to research the "Fang Lizhi phenomenon." He said to Deng Pufang: "How come when we're so nice to those intellectuals they turn around and oppose us? And why is it that those who oppose us win such great applause? Fang Lizhi is like that and now so is Qian Jiaju. How do we explain this? It's something that deserves study. I myself call it the 'Fang Lizhi phenomenon.' What can we do to avoid this kind of phenomenon in the future?"

Zhao Ziyang knew that Deng Xiaoping also didn't like Fang Lizhi and certainly Zhao expected Deng Pufang to pass the message along. In general, Zhao was ambivalent toward intellectuals. He only liked the kind of advisory intellectuals who worked at his institutes and was very cautious toward more independent-minded ones.

In this way, Zhao Ziyang narrowed his own basis of power. He ended up with a power structure designed by his advisers consisting of a single leader supported by a bunch of subservient power elites. Therefore, around the time of the 1987 Thirteenth Congress when Zhao Ziyang's power was at its peak, he relied primarily on Deng Xiaoping and the temporary alliance with the anti–Hu Yaobang cabal. When Deng Xiaoping realized the necessity of forcing the passage of price reform, his good feelings for Zhao turned cooler, and at the same time, the alliance between Zhao and the anti–Hu Yaobang cabal went up in smoke.

The behavior of Premier Li Peng following the failure of price reform was also of extreme importance. Li Peng, whom Zhao looked down upon, was determined to form an alliance with the Chen Yun clique in order to challenge Zhao Ziyang's power. Zhao Ziyang's advisers had certainly noted the importance of these intervening changes in 1988, but the prescription they raised against such a challenge was summed up in the catch phrase "new authoritarianism," a tactic that ended by completely isolating Zhao Ziyang.

In the "Commentary on the New Authoritarianism" [*Xin quanweizhuyi shuping*] that plagiarizes the beginning of the *Communist Manifesto* it was written:

> Perhaps sensitive people have long noticed that there is a weird specter flapping its wings flying through the forest of ideology, and that is new authoritarianism.
> …
> At the forum commemorating the ninetieth anniversary of the 1898 Reform Movement,* Ms. Dai Qing made an astonishing pronouncement indicating that the reform and modernization on mainland China requires a politically powerful person, a kind of politically powerful person who has emerged in the various East Asian countries over the last decade. …
> The new authoritarianism does not emphasize the body politic, but the leader. A democratic body politic may or may not generate leaders with authority as does the totalitarian system. In reality, various ways exist for a great leader to emerge who is able to lead a country to realize its modernization smoothly. Some are elected, some inherit power, some are appointed, and some come to power as a result of a coup d'état. We can find many relevant examples in contemporary world history. …
> The new authoritarianism does not only emphasize the leader, but also focuses on the clique of decisionmakers who enjoy cordial collaboration with the leader.
> In addition, the new authoritarianism also emphasizes wise views, decisive actions, and the power to eliminate any obstacles along with a super reactive ability.[4]

---

*A last-ditch attempt at political, economic, and military reform near the end of the Qing dynasty (1644–1911) that was effectively terminated by the interventions of the Empress Dowager Cixi.

Dai Qing's astonishing pronouncement goes something like this:

"Only with accumulated power and the use of autocratic authority can things be carried out with dispatch." That seemed to have been the pattern followed by the late president of Taiwan, Chiang Ching-kuo, for the last ten or twenty years of his life; it may well be the only model we have to follow today. When Chiang died, mourners lined the streets in the thousands, waiting as his hearse went past. All the fresh flowers on an island renowned for its abundance of flowers were sold out. Why? He arranged for an end to the rule of his own family and lifted the bans on opposition parties and restrictions on the press. "All right, I am an autocrat, but I am the last. I am using my power to ensure the introduction of democracy. ..."

Given our unique situation, only an enlightened autocrat can bring an end to autocracy in China.[5]

The article by Zhao's adviser Chen Yizi "The Developmental Model for Establishing a 'Hard Government and Soft Economy'" was even more specific. He proposed that the developmental phase in which the average per capita income is between $300 and $4000 "requires the concentration of political power and the dispersion of economic power, to place in leadership positions minority elites who represent the interests of the majority and control the direction of the state, and to realize, in the middle of the next century, the goal of a market economy and democratic politics."[6] Which is to say that the Chinese people must, for another half century, submit to a despotic totalitarian regime and struggle painfully at the hands of a grandiose leader and a minority of "elites" before being able to enjoy the gift of a market economy and democratic politics. The marvelous scenes proposed by the Chinese partisans of the "new authoritarianism" can be summed up in a few words:

The partisans of "new authoritarianism" believe in their hearts the wise and heroic leader is Zhao Ziyang, not Deng Xiaoping. The interventions of a Deng Xiaoping, which may be compared to those of the Empress Dowager Cixi of the Qing dynasty, must cease; a group of elites in profound and tacit agreement with the wise leader, the councillors of Zhao Ziyang, will dictate the course of China's development until the middle of the next century and only then return political power to the people.

Not since the days of Yüan Shih-k'ai in the 1910s has a theory of such despotic dictatorship been called for in black and white. Even when Chiang K'ai-shek proclaimed that it was necessary to have "one doctrine, one leader, and one party," he said that it was a necessary thing during a transitory period of "political tutelage [*xuncheng*] and war and chaos, but promised to pass rapidly to constitutional government" [*xianzheng*]. Even the CCP itself has always advocated democracy despite the fact that it implements the most ruthless dictatorial autocracy.

It's precisely this kind of bare-faced totalitarian character of their theory that isolated Zhao Ziyang and his advisers and put them in an unfavorable situation. But they were so confident in their wisdom and strategy that they were unable to notice how desperate their situation had become. Literally intoxicated by their theory, they lost all sense of reality. From the following conversation with one of Zhao's advisers we can see the degree their drunkenness attained:

Question: We at the lower levels of the Party think that the fall from power of Hu Yaobang effectively eliminated one wing of the reform group. It also caused the Zhao Ziyang pragmatist group to lose its protective screen, thereby making it more difficult to carry reform forward. How do you see it?

Answer: The problem is not as you have described it. Hu Yaobang's fall from power and Comrade Ziyang's taking over both the Party and government made it easier to take initiatives. Following Hu Yaobang's resignation, various factions lacked a leader and naturally they clung to Zhao Ziyang. Comrade Ziyang did not stir things up and instead acted with great wisdom and used effective tactics in attracting Hu Yaobang's people to his side. After Zhu Houze and Ruan Chongwu were dismissed from their positions, Comrade Ziyang gave them posts at the State Council. Although their positions were not as important as before, this kind of protection acted to win Hu Yaobang's people to his side.

A big politician and top leader must have a sense of detachment—to stay above various cliques and schools and have the ability to manipulate them. Comrade Xiaoping had such an ability and so does Comrade Ziyang.

Zhao Ziyang understands Chinese politics whereas Hu Yaobang didn't. Because of this, Comrade Ziyang places great emphasis on maintaining relationships with various factions, especially the relationship with the conservatives who oppose reform. Keeping things to himself, he does not set others against him. Hu Yaobang, on the contrary, oversimplified Chinese politics.

Question: As you just mentioned, Zhao Ziyang places great emphasis on personal relationships, especially with the conservatives. This is a very interesting point. How's his relationship with Bo Yibo?

Answer: Comrade Ziyang once told us the importance of converting resistance into initiative, a very wise strategy. The more conservative a person is, the harder Zhao Ziyang tries to win him over. For instance, on the issue of a contract system among medium and small-scale enterprises, Zhao Ziyang asked Peng Zhen and Bo Yibo for advice. Those old folks need to be respected and what they fear the most is to be ignored. Once you understand that mentality and frequently seek their advice and opinions, it's much easier to get things done.

In reality, Peng Zhen, Bo Yibo, and the like have no real wisdom and are unable to come up with specific agendas. Once you propose an agenda and report it to them, they will then see you as a subordinate and will agree with you. Whenever we conduct activities such as forums we usually go to Bo Yibo and ask him to attend and give a speech. And in his speeches, he at least mentions words like "reform and opening up." Prior to publishing any materials, we would first let Bo Yibo have a look. If he does not come up with explicit oppositional views, we then disseminate it throughout the country. The biggest advantage to doing things this way is to console them and prevent them from speaking out.

As for the reform agenda and propaganda materials, once they have read them in advance and have given their approval it's very difficult for them to publicly oppose these later. Hu Yaobang did not do well in this regard. He did not show any respect toward those old folks and offended them.

Question: What about Zhao's relationship with Yang Shangkun? It seems that Yang Shangkun has become increasingly important.

Answer: Comrade Ziyang also gives great emphasis to his relationship with Yang Shangkun and to win his support and understanding always consults him on important issues. You are right. Yang Shangkun's role is very important, for we can say that if it had not been for Yang, Hu Yaobang would have never fallen from power.

Question: A lot of Beijing folks say that the antagonism between Zhao Ziyang and the conservatives is becoming increasingly strained. A few days ago a slogan appeared in Beijing that goes something like this: "Down with Peng [Zhen], Bo [Yibo], Hu [Qiaomu], and Deng [Liqun]." I heard from someone who is close to Peng Zhen, that Peng and Hu Qiaomu and others suspect that the slogan was invented by Zhao Ziyang's people and therefore they now hate him. What do you think of this?

Answer: In fact, the antagonism in different views is widely known. However, I don't think that the conflict between Comrade Ziyang and Peng Zhen and Bo Yibo has gone public. The conflict between Comrade Ziyang and Hu Qiaomu, Deng Liqun, and Xiong Fu has been publicized to a certain extent, but we cannot be held responsible.

Comrade Ziyang has warned us to be poised when confronting trouble and self-restrained. We did not interfere with Hu Qiaomu and Deng Liqun's territories. To our surprise, the trees may prefer calm, but the wind will not subside. Those people aim at invading our territory and have come up with such criticisms as "the fundamental source of bourgeois liberalism is found in the economic realm; a commodity economy is the origin of bourgeois liberalism; those who talk about capitalism are criticized, whereas those who practice capitalism are left free." Comrade Ziyang has had no choice but to halt this wind.

Question: The reason why Hu Qiaomu, Deng Liqun, and Xiong Fu are so savage is that they have their backstage supporters, namely Peng Zhen and Bo Yibo. In addition, they also have the support of the leftist, high-ranking generals in the military. I'm not sure if Zhao Ziyang and you people are sufficiently vigilant on this matter.

Answer: As I have said, Comrade Ziyang has emphasized his relationships with Yang Shangkun and also with other high-ranking generals.

Question: To tell you the truth, the reason why I'm here today is that I've heard some unsettling news. That is, a group of middle-aged and young military officials who are the offspring of high-ranking leaders frequently talk about Zhao

Ziyang and you advisers in private. They have said: "Let them do what they want. Sooner or later they will get into trouble. At that point, one Deng Liqun will solve all the problems. Don't worry, the world will be ours sooner or later!" These people are extremely ambitious. I've heard that they are connected with Bo Yibo, Wang Zhen, Chen Yun, and the like. On this matter you people must be super cautious and defend yourselves.

Answer. We're not country bumpkins. In particular, Comrade Ziyang's political acumen is extremely well honed. I can tell you that Comrade Ziyang once gave us a hint: "Let's deal with each other like gentlemen and not become easily agitated. We'll mind our business and they will mind theirs. If, however, they don't respect us or act in an unruly manner, I, old Zhao, will not wait to be killed. When necessary we must employ appropriate measures."[7]

In point of fact, this kind of political strategy practiced by Zhao Ziyang and his political advisers was effective during the phase of uniting the conservatives against Hu Yaobang. But it became ineffective once Hu Yaobang fell from power. The conservatives may have united with Zhao Ziyang in opposing Hu Yaobang, but they would not join him in opposing Deng Liqun. The conflict between Zhao Ziyang and Deng Liqun, especially after Deng Liqun's defeat at the 1987 Thirteenth Congress, increased the vigilance of the conservatives against Zhao Ziyang. It was in the midst of all this that the propaganda concentrated by Zhao Ziyang and his advisors on the "new authoritarianism" attracted general attention.

At the beginning of this chapter, I described the common points of agreement between Zhao Ziyang and Deng Xiaoping on the theory of "new authoritarianism," that is, the one center and two basic points. Now, I would like to note their differences. Deng Xiaoping's own concept of "new authoritarianism" primarily emphasizes the "Party's leadership," that is, upholding the one-party totalitarian system. It does not include the concept of a power struggle inside the Party. Deng Xiaoping believed that although he did not hold any supreme leadership position, it was obvious that he enjoyed the highest authority. As he described it, the core of the first generation was Mao Zedong, and the core of the second generation was himself. As for Zhao Ziyang's version of "new authoritarianism," under the premise of affirming Deng Xiaoping's one-party totalitarian system, Zhao also emphasized two other aspects.

First is the so-called decisive and dictatorial aspect of government and the struggle against "Empress Cixi's intervention in politics," which were aimed at shifting totalitarian power into Zhao's hands. Who was meant by the metaphor "Empress Cixi"? Some people say it stands for Deng Xiaoping. Others say it refers to the entire "gang of old men" who constantly interfere in politics. Either way, it's basically the same.

The most explicit on this point was Zhao's adviser Wu Guoguang. As soon as he arrived in California, in February 1989, Wu gave an interview in which he asserted that "the most urgent task at present in China is to concentrate all power of the Party, government, and military in the hands of one leader—Zhao Ziyang." During the defeat of price reform, from early 1988 to spring 1989, the propaganda on "new authoritarianism" by Zhao Ziyang and his advisers reached a tremendous pitch, heard all the way from China to Hong Kong and overseas. One Hong Kong magazine, for instance, published an article entitled "What if Zhao Ziyang becomes a dictator?" that seemed to echo Wu's interview.

This propaganda offensive for "new authoritarianism" carried out by Zhao Ziyang's advisers, who themselves believed they thoroughly understood Chinese politics, naturally rendered a great disservice to Zhao Ziyang. The Deng Liquns of China couldn't wait to send that treasure chest of precious documents to Deng Xiaoping. "Look at what Zhao Ziyang is trying to do!" Even if Deng Xiaoping at that time was willing to shift his power to Zhao, those old men surrounding Deng were unwilling to do so. They immediately decided to unite with Li Peng and take back whatever power Zhao Ziyang still had. According to the theory of "new authoritarianism" of Zhao Ziyang and his advisers, a real leader had to demonstrate real political wisdom to succeed, far from the eyes of the people, in garnering the powers held, in a scattered fashion, by Deng Xiaoping and the other old men. This theory ended in a diametrically opposite result: The latter joined forces to protect their own power, and then Zhao found himself isolated.

The second aspect Zhao emphasized was the so-called power elite politics [*quanli jingying zhengzhi*]. The "power elite" guiding the new authoritarian system that Zhao and his people proposed to establish refers to the formation of "a power elite clique." This would be constituted by "the political elite who are less than ten percent of the population" who were "the most knowledgeable, possessed the most vision, and were the most capable." They would be masters over "the eighty and ninety percent of the masses who have low levels of education, lack any ability to participate in politics, and don't understand citizen rights."[8] These "elites" are not chosen by the masses, but are appointed by the totalitarian dictator and are responsible solely to him.

It was precisely this "elite" politics, totally outside the control of the public and acting as a preserve for corrupt bureaucrats, that from now on sabotaged economic reform in China.

In 1987 after Hu Yaobang's fall from power, advocates of the "new authoritarianism" defended "official profiteering" and corruption claiming that it was beneficial to the development of a commodity economy in China. This encouraged a massive expansion of official profiteering and corruption that aroused a screaming popular opposition. Indeed, popular discontent played a key role in bringing about the attempted price reform in 1988 and igniting the democratic movement in 1989: In both situations, the Chinese people opposed the totalitarian government, which included Zhao Ziyang, who was now considered to be the very incarnation of corruption.

When in spring 1989, the student and democratic movement roared forth, Zhao Ziyang found himself trapped between two poles: On the one side was the government of Li Peng, supported by Deng Xiaoping, Chen Yun, and the "gang of old men"; on the other, the mass of students and those citizens who wanted to be rid of the despotic regime and realize democracy. And when Zhao finally realized just how isolated he was and rushed to Tiananmen Square to talk to the students, it was too late.

Notes

1. A writer who claimed that he interviewed Zhao Ziyang at the beginning of 1989 and who later wrote an article described how he inquired of Zhao whether he agreed with the theory of new authoritarianism and Zhao indicated that he didn't. However, the writer did not cite Zhao's own words in composing the article and because of this we can overlook this interview. Interested readers can consult the article by Li Xianglu, "Why the Separation of Powers is Correct," *The Chinese Intellectual* (*Zhishifenzi*) (New York), Autumn 1990.

2. The young theoretical advisers involved in Zhao Ziyang's think tanks all drew upon the work of the U.S. political scientist and Harvard professor Samuel P. Huntington. But in his own words Huntington has said that the problems China confronts in its current progression toward modernization do not derive from a lack of central power and that the advocates of "new authoritarianism" in China have distorted his writings. See *World Economic Herald* [*Shijie jingji daobao*], March 1989.

3. See Deng Xiaoping's two conversations, one with the president of Guinea, July 9, 1988, and the second with the U.S. Secretary of State George Schultz, July 15, 1988.

4. Wu Jiaxiang, "Discourse on New Authoritarianism," in *New Authoritarianism: Debate over the Basic Principles of Reform* (*Xin quanweizhuyi: Dui gaige lilun ganglingde lunzheng*), ed. Liu Jun and Li Lin (Beijing: Jingji Xueyuan Publishing House, 1989), p. 34 [Wu Jiaxiang was formerly a researcher at the Office of Policy Research (*Tiaoyanshi*) under the General Office (*Bangongting*) of the CCP Central Committee. He was purged along with Zhao Ziyang following the June 1989 military crackdown].

5. Dai Qing, "From Lin Zexu to Jiang Jingguo [Chiang Ching-kuo]," in *New Authoritarianism,* ed. Liu Jun and Li Lin, p. 86 [Translated in Geremie Barmé and Linda Javin, *New Ghosts, Old Dreams: Chinese Rebel Voices* (New York: Random House, 1992), pp. 188–189].

6. Chen Yizi, Wang Xiaoqiang, and Li Jun, "The Developmental Model for Establishing a 'Hard Government and Soft Economy,'" in *New Authoritarianism,* ed. Liu Jun and Li Lin, p. 246.

7. "Interview with Zhao Ziyang Think Tank Advisor," in *China Spring (Zhongguo zhichun),* no. 52 (October 1987): 9–13.

8. See Chen Yizi, *China: The Ten Years Reform and the 1989 People's Movement* (*Zhongguo: Shinian gaige yu bajiu minyun*) (Taipei, Taiwan: Lianjing Press, 1990), p. 188.

13

Tragedy for Democracy in Tiananmen Square

On April 15, 1989, Hu Yaobang died.

At a commemorative service for him at Columbia University in New York City, I described him as the "principal representative of the democratic forces in the Party and the last of the intellectuals attached to an ideal of liberty and democracy who in the history of the Chinese Communist Party rose like a meteor to the level of supreme leadership."

The falling of this star shook the earth in China. A democratic movement of immense scope swept from the capital through the entire country. This democratic movement was not simply a continuation of the April Fifth movement of 1976. Its members no longer placed their hope on any one leader of the Chinese Communist Party, no matter how wise he was. The primary goal of the April Fifth movement had been to oppose one faction inside the CCP, the "Gang of Four," and to some extent to condemn the dying Mao Zedong who had supported the "gang." At the same time, however, it called for a new star—Deng Xiaoping—to rise up and rescue China from its crisis.

This time was different, however. With the death of Hu Yaobang the Chinese people lost their last illusions about the Chinese Communist Party leaders. On the campus of Peking University, there appeared the following poem on the day of Hu Yaobang's death:

> *The honest man is dead.*
> *The hypocrites live on;*
> *The enthusiast is dead;*
> *Indifference buried him.*
> *Hollow words, futility, mah-jongg, bridge,*
> *new authoritarianism ...*
> *Reform and its death*

This world is a new labyrinth.
Let me ask you, Yaobang: Is there still hope for China?

This poem expresses the psychological progress the Chinese masses made during the thirteen years that separated the death of Zhou Enlai from that of Hu Yaobang. The death of Zhou Enlai coincided with the people's loss of faith in Mao; that of Hu brought out into the open the utter disillusion of the people in regard to the Communist Party. To the masses, Hu Yaobang was the last reformer in the Party, an unlucky reformer. His defeat was the defeat of honesty at the hands of hypocrisy. He was a sacrificial lamb to the hypocritical and corrupt palatial totalitarian politics in the later years of the CCP. Bridge, the new authoritarianism, reform and its death—such were the terms in which the people judged the two other self-described "reformers" of the Party: Deng Xiaoping and Zhao Ziyang. This judgment corresponded to the facts. On December 30, 1986, those two reform leaders allied to force another reform leader to resign and thus showed that they placed their own power above reform and even the fate of China. This was what separated them fundamentally from Hu Yaobang. Their "reform" was nothing but hypocrisy. As soon as the reform began to touch their own power and self-interest, they didn't hesitate to sacrifice it. At the end of 1986, Deng Xiaoping and Zhao Ziyang had sacrificed Hu Yaobang. But now, in the new game of Deng Xiaoping, it was Zhao's turn to be sacrificed.

Let's observe the arrangement of political forces both in and outside the Party that were involved in this game. First, let's consider the CCP.

The first faction in the Party was that of the dogmatists. Before Mao Zedong acquired preponderance, they had long controlled the Party. Their backstage support was originally the Soviet Union and Stalin. In the Yan'an Rectification campaign in the 1940s, Mao Zedong attacked the major leader of that faction—Wang Ming—and lured the other two leaders, Chen Yun and Kang Sheng, to his own side with the promise of important positions: Chen Yun was appointed director of the Party Organization Department, and Kang Sheng was appointed director of both the Social Affairs Department [that is, the Secret Police] and the Security Department [*Baoweibu*]. In 1949 when the Communist Party gained power in China, Chen Yun and Kang Sheng continued to maintain their influence within the economic realm and in the ideological realm. In the early 1950s, Chen Yun had come up with the policy of the state monopoly of grain and introduced the Soviet model of the planned economy—the model according to which primary importance was given to military industry and heavy industry, accompanied in conformity with the Stalinist method, by the exploitation of the peasants. Today again, faithful to Stalin, this model recommends controlling the economy like a bird in a cage. In ideology also, Chen Yun copied and again copied from Stalin and his theorist, Andrei Zhdanov.* Chen Yun maintains to this day that despotism must reign in the ideological and cultural domains, and forbids freedom of opinion and publication. The so-called rightism of Chen Yun consists of nothing other than opposition to overly high targets of growth, but he cannot disguise the Stalinist traits that characterize his thought.

As for Kang Sheng, for a long time he reigned over a group of "anti-revisionist" scribblers at Diaoyutai in Beijing and maintained Stalinism and Zhdanovism in the ideological realm, against "Khrushchevian revisionism." This "anti-revisionism" group that was left behind after Kang Sheng's death produced the masterpiece of Hua Guofeng's "two whatevers" and the struggle against bourgeois liberalism so dear to Deng Xiaoping and Chen Yun. Prior to the 1978 Third Plenum, Hu Yaobang had a heart-to-heart conversation with the four top members of the "two whatevers" faction: Li Xin, Wu Lengxi, Hu Sheng, and Xiong Fu. Hu Yaobang said:

> You four people have played an extremely negative role in the liberation of thought, the role of a brake. As far as I'm concerned, this is because you've come too much under the influence of people like Kang Sheng. You have been tainted by the professional disease that poisons those like Kang Sheng and Wang Dongxing who are charged with security work. Those who engage in such work are overly suspicious. When they read articles, instead of focusing on the major theme, they only try to pierce the supposedly hidden meanings; they interpret them and reinterpret them trying to find a weakness that will allow a breakthrough attack. Kang Sheng passed his time reading between the lines looking for "allusions" without taking account of the real subject of articles and the general idea. He made a sort of talent of looking for a particular point that he could attack. He had learned this from Stalin, from Zhdanov and the KGB, and acted thus from the time of the Yan'an era.

After the Third Plenum, these tenors of the "two whatevers" rallied to the side of Deng Liqun. Initially, Deng was the same as them in that he had also served in Kang Sheng's "anti-revisionism" corps.

Stalinist dogmatism at the heart of the Communist Party in China thus goes back a long way in its history. But the importance of this force in the era of Deng Xiaoping has far surpassed its power in the era of Mao Zedong. Although he used these dogmatists, Mao Zedong was a self-proclaimed inde-

---

*A staunch Stalinist and cultural conservative, Andrei Zhdanov launched virulent ideological witchhunts in the Soviet Union, such as the 1947–1948 campaign against "cosmopolitanism," that is, Russian Jews in the Soviet Communist Party. See Seweryn Bialer, *Stalin's Successors: Leadership, Stability and Change in the Soviet Union* (Cambridge, U.K., Cambridge University Press, 1980), pp. 23–39.

pendent theorist and considered himself to be an original and independent thinker. On the whole, they needed him more than he needed them. Things were different with Deng Xiaoping, whose pragmatism never excited a deep study of theoretical problems and who reveals himself on this terrain to be pretty shaky. He turned the theory work over to the dogmatists. And though he intervened in the economic realm, in this sector also he delegated a good part of the power to the Stalinist economists in Chen Yun's system. That's why a rigid Stalinist dogmatist clique has installed itself at the heart of China's Communist Party: Yao Yilin and Song Ping were in charge of the economy (Song Ping was once the darling of Chen Yun and held concurrent positions charged with economic planning and organizing the administrative work of the Party); Deng Liqun and Hu Qiaomu ran the ideological and cultural realms, along with their bully boys Xiong Fu, Wu Lengxi, Hu Sheng, Lin Mohan, He Jingzhi, Wang Renzhi, and Xu Weicheng.

A second Party group of political significance is the "militarist faction" [*qiangganzi*], men who like to assert that "power is in the barrel of a gun." This faction never became an independent force capable of challenging the Party's power. On the contrary, its members have always been dependent on the dominant political faction. Prior to the 1935 Zunyi Conference,* they depended on the dogmatists; after that conference they shifted allegiance to Mao Zedong. Following Mao's death, they first depended on Hua Guofeng and then went over to Deng Xiaoping. Such conversions were not made freely, but resulted from political power struggles within the Party. That is to say, whoever controls the Party's absolute power then gains control of the "militarist faction." Precisely because he did not control absolute power in the Party, Lin Biao—although Mao's designated successor, vice commander of his army, and minister of National Defense—did not exercise enough authority to command the Trident airplane that was to whisk him from the country following his attempted coup. The militarists who played an eminent role in struggles for power were not, for the most part, great military leaders wreathed in victory, but men with keen political skills. Someone like Wang Zhen, a general of vulgar manners and incoherent vocabulary, is an example of the kind of hound with a keen sense of smell. He never achieved any military feats on the field of battle, but knew how to aim his guns toward the rear. No matter whether it was the empire of Mao Zedong or of Deng Xiaoping, he always managed to sniff the wind, and when he had to, play the bully, a not insignificant role in struggles for power. This "lovely bazooka," as Deng described him, could open fire on the dogmatists and on the liberals both and

---

*A conference held during the Long March at which Mao Zedong assumed sole command of the Red Army.

was just as indispensable to Mao Zedong as he became to Deng Xiaoping. Around the time of the fall of Hu Yaobang, as around that of Zhao Ziyang, he appeared in the vanguard, brandishing a knife.

The third faction at the heart of the Party is the democratic reform force. This force, which has pursued freedom and democracy and emancipation, originally constituted a powerful force in the Party. The two generations of CCP members who emerged out of the student democratic movements during both the anti-Japanese [1937–1945] and liberation [1945–1949] wars together formed this force. However, in all the political campaigns from 1942 to the present they have always been primary targets for attack by the dogmatist and militarist factions. That's why their position within the CCP has gradually weakened. Around the time of the 1978 Third Plenum, due to Hu Yaobang's efforts to liberate ideology and reverse the phony verdicts, this force was rejuvenated and developed to play a vanguard role in the reform and opening up of China. Eventually, however, this force was defeated by the alliance of the dogmatist and militarist forces. Hu Yaobang's forced resignation signaled the clear defeat of the democratic reform forces at the hands of the other two groups. Indeed, the critical regrouping of conservative political forces in the CCP at the beginning of 1987 laid the foundation of power for the June Fourth slaughter.

During the two-year period from Hu Yaobang's fall from power in early 1987 to his death in spring 1989 and the emergence of the democratic movement, the democratic reform forces in the CCP underwent a serious split. One group of the intellectual leaders from the democratic student movements of the 1940s, who had supported Hu Yaobang, shifted their support to Zhao Ziyang. Then, after Zhao came up with his "two basic points" in 1987 and defeated Hu Yaobang and Deng Liqun in succession, he pushed the "new authoritarianism" with its proposal for "economic freedom and political totalitarianism." This evolution put the democratic reform force in the Party in its weakest position since 1978 vis-à-vis the dogmatist and militarist factions.

At the same time, social democratic forces outside the Party gained unprecedented strength. As a major indication of this, democrats excluded from the Party and some who remained in it drew closer together. The members of these two forces corresponded with each other and supported each other in forming a new alliance against totalitarianism and corruption.

This alliance of democratic reform forces in and outside the Party during the emergence of the Xidan Democracy Wall and the Third Plenum played an important role in the historical turning point in China's march toward the ten-year reform. However, on March 30, 1979, when Deng Xiaoping proposed "upholding the Four Cardinal Principles" and ordered the arrest of Wei Jingsheng—the representative of the Xidan Democracy Wall—this temporary alliance was broken. Democratic forces in the Party represented by Hu Yaobang, though they maintained their own views on the heavy sentence meted out to Wei Jingsheng by Peng Zhen and supported by Deng Xiaoping, dared not come up with any direct opposition. From then on, adopting an attitude they had long since begun to entertain, the democratic forces in the Party avoided having any contact with the social democratic movement. During the entire period of the ten-year reform, these two forces were divided, a separation that enfeebled them both. On the one hand, the social democratic movement was placed in the difficult situation of being declared "illegal" and subject to frequent attacks by the public security sector that is totally subservient to the totalitarian system. On the other hand, the democratic reformers within the Party lost support from the social democratic forces and were weakened by joint assaults from the dogmatists and militarists.

This situation emerged at the beginning of 1989. Some of the famous free democrats excluded from the Party broke their ten years of silence and publicly petitioned and demanded the release of Wei Jingsheng, along with other political dissidents.* This political incident reflected the shift of the democratic movement in China from within to outside the Party. That is to say, even if Hu Yaobang had not suddenly died in spring 1989, the historical turning point of the Chinese democratic movement had already arrived. Hu Yaobang's sudden death merely accelerated something that was already occurring.

In the democratic alliance that emerged in 1978 between forces in and outside the Party, the leading role was played by democratic personages within the CCP. This alliance supported the democratic reform forces that ultimately defeated the dogmatist totalitarian forces represented by Hua Guofeng's "two whatevers" and permitted members of the alliance to direct the process of reform and opening up. Thus the social democratic movement outside the Party in 1978 primarily focused on supporting democratic reformers in the Party and did not possess a more extensive democratic goal. Although Wei Jingsheng warned against the conversion of reformers into new autocrats, not even he proposed specific ways to terminate the totalitarian system and achieve the transition to a more democratic order. Most people at the time weren't themselves mistrustful enough of Deng Xiaoping, and Wei Jingsheng's warnings went unheeded.

Today [in 1989] the situation is different. The isolated cry of Wei Jingsheng that ten years ago went unheeded has now become the cry of all. When in 1987 Hu Yaobang was forced to resign, Deng Xiaoping revealed his auto-

---

*See the February 16, 1989, "Open Letter to the Standing Committee of the National People's Congress and the Party Central Committee Calling for a General Pardon of Political Prisoners," in *China's Search for Democracy: The Student and the Mass Movement of 1989,* ed. Suzanne Ogden, Kathleen Hartford, Lawrence Sullivan, and David Zweig (Armonk, N.Y.: M. E. Sharpe, 1992), Document No. 6.

cratic nature to the masses, and the leader of the "reform faction," Zhao Ziyang, abandoned the banner of democracy and adopted his self-isolating notion of "new authoritarianism." Meanwhile, outside and in the Party many naive people dreamed that Hu Yaobang would be restored to power to relaunch democratic reform. But Hu Yaobang's death in April 1989 destroyed the last dreams of these people. Nobody, either in or outside the Party, could imagine any other CCP leader who had the strength to guide the democratic movement forward. The performance of the CCP ruling clique, which over the past six years [1983–1989] ceaselessly purged free democrats from Party ranks, has become more and more totalitarian and corrupt. Apart from expanding its own power, it is a narrow-minded political clique that has lost any sense of morality or standards. It would be pointless to wait for this political clique to cure itself of totalitarian corruption. Hu Yaobang was the last idealist among CCP leaders, the last to have attempted to cure the cancer of the CCP's corruption and despotism. And for precisely this reason, he was hounded from the circle of power, accused of "liberalism," and died tormented by regrets.*

Also, no matter what the participants thought in their heart of hearts, the demonstrators of the 1989 democracy movement could not brandish the slogan "Support the Communist Party." For tactical reasons, some movement leaders tried on occasion to take cover behind this slogan, as behind a screen, but these efforts seemed stripped of sincerity and altogether comic in the eyes of the masses and the officials. For it was obvious after the death of Hu Yaobang in April that it was impossible to count on healthy forces in the Party to give a boost to the great goals of the movement, eradicating despotism and punishing corruption. The democratic forces within the CCP could only rely on uniting with the social democratic forces outside the Party. Only by doing so could they have defeated the totalitarian, corrupt forces within the CCP. This is why from the very beginning of the democratic movement in 1989, it attired itself in a very keen political character, which was unprecedented in the Party as well as in civil society. Even the various political forces implicated in this movement didn't seem to perceive this extreme politicization more clearly than their adversaries.

On April 22, the day of official mourning for Hu Yaobang, various political forces from both in and outside the Party gathered in and around the Great Hall of the People in Beijing in the following fashion:

Inside the building could be found the forces of the Party leaders. These were composed of:

---

*Hu Yaobang reportedly suffered his fatal heart attack during a heated Politburo discussion over the future course of reform.

1. *The Dogmatists.* The political influence of the Chen Yun dogmatist clique had obviously grown in strength. After Hu Yaobang fell from power, opportunists who had once been associated with Zhao Ziyang, such as the Propaganda Department head Wang Renzhi, and the vice president of the Central Party School, Gao Di (after "June Fourth" he would be appointed director of the *People's Daily,* replacing Qian Liren), put their fingers to the political wind and joined with Deng Liqun and Hu Qiaomu. Thus the dogmatist force expanded its influence in the culture, education, and propaganda sectors. Although Zhao Ziyang managed to dismantle Deng Liqun's Research Office of the Secretariat and changed the *Red Flag* into the journal *Seeking Truth* [*Qiushi*], this did not weaken by one iota the strength of the dogmatist forces in the ideological realm. That's because, refusing to ally himself with the liberal democratic forces in the Party, Zhao Ziyang put his confidence in the "elites," the adepts of "new authoritarianism" who had neither the ability nor the possibility of managing ideology. Thus he could only hope that the forces of dogmatism originally under Deng Liqun and Hu Qiaomu would throw their support to him. Indeed, Zhao received temporary and superficial support. For instance, Wang Renzhi once expressed his loyalty to Zhao Ziyang and wrote an article supporting Zhao's views that was published in the *People's Daily* with Zhao's approval. However, once the direction of the political wind changed in favor of the dogmatists, Wang Renzhi immediately did a somersault from Zhao Ziyang's lap back into Deng Liqun's.

In the economic realm, the dogmatist clique used the opportunity created by Zhao Ziyang's role as Party general secretary and Li Peng's control of the government to win over Li Peng and Vice Premier Yao Yilin. Out of this was formed the economic dogmatist force that challenged Zhao Ziyang. When on April 22, Zhao Ziyang was reading the words of mourning for Hu Yaobang in the Great Hall of the People, he was already surrounded by conservatives, on the ideological plane as on that of the economy.

2. *The Militarists.* Represented by Wang Zhen and Yang Shangkun, the militarists had supported Deng Xiaoping and Zhao Ziyang in opposing Hu Yaobang in 1986–1987 and now in 1989 they were ready to once again unite with the dogmatists to dump Zhao and support Li Peng. Originally, Yang Shangkun was a member of the Twenty-Eight Bolsheviks in Moscow under the Wang Ming dogmatists, but after Wang Ming's fall, Yang rallied to Mao. In 1945 Yang Shangkun left the army and became the director of the General Office of the Central Committee, where he served for many years. From this position, he maintained a close relationship with Deng Xiaoping when he was secretary in chief and later general secretary of the Central Committee. Besides, Yang Yingong, the older brother of Yang Shangkun, had been one of the first communists in the heroic era, and the young Deng Xiaoping had been under his influence. In 1978 when Luo Ruiqing died, Deng Xiaoping was unable to find a successor to manage the routine work of the Central Mili-

tary Commission. Geng Biao was temporarily in charge but didn't do a good job, and thus Deng chose Yang Shangkun. Although Yang did not have much of a reputation in the eyes of the military and Deng had little appreciation for his military abilities, he trusted Yang politically: He believed that Yang would always be loyal to him. Although Wang Zhen also did not hold much military power, he was fond of interfering in politics as a military person and Deng was willing to use him as his "bazooka" in his power struggles in the Party. During the April 22, 1989, ceremony in the Great Hall, these two people—one the president of the PRC and the other the vice president—were staring at Zhao Ziyang like vicious tigers stalking their prey as Zhao read the words of mourning without showing the slightest emotion.

3. *The Reformers.* The reform force opposed to the dogmatists and militarists in the Party was split and weakened. With Hu Yaobang's fall from power, the democratic reform force lost its political leader. Zhao Ziyang, however, did not trust the intellectual free democrats in the Party, for he believed that their independent way of thinking made them hard to manipulate. He preferred to rely on his own, younger "intellectual elites." He found them smarter, more sensitive, better at understanding his intentions, and perfectly capable of finding in works classical and modern—Marxist or otherwise—theoretical arguments indispensable to the operation of his projects. In addition, the various agendas designed by those "think tanks" focused on the short term and thus were eye catching and gained the necessary support to solidify Zhao's power.

4. *The "New Authoritarians."* The new "intellectual elite," who separated themselves from the reformers, laughed at the other intellectual free democrats as obsolete "traditional democrats, utopian democrats, or romantic democrats." Thus they put those free democrats in a position where they pretty much had to support Zhao's reforms, but without receiving any attention.

Deng Xiaoping was also at the Great Hall of the People for Hu Yaobang's official mourning. Putting himself above the various factions as a spectator like Mao Zedong, Deng helped one or another of the factions in their keen competition against each other for his support while maintaining his own freedom to unleash the cat to catch the mouse whenever he was so inclined.

Outside the Great Hall of the People stood students from the great universities and colleges of the capital. University students in China indeed are the most sensitive barometer of the political forces. The goals proposed by the university students, namely opposition to totalitarianism and corruption, are the two common goals of the various social-political forces dissatisfied with the CCP power-holding clique. And these two big goals were represented by the slogan of "Down with official profiteering." Recently, quite a few overseas "elites" have issued condemnations like the following: "The 1989 democratic movement was not a true democratic movement, Chinese university students know nothing of democracy, and the slogan of down with official profiteering is an attack on reformers." This kind of aristocratic condemnation can only indicate how alienated the speakers are from the feelings of the Chinese people. Reform in the eyes of those "elites" does not aim at fundamentally changing the overall totalitarian system in the political, economic, cultural, and social realms. For them reform is nothing but a revision to enable the totalitarian system to make it possible for these minority "elites" to seek more personal benefits. A principal difference in both ideology and politics existed from the very beginning of the 1989 democratic movement, and that is the conflict between the demand by the Chinese people for freedom and democracy and the pursuit of "new authoritarianism" by the minority elites. At present, this conflict has only been transported abroad, where it now divides Chinese exiles who fled overseas after the June Fourth slaughter.

The kind of confrontation that occurred in April 1989 in and outside the Great Hall of the People among various political forces was a new phenomenon in contemporary Chinese politics. It reflects the fact that the conflict between factions in the CCP has now expanded beyond a pure inner-Party struggle and combined with political struggles outside the Party. This combination is indeed very complicated.

The democratic reform force of the Party shares the political orientation of the student movement that amassed outside the Great Hall of the People. This has been vividly described in a poem by the Beijing journalist Ge Yang:*

This Side and That

> *One world cut in two*
> *Separated by the wall of violence*
> *Here, all is icy indifference*
> *On that side is an ocean of truth and emotion*
> *On this side lies Yaobang's corpse*
> *On that side lies Yaobang's soul*
> *We are all from that side*
> *Without that side there is no this side*

This poem was composed by Ge Yang after she bade farewell to Hu Yaobang in the Great Hall of the People and stood next to the wall of violence and faced the ocean of truth, seeming not to see the isolated encounters between the demonstrators and armed soldiers and police. Since they had lost Hu Yaobang as a political leader in 1987, this part of the true democratic reform force had lost any sense of guidance and had become a wandering no-

---

*Ms. Ge Yang was the editor in chief of the highly acclaimed liberal journal *New Observer* (*Xin guancha*).

madic tribe fighting in isolation on a narrow battlefront. Although they bravely supported the democratic movement, their position in the CCP had become so marginal that they no longer carried any weight.

The "new authoritarian" reform faction led by Zhao Ziyang also attempted to use the student democratic movement to consolidate its own position in the Party's power struggle. After the defeat of the price reform launched by Deng Xiaoping in 1988, the challenge from the alliance between the dogmatists and militarists against Zhao Ziyang became public. Deng Xiaoping's support gradually shifted from Zhao Ziyang to Li Peng. And "new authoritarian" advisers serving under Zhao Ziyang one after another left China for what they called "the great victorious escape." It was in the midst of all this that the student movement burst forth. Those "new authoritarian" advisers who had not gone abroad planned their last battle: They decided to use the student movement to overcome the alliance of the dogmatists and the militarists while also gaining support from Deng for Zhao Ziyang. That is, they wanted to make Deng Xiaoping believe that only Zhao Ziyang, not Li Peng, had the capacity to handle the student movement and stabilize the situation, thereby shifting authority from Li to Zhao. At the same time, they prepared their route of retreat, to be able to save themselves by going overseas in case of defeat.

The hard-liners (the dogmatists and militarists) also planned to use the student movement to grasp the power held by Zhao Ziyang just as they had profited from the student movement in the end of 1986 by forcing Hu Yaobang to resign. They claimed that the student movement was the result of Zhao Ziyang's support of liberalism and even went so far as to accuse Zhao Ziyang of guiding the student movement, along with the U.S. CIA.

Democrats outside the Party themselves trusted neither Deng Xiaoping, who conducted reform like a bridge party, nor Zhao's reform through "new authoritarianism." Hu Yaobang's death symbolized for them the death of reform under the CCP's one-party dictatorship. For them, the failure of political reform confirmed that this Party had long been suffocated by the forces of totalitarianism and corruption and no longer possessed the internal vitality to promote reform. The student democrats and the urban population that followed them were a new political phenomenon, because apart from the deceased Hu Yaobang, they no longer supported any CCP leaders. They attempted to organize their own political forces in an autonomous way to compete on an equal footing with the CCP. The various autonomous organizations that appeared in the course of the movement, as well as the efforts during the demonstrations in April and May 1989 to negotiate with the Chinese government on an equal footing, were elements virtually unknown to past democratic movements.

Then what were Deng Xiaoping's options? What choice would he make in confronting these various political forces in and outside the Party? He could no longer play his pragmatic game of seeking political equilibrium. He had gradually separated himself from three of the four forces. First, in eliminating Democracy Wall and arresting Wei Jingsheng in 1979, he had broken with the social democratic force. Then he broke with the democrats in the Party when he forced Hu Yaobang to resign. And last, he broke with the "new authoritarianism" of Zhao Ziyang. Thus there was only one route open to him: to ally himself with the old totalitarian system composed of the dogmatists and militarists—with Chen Yun, Peng Zhen, Bo Yibo, and Yang Shangkun. Once that alliance of the most conservative forces—barbarous and cruel—was secured, the military crackdown in June 1989 against the democratic movement was inevitable.

If the leaders of the democratic movement on Tiananmen Square had perceived what was, really, after the death of Hu Yaobang, the rapport of political forces both in and outside the Party and had chosen an appropriate strategy—if in other words, they had known how to form a grand alliance with all forces opposed to dictatorship and corruption both in and outside the Party in order to attack them together—the movement could have gained the most extensive sympathy with society at large and would have had a chance of success. If the democratic forces in and outside the Party and the partisans of the "new authoritarianism" had realized that their mutual isolation would lead to their destruction and instead had united, it would have been possible for them to use their unity to defeat the alliance of the dogmatists and militarists.

But in spring 1989, on Tiananmen Square, there was only an alliance of totalitarianism and corruption, and their adversaries were dispersed. That was one of the causes of the failure of the democratic movement and the June Fourth slaughter. Certain "democratic movement leaders" have said in their exile that "the defeat of the 1989 democratic movement was inevitable because China hasn't any private property and the middle class wasn't powerful enough." This way of seeing democracy as the patent of a certain class under a certain system is itself a violation of democratic principles. Because if such a conclusion could be established, then the 1989 democratic movement itself should have been canceled and no democratic movement should occur until private ownership and a powerful middle class emerge. If that's the case, the "overseas democratic movement" is aimless and should have "discarded the democratic banner" long ago and devoted itself solely to accumulating capital and becoming middle class first. But it's unhealthy to use this defeatist and fatalistic view to avoid examining the responsibility of different political forces in the defeat of the 1989 democratic movement. What we should do today is make a serious study of past movements and prepare for China's future.

In retrospect, the crackdown on the 1989 democratic movement was not the only possible outcome. It was merely the worst among several possible scenarios. Looking at it today [in late 1989], two other possible outcomes could have occurred.

One possible outcome was that Zhao Ziyang, who was in the CCP's top position, could have changed his self-isolating position in support of "new authoritarianism," shifted to the democratic side favoring reform, united the three democratic forces in and outside the Party to defeat the antireform alliance, and thereby continued to push the reform forward. This outcome was not impossible. Even Zhao Ziyang's adviser Chen Yizi admits:

> In the course of the 1989 democratic movement, eighty percent of the cadres at and below the bureau level in both the Party and government organizations showed sympathy and support for the movement.* Among ministers and vice ministers, fully seventy percent were sympathetic and supportive. The most obvious thing was that from May 15 to 18, celebrities from all walks of life came out to show their support, hoping that the government would admit that the students were patriotic and carry out a dialogue with the students instead of relying on hard-line methods.† Those who first disagreed with the idea of using the military were the three vice chairmen of the National People's Congress who represented the military. Over eight hundred retired generals explicitly said that troops should not be used for any crackdown.[1]

Thus, although people both in and outside the Party knew that the April 26 editorial in the *People's Daily* accusing the student democratic movement of being "anti-Party, anti-socialist turmoil" [*dongluan*] reflected the views of Deng Xiaoping, still the majority of high-ranking cadres in the Party, government, and military remained unconvinced. When Zhao Ziyang returned from North Korea on April 30, he took on a very active role and twice expressed his view that the student movement should be treated leniently. This was expressed in his speeches given on May 3–4, the first a commemoration of the seventieth anniversary of the May Fourth movement and the second to representatives of the Asian Development Bank.‡ These won popular support both in and outside the Party and at home and abroad. Thus, it would not have been difficult for Zhao Ziyang to come out on top of the situation. With the exception of students from Peking University and Beijing Teachers' University, many students returned to class upon hearing these speeches. Zhao could have perfectly easily taken the initiative of holding a dialogue with the stu-

---

*The bureau (*siju*) is directly below the ministry (*bu*) and above the department (*chu*) in the hierarchy of the CCP and the government.

†Recognition of the students' patriotism and calls for a dialogue with the top leadership were two of the basic demands by student leaders throughout the 1989 Democracy Movement. See *China's Search for Democracy*, ed. Suzanne Ogden, Kathleen Hartford, Lawrence Sullivan, and David Zweig (Armonk, N.Y.: M.E. Sharpe, 1990), pp. 244–258.

‡See the text of Zhao Ziyang's two speeches in *Beijing Spring, 1989: Confrontation and Conflict, The Basic Documents*, ed. Michel Oksenberg, Marc Lambert, and Lawrence Sullivan (Armonk, N.Y.: M. E. Sharpe, 1990), pp. 244–258.

dents, making use of the gathered media intermediaries (TV, radio, newspapers, and other organs of opinion that remained under the control of Hu Qili and Rui Xingwen, both Zhao supporters). Zhao could also have gained active power over the legal organizations of the government (the chairman and vice chairman of the NPC, Wan Li and Xi Zhongxun, were both Zhao supporters). The pursuit of a dialogue with students, the launching of a great campaign of opinion, and the convocation of the National People's Congress where the situation could have been discussed and democratic reform measures for immediate application devised (for instance, a law on information and the press, the right of association, etc.), and together with these initiatives, a conciliatory attitude such as Zhao adopted would have permitted the situation to gradually stabilize. The military would have had no pretext to open fire, and Deng Xiaoping would have had to accept the existing situation.

Zhao Ziyang, however, did not pursue this course. He never intended to unite with the democratic forces in society and the Party. His main worry remained the struggle for power within the Party, and he merely attempted to use the force of the student movement to consolidate his own position in his struggle with Li Peng. Thus, on the one hand, he gave the speech on leniency (that indicated there were two opposing views on how to handle the democratic movement in the Party), and on the other, knowing Li Peng would irritate the students, he asked Li and his underlings to carry out the dialogue with the students. In the meantime, as the atmosphere grew more tense, he stood on the sidelines, abandoning all initiative for a dialogue with the students, waiting for Deng Xiaoping to make a new choice, which is to say, he thought that once Deng saw that Li Peng was unable to deal with the situation, Deng would transfer power back from Li Peng to Zhao. Then, Zhao thought, the moment would come for him to deal with the movement.

But Zhao Ziyang misjudged Deng Xiaoping. Deng Xiaoping interpreted Zhao Ziyang's attitude—and notably the revelations that he made to Gorbachev on the content of the so-called secret resolution of the First Plenum of the Thirteenth Congress (the one that said that Deng Xiaoping remained the "witness" who held the power of supreme decision)—as an indication that Zhao wanted to force Deng to sacrifice his own personal power. Deng would rather have mobilized tens of thousands of troops to retake Tiananmen Square than display any weakness in the face of a person who was trying to snatch his power. As always, he showed himself to be intractable, manifesting yet again a character trait that had for him the value of having been characterized by Mao as "patron of the steelworks."

Zhao Ziyang's total misjudgment of Deng resulted in his own fall from power. After the June crackdown, when Deng's daughter Deng Nan returned to work at the State Science and Technology Commission she uttered just two lines: "June Fourth was the result of an impossible choice" and "Who would have thought that Zhao Ziyang was a man so vile." By "a man so vile" she meant that Zhao had wanted to take possession of the power held by Deng.

Of course, the first of the possible outcomes, whereby Zhao would have dropped his concept of "new authoritarianism," would have produced the best possible results. Zhao Ziyang should be held accountable for his failure to take this road. His antidemocratic theory plus his illusory belief that he could win a victory in inner-Party struggles proved him incapable of making an accurate choice in accordance with the forward direction of Chinese history.

The second possible outcome would have required concessions by the students. That is, after Li Peng formally announced martial law on May 19, 1989, the students would have had to terminate the movement and return to their campuses. This course of action without doubt would have obviated the large-scale slaughter on June 4, but it would not have saved Zhao Ziyang. The dogmatists and the militarists of the Party as usual would have overshadowed him. Dictatorial power would have prevailed, and student leaders would have been arrested as political persecution continued. This also would have been a defeat, but less blood would have flowed.

Zhao Ziyang's political miscalculation and the students' persistence in occupying the square step by step pushed the 1989 democratic movement in China toward a third conclusion, far more tragic. With respect to Zhao Ziyang and the students both, Deng Xiaoping had reached the end of his patience. He seemed to sink into memories of the Huaihai battle he had won some forty years earlier during the civil war. His military genius complex became vastly overheated, and he decided to mobilize tens of thousands of troops to carry out a new "Huaihai battle to encircle and annihilate the trouble." In the course of his long life, this was probably the last opportunity available to him to demonstrate his military prowess. In reality, he had been tempted to try it out two years earlier during the student movement at the end of 1986, when he had proposed a declaration of martial law, and he had also praised General Jaruzelski, who had decreed a state of emergency in Poland against Solidarity. This time Deng would not let an opportunity go by that threatened never again to present itself.

So, on an order of Deng Xiaoping, tens of thousands of troops were seen moving toward the capital headed for Tiananmen Square. Unarmed and completely worn out, some tens of thousands of students occupying the square were hardly comparable to the well-armed Nationalist army that forty years earlier Deng had confronted in the Huaihai battle. However, this unarmed and worn-out force represented "the great climate in the world" as well as "the small climate in China." It represented the historical mainstream of the democratic movement throughout the world and in China.

Forty years earlier Deng Xiaoping had defeated the Nationalist troops at one stroke. But forty years later, Deng Xiaoping had trouble even approaching the square. Tens of thousands of troops were blocked on the outskirts of the city for over fifteen days by the peaceful and nonviolent masses. Only by giving the absolute order to carry out a slaughter in the city, threatening the soldiers that "whoever does not carry out the order will be executed according to military law," and engaging in distorted propaganda, was Deng able to stimulate the beastly character of some troops, thereby creating the enormous inhumanity of the June Fourth slaughter.*

No matter how many people Deng slaughtered—and to this day he still jealously guards the secret number—Deng Xiaoping has not destroyed the main body of the democratic force. On the white headbands worn by the masses blockading the soldiers was written: "Do you have 1.1 billion troops?" That was the best answer in reply to Deng Xiaoping's condescending attitude toward the masses. Deng Xiaoping will one day understand that this new "Huaihai battle" launched against the Chinese people will remain attached to his skin for the rest of his life, for he can never wash away the shame. And the masses he disdains are countless and the lives of dictators have limits. Some day on the ruins of this most ruthless and degenerate "Huaihai battle," a free and democratic China will emerge, irrigated by the fresh blood of the 1989 peaceful democratic movement.

Notes

1. Chen Yizi, *China: The Ten Years Reform and the 1989 People's Movement* (*Zhongguo: Shinian gaige yu bajiu minyun*) (Taipei, Taiwan: Lianjing Press, 1990), p. 163.

---

*This included such heinous acts as soldiers spraying buildings with machine gun fire, the use of lethal dum dum bullets, and the killing of unarmed students at point-blank range. See various eyewitness accounts of the massacre in *China's Search for Democracy*, ed. Suzanne Ogden, Kathleen Hartford, Lawrence Sullivan, and David Zweig (Armonk, N.Y.: M.E. Sharpe, 1992), Documents No. 180–196.

14

The Defeat of Violence and the Last Days of the Empire

The June Fourth slaughter destroyed the Deng Xiaoping empire. The new "Huaihai battle" launched by Deng Xiaoping—the Tiananmen battle—was from a purely "military perspective a victory." Several tens of thousands of troops armed with tanks, machine guns, and cannons surrounded the capital city for more than fifteen days, then launched an attack on unarmed students and city residents and marched through pools of blood to occupy Tiananmen Square, which had formerly belonged to the people. But in counterpoint to this military success, Deng Xiaoping met a veritable "political Waterloo."

In retrospect, one can see that Deng Xiaoping had established his empire with the 1979 war to "punish" Vietnam. During the more than three months that elapsed between the Third Plenum in December 1978 and the end of the war against Vietnam, China could have taken either of two possible roads.

One was toward liberal democracy. Between winter 1978 and spring 1979, the Beijing Xidan Democracy Wall and the nationwide democratic movement had already formed an alliance with the democratic reform force in the Party, and together they defeated the dogmatist "two whatevers" at the Third Plenum and created the possibility of ending China's experience with dictatorship and moving the country toward democracy. In one fell swoop, Deng Xiaoping became the leader of the forces for democracy inside and outside the Party. He not only united the democratic reform forces in the Party but also supported the democratic movement that had gained strength among the masses, winning him the support of the vast majority of farmers, workers, intellectuals, and most social classes. The power of the dogmatist and militarist factions in the hierarchy of the CCP was comparatively weak and on the defensive at the time, owing to the catastrophic "Cultural Revolution" and the smashing of the Lin Biao and the Jiang Qing cliques. The conditions were ripe for a democratic and economically open China in the spring of 1979, when the democratic reform forces inside and outside the Party were still unified.

The other road open to China led toward a new dictatorship, one that would replace the old-style autocracy. The Third Plenum had ended the rule of the "two whatevers" and marked the failure of the old totalitarian system of the Maoist era still being pushed by dogmatist forces represented by Hua Guofeng and Wang Dongxing. But that was not the end of the road for the dogmatist faction in the CCP. This faction, represented by Chen Yun and Kang Sheng, had become increasingly splintered during the ten-year "Cultural Revolution." Some of the dogmatist forces under Kang Sheng had shifted allegiance to Deng Xiaoping when he returned to power for the second time, as Kang Sheng lay on his deathbed. Those people included Li Xin, Deng Liqun, Wu Lengxi, Xiong Fu, Hu Sheng, and others. Under the leadership of Mao Zedong's former secretary Hu Qiaomu, they recruited liberal intellectuals from the former Central Propaganda Department such as Yu Guangyuan and Lin Jianqing and formed the Research Office under the State Council that functioned as the "squad of scholars" [*xiucai banzi*] of the then Vice Premier Deng Xiaoping (at the time when Premier Zhou Enlai was ill).

After Kang Sheng died, this group once again split, this time over the campaign to "criticize Deng and oppose the rightist trend of reversing the verdicts." Some surrendered to Jiang Qing. One such person was Hu Qiaomu, who turned over a great pile of documents to Jiang Qing based on notes he had taken in "private conversations" with Deng. Others, however, such as Li Xin, Hu Sheng, Wu Lengxi, and Xiong Fu, threw in their lot with Hua Guofeng and Wang Dongxing. Still others, such as Deng Liqun and the liberals Yu Guangyuan and Lin Jianqing, joined Deng Xiaoping on the sidelines. When the "Gang of Four" was smashed, this troupe underwent reform. Li Xin, Wu Lengxi, Xiong Fu, and others joined up with Hua Guofeng and embraced the "two whatevers." Yu Guangyuan and Lin Jianqing and other liberals, such as Zhou Yang, Hu Jiwei, Tong Dalin, and Wu Mingyu, supported the debate over the criterion of truth launched by Hu Yaobang and opposed the "two whatevers."

Deng Liqun, however, kept his distance from both the "whatevers" faction and the liberal faction. Seeing that not even death would expiate all of Kang Sheng's crimes, Deng Liqun realized the futility of joining up with either the Kang Sheng faction or with Wang Dongxing. Instead, he warmed up to Chen Yun's dogmatist faction, and relying on his old relationship with Wang Zhen, established when they served together in Xinjiang, he prepared to set up a new alliance between the dogmatist and militarist factions in order to deal with the rapidly emerging free democratic forces inside and outside the Party.

Deng Liqun's first move was to go to Deng Xiaoping with Wang Zhen to plead on behalf of Hu Qiaomu, to beg Deng to forgive Hu's earlier betrayal of Deng Xiaoping to Jiang Qing. They beseeched Deng Xiaoping to "let bygones be bygones," so that Hu Qiaomu could be utilized. That was a successful move. Then Deng Liqun established a "theory squad" to take the place of the other "theory squad" composed of Wang Dongxing's "whatevers" faction. This would also check the theory support group of the democratic faction that had gathered around Hu Yaobang. Later, in the many antiliberalism campaigns, Deng Liqun insisted time and again that the theory squad had been separated and had gone different ways ever since the 1978 Third Plenum. This involved an important split in the alliance consisting of the dogmatist faction represented by Hu Qiaomu and himself, the Chen Yun dogmatist aggregate that included "the State Planning Commission and Petroleum group" (composed of Yao Yilin, Song Ping, Yu Qiuli, and Kang Shi'en),* part of the "militarist" faction (Wang Zhen and Wei Guoqing), and the free democratic forces gathered around Hu Yaobang. The political goal of Deng Liqun and his allies was now to replace the old totalitarian system with a new one and oppose the development toward freedom and democracy. Their program was to uphold the Four Cardinal Principles and oppose bourgeois liberalism.

During the more than three months from the Third Plenum to the end of the war to "punish" Vietnam in March 1979, it was commonly believed throughout the nation that development toward democracy would occur. Deng Xiaoping at the Third Plenum had explicitly proposed that "To ensure people's democracy, we must strengthen our legal system. Democracy has to be institutionalized and written into law, so as to make sure that institutions and laws do not change whenever the leadership changes or whenever the leaders change their views or shift the focus of their attention."[1] It seemed that the only remaining task was to determine the specific characteristics of a democratic and legal system. Prior to his visit to the United States, at the Conference on Guidelines in Theory Work, Deng Xiaoping supported utilizing what's good in bourgeois democracy and finding ways in China to make people feel that they are the rulers of the country. He thus indicated again more clearly that it was necessary to take inspiration from the successful experiences of bourgeois democratic countries in order to elaborate a correct democracy for China. Clearly, during that period Deng Xiaoping's views and intentions were focused on abolishing the totalitarian system of the Mao Zedong empire to build a democratic political system that would guarantee the modernization of China. In other words, at that time Deng Xiaoping indeed was on the side of the free democratic forces both in and outside the

---

*This group traced its name to members' involvement in the 1960s development of the famous Daqing oil fields. By the 1980s they controlled much of the State Planning Commission, where they were responsible for Soviet-style economic planning. See Kenneth Lieberthal and Michel Oksenberg, *Policy Making in China: Leaders, Structures, and Processes* (Princeton: Princeton University Press, 1988), p. 46.

Party. And that is why he refused to give the speech drafted for the Third Plenum by Hu Qiaomu and instead delivered the one prepared by Hu Yaobang.

But the war against Vietnam changed the balance of forces on China's political stage, and it also changed Deng Xiaoping's thinking and focus.

Let's imagine that the war against Vietnam had unfurled as the victory forecast by Deng Xiaoping, delivering a hard blow in short order. Aided by the crisis in Cambodia, benefiting from the unanimous support of the country, Deng Xiaoping perhaps would not have had to change his opinion or modify his objective of modernization; the alliance between democrats and liberals in and outside the Party would not have been broken, and the coalition of dogmatists and militarists would not have been powerful enough to transform the process of democracy and liberalism. But as it happened, China did not defeat Vietnam, and the Cambodian crisis resolved nothing. Instead, the weakness of the Chinese military was displayed for all the world to see. This embarrassing war caused intense feelings of dissatisfaction in and outside the Party. But the dogmatist and militarist factions inside the Party skillfully exploited this limited discontent, making a mountain out of a molehill as they aimed at "changing the leadership's views and intentions" in order to pull China back from the democratic road to a new type of totalitarian system. This punitive war against Vietnam thus had three historic consequences.

First, the military defeat not only deprived this war of its "punitive" aspect, it also caused China to lose its status as a major world military power. In the 1950s and early 1960s, troops under Mao Zedong fought the U.S. army in Korea to a standstill and rapidly defeated the troops of the Nehru government of India, thereby achieving status as a major world military power. The war to "punish" Vietnam that followed Deng's visit to the United States was obviously aimed at winning China a reputation as a major world power. This objective was not achieved.

Second, though this war was a failure militarily, it achieved success in international politics by virtue of the fact that the Soviet Union failed to act; thus, the war helped create the Deng Xiaoping era in international politics. That is to say, Deng Xiaoping's willingness to confront Brezhnev militarily earned the great appreciation of the United States, which had surely given its tacit agreement to this operation. Thus, regardless of the military outcome, the war established a strategic relationship between the United States and China vis-à-vis the Soviet Union.

Third, in terms of domestic politics, the war consolidated the alliance between the dogmatist and militarist factions and effectively terminated the alliance of the free democratic forces in and outside the Party. The criticism formulated by critics like Wei Jingsheng against the "punitive" war and against Deng Xiaoping himself were used by Deng Liqun and Hu Qiaomu to incite Deng Xiaoping to struggle against the "right" and change not only his opinion but also his objective. Deng decided to make the arrest of Wei Jingsheng and to outlaw the Xidan Democracy Wall. He broke with the free democratic forces outside the Party and warned the reform wing and the democrats in the Party against having contacts with them. Henceforth, he ceased to rely on the democratic faction but turned instead to the dogmatists and the militarists.

Just as in the Mao Zedong era the Korean War blocked the recently inaugurated "New Democracy" and provoked a return to the Stalinist type of totalitarian system, the Vietnam war launched by Deng Xiaoping once again blocked democracy and turned China into a new totalitarian empire. However, the two historical processes present differences. China's involvement in the Korean War stemmed from the decision made by Mao in response to international pressure from three sides: Stalin, Kim Il Sung, and MacArthur, whereas the war to "punish" Vietnam was launched on Deng's own initiative. Further, under the economic sanctions imposed by the West following the Korean War, in order to break its isolation, China had no other choice but to turn to the Soviet Union and adopt the Stalinist system. Deng Xiaoping, however, even after the war against Vietnam, possessed ample free choices in terms of the future development of China.

To a great extent external influences forced Mao to change his decision at the 1945 Seventh Party Congress, that is to abandon the "New Democracy," which was in actuality more compatible with China's conditions and the will of the people, and return to the dogmatist and "populist" standpoint that he had initially opposed and adopt Stalinist "socialism." By contrast, Deng Xiaoping renounced democracy for the sole reason that the leader "had changed his views or shifted the focus of attention," to cite a formula he used at the 1978 Third Plenum. A personal factor played a decisive role in this unfortunate conversion. After the war in Vietnam, Deng was not subject to international pressure (from either the East or West), nor was he faced with sanctions as Mao was after Korea. On the contrary, both East and West actively expressed their desire to develop relations with China and both East and West supported reform and opening in China. Deng remained entirely master of the move toward democracy that he had launched before the war. Certainly, under the pressure of Chinese public opinion that demanded democracy and reform, Deng Xiaoping had three new chances, in 1980, 1986, and 1987, to go back to the problem of democracy.

But Deng Xiaoping never practiced what he preached by truly preparing for the establishment of a democratic political and legal system in China. On the contrary, he constantly altered his "views or focus of attention," and each time he engaged in a greater betrayal of democratic goals and a greater strengthening of the totalitarian empire. It all came about as I described in the Introduction to this book: "Sometimes he acted with a clear mind; at other times he appeared befuddled, driving both forward and backward in the huge cart of China's reform and opening up to the outside world. This changeable-

ness made people both hopeful and desperate." How do we explain this behavior?

I think that the political ambiguity of Deng's personality has proven to be
an insoluble contradiction between his rational deliberative style and his passion for violent military action and for patriarchal dictatorship, a passion
deeply anchored within himself that he can't get rid of. His taste for patriar-
chy, tied to his "patron of the steelworks" complex, as Mao put it, have led
him to act in ways contrary to his rational deliberations. He did not want the
highest leadership position, but he wouldn't allow anyone else to assume the
role of patriarch into which he fitted so well. So he changed in reality into a
"backstage ruler," single-handedly running military and political affairs and
making the transition to a new political system impossible even though the
position of the highest leader under the old system no longer existed. After
June Fourth, Deng declared that he himself was "the core of the second generation of leaders," demonstrating that he was quite conscious of his own patriarchal interference, though it clearly contradicted his self-professed rational
deliberations. The dogmatist and militarist factions in the Party exploited this
weakness of Deng Xiaoping's by "carrying him in a palanquin" and "singing
his praises." They made him into this grand patriarch so that a bunch of old
men could become at least small patriarchs and treat the legal leaders of the
Party the way mothers treat their daughters-in-law.

Closely connected to Deng Xiaoping's patriarchal complex was his military
complex. Whenever China was confronted with difficulties that could not be
solved solely by administrative means, Mao Zedong relied on mass campaigns. Deng, however, always turned to military solutions and violence. This
taste for patriarchal autocracy and military violence was Deng Xiaoping's
Achilles' heel. Eventually it betrayed his rational deliberations. It caused his
conflict with Hu Yaobang, for Hu Yaobang recognized that problems of public order and social problems were normal phenomena that should not raise
any concern in a big country and that a method of comprehensive treatment
should be adopted along with solving problems through normal legal procedures. Deng Xiaoping, however, advocated all kinds of extreme notions, such
as "everyone that comes should be seized; counterattack should be heavy, severe, and rapid; kill a few and seize a few; send them to the remote regions of
Xinjiang, Ningxia, Gansu and revoke their residence permits in Beijing." And
he found Hu Yaobang too "soft."

From spring 1979, after the war against Vietnam, the arrest of Wei
Jingsheng, the closing down of Democracy Wall, and the decision to split
away from the democratic force outside the Party, over the next ten years of
reform, Deng Xiaoping would on numerous occasions and at key junctures
perform a complete turnaround and end up destroying the results of the reform and opening up to the outside world that he had initiated. In every case
his patriarchal and military complex overwhelmed his rational deliberative

side with the most severe case coming in 1989 during the "Tiananmen battle." This was a vicious illustration of Deng's patriarchal and military complex negating his rational deliberative side—the last days of madness for the Deng Xiaoping empire.

What we see here is a big contradiction: Ten years of reform and opening up combined with ten years of control by the autocratic system of the Deng Xiaoping empire. This contradiction has already caused a great debate among the various political factions in China. The basic points of contention are these: What kind of political system should China select for its reform, opening up, and modernization? Should a democratic system be adopted or should the autocratic system be continued? The outcome of this debate, in which the victors will be either the liberal democrats or the partisans of despotism and dictatorship, will profoundly influence China's destiny in the twenty-first century.

As for China at the end of the twentieth century, we have already seen how the empires of Mao Zedong and Deng Xiaoping have mutually ensnared each other in large and small ways. The two empires are alike in that both Mao Zedong and Deng Xiaoping proposed freedom and democracy for China, and both united with democratic forces in and outside the Party to oppose totalitarian autocracy. This was the principal reason for the popular support that allowed both men to take power. But they soon moved in totally different directions and established their own totalitarian empires. And both empires ended with the suppression of a free democratic movement in Tiananmen Square.

The perspective of a half century shows that for China the entire twentieth century has been a struggle dominated by a duel between democratic destiny and dictatorial destiny. Since the foundation of the Republic of China after the revolution of 1911, up to the dispatch of military force by Deng Xiaoping to occupy Tiananmen Square in 1989, China's fate was one in which autocratic China consumed democratic China. Yüan Shih-k'ai, Chiang K'ai-shek, Mao Zedong, and Deng Xiaoping: Does such a succession signify that China is an unusual land, unfit for the blossoming of a democratic regime, on which only dictatorial empires, one after the other, are thrust?

Yüan Shih-k'ai's U.S. adviser Frank J. Goodnow promoted the idea that conditions in China were not conducive to democracy.* In saying this, he meant that a civilization based on Confucianism was diametrically opposed to civilizations whose foundations were Christian. Western theorists have subse-

---

*A U.S. political scientist, Frank Goodnow composed a treatise on the unsuitability of republican government for China that evidently reinforced Yüan Shih-k'ai's ill-fated inclinations to monarchical status in the mid-1910s. See Benjamin Schwartz, *In Search of Wealth and Power: Yen Fu and the West* (New York: Harper & Row, 1969), pp. 224–226.

quently explained that countries with "communist systems" cannot make the transition to a free and democratic system. These two theories have been shaken by recent developments in East Asia and Eastern Europe and other regions where countries have begun the historical process toward democracy. The destruction of imperial autocracy in East Asia and Eastern Europe marks a turning point in history: It demonstrates that violence is ineffective and heralds the end of these autocratic empires.

The concept of "empire" designates two phenomena: One is an internal political structure in which power is concentrated in the hands of a single autocrat; the other is stigmatized by the power of hegemonic ambition and the practice of aggression and the annexation or the control of other nations or countries. These two aspects generally go hand in hand, as was the case in Hitler's Third Reich or Stalin's empire. But it does not always have to be thus: There is also the "puppet emperor" who claims authority over domestic affairs but is "an official under a feudal ruler" on external matters.

Dictatorships are tied to violence. Every dictatorial empire maintains its domination thanks to its own system of violence or the violence of its ruler. Violence constitutes the very foundation of a despotic imperial system. The defeat of violence will bring about the collapse of the imperial system. This is a phenomenon of the 1980s. In the course of history, the survival of an imperial despotic system has always been tied to the use of violence by a dictator eager to conquer, to plunder and control the land, natural resources, markets, and slave labor in order to turn them into his personal wealth and power. As the traditional Chinese saying puts it, "Everything on earth belongs to the emperor, all peoples are the emperor's subjects."* Imperial expansionism is for the purpose of "taking advantage of the space of life and of power."

But today this law of history is no longer valid. Human intelligence and creativity have now attained a dramatically new stage. A system in which land, mineral products, and all kinds of natural resources are produced by slave labor can no longer form the basis of national power and increased wealth of a country. These elements play a role less and less important for survival. And the realization of human intelligence and creativity are more and more a determining factor in national power. That is to say, the ability of a nation and people to survive in the contemporary world no longer has to depend on violence to plunder territory or enslave other people; rather it is enough for each individual to develop his or her innate intelligence and creative power to establish superiority in competition. Recourse to violence, in one's own country or abroad, can only engender limited results. The exploitation of a prisoner or

---

*The traditional Chinese notion was that all humans, Chinese and non-Chinese alike, were subjects of the Chinese emperor—the emperor at the "center of the world."

a slave is limited to the use of his or her physical being. On the other hand, profiting from the infinite creativity of a person implies that she or he must be free. Expanding the machinery of violence in the contemporary world now has only an insignificant effect on society's wealth, natural resources, and human intelligence and creativity, and it is a kind of irrational counterdevelopment of production. The era of the empires that depended on war and violence to expand cannot be restored. Mankind is on the verge of entering a new historical epoch, an epoch in which violence is not an effective tool for external relations or solving internal political problems. The termination of the autocratic empire system and the peaceful evolution toward a free democratic system is the only course of development for contemporary civilization.

However, people are still in the habit of putting on old spectacles to make judgments on new historical developments. The theory by which China is an exception to contemporary developments in civilized societies, suggesting that a free democratic system does not fit in with the country's special characteristics, is continually promoted by groups as diverse as the autocrats in control of China and the overseas "democratic movement" elites.

In the recent "trial" of members of the 1989 democratic movement, the Li Peng government complacently asserted that the June Fourth slaughter was "correct": Don't you see that today China is more "stable" than the former Soviet Union and Eastern Europe? This is the result of using force to suppress the "turmoil" and "riot"! "The Chinese people only need the right to survive! The rights of man, of freedom, of democracy, that's all poppycock!"

Meanwhile, the overseas "democratic movement" elites form "research centers" to meticulously develop theses in which they expound the reasons why the democratic system is inappropriate to China's special conditions and how the development of democratic progress in East Asia and Eastern Europe have "traversed different roads":

> That which makes China different is partly its old original Confucian culture; a culture very different from the Christian culture that brought the ferments of modernization; and partly that it's a huge country dominated by a communist system. China is a traditional society but is also a society that has undergone a communist revolution. It is a communist country, but also a communist country in an ancient East Asian culture. China cannot go through the economic modernization and political democratization that have occurred in the noncommunist countries of East Asia. Nor can China undergo the same process of political democratization that communist countries outside East Asia did in jettisoning the communist one-party, autocratic system and then beginning the process of economic modernization.[2]

So what of China?

These overseas "democratic movement" elites assert that a new autocracy "guided by power elites" will be established after the communist totalitarian system in China is ended (though they avoid discussing just how this will occur, sometimes hinting that the situation must change after the death of the old man). The new autocracy will be composed of a "political elite from the top ten percent" possessing "the most knowledge, vision, and ability" that will organize a "power elite clique to rule the eighty-five or ninety percent of the masses who are poorly educated, incapable of participating in government, and don't understand citizen rights."[3]

In 1989 even before the blood shed in the June Fourth massacre had dried, these self-proclaimed "1989 democratic movement" elites had already, as Columbia University Professor Andrew J. Nathan described in his book *China's Crisis*, "transferred much of the onus for an acknowledged catastrophe from the shoulders of those who wrought it to the backs of those who suffered it."[4] Their published "monographs" and "essays" reprimand in a single voice the vast majority of China's farmers, workers, students, and intellectuals for having brought disaster to the "reform." "Of China's eight hundred million peasants, three hundred million or so are culturally backward, and the unique political characteristic of a peasant-based society is manifested in the power of the monarch"[5]; "the most intense attitude of the workers in the midst of the reform is a fear of loss, while they are highly suspicious of economic liberalization"[6]; "the character of the student movement was in the end the basis for its destruction."[7] In the view of these elites, supporters of the "reform" consisted only of "the group of entrepreneurs and private vendors [*getihu*] who have a newly created interest in the economic liberalization" and "a small group of theorists among young intellectuals."[8]

These new self-proclaimed theorists of "new authoritarianism" and "liberalism" argue that if China were to implement democracy prematurely chaos would result: If a measure of freedom of speech and press were allowed, the vast majority of farmers, workers, intellectuals, and students would emerge as an "opposition faction" [*fanduipai*] to the "reform." Of course, if free elections were allowed, these "elite groups" would have little chance of being elected. Because of this, they advocate that China can only create a system of "a minority elite holding leadership positions to manage the development of the nation."[9] They consider reform, freedom, order, and stability to be diametrically opposed to democracy. They consider their principal adversaries to be those who advocate a system at once free and democratic in China and they adorn them with the epithet "universalist democrats" [*fanmin-zhuzhuyizhe*].[10]

Thus, after enduring forty years of the empire of Mao Zedong and Deng Xiaoping's autocracy, must the Chinese people now suffer through yet a "third empire"? Both the current holder of power, the Li Peng government, and those preparing for "new authoritarianism" nourish the same dream of empire. But this dream, no matter how wonderful it may be for some, has no chance of surviving.

To begin with, the foundation of the empire rooted in war and violence has already been destroyed. Deng Xiaoping's final "Tiananmen battle" was the greatest failure in the entire life of this famous general who fought the battles of Huaihai and the Yangtze River Crossing and also inaugurated the ten-year reform and opening up to the outside world. Deng Xiaoping has been defeated and returned to power three times—defeated once by Wang Ming and twice by Mao Zedong—and each time he returned it was considered a political miracle. This fourth defeat, however, was self-inflicted, and he will never recover. The June Fourth slaughter was the death knell of the Deng Xiaoping empire, the last Chinese empire. The attempt by Deng Xiaoping to have the newly installed General Secretary Jiang Zemin, whose hands were unstained by bloodshed on June Fourth, repair the empire, was itself an indication that Deng had lost confidence in the results of war and violence. They can no longer serve any purpose in China.

Further, after Deng Xiaoping, who could then pretend to the rank of dictator? As I have written here, Deng Xiaoping is not someone who longs for formal power. During these ten years, the number of people who called on Deng to become Party chairman or state president was far more numerous than those who called on Yüan Shih-k'ai to proclaim himself emperor. Nevertheless, Deng refused to assume these positions, explaining, "It's not that I'm not qualified for this, but considering the overall situation, I think it would be better for me not to take it on." That came from the bottom of his heart. However, the problem was precisely that he was "qualified for this" [*zige*]. Although not an "emperor," others wanted him to be a "crownless emperor," or "backstage ruler." He ended by accommodating himself to them, though it made life impossible for those who were truly "crowned"—Hu Yaobang and Zhao Ziyang—and who one after another had to step down. Deng Xiaoping's "status" was a consequence of history and his military victories and the toughening that was also a product of the three disgraces he suffered. But today war and violence have become ineffective and can no longer produce a "supreme ruler." Deng Xiaoping is the last. Dai Qing once asserted "All right, I am an autocrat, but I am the last. I am using my power to ensure the introduction of democracy."[11] Such an assertion is bound to get nowhere in China. Neither Li Peng, Jiang Zemin, nor Zhao Ziyang have the "status" to dominate a "third empire." And the "young" theorists of "new authoritarianism" have even less.

Finally, the greatest historical legacy of the June 1989 democratic movement is that the Chinese masses are no longer fond of personality worship. Mass personality worship was one of the primary social conditions of the long domination of the dictatorial system in China. The combination of personal worship from below and violent rule imposed from above sometimes gave tyrannical politics a misleading aura. Both the 1976 April Fifth movement that preceded the end of the Mao Zedong empire and the 1978–1979 Democracy

Wall movement provided Deng with a new holy halo and baptized him "Deng the upright magistrate" [*Deng qingtian*]. What was unique about the 1989 democratic movement was that the people were now conscious enough not to lay hope on the "wisdom" of a certain Party leader but instead placed hope in their own power and looked to the independence and wisdom of the democratic movement to reform the old system and create a new one.

But the ineffectiveness of violence and the end of the empire do not automatically produce success for a democratic system. Although Deng no longer possesses the status of a human autocrat, the power of the cliques who love autocracy and oppose freedom and democracy cannot be overlooked. Therefore, the movement to terminate the autocratic system and bring about a democratic system should seek the most broad-based alliance on a national basis, including farmers, workers, students, intellectuals, and people who favor freedom and democracy in industry and commerce and from all walks of life. This should include CCP members and the military who also favor freedom and democracy. Such an alliance is the basis for ending the autocratic empire and establishing a free and democratic system. Only by forming such an alliance will it be possible to compel the forces of autocracy to give up their reliance on ineffective violence and accept the fundamental reform of the political system through peace, rationality, and nonviolence.

Isn't it true that those "young" theorists of "new authoritarianism" are putting considerable effort into opposing "universal democracy" and advocating that the "democratic banner be discarded"?

The forces for freedom and democracy should accept the challenge of "new authoritarianism," for democracy must be "universal," so universal that it will affect everyone, including those advocates of "new authoritarianism." Since the advocates of "new authoritarianism" oppose proponents of "universal democracy," the latter should unite with the former. We must help every Chinese become his or her own ruler, a ruler of the country and society. This is the principle of the universality of democracy.

The application of democracy throughout society is the first principle of a modern democratic system. That is to say, democracy does not distinguish between East and West, capitalism or socialism, bourgeoisie or proletarian, commoners or elites. Democracy is the creature of all the people. Without accepting the principle of the universal application of democracy, the development toward autocracy is inevitable.

Both the Nationalists and the communists have gone through the same historical experience: By the negation of universal democracy they both took the road of dictatorship and totalitarianism. Sun Yat-sen proposed the "Three Principles of the People" and on that basis in 1912 established the "Republic of China." But the Nationalist Party embarked on the road toward dictatorship and totalitarianism as soon as Sun Yat-sen discarded the principle of universal democracy. Sun Yat-sen believed that "the slave system in China has been in existence for thousands of years and the common people do not yet know that they should assume the role of ruler. Therefore, we have no method other than coercion to force them to become the ruler and teach them to practice it. This is what I mean by political tutelage."[12] For Sun Yat-sen, when after a period of tutelage, the slaves learned how to comport them-selves as masters, the Nationalist Party would "return political power to the people." He said, "After independence, and when people's rights are consoli-dated, I will renounce political power to once again become a simple citizen. Affairs shall be run by the sovereign will of the people. I will establish neither a dictatorship nor an enlightened despotism. I love freedom as much as my life, and my sincerity above all will be evident for all to see."[13] Little did he guess that after his death another tutor, Chiang K'ai-shek, would take pleasure in this tutelage, and the more he practiced it, the more he believed that he was a genius and the masses were stupid; and that finally, political tutelage, would be practiced into the foreseeable future. Thus there came about the twenty-two-year political tutelage of Chiang K'ai-shek [1927–1949] that was de-feated by Mao Zedong, who flaunted the project of building a "free and democratic China."

Mao Zedong began by making his stand on freedom and democracy; he preached Lincoln's idea of "by the people, for the people, and of the people" and Roosevelt's four freedoms, implicitly acknowledging the universal char-acter of democracy. Starting from 1949, however, he began restricting the principle, changing it into the "People's Democratic Dictatorship." In fact, Mao Zedong was quite frank, in that he publicly announced this so-called People's Democratic Dictatorship. When anyone said to him, "You are dicta-torial," he replied, "My dear sirs, you are quite right, that is just what we are."[14] But no dictatorship, once in place, can be retracted, so that over time Mao discarded ideas of freedom and democracy in order to establish the so-called overall dictatorship of the proletariat in all realms.

The "new authoritarians" and the "liberals" propose an "elite democracy" that "allows some people to become democrats ahead of others." Since the masses know nothing about democracy, the leaders and elites have to carry out "political tutelage." However, they are not as frank as Mao Zedong. This "elite democracy" is nothing other than a dictatorship exercised by the elite. If one defends the idea that democracy can't be universal and that it is only granted to some people or a certain class, one may as well say that society has to be made up in part by masters and for the rest by slaves. This is not modern contemporary democracy. On this point, there cannot be a different standard between East and West, nor do there exist any fundamental differences stem-ming from different races or cultural traditions. Political systems can take vari-ous forms in different nations, for instance the parliamentary system [*yihuizhi*], the congressional system [*guohuizhi*], and the system of the Peo-ple's Congress. In that sense, there can be differences between East and West.

The system on the European continent is different from that of Great Britain, which in turn is different from the U.S. system in the relative balance of power between the various branches. However, as to whether the ultimate source of power is derived from an independent citizenry or a minority holding privileged power—that is the fundamental difference between modern democracy and modern autocracy.

A principle of modern democracy is that it is based on human rights. Democracy cannot be separated from human rights or from freedom for the individual. This is the difference between the modern democratic system and the direct democracy of the city states of ancient Greece. Under the system in ancient Greece, slaves had virtually no rights and were not considered citizens. Even Socrates, a free thinker, was sentenced to death by the "democratic system" for adhering to free thought. This was a case of "democracy by violent people" [*baomin minzhu*], that is, an autocracy by violent people. A political system that is not based on human rights will not only generate the dictatorship of a tyrant but can also become a tyranny of the people. A "democracy" that only acknowledges the principle that the minority obeys the majority while ignoring the human rights of each individual can easily become an autocracy of a despotic people, such as the so-called big democracy of the "Cultural Revolution" in which people were arbitrarily slaughtered and even cannibalized at the hands of the majority.

Advocates of "new authoritarianism" polarize democracy and freedom, democracy and order, and democracy and stability, a view that indicates just how little they understand the basic principles of democracy. They merely take democracy as a kind of "rules of the game" [*youxi guize*], in which both the majority and minority can play. But they forget, intentionally or not, the two fundamental principles: universal democracy and human rights. That's why they propose that a democratic system cannot apply to a country like China, all the while zealously struggling to keep those "rules of the game" up to date and proposing to "forge a constitution," or even better, "revise" one. Perhaps they are preparing for the future "elite democracy"?

In reality, the difficult labor of producing a democratic system in China does not stem from the lack of a constitution or "rules of the game." In this century, China has had eleven constitutions: one in the Qing dynasty (1908); three at the beginning of the Republic of China (1912, 1913, and 1923); two by the Nationalists (1931 and 1946); and five by the Communists (1931, 1954, 1975, 1978, and 1982). China also does not lack a variety of different political systems: The Nationalists practiced their "five-branch constitution" (besides the executive, legislature, and judiciary, there were also the control and examination *yuan*); the CCP has had three formal divisions of power, among the State Council, the National People's Congress, and the Supreme Court. But although in reality this boiled down to "one party, one leader, one doctrine," it denied the principle of universal democracy and protection of human rights and refused to guarantee human rights, which enabled the political party, the leader, and the minority elites to usurp power over people's lives and property.

That's why, in a summary of the twentieth century, dictatorial China devoured democratic China. The most important lesson of this history is that we must put an end to the autocratic system of "one party, one leader, one doctrine." We must push for the establishment of a modern democratic system based on the principle of universality and human rights. This is the most fundamental premise and guarantee for the achievement of modernization in China. We should begin by striving for the protection of the freedom and rights of each citizen as guaranteed by the current PRC state constitution and to form a powerful alliance among the forces of freedom and democracy in a legal struggle to achieve democracy.

This includes a struggle for legal rights in freedom of speech, the press, publication, and creativity, as well as academic freedom. We should not believe that these freedoms are a monopoly of intellectuals. Each class, each individual, and each interest group—farmers, workers, students, soldiers, industrialists, and business people—all have an independent will, independent demands, and independent hopes that need to be freely expressed. Therefore, the need for free expression is obviously the need for forming a powerful alliance of free and democratic forces.

We must also struggle for more universal rights, including freedom of belief, religion, and association and free elections. In addition, there is a need to push for the right of subsistence, housing, and employment that Li Peng boasts about guaranteeing, because human rights cannot be divided. The Chinese want to live life as masters and not any longer as slaves. To be master means one has the right to choose one's own public servants and to dismiss them if they turn against one.

These ten years of reform and opening up have profoundly changed the social structures of "great unity, independence, and unbreakable stability." It has engendered a new generation of farmers, workers, entrepreneurs, and intellectuals of independent consciousness. Therefore, to condemn the younger generation for having lost all moral sense is unjustifiable. The democratic student movement in 1989 that extended to more than three hundred cities and towns on the contrary bears proof of this generation's sense of values. It formed the vanguard of the democratic and liberal forces that attempted to put an end to dictatorship and imperialism in twentieth-century China. The bloody tragedy in Tiananmen does not represent the victory of the imperial system. On the contrary, it signifies the last palpitations of a desperate struggle. Silence imposed by guns cannot last. No matter that the government of Li Peng and his advocates of the "new authoritarianism" make a big stink today: The day will come when the people will break their silence to annihilate the dictatorial and imperial system.

After the June Fourth slaughter, Deng Xiaoping announced that he would transfer his illegal supreme power to a third successor—what he called the "core of the third generation," Jiang Zemin. From a historical point of view, the Deng Xiaoping empire has already come to an end. After the June Fourth massacre, China entered the "post-Deng" era, a period of transition between "life and death." The dictatorial system is out of breath, but it is not yet deceased. The seeds of a free and democratic system have been planted, but it lies in the womb, as yet unborn. Each and every Chinese must contribute fully to ensure its peaceful birth.

Notes

1. Deng Xiaoping, "Emancipate the Mind, Seek Truth from Facts, and Unite as One in Looking to the Future," in *Selected Works of Deng Xiaoping: 1975–1982 (Deng Xiaoping wenxuan: 1975–1982)* (Beijing: People's Publishing House, 1983), p. 136.

2. Wu Guoguang, "Liberalism: The Basic Guideline for Redirecting the Promotion of China's Modernization," Contemporary China Research Center Paper, Number 2.

3. Chen Yizi, *China: The Ten Years Reform and the 1989 People's Movement (Zhongguo: Shinian gaige yu bajiu minyun)* (Taipai, Taiwan: Lianjing Press, 1990).

4. Andrew J. Nathan, *China's Crisis: Dilemmas of Reform and Prospects for Democracy* (New York: Columbia University Press, 1990), pp. 196–197.

5. Chen Yizi, *China: The Ten Year Reform.*

6. Wu Guoguang, "Liberalism."

7. Ibid.

8. Ibid.

9. Chen Yizi, Wang Xiaoqiang, and Li Jun, "The Developmental Model for Establishing a 'Hard Government and Soft Economy,'" in *New Authoritarianism: Debate over the Basic Principles of Reform (Xin quanweizhuyi: Dui gaige lilun ganglingde lunzheng)*, ed. Liu Jun and Li Lin (Beijing: Jingji Xueyuan Publishing House, 1989).

10. Wu Guoguang, "Liberalism."

11. Dai Qing, "From Lin Zexu to Jiang Jingguo [Chiang Ching-kuo]," in *New Authoritarianism*, ed. Liu Jun and Li Lin [Translated in Geremie Barmé and Linda Javin, *New Ghosts, Old Dreams: Chinese Rebel Voices* (New York: Random House, 1992), p. 189].

12. Sun Yat-sen, "An Explanation of Political Tutelage" (Speech to the Nationalist Party Gathering in Shanghai, November 9, 1920), in *The Complete Works of the Founding Father (Guofu quanji)* (Taipei, Taiwan: Party History Committee of the Chinese Nationalist Central Party Committee, 1985), vol. 2, p. 399.

13. Sun Yat-sen, "Proclamation Explaining the Task of a 'Government of National Construction' (1924)," in *The Complete Works*, vol. 1, pp. 925–926.

14. Mao Zedong, "On the People's Democratic Dictatorship," in *Selected Works of Mao Zedong (Mao Zedong xuanji)* (Beijing: People's Publishing House, 1977), vol. 3, p. 417.

Epilogue to the English Edition

Just at a time when rumors that Deng Xiaoping was seriously ill or had actually passed away were so pervasive in the media that they affected the stock market (in fact he was peacefully celebrating his eighty-ninth birthday), my good friend Peter Rand informed me that he and his two friends Nancy Liu and Lawrence Sullivan had completed translating the English version of this book, and he asked me to write an epilogue.

Deng Xiaoping: Chronicle of an Empire covers the period of Deng Xiaoping's rule up to June 1989, when he had not yet reached the age of eighty-five. In the four years since then, the clock has stopped on the history of Deng's empire. So much so, indeed, that Deng's systematic practice of opposing "rightists" in odd-numbered years and taking on "leftists" in even-numbered years has been suspended. Between 1989 and 1991, Deng's "Jiang [Zemin]–Li [Peng] structure" seemed determined to follow the conservative inclinations of Chen Yun, Wang Zhen, and Deng Liqun in order to carry out the contractional policies of "administrative rectification and readjustment" [*zhili zhengdun*] in the economic sphere and "opposing peaceful evolution" [*fan heping yanbian*] in the political realm.* Their mutual celebration of the 1991 three-day military coup in the Soviet Union amounted to a confession of their dream to restore a Stalinist and Maoist empire in China.

But the economic forces released during China's ten-year reform made it impossible to push the country's economy back into the bird cage of the old planned economy. Both the Chen Yun clique—the old venerated vanguard of Stalinism—and the "prince's faction" [*taizidang*]† of the Chen Yuan genera-

---

*This notion was disseminated by opponents of "bourgeois liberalism" in the September 1991 internal CCP document "The Struggle Between Peaceful Evolution and Counterpeaceful Evolution is a Class Struggle in the World Arena." It contained criticism of Western countries, particularly the U.S. under the Bush administration, for their alleged campaign to foster a "peaceful evolution" of China from a communist dictatorship to a Western-style parliamentary democracy.

†For an analysis of this group's influence in contemporary politics, see Ho Pin and Gao Xin, *The Chinese Communist "Prince's Faction" (Zhonggong "Taizidang")* (Taiwan: Shibao wenhua, 1992), English trans. by Allyson Lee, *Princes and Princesses of Red China* (Toronto: Canada Mirror Books, 1993).

tion attempted at home and abroad to advance the notion that the size of the bird cage "could be expanded or reduced and be given all kinds of flexibility." Try as they did very hard to advertise how much security the cage afforded those inside it, their efforts had almost no effect on the reality in China. Along with the collapse of the coup in the Soviet Union, the policies of "administrative rectification and readjustment" and "opposing peaceful evolution" of the Jiang-Li structure failed miserably. The market economy smashed the "ideological forbidden zone" that once upon a time had prohibited inquiry into whether an initiative was "in the nature of capitalism or socialism." And the continuing development of a market economy signaled a historic shift of focus from the central to the local economic level and from an economy managed by the state to one managed by the people. Deng Xiaoping's tour of the southern provinces early in 1992 was itself the upshot of this historic change.

But Deng Xiaoping's individual views haven't changed one iota since "June Fourth." His speeches on the 1992 southern tour contained nothing new. His most important comment during this *Wanderjahr* was that people should "guard against rightism, but should mainly guard against leftism." At the time, it was said that this line could not be found in the record of Deng's speech, but that it had been added by the note taker as a summary. What Deng did say was this: "I am not a leftist." Then Mao Mao [pen name for Deng Rong], one of his daughters,* exclaimed: "You aren't a rightist either!" To be more accurate, the transcript should state that Deng is "not a leftist" in the economic sphere, where "[we] should mainly guard against leftism," and in the political sphere he is "not a rightist," in the sense that he will "guard against rightism." Over the past decade or so, Deng has always lingered at the crossroads of an open economy and a closed political system—he has been willing neither to move one step forward nor to retreat one step back.

But great changes have already taken place in the political situation surrounding Deng. The political structure of centralized power has been weakened. The "third generation" of leaders of the "Jiang-Li structure" appointed by Deng following the June Fourth massacre is a farce. It's a group composed of a bunch of incompetent individuals who have yet to establish any trust at home or abroad, who have relied on Deng's support but who in actuality he dislikes. Around the time of the attempted coup in the Soviet Union, Jiang Zemin literally became Deng Liqun's public address system. His speech on July 1, 1991, on the seventieth anniversary of the CCP, advocated "viewing opposition to peaceful evolution as the central political task." This was prepared by Deng Liqun and drafted by Teng Wensheng. Deng Liqun

---

*See Mao Mao, *My Father, Deng Xiaoping* (*Wode Fuqin, Deng Xiaoping*) (Beijing: Central Party Literature Publishing House, 1993), vol. 1.

bragged that it was the "new *Communist Manifesto*," and he arranged for the entire CCP to engage in an intensive study of the document that effectively launched the nationwide campaign of "opposing peaceful evolution." That campaign not only met with pervasive resistance at the local level but also provoked Deng Xiaoping's rage. In fact, his 1992 southern tour was a direct consequence of this campaign. He set out on his junket accompanied solely by members of his family to demonstrate his distrust of the "Jiang-Li structure." Clearly the reform forces in the Party have been systematically excluded from the "Jiang-Li structure" ever since the two big purges of the CCP in recent years—Hu Yaobang's forced resignation in 1987 and the June 4, 1989, massacre. Until then, Deng had relied on a political scheme in which every other year the reform forces at the center countered the conservative forces, but this no longer worked. Now Deng had to mobilize support at the local levels to help him encircle the center and force Jiang and Li to surrender. The weakening of the central reform forces did not, however, translate into the consolidation of the conservative forces. The deaths of Hu Qiaomu and Wang Zhen in 1992 and 1993, respectively, along with the retirement of Yao Yilin and Song Ping have seriously affected the influence of the Chen Yun clique. The only one left is that malodorous stuffed shirt, Deng Liqun. Moreover, recently Jiang Zemin has become more suspicious of him, warning his subordinates to "keep their distance from Comrade Liqun."

There has also been an increase in the power of the local levels in their confrontations with the center. The historical progression in China since June Fourth indicates that after the reform forces at the center were smashed, local reform forces took up the slack and acted as a force to counterbalance the center. Such counterbalancing, in fact, prevented the "Jiang-Li structure" from using "administrative rectification and readjustment" in 1989–1990 to pull the Chinese economy back from the market to a more centrally planned system. Moreover, this counterbalancing obstructed the 1991 attempts of Jiang Zemin and the Chen Yun clique to restore the Stalinist system of "ideological control in carrying out the campaign of 'opposing peaceful evolution.'" Finally, this counterbalancing gave support to Deng Xiaoping's effort on his southern tour to promote the market economy. Such counterweighting of the central government by local powers was a political by-product of the shift from a planned to a market economy. It is a new factor in stabilizing the political situation in China, and it will continue to play that role in the future.

Additionally, let's consider the growth and expanding consciousness of political forces among the people. Deng Xiaoping's June Fourth massacre and the arrest, trial, imprisonment, and exile of dissident forces failed to "completely eliminate" the free democratic forces; on the contrary, the free democratic forces in China have grown and matured under the killing knife of the empire. The resort to a violent crackdown, and the continued reliance on surveillance and media blackouts, along with the use of military police, can no longer prevent the dissemination of "dissenting views" among the people. They no longer fear the appellation of "dissenting views" or "counterrevolutionary views," and indeed these viewpoints are now more popular than the "official standpoint" and the "revolutionary standpoint." As soon as political dissidents are released from prison, they cease to be seen by the public as "those with whom there must not be any contact." On the contrary, they quickly become the vanguards, whom the people most respect. Even more valuable, a mature common understanding has formed among political dissidents of different age groups, in prison or in exile abroad, from Wei Jingsheng and Liu Qing to the 1989 student movement leaders Wang Dan and Chai Ling, about the need to face the realities of mainland China, to promote political reform through the implementation of the principles of the current state constitution, to gradually realize democracy and create a legal system, and to terminate one-party rule. Such a choice is consistent with the common popular desire in China and among the rational reform forces still in the Party to maintain social stability.

These changes in the Chinese political climate call for people to reexamine the sophism that the prosperity and security of China depend solely on Deng Xiaoping the individual. Unfortunately, that old way of thinking is still popular in the political realm in China and among the military, not to mention the news media in Hong Kong, Taiwan, and the West, where it is commonly believed that "once Deng dies, great chaos will prevail." Those both in and outside the Communist Party opposed to reform in China still take advantage of this silly superstition to effectively prevent China from moving ahead toward political reform. Their only morsel of evidence is the old cliché that used to be spouted by Western colonialists: "The Chinese people are backward and low class." Note here the content of a speech given by a self-proclaimed "political dissident," presented recently at Harvard University:

> Present-day China (which includes intellectuals and primarily intellectuals) is a society in which social decadence prevails. People will do anything to make a fortune and to become rich. Before I came abroad, I heard a saying in China that describes the "three new ways peasants become rich: They rob ancient tombs, steal electrical cables from factories, and become prostitutes." The peasants are not alone. Throughout China, people who are anxious to become rich have become quite frightening, and except for their fear of the harsh laws imposed by the Communist Party, they feel no other fear or taboos. At present, the only way to maintain social order is to ensure the application of harsh laws. For once the tight external controls imposed by the police, the courts, and prisons founder, China will become a human hell controlled by wolves.
>
> Moreover, discontent, anger, and hatred, along with tension between various social and ethnic groups, is far more serious in China than it was in the former Soviet Union. Once the suppression by dictatorship is ended, the explosion of these

sudden and violent destructive forces will be severe enough to overwhelm a democratic system.[1]

Such arguments are familiar to Chinese officials. Deng Xiaoping himself once commented: "You Westerners blame China for not exercising human rights and human freedom. I can open the gate and allow two million people [to emigrate to the United States]. Dare you take all of them?"* This was the comment of a Chinese official. But the remarks uttered by the "political dissidents" achieve sensational results far more effectively. Nevertheless, they are nothing other than sensational remarks.

First, these statements don't contain even the tiniest grain of truth. The entire world has witnessed the enormous outpouring of commercial products for both domestic and foreign consumption released by the market economy in China. These products have not been robbed from ancient tombs and they don't consist of stolen electrical cables. They aren't the benefactions of prostitutes, either. They are the artifacts of the labor and wisdom of hundreds of millions of Chinese people, including millions, who emancipated from the land, plunged head first into the free labor market. This "floating population" is the real genius behind China's economic prosperity. Of course, criminal acts like the "robbing of ancient tombs" indeed have occurred, just as they do in other societies. But it's senseless slander to characterize those criminal acts conducted by a minority of people as "the common way peasants become rich" or as a "pervasive disease afflicting all of China."

Further, these arguments are blatantly illogical. That's my next point. Just what is the rationale behind the argument that "once the suppression by dictatorship is ended" and "the tight external controls imposed by the police, the courts, and prisons founder, China will become a human hell controlled by wolves"? How is it that "violent and destructive forces" can be "handled" by a totalitarian system but "will overwhelm" a democratic system? According to this "logic," only totalitarian control can maintain the legal system and social order, and a democratic system has no connection whatsoever to law and social order. This is sheer nonsense. A democratic system does not eliminate the role of the police, the courts, and the prisons. On the contrary, it deploys them more effectively. Once the shift is made from totalitarian control to a constitutional democratic system, the function of the police, the courts, and the prisons will also change. These agencies will no longer be used to ar-

---

*Deng made these remarks during the Carter presidency after questions were raised in the U.S. Congress regarding the freedom of the Chinese people to emigrate, a stipulation of the Jackson-Vanik Amendment that was, of course, originally aimed at the Soviet Union.

rest, put on trial, and imprison political and ideological prisoners. No longer will they serve as instruments by which the totalitarians arbitrarily suppress opinions at will and violate human rights. These agencies will "lose" their mandate to provide trumped up, phony verdicts, and instead they will concentrate their energies on punishing real illegal acts while strengthening the legal system and maintaining social order. They will deal with the true wolves in society. So to describe China's conversion to a constitutional democratic system as one that leads to "mob politics" like the lawlessness of the "Cultural Revolution" is to mix up two things—mob rule and constitutional democracy—that are fundamentally at odds with one another. "Mob politics" during the "Cultural Revolution" was the direct product of Mao Zedong's monarchical, totalitarian system [*baojun zhuanzhi*]. Only by terminating the lawlessness inherent in the totalitarian system and bringing about the conversion to a constitutional democracy can a resurgence of mob politics be avoided in China.

Next let me say that those arguments represent the last desperate efforts of a small privileged elite to prop up the totalitarian system after Deng's demise. Because not only does that semitotalitarian and semimarket economy of the Deng Xiaoping empire protect the old privileged classes and bankrupt agencies of the planned economy—it also nourishes the next generation of that privileged class, the nouveaux riches of the market economy. A full analysis has yet to be made of the phenomenon of "making a fortune and becoming rich" in the Deng Xiaoping empire. Due to the semimarket economy, working people and the educated classes now have the possibility of making a fortune based on their labor and knowledge. That has been the true source of economic development and prosperity in contemporary China, and it's also the basis for stability and progress. On the other hand, thanks to the semitotalitarian system, bankrupt agencies of the planned economy and the nouveaux riches have been given the opportunity to steal state property and social wealth through the happenstance of political privilege. In fact, the origins of the June Fourth massacre may be found in the resistance mounted by these two privileged groups against any democratic changes in order to protect their vital interests. Thus, to no one's surprise, since the crackdown an alliance between these two groups has reinforced the structure of the totalitarian system that allows them to steal social wealth. It's an alliance that treats the government as if it were one big "family" [*jia*] based on blood ties: Chen Yun and his son Chen Yuan, Wang Zhen and his son Wang Jun, Yao Yilin and his son-in-law Wang Qishan, Rong Yiren and his son Rong Zhijian—political power combined with money is passed on from one generation to the next. These people don't have to "rob ancient tombs, steal electrical cables, and become prostitutes." And neither Jiang Zemin's much heralded "anticorruption" drive nor Zhu Rongji's policy of "administrative rectification and readjustment" will touch them, because Jiang Zemin, Li Peng, and Zhu Rongji all need the support of these key figures.* Even a Soviet–East European–style collapse would not threaten them.

These people have no fear of "riots," because they can "kill two hundred thousand people in exchange for twenty years of stability" (a line initially said to have been uttered by Deng Xiaoping after June 4, 1989, although further inquiry reveals that it actually came from Yao Yilin's son-in-law, Wang Qishan). And if killing becomes ineffective, they have another means at their disposal. Just like the cunning bunny with three holes in which to hide, they have stashed vast amounts of capital in Hong Kong and overseas. Their greatest fear is the implementation of democracy in China, because only when there is a constitution and a legal system superior to privilege, these privileged wolves won't be able to steal the national wealth. This is the reason why these various privileged groups have forged their alliance and why deep down they detest democracy.

Finally, these arguments all represent an effort to restore the old empire or build a new empire, but none of them have held water very long. From General Secretary Jiang Zemin's "New *Communist Manifesto*" to Chen Yuan's September 1991 "Realistic Responses and Strategic Options for China Following the Soviet Union Upheaval," these various efforts to defend the totalitarian system peaked during 1991. Jiang Zemin used the June Fourth massacre and the "upheaval in the Soviet Union" in an attempt to restore the Stalinist-Maoist empire and he even tried to wipe out the semimarket economy pushed by Deng Xiaoping. At the same time, Chen Yuan challenged Jiang Zemin at the 1992 Fourteenth Party Congress with his attempt to establish a new empire in which the "prince's faction" would establish its control over state property and national wealth. But both Jiang and Chen Yuan were hit by the blow of Deng's southern tour.

Then came the turn of the "political dissidents." Even before the 1989 democracy movement, calls had been heard from these dissidents supporting the totalitarian system. The most famous was by Ms. Dai Qing, who as noted above enthusiastically endorsed the idea of a "last autocrat." Now they are playing the same old tune. But the atmosphere has radically changed. Five years ago they at least had an object for their love and respect who was just waiting to enter the stage. Who can they call on now? They themselves don't know. At a recent symposium held at Princeton University, someone made

---

*Thus an investigation of the Great Wall Corporation was halted in 1993 when it threatened to implicate relatives of top leaders, including Deng Xiaoping, though later the general manager, Shen Taifu, was executed in 1994.

the claim that "a Napoleon is bound to emerge on mainland China." When asked whence such a figure would emerge, the commentator replied: "From the corps of young military officers." This would amount to nothing more than a Latin American–style military coup in which the "government is overthrown by a battalion of troops, two tanks, and half a dozen officers." It is but a vague dream, in which the 1.1 billion Chinese appear as a "mob" or as "jackals and wolves all over China." Attention neototalitarians: So you want a return to the ancien régime? If you try, 1.1 billion jackals and wolves will sweep you away with one stroke!

These fantasies can frighten only a small number of people with weak nerves. During my five-year stay abroad, I have encountered quite a number of relatives and friends, both Chinese and foreign, who travel frequently to China. All have witnessed the critical transformation that I have depicted in this book, and not one of them believes that once the shackles of the totalitarian system are broken China will become a human hell, or a "yellow peril" that will engulf the entire world.

There are, of course, a number of problems on mainland China, among them a chaotic financial system and pervasive corruption. But these are not the result of the "backward and low-class" character of the Chinese people. These are birth defects inherent to a privileged class born of the union of a semimarket economy and the semitotalitarian system of the Deng Xiaoping empire. Without a change in this self-contradicting system, it will be impossible to establish a sound market economy and a comprehensive institutional structure. And without changes in the system of privileges, Zhu Rongji's attempt to restore financial order and Jiang Zemin's effort to root out corruption will go nowhere. In order to enable the semimarket economy to become a complete market economy, the malignant tumor of the system of privileges must be removed and changes in the direction of an institutionalized democratic system must be realized.

The preconditions for promoting such changes already exist. As long as Deng Xiaoping is alive, progress toward such changes will be slow, but once Deng is no longer around the pace of change will certainly accelerate. Deng's nerves were frayed by the shadow of the so-called big democracy of the "Cultural Revolution"; as a result, he couldn't distinguish between the reality of the Tiananmen demonstrators in 1989 and the rampaging Red Guards of 1966. This led to the crackdown on the students in the square, who were demanding the creation of institutional democracy. In the years since June Fourth, that shadow continues to cast a pall over him and effectively prevents him from taking the first steps toward political reform. If it can be said that his 1992 southern tour was his last advance, then he merely managed to push aside the obstacles of the old planned economy and failed to budge the rock blocking institutional reforms. About the importance of removing that obstacle, he himself has said:

We must strengthen our legal system. Democracy has to be institutionalized and written into law, so as to make sure that institutions and laws do not change whenever the leadership changes, or whenever the leaders change their views.[2]

Deng's ultimate tragedy is that he cannot remove this obstacle. But the Chinese people will undoubtedly be able to move it aside and leave Deng Xiaoping in their wake.

Notes

1. "A Political Dissident's View of Post-Deng China," *Contending* (*Zhengming*), no. 8 (1993).

2. Deng Xiaoping, *Selected Works of Deng Xiaoping: 1975–1982 (Deng Xiaoping Wenxuan: 1975–1982)* (Beijing: People's Publishing House, 1983), p. 136.

Glossary of Dramatis Personae

Ba Jin: Born in 1904, Ba Jin has been a major literary figure in China since the 1930s. An anarchist since his student days in France, Ba Jin is the author of such famous novels as *The Family* (*Jia*) and translator of Turgenev's *Fathers and Sons*. Since 1949 he has served in the National People's Congress and as vice chairman of the All-China Writers' Association.

Bai Hua: A member of the PLA, Bai Hua was labeled as an "anti-socialist element" during the 1957 anti-rightist movement and attacked during the Cultural Revolution. He returned to the army in 1977, but his film script *Bitter Love* was criticized in 1981. He is a member of the All-China Writers' Association and in 1988 visited France.

Bao Tong: A close adviser to General Secretary Zhao Ziyang, Bao Tong became a member of the CCP Central Committee at the 1987 Thirteenth Party Congress and in 1988 headed the Research Center for the Reform of the Political Structure. After the 1989 Beijing massacre, Bao was arrested and imprisoned.

Bo Yibo: Born in 1908, Bo Yibo became a member of the CCP Central Committee in 1945 and the Politburo in 1956. Throughout the 1950s and early 1960s he served in various posts dealing with the economy, such as minister of finance and chairman of the State Planning Commission. Purged during the Cultural Revolution, Bo was rehabilitated in 1978 and assumed key positions in the government overseeing the economy and in the Party organization. In 1987 he joined the Central Advisory Commission in nominal "retirement."

Chen Boda: Deceased in 1975, Chen Boda served as political secretary and ghost writer to Mao Zedong in the Yan'an period. During the early 1950s he was involved in CCP propaganda work and was vice president of the Marxism-Leninism Institute in Beijing. In 1956 he was appointed to the Politburo and became deputy director of the Propaganda Department, where he served as editor in chief of the *Red Flag* (*Hongqi*). A radical during the Cultural Revolution, he headed the Cultural Revolution Small Group with Jiang Qing until purged in 1970.

Works consulted in preparation of this glossary include: *Who's Who in the People's Republic of China,* ed. Wolfgang Bartke, 1st ed. (Armonk, N.Y.: M. E. Sharpe, 1981), 2d and 3d ed. (Munich: K. G. Saur, 1987 and 1991); Donald W. Klein and Anne B. Clark, *Biographic Dictionary of Chinese Communism, 1921–1965* (Cambridge, Mass.: Harvard University Press, 1971); *Biographical Dictionary of Republican China,* ed. Howard L. Boorman (New York: Columbia University Press, 1968); *Who's Who in Communist China* (Hong Kong: Union Research Institute, 1970).

Chen Junsheng: From the Northeast, Chen Junsheng served in the 1970s in the Heilongjiang province CCP and in 1987 he headed the fire-fighting leading group in the province. In 1988 he became a state councillor.

Chen Yizi: In 1987 Chen Yizi became the director of the Institute for the Reform of the Economic Structure under the State Commission for Restructuring the Economy. In June 1989 he was accused by the Chinese government of responsibility for fomenting student unrest and fled China. In September, Chen, along with Yan Jiaqi, took part in Paris in the formation of the Federation for a Democratic China.

Chen Xilian: Born in 1913, Chen Xilian rose to prominence in the communist armies in the 1920s and 1930s where he was closely associated with Lin Biao and Liu Bocheng. Chen became commander of the Beijing Military Region in 1974 and a member of the Central Military Commission in 1977. He was removed from his post as a Politburo member at the 1980 Fifth Plenum of the Eleventh Party Congress and appointed to the Central Advisory Commission in 1982.

Chen Yuan: Son of China's economic czar and perennial political conservative Chen Yun, Chen Yuan was trained as an engineer at Qinghua University and was Party secretary in a west Beijing district. He was appointed to the Standing Committee of the Beijing CCP in 1984 and became vice governor of the People's Bank in 1988.

Chen Yun: Born in 1905, Chen Yun became active in the early 1920s in the trade union movement along with Liu Shaoqi and joined the CCP in 1925. He became a member of the CCP Central Committee in 1934 and worked in the CCP Organization Department. In the mid-1930s he was in the Soviet Union and returned to China in 1937, accompanying Wang Ming and Kang Sheng. In 1940 he became active in economic issues and worked in Manchuria. Throughout the 1950s and 1960s he served in the Politburo and in various posts dealing with the economic planning system. Chen nominally retired in 1987.

Dai Qing: The adopted daughter of Ye Jianying, Dai Qing was trained as a missile engineer, became a Red Guard activist during the Cultural Revolution, and underwent secret service training in the military. In the early 1980s, she became a journalist at the *Enlightenment Daily* and initiated investigative reporting of intellectual persecution in the history of the CCP, including the cases of Wang Shiwei, Liang Shuming, and Chu Anping. She is a strong advocate of freedom of the press and environmental protection and has collected documents from many scientists and economists opposed to the Three Gorges dam project. In 1989 Dai was imprisoned after the June 1989 crackdown as her book on the Three Gorges dam, *Yangtze! Yangtze!* was banned for allegedly contributing to the "turmoil." Later released, Dai has since been a Nieman Fellow at Harvard University and a fellow at the Freedom Forum, School of Journalism, Columbia University.

Deng Liqun: Born in 1914 in Mao Zedong's native province of Hunan, Deng Liqun worked in the early 1950s in Xinjiang province, where he assisted in putting down Muslim resistance to communist rule. Later serving as secretary to Liu Shaoqi, Deng was purged in the Cultural Revolution but returned in 1975 to serve on the State Council and as vice president of the Academy of Social Sciences. In the early 1980s, he headed the Policy Research Office under the Party Secretariat and was a member of the Central Commission for Guiding Party Consolidation.

Deng Pufang: The son of Deng Xiaoping, Deng Pufang graduated from the physics department at Beida and in 1968 was crippled by Red Guards. Throughout the

1980s he has served in various national and international organizations for disabled persons.

Deng Xiaoping: Born in 1904 in Sichuan province, Deng Xiaoping was the eldest son of a landowner. In 1920 he traveled to France as a work-study student and joined a Chinese socialist youth organization. Upon returning to China, in 1924 he joined the CCP and assumed his first position as an instructor at the Xi'an Military and Political Academy established under the auspices of the warlord Feng Yuxiang. In 1929 he helped organize communist military forces in the southwestern Guangxi province and became a political commissar. During the 1945–1949 Civil War, Deng was a member of the Second Field Army in the Crossing the Yangtze River and Huaihai battles. In 1952 he was appointed a vice premier and in 1956 a member of the Politburo Standing Committee and head of the Party Secretariat. He was condemned in the Cultural Revolution for having previously criticized the personality cult of Mao Zedong and for his "liberal" policies on agriculture. He first appeared after the Cultural Revolution in 1973 as a vice premier and in 1975 was reappointed to the Politburo Standing Committee, only to be dropped again in 1976 following the April Tiananmen incident. Deng reappeared in July 1977 and assumed all previous posts, plus People's Liberation Army chief of staff, and in 1981 became chairman of the Central Military Commission. In November 1987 he "retired" from all posts, except the Military Commission. He plays bridge.

Fang Lizhi: A theoretical physicist and one of China's most eminent scientists, Fang Lizhi has been a constant critic of the CCP dictatorship. Fang was denounced by Party leaders for allegedly instigating student demonstrations in late 1986 that resulted in the removal of Hu Yaobang as general secretary. Purged from the CCP in 1987, Fang wrote an open letter to Deng Xiaoping in January 1989 calling for an amnesty for all political prisoners, particularly Wei Jingsheng. After the June 1989 crackdown, Fang sought refuge in the U.S. Embassy and was later allowed to leave China for the West.

Fang Yi: A vice mayor of Shanghai and vice minister of Finance in the 1950s, Fang Yi became a vice chairman of the State Planning Commission in 1961. Evidently protected by Zhou Enlai during the Cultural Revolution, Fang was elected to the Central Committee in 1973 and in 1977 became a member of the Politburo and vice president of the Academy of Sciences. In 1978 he became minister of the State Science and Technology Commission and a vice premier, and from 1982 to 1988 he was a state councillor.

Fei Xiaotong: Born in 1910, Fei Xiaotong studied at London University and worked at Harvard University in the mid-1940s. He has been chairman of the China Democratic League, one of the small satellite parties in China, and published several books on Chinese rural life and minority groups. Fei accompanied Hu Yaobang on a 1986 trip to the West.

Feng Wenbin: A prominent member and leader of the Communist Youth League since 1925, Feng Wenbin in 1952 was replaced as head of the Communist Youth League by Hu Yaobang. After dropping out of the national political limelight for more than twenty years, in 1979 Feng became vice president of the Central Party School in Beijing. In the early 1980s he was appointed first deputy director of the General Office of the CCP and head of the Party History Research Center.

Gao Di: Beginning in the 1950s as a county Party secretary in Jilin province, Gao Di in 1983 rose to become Jilin province Party secretary and in 1985 a member of the Central Committee. In 1988 he was appointed vice president of the Central Party School and visited North Korea. In 1989 following the Beijing massacre he became director of the *People's Daily*.

Gao Yang: A municipal and provincial Party official in China's northeast throughout the 1950s, Gao Yang became minister of the Chemical Industry in 1962 until purged in the Cultural Revolution. In 1979 he became minister of State Farms and Land Reclamation (formerly headed by Wang Zhen) and in 1982 Party secretary of Hebei province. From 1987 to 1989 he was president of the Central Party School in Beijing.

Geng Biao: A Long March veteran, Geng Biao in 1960 became a vice minister of Foreign Affairs and in 1969 was elected to the Central Committee at the Ninth Party Congress. In 1971 he became the director of the International Liaison Department of the CCP and in 1977 was appointed to the Politburo. In 1978 he became a vice premier and in 1981 minister of National Defense. In 1982 he joined the Central Advisory Commission.

Gu Mu: A member of the League of Left-Wing Writers in Beijing in the 1930s, Gu Mu was a vice minister of the State Economic Commission in the 1950s and in 1965 headed the State Capital Construction Commission. After disappearing in the Cultural Revolution, he was elected to the Central Committee in 1973 and resumed his post at the Capital Construction Commission and from 1982 to 1988 was a state councillor. In 1986 he headed the Leading Group in Charge of Foreign Investment in China and in 1988 joined the Chinese People's Political Consultative Conference.

Han Zhixiong: A young worker, Han Zhixiong in 1976 was arrested and imprisoned after giving a speech denouncing the "Gang of Four" during the April Fifth Qing Ming festival demonstrations on Tiananmen Square. After the smashing of the "gang," Han was released and wrote an article memorializing the April Fifth Movement in the newly restored journal *China Youth* that provoked the rage of Wang Dongxing. Hu Yaobang met with Han soon after and recommended him as a member of the Central Committee of the Communist Youth League.

He Dongchang: Trained as an aeronautical engineer, He Dongchang in the 1950s was the Party secretary of Qinghua University. Branded a "counterrevolutionary" in the Cultural Revolution, he was appointed in 1978 to the Central Discipline Inspection Commission and in 1979 became vice president of Qinghua University. In 1982 he was appointed minister of Education and a member of the Central Committee. In 1988 he was chairman of the National Academic Degrees Committee.

He Jingzhi: A leftist writer, in 1945 He Jingzhi wrote the libretto for the revolutionary opera *The White-Haired Girl* (*Baimao nu*) and in 1951 received the Stalin Literary and Art Award. In the early 1980s, he became vice minister of Culture and vice chairman of the All-China Writers' Association. He was appointed acting minister of Culture following the 1989 Beijing massacre.

Hu Fuming: Author of the seminal article "Practice Is the Sole Criterion of Truth" published on May 10, 1978, in the CCP Central Party School publication *Theory Trends,* Hu Fuming was chairman of the philosophy department at Nanjing University and deputy secretary of the department's Communist Party branch. The republication of the article under Hu Yaobang's tutelage on May 11, 1978, in the *Enlightenment Daily* and shortly thereafter in the *People's Daily* provoked the final battle between the reformist faction in the CCP and hard-line leftists led by Wang Dongxing that ultimately led to the latter's political demise. Deng Xiaoping's support for "reviving the practice of seeking truth from facts" at the September 1977 Eleventh Party Congress provided crucial political backing for Hu Yaobang and political reform in the late 1970s.

Hu Jiwei: In 1954 Hu Jiwei became deputy editor and then in 1958 deputy editor in chief of the *People's Daily,* the official organ of the CCP Central Committee. Hu disappeared during the Cultural Revolution but in 1982 returned to the *People's Daily.* He was criticized in July 1989 for supporting the student demonstrations in May-June.

Hu Ping: In 1983 Hu Ping was appointed governor of Fujian province and in 1985 became vice secretary of the Fujian province Party committee. In 1987 Hu became vice minister of the State Economic Commission and in 1988 minister of Commerce.

Hu Qiaomu: Born in 1912, Hu Qiaomu came from a politically prominent family of wealthy landowners. He joined the CCP in 1935, working with Jiang Nanxiang in the fields of journalism and propaganda in Shanghai and Shaanxi province. In 1945 Hu succeeded Chen Boda as secretary to Mao Zedong and also headed the New China News Agency. He became a member of the Central Committee in 1956 and deputy director of the Propaganda Department. Publicly criticized by Red Guards during the Cultural Revolution, he reappeared in 1974 as a member of the Party Secretariat and Central Committee. In 1982 he became honorary president of the Academy of Social Sciences and in January 1984 published his article "On Humanism and Alienation." He nominally retired from his positions in November 1987 and served as honorary head of the Shakespeare Research Society until his death in 1992.

Hu Qili: A mechanical engineer and long-time active Communist Youth League member, Hu Qili was branded as a follower of Liu Shaoqi during the Cultural Revolution and subsequently purged. He returned in the mid-1970s as a county Party secretary in Ningxia province and then vice president of Qinghua University. In 1982 he became director of the General Office of the CCP; in 1985 he accompanied Hu Yaobang to Australia and became a member of the Politburo. In 1988 he was put in charge of the Propaganda and Ideological Work Leading Group under the Central Committee. In June 1989 Hu was removed from the Politburo standing committee and other posts for allowing journalists free rein during the student demonstrations but reemerged in April 1990 at a meeting of the National People's Congress.

Hu Sheng: President of the Academy of Social Sciences and of the Party History Research Center under the CCP Central Committee, Hu Sheng was instrumental in drawing up the Basic Law of the Macao Special Administrative Region.

Hu Shi [Hu Shih]: One of China's most prominent liberal intellectuals, Hu Shi was a disciple of John Dewey and a major promoter of vernacular Chinese literature in the 1920s. He attended Cornell and Columbia universities, studying at the latter under Dewey and writing his doctoral dissertation on pragmatic tendencies in ancient Chinese thought. Hu was an enthusiastic advocate of experimentalism and a sometime critic of the Nationalist government. He was Nationalist China's ambassador to the United States from 1938 to 1942 and became president of the Academia Sinica in Taiwan. He died in Taiwan in 1962.

Hu Yaobang: Born in 1915 in Hunan province, Hu Yaobang became a Red Army soldier at the age of 15 and in 1933 engaged in youth work for the Central Party leadership in the Jiangxi Soviet. During the Civil War (1945–1949), he served in the Political Department of the Second Field Army and later in the Southwest China Military and Administrative Council, both of which were organizations dominated by Deng Xiaoping. In 1957 he headed the then recently reorganized Communist Youth League and was later attacked during the Cultural Revolution. Hu reappeared in 1972 and in 1977 became a member of the CCP Central Committee and the director of the CCP Organization Department. In 1978 he entered the Politburo and headed the Propaganda Department and then in 1980 became general secretary of the Secretariat. He was appointed the third and last chairman of the CCP until this position was eliminated in 1982. Hu remained general secretary until his dismissal in early 1987. Hu's death in April 1989 sparked the student demonstrations that culminated in the June 4, 1989, Beijing massacre.

Hua Guofeng: Born to an extremely poor peasant family, Hua Guofeng joined the Red Army at the age of 15 and in 1949 became a county Party secretary in Hunan. After overseeing the rapid formation of agricultural cooperatives in his county, Hua was appointed on Mao Zedong's personal recommendation as Hunan Party secretary and during the Cultural Revolution headed the province's Revolutionary Committee. After supporting construction of a mausoleum in Hunan for Mao Zedong's first wife, Yang Kaihui, Hua was transferred to Beijing and headed a special group to investigate the Lin Biao affair. Appointed to the Politburo in 1973 and minister of Public Security in 1975, Hua became premier in 1976 and was personally designated by Mao to succeed him as Party chairman, a post Hua assumed in October 1976. Hua was replaced in September 1982 at the Twelfth Party Congress but retained his position on the Central Committee. Hua's inscription (in gold) still adorns the Mao Zedong Memorial Hall (*Mao Zedong jinian tang*) in Tiananmen Square. Two workers reportedly died from toxic fumes while affixing the gold.

Ji Dengkui: Ji Dengkui rose up through the ranks of the Party municipal and provincial apparatus in Henan province and during the Cultural Revolution played an active role in setting up the Henan Revolutionary Committee. Also during the Cultural Revolution, Ji became a vice premier and supporter of Jiang Qing; he was purged in February 1988.

Jiang Liu: Jiang Liu was identified in 1987 as chairman of the Education Department of the Central Party School in Beijing.

Jiang Nanxiang: A graduate of Qinghua University, Jiang Nanxiang joined Hu Qiaomu during the Yan'an period in editing the journal *Chinese Youth.* In 1952 he became dean and later president of Qinghua University and in 1957 first Party secretary of the Party Committee at Qinghua. As minister of Education in 1965 he was attacked as a supporter of the Beijing Party Committee head Peng Zhen and disappeared until 1974. From 1979 to 1982 he was minister of Education and in 1982 became first vice president of the Central Party School.

Jiang Qing: Mao's wife and later member of the so called Gang of Four, Jiang Qing was born in Shandong province under the name of Li Yunhe. In the 1930s she was a film actress in Shanghai. After divorcing her first husband (who in later years opened a Chinese restaurant in Paris), Jiang Qing traveled to Yan'an in 1938 where she met Mao, and despite reservations of the Central Committee, married the chairman after he secured a divorce from his third wife. Although Mao initially promised that Jiang Qing would stay out of politics, Jiang became active in 1965 when Yao Wenyuan (a later cohort in the "Gang") directed his acid pen at the drama *The Dismissal of Hai Rui from Office* that Yao suggested was a veiled attack on Mao. During the Cultural Revolution, Jiang Qing assumed a prominent role in the Cultural Revolution Small Group led by Chen Boda and in 1967–1968 egged on Red Guards to launch vicious assaults on the Party and army. With the purge of Chen Boda and the demise of Lin Biao in 1970–1971, Jiang's influence waned; she focused increasingly on foreign policy. In October 1976 she was purged with the other three members of the "gang" (Zhang Chunqiao, Yao Wenyuan, and Wang Hongwen) and in 1981 was sentenced to death (with a two-year reprieve) for her role in the Cultural Revolution. Her suicide in prison in 1991 was noted in the Chinese press but ignored on Central China TV.

Jiang Zemin: Currently general secretary of the CCP, president of the PRC, and chairman of the Central Military Commission, Jiang Zemin is the third successor chosen by Deng Xiaoping, following Hu Yaobang and Zhao Ziyang, both of whom were purged. Jiang is from Shanghai and has a degree in electrical engineering. Early in his career Jiang worked as a trainee in the Stalin Automobile Factory in Moscow and in the 1950s and 1960s was director of a number of industrial plants in Shanghai. In 1971 he entered the central government in the First Ministry of Machine Building and in the early 1980s headed the Ministry of the Electronics Industry. In 1985 he became mayor of Shanghai and in 1987 a member of the CCP Politburo. During the June 1989 student demonstrations in Shanghai he averted violence, mollifying students by reading them Lincoln's Gettysburg address. Following the massacre in Beijing, he was appointed by Deng as the "core" of the third generation of leaders.

Kang Sheng: Born in 1899 to a family of well-off landlords and now deceased, Kang Sheng was one of the most important CCP leaders involved in intelligence and security and also liaison with foreign communist parties. In the 1930s he was an underground Party operative in Shanghai, where he established early links with Li Kenong. He then went to Moscow, where he studied Soviet security techniques and was CCP representative to the Comintern. Returning to Yan'an in 1937 with Wang Ming, Kang was reinstated as a Politburo member and headed the growing security apparatus, including the Social Affairs Department, or secret police, and was also a top official at the Party School. During the early 1940s, Kang promoted the notorious "rescue campaign" aimed at ferreting out alleged Kuomintang spies and "Trotskyites" in the CCP, but ending with purging many innocent intellectuals, including Wang Shiwei who in 1947 was executed. In the late 1950s, Kang was involved with Deng Xiaoping in the growing dispute with the Soviet Union over ideological and other issues and at the same time strongly defended Mao's 1958–1960 Great Leap Forward policies. Kang's political star rose considerably in 1962 after the purge of Peng Dehuai, when Kang was appointed to the Party Secretariat headed by Deng. During the Cultural Revolution he served as a critical "adviser" to the radical faction of Jiang Qing and became a member of the Politburo Standing Committee. Kang collected art and after his death in 1975 his home in Beijing was converted to a Sichuan restaurant.

Li Chang: A member of the CCP underground at Qinghua University in Beijing during the 1930s, Li Chang became a prominent figure in the scientific arena after 1949 as president of Harbin Polytechnical University. He was denounced during the Cultural Revolution as a follower of Liu Shaoqi. In 1978 he became a vice president of the Academy of Sciences. In the early 1980s he was involved with the Research Society in Natural Dialectics.

Li Honglin: A former president of the Fujian Academy of Social Sciences, Li Honglin has been a constant critic of the "personality cult" in China and since the 1970s a strong advocate of political reform. He was deputy director to the theory bureau of the CCP Propaganda Department. In February 1989, he joined forty-two other intellectuals in signing an open letter to the CCP leadership calling for the release of political prisoners and greater freedoms throughout Chinese society. After June 1989 he was imprisoned; he was released in May 1990.

Li Peng: Currently the premier of China, Li is the "adopted" son of Zhou Enlai. Li Peng was born in Sichuan to parents active in the CCP, both of whom were executed during the early 1930s. From 1948 to 1954, Li was trained as a power engineer in the Soviet Union and from 1955 to 1979 worked in China in numerous positions in the power industry. In 1982 he became vice minister of the Ministry of Water Resources and Electric Power and the same year became a member of the Central Committee at the Twelfth Party Congress. In 1985 he was appointed to the Politburo and in 1987 to its Standing Committee. He became premier in 1988. In June 1989 he reportedly issued the order for troops to use force against prodemocracy demonstrators.

Li Ruihuan: Trained as a construction worker in the 1950s, Li Ruihuan cut his teeth during the Great Leap Forward as a member of the young carpenters' shock brigade building the Great Hall of the People in Tiananmen Square, one of the world's largest buildings. In 1976 he was the director of the work site for the Mao Zedong Memorial Hall and in 1979 was dubbed a model worker. In 1982 he became mayor of Tianjin and helped to clean up the city's notoriously polluted water supply. In 1987 he became head of the Tianjin City Party committee as well as member of the Politburo. With very little formal education, Li since 1989 has frequently weighed in on issues of ideology and culture.

Li Weihan (Luo Mai): An early associate of Mao Zedong in Hunan, Li Weihan traveled to France in 1920 for education, though he quickly returned to China for the CCP's founding conference in Shanghai in July 1921. In 1927 Li became a member of the Politburo but was quickly denounced as a "coward" for attempting to terminate the ill-fated Autumn Harvest Uprising. Li subsequently emerged in the early 1930s as a strong supporter of de facto Party leader Li Lisan and was an early opponent of the Twenty-Eight Bolsheviks out of Moscow. In Yan'an, Li headed the Communist Party School and was a top official in the Shaan-Gan-Ning Border Government. After 1949 Li became heavily involved in minority and nationality issues and also helped guide the early campaigns to seize private business and establish total state control of the economy. From his position in the CCP's United Front Department, Li in the late 1950s launched attacks on "rightists" in China's eight satellite parties, including his own brother, but in 1964 was removed from his post and later attacked by Zhou Enlai for "capitulationism in united front work."

Li Yining: A 1955 graduate of the economics department at Peking University (Beida), Li Yining has written a book on the economic theories of the U.S. economist John Kenneth Galbraith and is a financial adviser to the China Investment Consulting Experts Committee.

Li Xiannian: Born in 1909 to poor peasants in Hubei, Li Xiannian was trained as a carpenter and then joined the communists in the late 1920s. Rising to the top of the CCP hierarchy as a military commander, Li became a member of the Central Committee in 1945 and after 1949 became mayor of Wuhan and a vice premier. He was made a member of the CCP Politburo in 1956 and became minister of Finance in 1957. He continued to serve in the Politburo throughout the Cultural Revolution and remained a central figure in economic and financial affairs through the 1980s. From 1983 to 1988 he was president of the PRC. He died in 1992.

Li Xin: A former secretary to Kang Sheng, Li Xin in the late 1970s was appointed deputy director of the Special Cases Investigation Group and was closely associated with Wang Dongxing, Hu Sheng, Wu Lengxi, and Xiong Fu. In the 1980s he was one of many "Party historians" involved in the Party History Research Center under the Central Committee.

Lin Biao: The "closest comrade in arms" during the Cultural Revolution of Mao Zedong and his constitutionally designated successor, Lin Biao died in 1971 during an alleged attempt to assassinate the chairman. Lin was a major military leader during the 1945–1949 Civil War, during which his siege of the northeastern city of Changchun led to the death of several hundred thousand people. After lengthy medical treatment in the Soviet Union, Lin became a marshal of the People's Liberation Army in 1955 and minister of National Defense in 1959 following the purge of Peng Dehuai. He emerged as an important political figure in 1964 at a People's Liberation Army Political Work Conference and was canonized as Mao's official successor in the 1969 Ninth Party Congress constitution. Lin and his entourage maintained an uneasy alliance with the radical faction surrounding Jiang Qing. Lin's notorious wife, Ye Qun, and his son, Lin Liguo, allegedly joined in the foiled assassination plot against Mao. Although the official line is that Lin Biao died in a plane crash while attempting to flee China, the rumor mill in Beijing has it that he was poisoned by Mao at a banquet.

Lin Jianqing: During the 1950s Lin Jianqing was editor in chief of the journal *Study* (*Xuexi*), which often contained elliptical criticisms of leftist ideology in the CCP and of Mao Zedong's growing personality cult. After returning from being purged during the Cultural Revolution, he was appointed in 1982 as deputy director of the Policy Research Office under the CCP Secretariat and a member of the Central Committee at the Twelfth Party Congress.

Lin Mohan: A member during the Yan'an period of the Marxism-Leninism Institute, he was also editor of the *Liberation Daily* (*Jiefang ribao*) and the journal *Chinese Culture* (*Zhongguo wenhua*). In the 1950s he became vice minister of Culture and in the early 1960s a deputy director of the CCP Propaganda Department. Branded a "counterrevolutionary" in 1967, he reappeared in 1978 as vice minister of Culture and in the mid-1980s became an adviser to the All-China Writers' Association.

Liu Binyan: After joining the underground CCP in the 1940s in Tianjin, Liu Binyan worked with the *Beijing Youth Daily* in the early 1950s and later the *People's Daily*. He was branded a "rightist" in 1957 for his scathing criticism of bureaucratism in China and sent to do labor on a state farm. After returning to work in the early 1960s, he was denounced again in the Cultural Revolution and then rehabilitated yet again in 1979. In 1985 he was elected vice chairman of the All-China Writers' Association and in 1987 was expelled from the CCP. Since 1988 he has been in exile in the West and was denounced in November 1989 in the *People's Daily* as the "scum of the Chinese nation." Liu's written works include *People or Monsters?* and *A Second Kind of Loyalty.*

Liu Bocheng: Born in 1892 and now deceased, Liu Bocheng was trained as an army officer at the time of the Republican Revolution in 1911 and was wounded several times, including the loss of an eye. Known thereafter as the "one-eyed dragon," he began to support the communists in the 1920s and went to the Soviet Union in the late 1920s for further military training. Liu commanded volunteer units during the epic Long March (1934–1935) and sided with Mao during his disputes with rival leaders promoted by Stalin and the Comintern. He was appointed to the Central Committee in 1945 and headed the Second Field Army, in which Deng Xiaoping served as a political commissar. In 1955 he was elevated to the rank of marshal and in 1956 became a member of the Politburo at the Eighth Party Congress. Liu reportedly was protected during the Cultural Revolution and retired from public life in 1977.

Liu Shaoqi: A native of Hunan province, Liu Shaoqi emerged as the first heir apparent to Mao Zedong in the 1950s, and Liu replaced Mao as state chairman in April 1959 in the political fallout over the disastrous Great Leap Forward. Author of "How to Be a Good Communist," Liu's political star rose throughout the early 1960s as he supported substantial loosening of state controls on the economy, especially agriculture, to help China recover from the Leap. Liu was attacked very early in the Cultural Revolution as "China's Khrushchev" and as "the Number One Party person in authority taking the capitalist road." He was replaced as Mao's heir by Lin Biao and was formally expelled from the CCP in October 1968. He later died ignominiously in a solitary cell.

Lu Dingyi: After joining the CCP in 1925, Lu Dingyi became active in the Communist Youth League and served as a propaganda cadre in the People's Liberation Army. A Long March veteran, he headed the Propaganda Department on and off throughout the 1940s and 1950s. In May 1956 Lu delivered his famous speech "Let a Hundred Flowers Bloom," in which he favored greater freedom of thought and expression, a proposal later embraced by Mao. He became a member of the Central Committee Secretariat in 1962 and in 1965 became minister of Culture. Branded a "counterrevolutionary" during the Cultural Revolution, he was rehabilitated in 1979 and took part in revising China's state constitution. In 1982 he became a member of the Central Advisory Commission and in 1986 wrote an article commemorating the 1957 Hundred Flowers.

Luo Ruiqing: One of the earliest members of the Red Army and a senior military and political officer throughout the 1930s and 1940s, Luo Ruiqing in the 1950s became minister of Public Security. He helped establish the system of "reform through labor" and defended the execution of alleged "counterrevolutionaries" in the early 1950s as having been carried out to "appease the rightful indignation of the people." In 1959, Luo rose up the ranks after the purge of Peng Dehuai; he became army chief of staff and was appointed to the Central Military Affairs Commission. In 1965 he was replaced and became a major target in the Cultural Revolution, during which time he sustained serious injuries at the hands of Red Guards. Rehabilitated in the late 1970s, he traveled in 1978 for medical treatment to West Germany, where he died from a heart attack.

Mao Zedong: Chairman of the CCP from 1935 until his death in September 1976, Mao Zedong from 1958 onward generally ceased attending Politburo meetings. His body has been preserved like those of Lenin and Ho Chi Minh and lies in a crystal sarcophagus in the memorial hall in Tiananmen Square, Beijing.

Nie Rongzhen: A participant in the 1919 May Fourth Movement and in the 1920s a natural science student in Belgium, Nie Rongzhen also studied in the Soviet Union in the 1920s. During the Long March he served under Lin Biao and in 1945 was elected to the Central Committee. In 1949 he helped "liberate" Beijing. In the early 1950s he was acting People's Liberation Army chief of staff and as one of China's ten marshals he became vice chairman of the National Defense Council. In 1958 he became chairman of the Science and Technology Commission and in 1967 a member of the Politburo. During the Cultural Revolution Nie was instrumental in developing China's nuclear weapon and in insulating the country's nuclear and missile program from interruption by Red Guards. In 1983 Nie was elected vice chairman of the Central Military Commission. He resigned from his posts in 1985 and died in 1992.

Peng Dehuai: Born in 1898 in Hunan, Peng Dehuai emerged as one of the top military figures in the CCP. It is said that when Peng was eleven his father fired a gun at him, and he showed his steely nerves by not flinching. Peng soon left his family and joined local military forces and in 1919 was profoundly influenced by the writings of Sun Yat-sen and the liberal ideas of the May Fourth Movement. Peng joined the CCP in the late 1920s and emerged as one of the foremost military figures in the communist movement, commanding CCP forces in a major battle with the Japanese in 1940 and leading the First Field Army during the Civil War. Peng then commanded Chinese forces during the 1950–1953 Korean War, where his troops fought U.S. forces to a standstill, but with extremely heavy losses on the Chinese side, including Mao Zedong's son. A strong supporter of a professional military in China, Peng helped introduce ranks in the mid-1950s and himself became a marshal. Peng's letter in August 1959 to Mao Zedong raising questions about economic policy in the Great Leap led to his purge. Efforts to rehabilitate Peng in the early 1960s provoked Mao's wrath, and during the Cultural Revolution Peng was denounced and paraded through the streets by Red Guards. Peng died in obscurity in 1974.

Peng Zhen: Born in 1902 to destitute peasants, Peng Zhen joined the CCP in 1923 and served as a political commissar in the Eighth Route Army. In 1945 he became a member of the Central Committee and the Politburo and after 1949 was mayor of Beijing until his purge in the Cultural Revolution. He reappeared in 1979 and was appointed chairman of the Legal Commission of the National People's Congress and reappointed to the Central Committee and Politburo. He "resigned" from all posts in 1987 but reportedly played a major role in June 1989 in sanctioning the crackdown on prodemocracy demonstrations.

Qian Jiaju: A graduate of the Department of Economics at Peking University in the 1930s, Qian Jiaju remained in China after the communist takeover as a leading figure in the Chinese People's Political Consultative Conference and in the China Democratic League, one of the eight largely powerless political parties in the People's Republic of China. In the 1957 Hundred Flowers, Qian criticized CCP policy toward science and in 1967 was branded as a follower of Liu Shaoqi. He reappeared in 1981 in the Democratic League and the CPPCC and became a major critic of the proposed gigantic Three Gorges dam project that was formally approved by the National People's Congress in 1992. A strong supporter of Mikhail Gorbachev's ideas, Qian also criticized Li Peng's economic austerity measures in 1988–1989. He now lives in a monastery in the United States.

Qian Weichang: A member of the commission that drafted the Basic Law of the Macao Special Administrative Region, Qian Weichang earned a Ph.D. in applied mathematics in the United States and once worked at the Jet Propulsion Lab. In the 1950s, he returned to China and became a dean and then vice president at Qinghua University. In June 1957 during the Hundred Flowers, he joined with Qian Jiaju in criticizing CCP policy toward science by coauthoring an article in the *Enlightenment Daily*. He was relieved of all posts in 1958 for suggesting that laymen should not be permitted to set guidelines for experts but was rehabilitated in 1960. Purged again during the Cultural Revolution, he returned in the 1980s and developed a new coding system for computerizing Chinese language characters.

Qiao Shi: Leader of the Shanghai student movement in the 1940s, Qiao Shi in the 1950s and early 1960s worked in the Communist Youth League and in the steel industry. In 1982, he was appointed director of the International Liaison Department of the CCP and in 1984 a director of the CCP Organization Department. In 1985 he became a member of the Politburo and the Party Secretariat and in 1987 a member of the Politburo Standing Committee. In 1989 he became president of the Central Party School and visited Romania, where he praised the great successes of the socialism of the Ceauşescu government two weeks before its collapse.

Qin Chuan: A propaganda cadre in the 1950s and 1960s, Qin served from 1978 to 1982 as deputy editor in chief of the *People's Daily* and editor in chief from 1982 to 1985.

Ren Zhongyi: A Party secretary of Harbin City and then Heilongjiang province Party committee in the 1950s and 1960s, Ren Zhongyi in 1977 became a member of the Central Committee and head of the Liaoning province Party committee. In 1980 he became Party secretary of Guangdong province. In 1985 he resigned his posts to join the Central Advisory Commission.

Rong Yiren: Chairman of the Board of Directors of the China International Trust and Investment Corporation (CITIC) and a managing director of the Bank of China, Rong Yiren helped develop China's economic ties with foreign nations after his reappearance in 1972 from the Cultural Revolution. In 1987 he was appointed honorary chairman of China's National Committee for Pacific Economic Cooperation.

Ruan Chongwu: A graduate in 1957 of the Moscow Motor Vehicle Machinery College, Ruan Chongwu in the early 1980s was an official in the Shanghai government and Party organizations. In 1985 he was appointed minister of Public Security and political commissar of the People's Armed Police. In July 1989 he became minister of Labor.

Rui Xingwen: A chemical engineer and in the late 1970s a vice minister of the military-related Seventh Ministry of Machine Building, Rui Xingwen became a vice minister of the State Planning Commission and member of the Central Party Secretariat. In 1988 he was deputy head of the Propaganda and Ideological Work Leading Group under the CCP Central Committee.

Song Ping: Born in 1917, Song Ping studied in the 1940s in Yan'an at the Central Party School and the Institute of Marxism-Leninism. In the late 1950s he became vice minister of the State Planning Commission and during the 1960s was put in charge of defense construction projects for inland areas (the so-called Third Front). He was active in the Cultural Revolution in Gansu province, where in 1976 he read Mao Zedong's eulogy. In 1983 he became a state councillor and minister of the State Planning Commission and in 1987 assumed the directorship of the CCP Organization Department. In June 1989 he became a member of the Politburo Standing Committee.

Song Renqiong: Graduate of the Whampoa Military Academy, Long March veteran, and associate of Liu Bocheng, Song Renqiong in 1942 organized the "Death Corps" in Shanxi province and in 1945 was elected to the Central Committee. In the early 1950s Song was in southwest China and in 1954 returned to Beijing, where he became a member of the National Defense Council. In the early 1960s Song became deputy secretary in chief of the Central Committee and minister of the Third Ministry of Machine Building. Throughout the Cultural Revolution he was repeatedly attacked by Red Guards but returned in 1979 to become director of the CCP Organization Department. In 1982 he was elected to the Politburo and in 1985 resigned to join the Central Advisory Commission. He plays volleyball.

Su Shaozhi: An economist by training, Su Shaozhi was one of China's leading Marxist theorists and proponents of reform and in the mid-1980s headed the Marxism-Leninism Mao Zedong Thought Institute. In December 1988 at a forum to commemorate the decade of reform, Su defended Wang Ruoshui and attacked conservative ideologues such as Hu Qiaomu. In February 1989 he signed an open letter calling for the release of political prisoners in China. He fled China after the June 1989 crackdown and has held several university posts in the United States.

Sun Changjiang: Trained as a philosopher, Sun Changjiang was once deputy director of the Theory Research Department of the Central Party School. He helped author the article "Practice Is the Sole Criterion of Truth," published in May 1978. When in 1982 Wang Zhen replaced Hu Yaobang as president of the Central Party School, the Theory Research Department was dismantled and Sun was ousted from the Party School and became a faculty member at Beijing Teachers' College. Sun subsequently became the editor in chief of the *Science and Technology Daily* (*Keji ribao*), but after the June 4, 1989, Beijing massacre he was ousted from this post.

Tan Zhenlin: A follower of Mao Zedong in the 1927 Autumn Harvest Uprising, Tan Zhenlin became a political commissar in the New Fourth Army. In 1958 he was appointed to the Politburo and in 1962 a vice chairman of the State Planning Commission. In 1967 he participated in the so-called February Adverse Current, an attempt to terminate the Cultural Revolution and outlaw the Red Guards. He was purged but reappeared in 1973 and was reappointed to the Central Committee.

Tian Jiaying: In 1955 Tian Jiaying was appointed to the Staff Office for the Chairman of the People's Republic, where he served as one of Mao Zedong's many secretaries. He committed suicide during the Cultural Revolution reportedly because of his split with Mao.

Tian Jiyun: From Guizhou province, Tian Jiyun in the early 1950s joined the CCP as head of a land reform team and in the 1970s after the Cultural Revolution became a financial expert in Sichuan province. In 1981 he became an official in the State Council and in 1982 was appointed to the Central Committee. He became a vice premier the next year. In 1985 he was elected to the Politburo and Party Secretariat and in 1987 became a member of the Politburo Standing Committee. In September 1989 he was put in charge of breaking up and merging companies and firms.

Tong Dalin: A specialist in science policy research, Tong Dalin in 1978 became a vice minister of the State Science and Technology Commission and in 1982 a vice minister of the State Commission for Restructuring the Economy. In 1993 he was the head of the Research Society for the Reform of the Economic Structure.

Twenty-Eight Bolsheviks: The Twenty-Eight Bolsheviks were a faction of Chinese revolutionary students trained in Moscow in the late 1920s and early 1930s led by Wang Ming and generally beholden to Stalinist policies toward the CCP. During their training at Sun Yat-sen University in Moscow, the Twenty-Eight Bolsheviks cut their political teeth by engaging in ruthless internal Party struggles against reputed Chinese "Trotskyites." On their return to China in the early 1930s, this group (also known as the Russian Returned Students) relied on Stalin's backing to take over the CCP's central organizations in Shanghai and later the Central Soviet in Jiangxi province. But as other top Party leaders gradually shifted their support to Mao Zedong and his theories of guerrilla warfare, the Twenty-Eight Bolsheviks, especially Wang Ming, lost power. However, some members of the Bolshevik faction, such as Yang Shangkun, survived politically and ultimately moved into high positions in the CCP hierarchy.

Wan Li: Born in 1916, Wan Li fought with communist forces throughout the 1930s and 1940s and after 1949 assumed various positions in the Beijing Party and government organizations. Branded during the Cultural Revolution as a follower of Liu Shaoqi, he reappeared in 1971 only to be dismissed, along with Deng Xiaoping, after the April 1976 Tiananmen incident. In the late 1970s, he reappeared again as first secretary of the Party committee in Anhui province, where radical changes in agricultural policy occurred with Wan's apparent blessing. In 1982 Wan was appointed to the Politburo and assumed the role of acting premier during Zhao Ziyang's travels abroad. In 1988 he became the chairman of the seventh National People's Congress Standing Committee. In 1989 during a visit to the United States in the midst of prodemocracy demonstrations in Beijing, Wan assured President George Bush that force would not be used against demonstrators.

Wang Dongxing: Since the 1930s, a member of various guard units for CCP leaders, including Mao Zedong, Wang Dongxing in 1955 was appointed vice minister of Public Security. During the Cultural Revolution he was appointed director of the General Office of the CCP Central Committee and became a member of the Central Committee in 1969 at the Ninth Party Congress. In 1973 he was promoted to the Politburo and in 1977 became a vice chairman of the CCP and member of the Politburo Standing Committee. As commander of the security forces in Beijing, Wang played a key role in arresting the so-called Gang of Four. In February 1980, he was removed from all Party and state posts but was made an alternate member of the Central Committee in 1982. In 1985 he joined the Central Advisory Commission.

Wang Heshou: Trained as an engineer at Tangshan Engineering College, Wang Heshou graduated in 1930 from Sun Yat-sen University in Moscow. In the 1940s he was a Party operative in the northeast. In the 1950s, he was Minister of Heavy Industry and in 1956 joined the Central Committee as an alternate member. After being purged in the Cultural Revolution, from 1978 to 1987 he was deputy secretary and then secretary of the Central Discipline Inspection Commission.

Wang Ming: Born Chen Shaoyu, but better known by his revolutionary nom de guerre, Wang Ming was the leader of the Twenty-Eight Bolsheviks faction that struggled with Mao Zedong for leadership of the CCP in the 1930s and 1940s. From a family of well-to-do peasants, Wang was trained in Moscow at Sun Yat-sen University and beholden to Stalinist policies toward the CCP. Throughout most of the 1930s he resided in Moscow as the Chinese representative to the Comintern. He returned to China in 1937, accompanied by Kang Sheng, and became the major proponent in the 1940s of united-front policies with the Kuomintang. Outflanked in internal Party struggles by Mao Zedong, Wang Ming became the target of Mao's relentless struggle against "foreign formalism" in the 1942–1944 Rectification campaign. By the Seventh Party Congress held in 1945, Wang and his Twenty-Eight Bolsheviks faction were totally defeated politically, though Wang Ming was retained in the last position on the CCP Central Committee. By the mid-1950s, Wang was back in Moscow launching public diatribes against Mao and his leadership of the CCP. Wang was a perennial supporter of the women's movement in China and helped formulate China's marriage law.

Wang Renzhi: A member of the Policy Research Office under the State Council from 1978 to 1982, Wang Renzhi became deputy editor in chief of the *Red Flag* until 1987, when he assumed directorship of the CCP Propaganda Department. In 1988 he became a member of the Propaganda and Ideological Work Leading Group. Wang was one of the last Chinese leaders to visit the old USSR.

Wang Renzhong: Now deceased, Wang was a Long March veteran who throughout the 1950s was an official in Hubei province and was later attacked during the Cultural Revolution. He reemerged in 1978 and became a member of the Central Committee and also became active in agricultural policy. From 1980 to 1982 he was director of the CCP Propaganda Department and an active member of the National People's Congress in financial and economic affairs.

Wang Ruoshui: Trained as a Marxist philosopher and from 1977 to 1983 a deputy editor in chief of the *People's Daily*, Wang Ruoshui wrote on alienation and criticized the "personality cult" of Mao Zedong. In February 1989, Wang signed a letter to CCP leaders calling for political liberalization. Visiting the United States in May 1989 during the outbreak of the prodemocracy movement in Beijing, he returned to China to participate in the demonstrations.

Wang Ruowang: After joining the CCP during the anti-Japanese war, Wang Ruowang traveled to Yan'an where he became involved with a wall newspaper called *Light Cavalry* (*Qingqidui*) that exposed the darker sides of the CCP. As a result he was exiled to Shandong by secret police chief Kang Sheng. Rehabilitated, he became a journalist in post-1949 China and was branded a "rightist" in 1957 for writing several "critical essays" (*zawen*) during the Hundred Flowers period. Rehabilitated once more in 1962, he launched into more criticisms of the CCP for its Great Leap Forward policies and was singled out for attack by Shanghai Party boss Ke Qingshi, an event that evidently contributed to the death of Wang's wife. Jailed in 1966 as a "counterrevolutionary," Wang was rehabilitated for a third time in 1979. At the height of the "literature of the wounded," describing the human suffering brought on by the Cultural Revolution, Wang wrote *Hunger Trilogy*. This largely autobiographical account portrays prison conditions as relatively less inhumane under the Nationalist regime in comparison to the communist period. A Party member for fifty years, Wang was expelled from the CCP in 1987. In 1989 he supported the prodemocracy demonstrations and was imprisoned for over a year in 1989–1990.

Wang Zhen: Born in 1908 to poor peasants and now deceased, Wang Zhen attended only three years of elementary school and then was forced to work on the railway. Wang joined the CCP in 1927 and two weeks after their marriage his wife was executed by the Nationalists. After fighting under the CCP General He Long, Wang became commander of the Yan'an garrison in the 1940s and was appointed by Mao to oversee rectification of intellectuals, including Wang Shiwei, who was executed on He Long's orders. After 1949 Wang was stationed in Xinjiang province, where with Deng Liqun he helped put down local resistance to communist control. In 1956 he was appointed minister of State Farms and Reclamation and became a member of the Central Committee. Wang retained his posts throughout the Cultural Revolution and in 1978 became a member of the Politburo and the Central Military Commission. From 1982 to 1987 he headed the Central Party School and in 1988 became the vice president of China. Wang apparently rode in a People's Liberation Army tank during the Beijing massacre in June 1989. He died in 1993.

Wei Guoqing: Born in 1906 Wei Guoqing joined the CCP in 1929 and rose through the military hierarchy in the Third Field Army of Peng Dehuai. In 1954 he contributed to the Vietnamese defeat of the French at Dien Bien Phu by directing Chinese-supplied artillery and returned to become Party secretary in his home province of Guangxi. In 1966 Wei became the political commissar of the Guangzhou Military Region and survived through the Cultural Revolution, though sometimes criticized by Red Guards. In the late 1960s and early 1970s he headed the Revolutionary Committee in Guangxi and ordered that "mass trials" be held that resulted in thousands of deaths by the persecuted who were often cannibalized. He was appointed to the Politburo in 1973, and from 1977 to 1982 was director of the General Political Department of the PLA. In 1985 he resigned his Party posts.

Wei Jingsheng: China's most prominent dissident, Wei Jingsheng came from an Anhui province cadre family and was trained as an electrician. During the Cultural Revolution he was a Red Guard and was also imprisoned. In 1979 at Beijing's Xidan Democracy Wall, Wei called on Deng Xiaoping to initiate a "fifth modernization" of democracy and human rights, arguing that Deng's four modernizations stressing economic development and scientific and military modernization were insufficient.

He was sentenced in October 1979 on charges of being a "counterrevolutionary" and for revealing "state secrets" to a foreigner and was sentenced to fifteen years' imprisonment, often in solitary confinement. Wei was released in 1993.

Wu De: A labor organizer in the 1930s and 1940s, Wu De in 1952 became president of Tianjin University and Tianjin's mayor. In 1956 he became a member of the Central Committee and in the early 1960s was a political commissar of the Jilin Military Region. Following the purge of the Beijing Party Committee at the start of the Cultural Revolution, Wu became a vice chairman of the Beijing City Revolutionary Committee and political commissar of the Beijing military garrison. In 1971 he became a secretary of the Beijing Party Committee and a member of the Cultural Revolution Small Group. He was appointed to the Politburo in 1973 and a vice chairman of the National People's Congress. In 1980 he was removed from all Party and state posts.

Wu Guoguang: A young member of one of Zhao Ziyang's "think tanks" and a journalist at the *People's Daily*, Wu Guoguang is now a graduate student in the United States at Princeton University.

Wu Jiang: Trained as a philosopher, Wu Jiang during the early 1960s was director of the philosophy department of the journal *Red Flag*. In the late 1970s, Wu was also director of the Theory Research Department of the Central Party School, where he assisted Hu Yaobang in criticizing the "two whatevers" and also participated in the debate over the "criterion of truth." In 1982, when Wang Zhen dismantled the Theory Research Department of the Party School, Wu was transferred to the Chinese Academy of Socialism (*Zhongguo shehuizhuyi xueyuan*), where he has served as the honorary vice president.

Wu Jinglian: A graduate of the economics department of Fudan University, Wu Jinglian in 1986 became director of the Economic, Technological, and Social Development Research Center under the State Council.

Wu Lengxi: From 1952 to 1965, Wu Lengxi was director of the New China News Agency (Xinhua) and in 1958 he also became editor in chief of the *People's Daily*. Like almost all cadres in the fields of culture and propaganda, Wu was purged in the Cultural Revolution but was rehabilitated in 1972. In 1982 he became minister of Radio and Television but was relieved of this post in 1985.

Wu Zuguang: One of China's premier wartime dramatists and author of over forty plays and film scripts, Wu Zuguang was labeled a "rightist" in 1957 and sent to northeastern China for physical labor. He returned in 1960 only to be sent back to the countryside in 1966, where he remained for ten years. In 1980 his play *Itinerant Players* was performed in Tianjin, but in 1987 Wu was once again criticized as a "bourgeois liberal" and expelled from the Party. In spring 1989 Wu joined other intellectuals in signing a petition to the CCP leadership calling for greater political freedoms in China.

Xi Zhongxun: A political commissar in the First Field Army during the Civil War and a director of the CCP Organization Department, Xi Zhongxun was elected to the Central Committee in 1956. In 1962 he disappeared as a result of his close association with Peng Dehuai. In 1978 he reappeared as a Party and military official in Guangdong province and in 1981 headed the National People's Congress Legal Commission. From 1982 to 1987 he was a member of the Politburo.

Xia Yan: Educated in Japan, Xia Yan joined with Lu Xun in 1930 in establishing the League of Left-Wing Writers. Xia translated into Chinese Maxim Gorky's *Mother* and wrote such film scripts as *Fascist Germs*. In 1949 he became deputy director of the Propaganda Department of the CCP East China Bureau and in 1954 vice minister of Culture. In 1965 he was labeled "bourgeois" for his film script *Lin's Shop*, which was based on a short novel by China's prominent writer Mao Dun, and was accused of serving as Liu Shaoqi's "agent" in literary and art circles. After the Cultural Revolution, Xia reappeared in 1977 and became an adviser to the Ministry of Culture until the early 1980s. In 1980 he was elected vice president of the Chinese PEN Center and in 1990 president of the Society for Japan Studies.

Xiang Nan: A long-time Communist Youth League member, Xiang Nan was also a specialist in agricultural machinery. He disappeared from public view from 1964 to 1977 and in 1982 was appointed as the Party secretary in the coastal province of Fujian. In 1987 he was relieved of his posts and joined the Central Advisory Commission and in 1990 became president of the Foundation of Underdeveloped Regions in China.

Xiong Fu: A journalist in central China in the 1950s, Xiong Fu was purged in the Cultural Revolution but returned to become editor in chief of the *Red Flag* from 1978 to 1987. In May 1982 he published an article in that journal titled "On the Principle of Democracy in the Relationship Between Leaders and the Masses."

Xu Weicheng: A member of the Communist Youth League, Xu Weicheng served in the late 1950s and early 1960s as an editor of *Youth News* in Shanghai. During the Cultural Revolution he was reportedly a member of the radical "rebel faction" (*zaofanpai*) of Red Guards and a protégé of the "Gang of Four." In the early 1980s, he became a member of the Beijing Party organization and in 1987 launched frenzied attacks in the *Beijing Daily* on intellectuals as part of the overall onslaught against "bourgeois liberalism." Xu apparently had a hand in crafting the April 26, 1989, *People's Daily* editorial (based on comments by Deng Xiaoping) that condemned the prodemocracy movement as a "planned conspiracy and disturbance." In 1990 he was elevated to deputy director of the CCP Propaganda Department.

Yan Jiaqi: A vice president of China's Political Science Society, Yan Jiaqi was trained in the 1950s as an applied mathematician and later studied philosophy. In the mid-1980s, Yan served in the Office of Political Reform and helped shape Zhao Ziyang's proposals for developing a modern professional civil service in China and for eliminating lifelong tenure of political leaders. After giving speeches in Tiananmen Square during the 1989 prodemocracy demonstrations, Yan fled China and in Paris founded the Federation for a Democratic China.

Yang Shangkun: Yang Shangkun was a member of the Twenty-Eight Bolsheviks trained in Moscow in the late 1920s and in the 1940s headed a drama troupe performing propaganda plays for communist troops. In 1945 he became head of the General Office of the CCP, a post he held until the Cultural Revolution. He became a member of the Central Committee in 1956 but fell out of favor with Mao in the early 1960s, reportedly after bugging the chairman's residence (a fact apparently discovered by one of Mao's many mistresses). In 1966 he was branded a "counterrevolutionary" and did not reappear until 1978. In 1982 he was appointed to the Politburo and became permanent vice chairman of the Central Military Affairs Commission and in 1988 became president of the People's Republic of China. During this period, Yang and his half-brother, Yang Baibing, became known as the "Yang family clique" for their influence in the military. Both lost their positions after the October 1992 Fourteenth Party Congress, allegedly after Deng Xiaoping caught wind of their plans to place all the blame for the 1989 massacre on Deng following his death.

Yao Yilin: Trained in chemistry and as a teacher, Yao Yilin led armed uprisings in eastern China in the 1940s. After 1949 he became vice minister of Commerce and negotiated trade agreements with the Soviet Union. In 1958 he was appointed to the Bureau of Finance and Commerce under the State Council and in 1960 minister of Commerce. Criticized in the Cultural Revolution as a "three-anti element of the Peng Zhen clique," he returned in 1973 and became involved in foreign trade issues and in 1977 became a member of the Central Committee. In 1980 he became director of the State Planning Commission and a member of the Finance and Economics Leading Group headed by Zhao Ziyang, and in 1985, was appointed to the Politburo. In 1988 he was acting premier during Li Peng's absence and chairman of the State Three Gorges Project Examination Committee.

Ye Jianying: Born in 1887 to wealthy merchants and now deceased, Ye Jianying was an instructor at the Whampoa Military Academy and joined the CCP in 1927. He studied military science in Moscow and participated in the Long March, siding with Mao Zedong's major nemesis, Zhang Guotao. In 1945 he became a member of the Central Committee and after 1949 became a vice chairman of the National Defense Council. In 1955 he was promoted to the rank of marshal in the People's Liberation Army and in 1966 was appointed to the Politburo. In 1967 he became vice chairman of the Central Military Commission and in 1973 a member of the Politburo Standing Committee. In 1975 he became minister of National Defense and in 1979 proposed the crucial Conference on Guidelines in Theory Work. In 1985 he resigned from his posts.

Ye Wenfu: A poet and a member of the military, Ye Wenfu became famous for his poem titled "General You Cannot Do That," in which he criticized a People's Liberation Army general for using his authority to expand his house and displace a children's kindergarten. Ye's speech at Beijing Teachers' University, warmly welcomed by students, offended the university Party committee and Beijing municipal government members, who singled Ye out as a typical case of "bourgeois liberalism." Ye was also personally criticized by Deng Xiaoping for the same "erroneous tendency."

Yu Guangyuan: A veteran of the December 9, 1935, student movement, Yu Guangyuan in the 1950s became actively involved in developing China's scientific establishment, especially in the field of physics and the philosophy of natural science. During the anti-rightist campaign he launched attacks against other philosophers and in 1962 became a professor at Beida. In 1967 he was branded a "counterrevolutionary" and purged but returned in 1977 as vice minister of the State Scientific and Technical Commission. In the early 1980s Yu headed a number of societies dealing with economic development and was elected to the presidium of the Academy of Sciences. The intellectual mentor of Yan Jiaqi, Yu in 1988 became president of the Society for the Study of Marxism-Leninism and Mao Zedong Thought. After the 1989 Beijing massacre, the *Beijing Daily* criticized Yu for "negating the people's democratic dictatorship."

Yu Haocheng: A vice president of China's newly established Political Science Society in 1982 and a legal and constitutional expert, Yu Haocheng also was head of the *Masses* (*Qunzhong*) publishing house run by the Ministry of Public Security. In February 1989 he signed a petition calling for greater freedoms and release of political prisoners and in June 1989 was put on the Ministry of Public Security's wanted list for his role in the prodemocracy demonstrations.

Zhang Chunqiao: A guerrilla fighter during the 1940s, Zhang Chunqiao in the early 1950s became managing director of the People's Liberation Army *Liberation Army Daily* in Shanghai. In 1959 he was appointed to the Politburo of the Shanghai City Party Committee and director of its Propaganda Department. In 1966 he was deputy head of the Cultural Revolution Small Group under the Central Committee and helped initiate demonstrations by Red Guard *zaofanpai*. Zhang headed the "Shanghai People's Commune," which later became the Shanghai Revolutionary Committee and in 1969 became a member of the Central Committee and the Politburo. In 1975 he became a vice premier and a director of the PLA General Political Department. In October 1976 he was arrested as a member of the "Gang of Four" and in 1981, like Jiang Qing, was unrepentant at his trial and was sentenced to death with a two-year reprieve.

Zhang Pinghua: A Long March veteran and a political commissar in the Eighth Route Army, Zhang Pinghua in the early 1950s became a prominent member of the Wuhan City Party Committee and the Hubei province Party Committee. He became a member of the Central Committee in 1956 and first Party secretary in Hunan until his purge in 1967 as a "counterrevolutionary double-dealer of Liu Shaoqi and Deng Xiaoping." He returned in 1971 and from 1977 to 1978 headed the CCP Propaganda Department. In 1982 he joined the Central Advisory Commission.

Zhang Xianyang: A research fellow at the Chinese Academy of Social Sciences, Zhang Xianyang was involved in criticizing the theory of the "two whatevers" and was one of the earliest critics of Mao Zedong's theories of "overall dictatorship" and "the continuation of the revolution under proletarian dictatorship." In 1987, Zhang was ousted from the CCP in the campaign of "struggle against bourgeois liberalism."

Zhao Ziyang: Born in 1919 to a landlord family in a county in Henan province where large numbers of Chinese Jews reside, Zhao Ziyang attended middle school and then joined the CCP in 1938. During the 1940s he worked in rural areas and after 1949 worked in the CCP's Central-South China Subbureau of the Central Committee. In 1955 he became deputy secretary of the Guangdong Party Committee and in the early 1960s proposed a system of countervailing powers in the CCP. In 1967 he was paraded through the streets by Red Guards but reappeared in 1971, becoming secretary of the Guangdong Party Committee in 1973. In 1976 he headed the Sichuan Party Committee and in 1979 was made a member of the Politburo. In September 1980 he was appointed premier and in 1987 became general secretary of the CCP. In June 1989 he was dismissed from the Politburo and all other posts but retained his Party membership.

Zhou Enlai: Perhaps the most astute and cosmopolitan politician among top CCP leaders, Zhou Enlai was born in 1898 to a well-to-do gentry family. Educated in Japan and Europe, Zhou was an early member of the CCP but throughout the 1920s and 1930s was frequently in conflict with Mao Zedong, a man whom Zhou would later faithfully serve for decades. During the 1920s, Zhou was heavily involved in military affairs, and by the 1940s he served as the CCP's highly skilled negotiator with the Kuomintang during the Second United Front (1937–1945) and in talks in 1945 aimed to ward off the subsequent civil war. Following the CCP victory in 1949, Zhou became China's chief diplomat and in 1951 engaged in intense efforts to avoid a confrontation with the United States over Korea. Serving concurrently as premier and minister of foreign affairs, Zhou emerged as a major figure on the world stage at the 1954 Geneva conference that ended the French-Vietnamese war and in 1955 at the Afro-Asian Conference in Bandung, Indonesia, where he proclaimed a period of "peaceful coexistence and anti-imperialism." In China's domestic politics, Zhou endorsed a liberalization of policies toward intellectuals in the 1950s and assumed initially a neutral position on the 1958–1960 Great Leap Forward. But when in 1959 the government finally realized it confronted an enormous crisis in grain production, it was Zhou who announced the low food supply figures, providing political cover for Mao Zedong, who had almost single-handedly promoted the Leap. Zhou Enlai's willingness to stick with Mao through thick and thin was apparent during the Cultural Revolution when Zhou reluctantly supported the widespread purges but made every effort to defend old colleagues from Red Guard attacks. Zhou also provided protection for China's historical relics, such as the Forbidden City, which were often targeted for destruction by the rampaging Red Guards. During the Lin Biao affair in 1971, Zhou evidently ordered the shooting down of Lin's Trident plane. Afterward, Zhou became a primary target of Jiang Qing and her supporters, who considered Zhou the major obstacle to their plans for political succession to Mao Zedong. Zhou contracted cancer in the mid-1970s and was evidently denied crucial medical assistance on orders from Mao. Zhou died on January 8, 1976. Three months later during the Qing Ming (Sweeping the Graves) festival, demonstrations in Tiananmen Square called for official commemorations of Zhou's death but were crushed by security forces. Demonstrators chanted "Long Live the People" and "Down with the era of Qin Shihuang."

Zhou Hui: Secretary in the 1960s of the Hunan province Party Committee, Zhou Hui disappeared in the Cultural Revolution. In 1978, he became Party secretary in Inner Mongolia and a member of the Central Committee. In 1982 he wrote an article praising the rural responsibility system. In 1987 he was relieved from his posts soon after the fall of Hu Yaobang.

Zhou Yang: Born in 1907 and now deceased, Zhou Yang in 1930 was secretary of the League of Left-Wing Writers in Shanghai and during the anti-Japanese War defended the concept of "literature of national defense" in controversies with Ba Jin and others. In the early 1950s Zhou joined in persecuting his old rival Hu Feng as a "counterrevolutionary" and during the Cultural Revolution was himself branded a "three-anti element" and publicly denounced with Lu Dingyi. Zhou reappeared in 1977 as an adviser to the Academy of Social Sciences, a vice chairman of the All-China Writers' Association, and until 1982, a deputy director of the Propaganda Department.

Zhu Rongji: Born in 1928, Zhu Rongji graduated from the electric motor engine department of Qinghua University and worked from 1951 to 1966 in the State Planning Commission. In the late 1970s he worked in the Ministry of Petroleum and then in 1983 was appointed vice minister of the State Economic Commission. In 1987 Zhu became a member of the Central Committee and in 1988 became mayor of Shanghai. After a stint at the China International Trust and Investment Corporation (CITIC), in 1991 he became a vice premier and was put in charge of cooling down the Chinese economy.

Zhu Houze: In the 1950s and early 1960s, Zhu Houze was involved in Communist Youth League work in Guiyang, Guizhou province. After being sent down to the countryside in the Cultural Revolution, in 1985 he became secretary of the Guizhou Party Committee and director of the CCP Propaganda Department the same year. In 1987 he was relieved of this post and became deputy director of the Rural Development Research Center under the State Council. In 1988 he became secretary of the Federation of Trade Unions but was purged after the fall of Zhao Ziyang.

Zhu Muzhi: Director of the New China News Agency in the 1950s, Zhu Muzhi became a member in the 1960s of the All China Journalists Association. After the Cultural Revolution, he was elected to the Central Committee in 1973 and in 1977 became a deputy director of the CCP Propaganda Department and in 1978 a member of the Central Discipline Inspection Commission. From 1982 to 1986 he was minister of Culture and in 1988 became a member of the Propaganda and Ideological Leading Group under the Central Committee.

Zou Jiahua: A graduate of the Moscow Engineering Institute, Zou Jiahua served in the 1950s and 1960s as a director of a machine tool plant in Shenyang City and then worked in the First Ministry of Machine Building. In 1974 he was identified as a member of the People's Liberation Army Science and Technology Commission for National Defense and in 1977 was elected as an alternate to the Central Committee. In 1983 he became vice minister of the Commission of Science, Technology, and Industry for National Defense and in 1985 minister of Ordnance Industry. In 1988 he became a state councillor and minister of Machine Building and the Electronics Industry and in 1989 head of the State Planning Commission and in 1991 a vice premier.

About the Book and Author

In 1978, Deng Xiaoping, China's paramount leader, launched the economic reforms that turned the world's most populous nation into an economic dynamo. Yet Deng also shaped the destiny of a China that to this day is locked in the iron embrace of the Chinese Communist Party and its ancient, intractable leaders—even though early in his regime Deng had held out to the Chinese people the promise of democratic reforms. Such is the "empire" of Deng Xiaoping. It is at one and the same time the world's third largest economy and a country imprisoned behind the bars of a political structure created by the founding "emperor," Mao Zedong.

This book tells the inside story of the ideological *mano a mano* leadership battles that have made today's China a nation of great economic vitality and political despotism. Ruan Ming, a former associate of Deng Xiaoping's first designated successor, Hu Yaobang, was uniquely placed to view these battles with an experienced—and sardonic—eye. In 1978 he contributed to Deng's pathbreaking Third Plenum speech, which launched China's reforms. Throughout the 1980s, Ruan Ming joined with liberal reform forces in the CCP to push Deng toward both economic and political liberalism; this futile effort ultimately led to Ruan's purge from the CCP and relocation to the United States.

In this revealing chronicle, although Deng Xiaoping is portrayed as a leader with some liberal political intentions, Ruan shows him to be utterly crippled by deep insecurities that have doomed any effort to break with his powerful cohorts in the "gang of old men"—those conservative manipulators in the Chinese Communist Party who oppose political change of any kind.

Born in 1931, **Ruan Ming** received a B.A. in mechanical engineering from Yanjing University in 1952. He was deputy director of the Theoretical Research Department in the Central Party School of the Chinese Communist Party until he was expelled from the party in 1983. Since 1988 he has been a visiting scholar at Columbia University, the University of Michigan, Princeton University, and Harvard University, and a member of the Princeton China Initiative.

About the Translators and Editors

Nancy Liu is a graduate student in speech pathology at Columbia University. **Peter Rand** is a freelance writer and the author of the forthcoming book *China Hands*. He is also an affiliate of the Fairbank Center for East Asian Research at Harvard University. **Lawrence R. Sullivan** is associate professor of political science at Adelphi University and a research fellow at the East Asian Institute, Columbia University.

Index